WILLIAM SHARP AND "FIONA MACLEOD"

William Sharp and "Fiona Macleod"

A Life

William F. Halloran

https://www.openbookpublishers.com

© 2022 William F. Halloran

This work is licensed under a Attribution-NonCommercial 4.0 International (CC BY-NC 4.0). This license allows you to share, copy, distribute and transmit the text; to adapt the text for non-commercial purposes providing attribution is made to the authors (but not in any way that suggests that they endorse you or your use of the work). Attribution should include the following information:

William F. Halloran, *William Sharp and "Fiona Macleod": A Life*. Cambridge, UK: Open Book Publishers, 2022, https://doi.org/10.11647/OBP.0276

Copyright and permissions for the reuse of many of the images included in this publication differ from the above. This information is provided in the captions and in the list of illustrations.

In order to access detailed and updated information on the license, please visit https://doi.org/10.11647/OBP.0276#copyright. Further details about Creative Commons licenses are available at http://creativecommons.org/licenses/by-nc/4.0/

All external links were active at the time of publication unless otherwise stated and have been archived via the Internet Archive Wayback Machine at https://archive.org/web. Digital material and resources associated with this volume are available at https://doi.org/10.11647/OBP.0276#resources

Every effort has been made to identify and contact copyright holders and any omission or error will be corrected if notification is made to the publisher.

ISBN Paperback: 9781800643260
ISBN Hardback: 9781800643277
ISBN Digital (PDF): 9781800643284
ISBN Digital ebook (epub): 9781800643291
ISBN Digital ebook (azw3): 9781800643307
ISBN XML: 9781800643314
DOI: 10.11647/OBP.0276

Cover image: William Strang, William Sharp (c. 1897), etching, printed by David Strang. Photograph by William F. Halloran of author's copy (2019).
Cover design: Anna Gatti.

For

Mary Helen Griffin Halloran

intelligence, patience, compassion

Contents

Acknowledgements	ix
Preface	xi
Chapter One: 1855–1881	1
Chapter Two: 1882–1884	9
Chapter Three: 1885–1886	19
Chapter Four: 1887–1888	31
Chapter Five: 1889	43
Chapter Six: 1890	53
Chapter Seven: 1891	61
Chapter Eight: January–June 1892	79
Chapter Nine: July–December 1892	93
Chapter Ten: 1893	111
Chapter Eleven: 1894	127
Chapter Twelve: January–June 1895	147
Chapter Thirteen: July–December 1896	169
Chapter Fourteen: January–June 1896	189
Chapter Fifteen: July–December 1896	205
Chapter Sixteen: 1897	223
Chapter Seventeen: 1898	243
Chapter Eighteen: January–June 1899	265
Chapter Nineteen: July–December 1899	283
Chapter Twenty: 1900	295
Chapter Twenty-One: 1901	315
Chapter Twenty-Two: 1902	333
Chapter Twenty-Three: 1903	349
Chapter Twenty-Four: 1904	365
Chapter Twenty-Five: 1905	387

Appendix 1: William Butler Yeats and Elizabeth Amelia Sharp	413
Appendix 2: Catherine Ann Janvier and Roselle Shields	421
Bibliography	425
List of Illustrations	429
Index	441

Acknowledgements

I am indebted to the following for their permissions and their insights: Noel Farquharson Sharp, Rosemarie Fanning Sharp, Robin Sharp, Caroline (Sharp) Schwartz, Esther Mona Harvey, and the Special Collection Librarians of the following institutions:

The American Antiquarian Society; Baylor University's Armstrong Browning Library; The British Library; The Brown University Library; The Library of Colby College; Columbia University's Rare Book and Manuscript Library; The Edinburgh City Libraries; Harvard University's Houghton Library; The Huntington Library of San Marino California; Indiana University's Lilly Library; The Library of Congress; The Manx Museum on The Isle of Mann; The National Library of Scotland; The Newberry Library; The New York Public Library's Berg Collection; New York University's Fales Library; The Northwestern University Library; The University of Oxford's Bodleian Library; Pennsylvania State University's Pattee Library; The Pierpont Morgan Library in New York City; Princeton University's Firestone Library; The Sheffield City Archives; The Smith College Library; The Stanford University Library; The State University of New York at Buffalo Library; The Library of Trinity College Dublin; The University of British Columbia Library; The University of California Berkeley's University Research Library; The University of California Los Angeles's William Andrews Clark Memorial Library; The University of Delaware Library; The University of Illinois Urbana-Champaign Library; The University of Leeds's Brotherton Library; The University of Texas Austin's Library and its Henry Ransom Humanities Research Center; The University of Toronto's Thomas Fisher Rare Book Library; The University of Wisconsin-Milwaukee's Golda Meir Library; Yale University's Beinecke Library.

This project would not have come to fruition had it not been for Warwick Gould, Emeritus Professor and Founding Director of the

Institute for English Studies at the University of London. It was he who supported the first iteration of the Sharp letters as a website supported by the Institute, and it was he who suggested Open Book Publishers as a location for an expanded edition of *The Life and Letters of William Sharp and Fiona Macleod*. His support and friendship have been a beacon of light.

Finally, and most important, through the many years of my involvement with William Sharp, my wife — Mary Helen Griffin Halloran — has been endlessly patient, encouraging, and supportive. This work has benefited from her insights and her editorial skills.

Preface

Who Was William Sharp?

William Sharp was born in Paisley, near Glasgow, in 1855. His father, a successful merchant, moved his family to Glasgow in 1867; his mother, Katherine Brooks, was the daughter of the Swedish Vice Consul in Glasgow. A talented, adventurous boy who read voraciously, he spent summers with his family in the Inner Hebrides where he developed a strong attachment to the land and the people. In the summer of 1863, his paternal aunt brought her children from London to vacation with their cousins. Months short of his eighth birthday, Sharp formed a bond with one of those cousins, Elizabeth Sharp, a bright girl who shared many of his enthusiasms. Their meeting led eventually to their engagement (in 1875) and their marriage (in 1884).

After finishing school at the Glasgow Academy in 1871, Sharp studied literature for two years at Glasgow University, an experience that fed his desire to become a writer. Following his father's sudden death in August 1876, he fell ill and sailed to Australia to recover his health and look for suitable work. Finding none, he enjoyed a warm and adventurous summer and returned in June 1877 to London where he spent several weeks with Elizabeth and her friends. A year later he settled in London and began to establish himself as a poet, journalist, and editor. Through Elizabeth's contacts and those he made among writers, including Dante Gabriel Rossetti, he became by the end of the 1880s a well-established figure in the literary and intellectual life of the city. During this decade he published biographical studies of Rossetti, Percy Bysshe Shelley, and Robert Browning; three books of poetry; two novels; many articles and reviews; and several editions of other writers. None of those publications brought the recognition he sought. By 1890 he had accumulated enough money to reduce his editing and reviewing and devote more time to poetry and prose.

That autumn he and Elizabeth went to Heidelberg for several weeks and then to Italy for the winter. In January, Edith Wingate Rinder, a beautiful young woman and the wife of Frank Rinder, accompanied her aunt, Mona Caird, a close girlhood friend of Elizabeth, on a three-week visit to Rome. There Edith spent many hours exploring the city and surrounding area with Sharp who fell deeply in love with her. Inspired by the joy he felt in her presence and the warmth and beauty of the country, Sharp wrote and printed privately in Italy a slim book of poems, *Sospiri di Roma*, that exceeded in quality those he had written previously.

After returning to England in the spring of 1891 and under the influence of his continuing relationship with Edith, Sharp began writing a prose romance set in western Scotland. When he found a publisher (Frank Murray in Derby) for *Pharais, A Romance of the Isles*, he decided to issue it pseudonymously as the work of Fiona Macleod. In choosing a female pseudonym, Sharp signaled his belief that romance flowed from the repressed feminine side of his nature. The pseudonym also reflected the importance of Edith in the novel's composition and substance. Their relationship is mirrored in the work's depiction of a love affair doomed to failure. Finally, it disguised his authorship from London critics who, he feared, would not treat it seriously if it appeared as the work of the prosaic William Sharp.

Pharais changed the course of Sharp's life. Along with *The Mountain Lovers*, another west of Scotland romance that followed in 1895, it attracted enthusiastic readers and favorable notices. When it became clear that his fictional author had struck a sympathetic chord with the reading public and the books were bringing in money, Sharp proceeded to invent a life for Fiona Macleod and project her personality through her publications and letters. In letters signed William Sharp, he began promoting the writings of Fiona and adding touches to her character. He sometimes functioned as her agent. To some, he asserted she was his cousin, and he implied to a few intimate friends they were lovers. In molding the persona of Fiona Macleod and sustaining it for a decade, Sharp drew upon the three women he knew best: Elizabeth, his wife and first cousin; Edith Rinder, with whom he had developed a deep bond; and Elizabeth's friend and Edith's aunt, Mona Caird, a powerful and independent woman married to a wealthy Scottish Laird. He enlisted his sister Mary Sharp, who lived with their mother in Edinburgh, to supply the Fiona handwriting. His drafts of Fiona Macleod letters went to her for copying and mailing from Edinburgh.

For a decade before his death in 1905, he conducted through his publications and correspondence a double literary life. As Fiona, he produced poems and stories which, in their romantic content, settings, characters, and mystical aura, reflected the spirit of the time, attracted a wide readership, and became the principal literary achievement of the Scottish Celtic Renaissance. As Sharp, he continued reviewing and editing and tried his hand at several novels. As Fiona's chief advocate and protector, he deflected requests for interviews by insisting on her desire for privacy. If it became known he was Fiona, critics would dismiss the writings as deceptive and inauthentic. Destroying the fiction of her being a real woman, moreover, would block his creativity and deprive him of needed income. So, he persisted and maintained the double life until he died. He refused to disclose his authorship even to the Prime Minister of England to obtain a much-needed Civil List pension. The popular writings of Fiona Macleod may have obtained Parliament's approval, but not those of the journeyman William Sharp

His rugged good looks and exuberant manner obscured the fact that Sharp had been ill since childhood. Scarlet fever in his youth and rheumatic fever as a young man damaged his heart. In his forties, diabetes set in, and attacks increased in frequency and seriousness. Given his declining health after the turn of the century, though interrupted by occasional bursts of exuberant creativity, his death in December 1905 was not a surprise to his family and close friends. It occurred while he and Elizabeth were staying with Alexander Nelson Hood, the Duke of Bronte, at his Castello Maniace on the northwest slopes of Mount Etna in Sicily. Sharp is buried there in the estate's Protestant Cemetery where a Celtic cross marks his grave.

Biographies of William Sharp

The first book-length account of William Sharp's life was written by his wife, Elizabeth Amelia Sharp. Her *William Sharp (Fiona Macleod): A Memoir* was published in 1910 by William Heinemann in London and Duffield and Company in New York. Comprehensive and beautifully written, this book contains all Elizabeth wanted to say about her husband, and it remains an essential source of information about his life. The next book-length effort to understand Sharp and his creation of Fiona Macleod was Flavia Alaya's *William Sharp — "Fiona Macleod"* published by the Harvard University Press in 1970. This work depends on Mrs. Sharp's *Memoir* for the basic facts of Sharp's life and work, but it differs in intensions. The author's insightful reading both of Sharp's writings and that of his European and American contemporaries enabled her to place Sharp in the historical context of Late Victorianism. In this book, Sharp emerged from obscurity into a writer to be read for the quality and range of his work and for his insights into the cultural landscape of the late nineteenth and the early twentieth centuries.

The next bibliographical study of Sharp — Steve Balmires's *The Little Book of the Great Enchantment* — was published by R. J. Stewart Books in Arcata, California in 2008. This book profits immensely from Mr. Balmires's ability as a storyteller, his knowledge of the Gaelic language and Celtic civilization, and his access to my first rendition of Sharp's life and letters known as *The William Sharp "Fiona Macleod" Archive* sponsored by the Institute of English Studies in the School of Advanced Study in the University of London. (The *Archive* has been superceded by my three volume *Life and Letters of William Sharp and "Fiona Macleod"* published by Open Book Publishers in 2018–2020.) What may be a limitation of this book for some readers is the author's treatment of William Sharp and Fiona Macleod as two separate individuals. Beyond that, the reader's ability to "suspend disbelief" may be tested by the author's assertion that Fiona was a product of the realm of fairies, and her writings were a "personal, first-hand account of her own Fairy tradition." Fairies were and for some are still a constant among the people of the Inner and Outer Hebrides. Mr. Balmires professes to share their belief in spirits who make themselves known in the material world with negative as well as positive results.

Professor Terry L. Meyers published in 1996 a short but important book with a very long title: *The Sexual Tensions of William Sharp: A Study of the Birth of Fiona Macleod Incorporating Two Lost Works, "Ariadne in Naxos" and "Beatrice"* (New York: Peter Lang). Drawing on recent studies of gender identification and male and female homosexuality in the late nineteenth century, Meyers observed that repressed homosexuality was the source of Sharp's sexual tensions. He presented the two lost works as additional evidence that Sharp, from an early age, recognized feminine traits in his make-up and identified with the plight of women. In the mid-nineties he compartmentalized his masculine and feminine inclinations and invented a woman through whom he could give voice to the latter. That bifurcation, the presence of two individuals, one male and the other female, Meyers observed, became a means of alleviating, as he acutely concludes, though not eliminating, Sharp's sexual tensions. Sharp recognized the complexities of gender identification and the varied combinations of masculine and feminine traits in his associates. He was sexually attracted to both women and men. Though there is ample evidence of its overt expression in his realtions with women, there is no such evidence in his relations with men. Lack of evidence, of course, does not preclude its occuring.

This biography of William Sharp has a lengthy and checkered ancestry. It began when Professor Lionel Stevenson in the Duke University Department of English suggested I look at William Sharp, whom I had never heard of, as I explored topics for a doctoral dissertation. I did so and admired the quality of some of his writings. More important, I became fascinated by what was known or assumed about his personal life. A grant from the Duke Graduate School enabled me to travel to London where I met William Sharp's nephew and Literary Executor, Noel Farquharson Sharp, and to Edinburgh where I examined the Sharp manuscripts in the National Library of Scotland. That trip was the first of many to England and Scotland where I have been welcomed by people with various ties to the writer. Upon arriving at the University of Wisconsin-Milwaukee (UWM) in 1966 as a member of its English Department, I began to collect copies of Sharp's letters — those signed William Sharp and those signed Fiona Macleod — from libraries and private collectors. With the help of graduate students and support from the UWM Graduate School, I eventually collected and annotated copies of hundreds of letters written to a wide range of British, American, and European literary figures with whom Sharp corresponded between 1870 and 1905.

As the number of letters grew, I abandoned all hope of having them published. In the mid-1990s, I met Professor Warwick Gould, the eminent Yeats scholar who founded the Institute for British Studies in London University. He suggested I prepare the annotated Sharp letters to insert chronologically on a website supported by his Institute. I did so, and that website, known as *The William Sharp "Fiona Macleod" Archive*, was completed in 2010, and it has been consulted by many scholars interested in Sharp and his friends. In 2017, Professor Gould suggested I prepare a proposal to publish the letters and send it to Open Book Publishers in Cambridge, England. When that proposal was reviewed and accepted, I returned to the letters, checked the transcriptions, expanded the annotations, and reworked the introductory section for each chapter of letters. The happy result was *The Life and Letters of William Sharp and "Fiona Macleod,"* twenty-five chapters arranged chronologically in three volumes which are available from Open Book Publishers' website without charge and in hard or soft copies for a modest price (*Volume 1: 1855-1894* is available at https://doi.org./10.11647/OBP.0142; *Volume 2: 1895-1899* at https://doi.org./10.11647/OBP.0196; V*olume 3: 1900-1905* at 10.11647/OBP.0221). The first volume was published in 2018, and the final two in 2020.

After finishing that project, I realized the introductory essays — the "Life" sections of *Life and Letters* — were an incipient biography buried in three large volumes of transcribed and annotated letters where they are likely to be read only by scholars interested in the period. I was, nonetheless, astonished to see recently that the three volumes of *Life and Letters* have been viewed online 9,000 times and downloaded 2,500 times. That aside, this compilation of the revised twenty-five chapters is more readable, both online and as a printed volume. Lacking annotations and strictly chronological, it is closely tied to *Life and Letters*. Quotations from and references to Sharp's letters are not annotated, but their dates are evident in the text. Readers may download the appropriate volume and chapter of *Life and Letters* to read the full letter, consult annotations to that letter, and use one of several widely used search engines to learn more about people and places. Page numbers of quotations from and references to other books and articles are given in parentheses. Since much of the information about Sharp's life is derived from Elizabeth

Sharp's *Memoir*, its page numbers are often omitted to enhance readability. Publication details of books and articles mentioned in the text may be found in the Bibliography. Books and articles by William Sharp are not included in the Bibliography. They await a full-scale bibliography, a major undertaking beyond the scope of this biography. The best listing of Sharp's writings remains that at the end of the two-volume edition of Elizabeth Sharp's *Memoir*.

Constrained by its ancestry, this biography focuses on Sharp's life and draws heavily on his extensive correspondence, Elizabeth Sharp's *Memoir*, and accounts by his contemporaries. It portrays his daily comings and goings, his interactions with publishers in Europe and America, his beliefs, his values, and his physical and mental condition. The letters reveal more than has previously been known, and from them Sharp emerges as a handsome, intelligent, talented, sensitive, and conflicted man. Difficult to pin down with precision, he was immersed in the crosscurrents of ideas and the artistic and social movements of his time. He took part in spiritualist efforts to affirm the existence of life after death, and he embraced innovative ideas about the place of women in society, the constraints of marriage, the fluidity of gender identity, and the complexity of the human psyche. Those issues and many others are addressed in his letters and, sometimes indirectly, in his writings. They are laid out in this volume in such a way that they may form the basis for a more comprehensive study of his life and work.

A singular contribution of this biography is its description of the autobiographical content of the writings of Fiona Macleod, of the remarkable extent to which Sharp used the feminine pseudonym and stories and myths from the Gaelic past to disguise his telling and retelling the complex story of his love affair with an exceptional woman who was not his wife. This revelation adds, I believe, depth and poignancy to the pseudonymous stories and poems.

Neither the annotated letters and introductions in *Life and Letters* nor the revised introductions that form this biography would have been possible without the tools bestowed on historians and literary scholars by computers and the internet. Nor would they be available without the foresight and generosity of Open Book Publishers which offers them to the public free of charge.

Chapter One
1855–1881

William Sharp was born on September 12, 1855, at 4 Garthland Place in Paisley, Scotland. He was the oldest in a family of five daughters and three sons. His father, David Galbreath Sharp, was a partner in a mercantile house, and his mother, Katherine Brooks, was the daughter of the Swedish Vice Consul in Glasgow. Sharp spent the summers of his childhood in the West country — on the shores of the Clyde, the sea coast, and the Isle of Arran. He swam, rowed, sailed, and cultivated a passionate love of nature inherited from his father. His Highland nurse, Barbara, told him tales of fairies, Celtic heroes, and Highland chieftains. These stories and the old Gaelic songs seeded his imagination with materials that came to fruition years later when he began writing the tales and poems published under the pseudonym "Fiona Macleod." Fanciful as a child, Sharp often imagined himself a marauding Viking or a brave Gaelic warrior. He developed early the sense of an invisible world and communicated freely with invisible playmates. The God he learned about in church was "remote and forbidding," but in the woods of the Inner Hebrides "he felt there was some great power behind the beauty." The "sense of the Infinite touched him there." When he was six, "he built a little altar of stones, [...] and on it he laid white flowers in offering" to a benign and beautiful Presence who ruled the natural world (*Memoir*, 6).

In 1863, when he was seven, his aunt brought her three children from London to spend some time with the Paisley Sharps who had rented a house for the summer at Blairmore on the Gare Loch in western Scotland. One of those children was Elizabeth Amelia Sharp. Years later she recalled her cousin William, who would eventually be her husband, as "a merry, mischievous little boy [...] with bright brown curly hair, blue-gray eyes, and a laughing face [...] eager, active in his endless invention of games and occupations." Until he was eight, he was educated at home by a governess. In the fall of 1863, he was sent to Blair Lodge, a boarding school in Polmont Woods between Falkirk and Linlithgow. Four years later, the Sharps moved from Paisley to Glasgow and enrolled William as a day student at Glasgow Academy. In the summer of 1871, when he was fifteen, he developed a severe case of typhoid fever and was sent to the West Highlands to recover. There he formed a friendship with Seumas Macleod, an elderly fisherman whose tales and beliefs found their way into the stories and poems he began publishing in the 1890s as the work of another Macleod whose first name, Fiona, was an abbreviation of Fionnaghal, the Gaelic equivalent of Flora. In the fall of 1871, at age sixteen, he entered Glasgow University. An eager and perceptive student, he excelled in English literature, which he studied under Professor John Nichol who became a close friend.

His most memorable summer was his eighteenth. Wandering near the Gare Loch close to Ardentinny, he encountered and joined a band of gypsies. Without explaining his absence or communicating his whereabouts, he roamed with them for weeks. With his light brown hair, he became their "sun-brother," and he absorbed much of their bird-lore and wood-lore and the beliefs they derived from the patterns of the stars and the winds. This magical experience, free and unconventional, informed his later publications, especially *Children of Tomorrow* and *The Gypsy Christ*. Understandably his parents were distressed upon learning their son had "gone with gypsies." When they located him, he relented and returned in the fall of 1872 to his classes at Glasgow University. Worried about his dreaming nature and interest in literature, his father at the close of the 1872–1873 academic year placed him in the Glasgow law office of Messrs. Maclure and Hanney with the hope he might take to the legal profession. Though he left the University after two years, he was found "worthy of special commendation" at the end of his second year. He had taken full advantage of the University's library, and during his two years as a legal apprentice he continued to "read omnivorously," according to Elizabeth, in "literature, philosophy, poetry, mysticism, occultism, magic, mythology, folklore." He developed "a sense of brotherhood with psychics and seers of other lands and days. His reading precipitated a radical shift from the Presbyterian faith in which he was raised toward a belief in the unity of the truths underlying all religions.

Sharp's second meeting with Elizabeth took place in August 1875 when the London Sharps invited him to spend a week with them at Dunoon on the Clyde where they were on holiday. Of that occasion, Elizabeth wrote,

> I remember vividly the impression he made on me when I saw the tall, thin figure pass through our garden gateway at sunset — he had come down by the evening steamer from Glasgow — and stride swiftly up the path. He was six feet one inch in height, very thin, with slightly sloping shoulders. He was good looking, with a fair complexion and high coloring; gray-blue eyes, brown hair closely cut, a sensitive mouth, and a winning smile. He looked delicate but full of vitality. He spoke very rapidly, and when excited his words seemed to tumble one over the other so that it was not always easy to understand him (*Memoir*, 17).

After a month in the West, Elizabeth and her sister visited the Glasgow Sharps in September, and before the end of the month, as Elizabeth recalled, she and William, both twenty years old and first cousins, "were secretly plighted to one another." They managed to spend a day together secretly in Edinburgh's Dean Cemetery where William confided "his true ambition lay not in being a scientific man, but a poet, that his desire was to write about Mother Nature and her inner mysteries." As Elizabeth recalled, "We talked and talked — about his ambitions, his beliefs and visions, our hopeless prospects, the coming lonely months, my studies — and parted in deep dejection," as they had no hope of seeing each other again until the next fall.

After Elizabeth returned to London, she received some of her fiancé's early poems, among them "In Dean Cemetery," a "pantheistic dream in fifty-seven stanzas" commemorating their day together. As the year proceeded, she received many more poems. In her *Memoir*, Elizabeth explained "why he chose such serious types of poems to dedicate to the girl to whom he was engaged." She was "the first friend he had found who to some extent understood him, understood the inner hidden side of his nature, sympathized with and believed in his visions, dreams, and aims." That sentence explains not only Sharp's initial attraction to Elizabeth, but also the foundation of their marriage which occurred several years later and lasted until Sharp died in 1905 at the age of fifty-five.

In August 1876, a year later, the two Sharp families rented houses next to each other in Dunoon which enabled Elizabeth and William to spend many happy days "rambling over the hills, boating and sailing on the lochs," talking over their very vague prospects, and reading and discussing his poems. The families' holiday was brought to an abrupt and unhappy end on August 20 by the untimely death of William's father, an event that was a great shock to William who soon suffered a physical breakdown that raised the danger of consumption. Hoping a complete change of environment might improve his health and spirits, his family arranged passage for him on a ship bound for Australia. He relished the experiences of the voyage and the new country, where he stayed with family friends and spent many days exploring Gippsland and the desert region of New South Wales. He decided to settle in Australia and began looking for suitable work. When that search failed, he changed course and booked passage on the *Loch Tay* which reached London in June 1877.

Sharp stayed for a time with Elizabeth and her parents at their London house on Inverness Terrace just north of Bayswater Road. This was his first experience of the city that would become his home. Elizabeth introduced him to her friends, among them Adelaide Elder and Mona Alison, who later married the Scottish Laird, Henryson Caird of Casseneary. Elizabeth's mother enlisted the help and influence of her friends to find work for Sharp, but there was no immediate success. At summer's end, he returned to Scotland, joining his mother at Moffat where she had taken a house, and he devoted himself through a lonely fall and winter to writing. Several poems composed during these months appeared in his first volume of poetry, *The Human Inheritance*, in 1882.

Less than a year after returning from Australia, in the spring of 1878 when he was twenty-two, Sharp returned to London and began work at the London branch of the Melbourne Bank, a position secured for him by Alexander Elder, the father of Adelaide. He rented a room at 19 Albert's Street near Regent's Park and spent weekends with Elizabeth and her family at 72 Inverness Terrace, but their engagement remained secret. Despite an earlier decision to refrain from publishing "until he could do it properly," Sharp became increasingly anxious to appear in print. He submitted a poem, "A Nocturne to Chopin," to *Good Words*. It was accepted and published in July 1878. Late that summer, Elizabeth convinced him to end the secrecy, which he thoroughly enjoyed, and tell her mother they were engaged. When she realized her daughter was determined, she reluctantly approved, but warned others would disapprove because they were first cousins. "From that moment," Elizabeth said, her mother "treated her nephew as her son."

On the first of September 1879, William, with an introduction from Sir Noel Paton, the Scottish Pre-Raphaelite painter and a friend of the family, appeared at the door of the famous poet and painter Dante Gabriel Rossetti. Rossetti welcomed the handsome and enthusiastic young writer who became a frequent guest at his home, 16 Cheyne Walk. Sharp soon gained acceptance into the circle of admiring friends who lightened the darkness of Rossetti's final years. He came to know Algernon Swinburne, Theodore Watts (later Watts-Dunton), Hall

Fig. 1 Dante Gabriel Rossetti in 1850 at age twenty-two. A portrait by William Holman Hunt (c. 1883), Wikimedia, https://commons.wikimedia.org/wiki/File:William_Holman_Hunt_-_Portrait_of_Dante_Gabriel_Rossetti_at_22_years_of_Age_-_Google_Art_Project.jpg, Public Domain.

Caine (another Rossetti acolyte), Robert Francillon, Julian Hawthorne, Rossetti's brother and sister, William Michael and Christina, and Philip Marston, a promising young poet who was blind and soon became Sharp's close friend.

Fig. 2 An albumen print of Dante Gabriel Rossetti. Taken by Charles Lutwidge Dodgson (Lewis Carroll) (1863), Wikimedia, https://commons.wikimedia.org/wiki/File:Dante_Gabriel_Rossetti_001.jpg, Public Domain.

In the summer of 1880, Mrs. George Lillie Craik, author of *John Halifax, Gentleman* and Philip Marston's godmother, entertained Sharp and Marston several times at her home, The Corner House, south of London in Shortlands, Kent. During one of those visits Sharp caught a severe cold after being drenched in a thunderstorm. Still ill, he went to Port Maddock in North Wales to visit Elizabeth and her mother who had rented a holiday cottage. There his cold descended into rheumatic fever which forced him to stay an entire month while Elizabeth and her mother nursed him back to health. The illness lasted through the fall and permanently damaged his heart. Despite her worry that Sharp — "weak and delicate" — would not take care of himself, Elizabeth accompanied her mother to Italy for the winter months. By mid-December Sharp was well enough to describe in a letter to Elizabeth a night he spent at the Oasis Club in Covent Garden with Francillon, Julian Hawthorne, and many other artists.

In 1881 Sharp published several articles in *Modern Thought* and increased his contacts with the Rossetti circle. One consequence of his deeper literary involvement was an abrupt end to his banking career. In late August, the Principal of the City of Melbourne Bank offered him the alternative of employment in a remote branch in Australia or resignation. Sharp chose the latter and went to Scotland for two months to visit relatives and friends, among them William Bell Scott and Sir Noel Paton. When he returned to London he spent several weeks looking for another position and finally obtained a post with the Fine Arts Society's Gallery in Bond Street. The Society had decided to establish a section on German and English engravings and hired Sharp, through the good offices of Mrs. Craik, to study the subject for six months and then become the section's director. Shortly after he began work at the Gallery, the society reversed course and withdrew from the project. At year's end, Sharp was again out of work.

His trip to Australia, his persistent ill-health, his relationship with the woman who would become his wife, his determination to become a serious writer, and his lack of interest in banking or any other business or profession defined Sharp's life into his mid-twenties. His prospects were dim at the close of 1881. But another factor turned the tide: the friends he made as a bright and handsome young Scotsman new on the London scene. Some came through Elizabeth, a young girl of means with a fine mind and a sound education. She had a group of similarly talented and knowledgeable friends who readily accepted Sharp into their circle, supported his ambitions, and encouraged his development. Others came through Dante Gabriel Rossetti, who in his final years fostered Sharp's development as a poet, confided in him through long opium-fueled nights, and welcomed him into his circle of accomplished and respected painters, poets, and editors. They smoothed Sharp's entry into the literary life of London where he would flourish and attain a position of prominence during the 1880s.

Chapter Two
1882–1884

In February 1882 Rossetti became ill and depressed, convinced he was near death. Hall Caine, his main caretaker, rented a house on the seacoast near Birchington in Kent in the hope that living near the sea away from the fogs and smoke of London would improve his health and spirits. He invited William Sharp and Theodore Watts for a weekend to help him break through Rossetti's gloom. In a February 13 letter to Elizabeth from Birchington, Sharp described an outing with Rossetti the previous day: "Oh, the larks yesterday! It was as warm as June, and Rossetti and Caine and I went out, and I lay in the grass basking in the sun, looking down on the shining sea, and hearing these heavenly incarnate little joys sending thrills of sweetness, and vague pain through all my being." Years later he expanded on the experience as one of his most cherished memories:

> It had been a lovely day. Rossetti asked me to go out with him for a stroll on the cliff; and though he leaned heavily and dragged his limbs wearily as if in pain, he grew more cheerful as the sunlight warmed him. The sky was a cloudless blue and the singing of at least a score of larks was wonderful to listen to. Everywhere Spring odours prevailed…. At first, I thought Rossetti was indifferent, but this mood gave way. He let go my arm and stood staring seaward silently, then, still in a low, tired voice, but with a new tone, he murmured, "It is beautiful — the world and life itself. I am glad I have lived." Insensibly thereafter the dejection lifted from off his spirit. And for the rest of that day and that evening he was noticeably less despondent (*Memoir*, 59–60).

Less than two months later, on April 9, Rossetti died. Sharp described his feelings to Elizabeth on the night before he went to Birchington for the funeral:

> He had weaknesses and frailties within the last six or eight months owing to his illness, but to myself he was ever patient and true and affectionate. A grand heart and soul, a true friend, a great artist, a great poet. I shall not meet with such another. He loved me, I know — and believed and hoped great things of me, and within the last few days I have learned how generously and how urgently, he impressed this upon others. [...] I can hardly imagine London without him.

Rossetti was more than a friend and mentor. Sharp's father rejected his son's artistic bent and died without reconciliation. Rossetti was the first of many who filled that void.

In the years before his death, Rossetti drew first Caine and then Sharp into his circle and depended on them for support and companionship. Soon after he died, both men decided to write a book about the great man. When Caine learned in July that Sharp was preparing a book, he complained bitterly. Since Sharp's book would cut into the sale of his book, he had decided to abandon it. Sharp's letters to Caine were not available to Elizabeth for her *Memoir*, and she mentioned him only twice. Their competing books on Rossetti might well have permanently damaged their relationship. A trove of Sharp letters to Caine preserved in the Manx Museum on the Isle of Man shows, on the contrary, they remained close friends for many years. After a brief period of strain in the summer of 1882, Sharp cleared the air in a letter that assured Caine his book would not be a biography, but "a Study of the Poet-Artist — for in deference to your own work I determined to make the biographical portion consist of only about ten pages or so. [...] I fail to see where the two will clash." Mollified by this explanation, Caine went ahead with his book — *Recollections of Dante Gabriel Rossetti* — which was published by Elliot Stock in September. Sharp's response to Caine preserved their friendship.

During July, William Michael Rossetti worked with Sharp on the dating and location of his brother's paintings. With that information in hand by early August, Sharp joined his mother and sisters in a rented cottage in western Scotland where he wrote the main body of the book. He finished it after returning to London, and Macmillan published *Dante Gabriel Rossetti: A Record and A Study* in December. The book's favorable reception provided a significant boost to Sharp's literary career. While his descriptions and analyses of Rossetti's paintings, poetry, and prose continue to be of some interest, the book's main lasting value is its

Fig. 3 Hall Caine, The Manxman, as caricatured in *Vanity Fair*. John Bernard Partridge (1896), Wikimedia, https://en.wikipedia.org/wiki/File:Hall_Caine_Vanity_Fair_2_July_1896.jpg, Public Domain.

Appendix, a detailed listing of the dates, subjects, and then current owners of Rossetti's paintings.

Sharp's first book of poems — *The Human Inheritance*; The *New Hope*; *Motherhood* — was published by Elliot Stock in 1882. He considered this book, according to Elizabeth, the beginning of the "true work of his life." As the title indicates, it consists of three long poems. "The Human Inheritance" has four sections which depict, in turn, childhood, youth, manhood/womanhood, and old age. "The New Hope" forecasts a spiritual regeneration of the world; and "Motherhood" attempts to show "by depicting the experience of giving birth" the commonality of experience among all living creatures. Sharp considered that poem, which Rossetti had praised, a major accomplishment. When Elizabeth was in Italy in 1880, she read parts of "Motherhood" to Eugene Lee-Hamilton, an aspiring poet who lived near Florence with his mother and sister, Violet Paget, who was gaining a reputation in England for her publications under the pseudonym Vernon Lee. They thought the poem's depiction of "giving birth" was not a fit subject for poetry. In response Sharp wrote a long letter to Lee-Hamilton and another to Paget in March 1881 justifying his effort to show in the poem that women shared with animals many experiences and feelings. The poem seems not to have produced much consternation when it appeared in the 1882 volume, perhaps because the entire volume evoked minimal notice and sank quietly out of sight. The care with which Sharp wrote and defended "Motherhood," however, signaled his life-long fascination with the inner lives of women. This poem was his first effort to penetrate and portray publicly the consciousness of a woman, a manner of thinking and feeling he felt deep within himself that culminated in 1892 in his creation of and identification with Fiona Macleod.

During 1882 Sharp earned small amounts for poems that appeared in the *Athenaeum*, the *Portfolio*, the *Academy*, the *Art Journal*, and, in America, *Harper's Magazine*. Toward the end of the year, he was down to his last penny. A forty-pound check from *Harper's* provided relief; then out of the blue a two-hundred-pound check arrived from an unknown friend of his grandfather who had heard from Sir Noel Paton that he was "inclined to the study of literature and art." Sharp was to use the money "to pursue his artistic studies" in Italy. With this windfall he left for Italy at the end of February 1883 and spent five months studying paintings by the major figures of the Italian Renaissance. He went first to Florence where he stayed with Elizabeth's aunt in her villa on the outskirts of the city, then to Venice where he met Ouida and William Dean Howells and formed a close friendship with John Addington Symonds, then to Sienna, and then to Rome before returning to Florence. He described much of what he saw in a series of lengthy letters to Elizabeth who had seen many of the paintings and frescoes during her trip to Italy in 1881. He studied the works carefully and shared his opinions of their relative merits. His association with Rossetti and others of the Pre-Raphaelite movement introduced him to many artists who preceded Raphael. In Italy he made direct contact with their paintings, and that experience provided a solid basis for the art criticism that occupied his time and attention in the years that followed.

When he returned to London, he wrote a series of articles for the *Glasgow Herald* on Etrurian cities. In August, he was in Scotland with his mother and sisters in a rented house on the Clyde. While there, he

Fig. 4 Photograph of William Sharp taken by an unknown photographer in Rome in 1883. Reproduced from *William Sharp: A Memoir*, compiled by Elizabeth Sharp (London: William Heinemann, 1910).

went over to Arran to visit Sir Noel Paton; from there he went on to Oban, sailed to Mull, and crossed the island to the small island of Iona which became a place of pilgrimage for him and figured prominently in his writings as Fiona Macleod. In September, the *Glasgow Herald*, on the strength of his Italian articles, invited him to become its London-based art critic, a post he held for many years before turning it over to Elizabeth.

On his way to Scotland in early August, he lost a large portmanteau which "in addition to new clothes got in London and valuable souvenirs and presents from Italy, contained all my MSS., both prose & verse, all my Memoranda (many of them essential to work in hand), all my Notes taken in Italy, my private papers and letters, some proofs, three partly written articles (two of them much overdue), my most valued books — and indeed my whole literary stock-in-trade pro-tem." After retracing his steps in cold, wet weather, trying to find the missing case, he had no choice but to accept its loss. He wrote to Hall Caine in August 1883:

> As a literary worker yourself you will understand what a "fister" this is to a young writer. I must take this buffet of Fate, however, without undue wincing — and tackle to again all the more earnestly for the severe loss and disappointment experienced. There's no use crying over spilt milk.

The portmanteau was found about a month after its loss and returned in a wet and damaged condition, but many of the poems and essays were recoverable, and some were published in *Good Words*, the *Fortnightly Review*, *Cassell's Magazine*, and the *Literary World*.

After returning to London from Scotland in September, Sharp contacted a cold that progressed into a second bout of rheumatic fever, further damaging his heart. His sister Mary came from Edinburgh to join Elizabeth in nursing him back to health. By November he was able to tell Caine:

> I am greatly better, so much so that I find it difficult to credit the doctor's doleful prognostications: I *feel* I must take care, but beyond that I have no immediate cause for alarm. The worst of it is that I am one day in exuberant health and the next very much the reverse. The doctors agree that it is valvular disease of the heart, a treacherous form thereof still further complicated by a hereditary bias.

He felt well enough to make light of the illness: "a fellow must 'kick' someday — and I would as soon do so 'per the heart' as, like no small number of my *forbears* in Scotland, from delirium tremens, sheep-stealing (in hanging days), and general disreputableness." Still, there was a problem: "Even if pecuniarly able, I am forbidden to marry for a year to come — and though waiting is hard now for us both, it is better even for my fiancée that nothing should be done which might result in what would be such a grief to her." Even if he had the requisite money, marriage would put too great a strain on his heart.

During the early part of 1884, Sharp prepared his second book of poems, *Earth's Voices*, which was published by Elliott Stock in June. Perhaps because he had become friends with more important literary figures, it was more widely noted than the earlier volume. He received a letter of praise from Walter Pater, whose judgment might have been tinged by the volume's dedication to him, and another from Christina Rossetti who liked several poems, especially those praising her brother. In a 1906 *Century* article, Sharp's friend Ernest Rhys praised some of the poems in *Earth's Voices*: "His writings betrayed a constant quest after those hardly realizable regions of thought and those keener lyric emotions, which, since Shelley wrote and Rossetti wrote and painted, have so often occupied the interpreters of the vision and spectacle of nature." Rhys found in one of the volume's poems, "A Record," "unmistakable germs" of "some of the supernatural ideas that afterward received a much more vital expression in the works of Fiona Macleod."

Sharp spent most of March and April in a Dover house loaned to him by Mrs. Craik who understood both his precarious finances and his need to recuperate away from the fogs of London. His friend and fellow poet Philip Marston (1850–1887), Mrs. Craik's godson who was partially blinded at the age of three, spent a week with him in April. Following Marston's death in 1887, Sharp published an edition of his poem, *For a Song's Sake*, in Walter Scott's Canterbury Series. In a "Memorial Introduction," he described in glowing terms the walks they took together near Dover in 1884 and Marston's excited response to the warm sea air and sounds he never heard in London. Sharp crossed to France in early May for the first of many visits to Paris as an art critic for the *Glasgow Herald*. He wrote excitedly to Elizabeth about the writers, painters, and other luminaries he was meeting, among them Paul Bourget, Alphonse Daudet, Emile Zola, Frederic Mistral, Adolphe Bouguereau, Fernand Cormon, Puvis de Chavannes, Jules Breton, and, curiously, Madame Blavatsky.

After returning from Paris, Sharp suffered another relapse that led him to ask Hall Caine on Sunday, June 15, 1884, if he could stay with him the following night. He was vacating his cold and damp rented rooms in Thorngate Road, and he had to leave them the next day. He could not stay with Elizabeth's family in Inverness Terrace until Tuesday. The letter shows how close Sharp and Caine were in this period and supplies a revealing insight into the malady Sharp could not escape:

> I have had, this afternoon, a narrow escape from rheumatic fever & must leave here at once. I think I have fought it down, but I must not risk such another chance. I have been crouching over a large fire and with my medicine have got the better of the cursed complaint. [...] If in any way inconvenient, a postcard will do if you only say all right on it. Wd. come in the evening — but must go west early in the day from here on an urgent matter. Can't say how thankful I am to have escaped this sharp and sudden attack, & there's no saying what a second bout would do.

> Excuse a hideous scrawl, but my hands are so chilled and pained I can hardly hold the pen — and have to write at a distance.

Caine replied at once. Sharp should come the next day to a house Caine rented in Hampstead where he would be well cared for by two ladies. According to Caine's biographer, Sharp spent that Monday night at Caine's house on Worsley Road, Hampstead — where he was looked after by Caine's fifteen-year-old mistress, Mary Chandler, and her maid. (*Hall Caine: Portrait of a Victorian Romancer*, 171.)

Caine had rented the Hampstead house for Mary Chandler because he did not want his family or others to know about his relationship with a very young girl who was pregnant with his child. Sharp was one of only a few close friends who knew about the arrangement. In an August 26th letter from Scotland, he asked Caine

> Is the hour of paternity drawing nigh? I wonder if MacColl would accept for the *Athenaeum* a sonnet on "Caine's Firstborn"? I must try. If a boy, please call it "Abel," or in case this would give rise to too many poor jokes, what do you say to "*Tubal*." Most people would simply think you had called him after "that fellow, you know, in one of George Eliot's poems"!

As it turned out, a baby boy was born on August 15th and named neither Abel nor Tubal, after the Tubal-Cain in *Genesis*, but Ralph after Ralph Hall, Caine's grandfather. The main purpose of the August 26th letter was to let Caine know about an upcoming change in his own circumstances:

> Just a line, my dear Caine, in the midst of pressure from urgent work and accumulated correspondence, to let you know (what I am sure you will be glad to hear for my sake) that at last my long engagement is drawing to a close, and that Lillie and I are to be married on All Saints Day — just about two months from date. What we have got to marry on, Heaven knows — for I don't: yet I hope a plunge in the dark will not in this instance prove disastrous. It is not a plunge in the dark as regards love and friendship — and that is the main thing.

The year of waiting prescribed by his doctor was up, and Elizabeth's parents were finally convinced her marriage to her first cousin was inevitable even though the newly married couple's financial circumstances remained uncertain. Sharp had proved himself a reliable and constant young man; indeed, his frequent presence at 72 Inverness Terrace, Bayswater, had made him part of Elizabeth's family.

On October 31st, after a nine-year courtship, Elizabeth and William were married at Christ Church, Lancaster Gate, London. They rented a flat at 46 Talgarth Road in West Kensington which was furnished by their families. They continued to make their way as writers and expanded their circle of literary and artistic friends. In her *Memoir*, Elizabeth included a list of luminaries whose "literary households" welcomed the newly married couple. Among the many were Walter Pater, Robert Browning, Mr. and Mrs. Ford Madox Ford, Mr. and Mrs. William Morris, Mr. and Mrs. William Rossetti, Mr. and Mrs. Oscar Wilde, and Sir Frederick Leighton, the painter whose beautiful home and studio just off the Kensington High Street is now open to the public. At the close of 1884, both Sharps embarked on a six-year period of editing and reviewing that placed them near the center of London's literary elite. Still, William continued to write poetry and harbored a desire to gain attention and praise for his imaginative writing in poetry and prose.

Chapter Three

1885–1886

Sharp remained healthy for most of 1885 and became more productive. He continued as London art critic for the *Glasgow Herald*, joined the staff of the *Academy*, and contributed articles to the *Art Journal*, the *Examiner*, the *Athenaeum*, and *Good Words*. He hoped a year or two of reviewing and editing would free him financially to concentrate on poetry and fiction. He wrote to Eugene Lee-Hamilton in early January to praise his recently published book of poems, *Apollo and Marsyas, and Other Poems*. In a separate letter to Violet Paget, Lee-Hamilton's half sister who published as Vernon Lee, he expressed his disappointment in her recent novel, *Miss Brown*, which portrayed some of Sharp's friends in a negative light: "You cannot be aware of the deep offense it has given to many good friends. […] If I had never read anything else of yours, 'Miss Brown' would effectually have prevented my ever reading or having the faintest curiosity to read anything from your pen." Then he tempered those harsh words:

> If it were not for my sincere admiration for you as a writer of much delightful, admirable, and original work — I should not have written to you as I have now done: but it is because of my admiration for the "Vernon Lee" whom I know that I refuse to recognize as genuine or characteristic a production in every sense inferior to anything she has done.

The severe criticism may have derived in part from Paget's negative response to Sharp's "Motherhood," parts of which Elizabeth read to her when she visited Italy in 1881. Yet Sharp's opinion of the novel reflected that of many others, including Henry James to whom she had dedicated the novel, and she came to regret her authorship. Though Sharp's relationship with Vernon Lee soured temporarily, that with Eugene Lee-Hamilton remained strong. Following the death of their mother in 1896, Lee-Hamilton found himself able to leave the reclining chair he had lain in for years, travel to America, and marry in 1898 the Anglo-Jamaican novelist Annie E. Holdsworth. Though Lee-Hamilton's health remained precarious, he with his wife and half-sister continued for several years to host British writers, Sharp among them, at their Villa Il Palmerino outside Florence.

When he wrote the letters to Lee-Hamilton and Violet Paget, Sharp was in bed with an illness that made him liable to his "old trouble" which we now know was rheumatic fever and which he defined as a rheumatic chill that "rather floored him." By February he had recovered enough to write a review of Walter Pater's *Marius the Epicurean* that appeared as the lead item in the 28 February issue of the *Athenaeum* (271–273). *Athenaeum* reviews were unsigned, but Sharp sent a copy to Pater who thanked him on March 1: "You seem to have struck a note of criticism not merely pleasant but judicious; and there are one or two points — literary ones — on which you have said precisely what I should have wished and thought it important for me to have said. Thank you sincerely for your friendly work!" He was pleased that Mrs. Sharp was also interested in the book as it was always a sign to him that he had to some extent succeeded in his literary work when it gained the "the approval of accomplished women." He hoped Sharp would contact him a week or so ahead of a projected visit to Oxford so they could plan to see as much as possible of each other (*Memoir*, 104–105).

Sharp first met Pater through Dante Gabriel Rossetti in the late 1870s, and their friendship was such by November 1882 that Pater began a letter to Sharp with a parenthetical: "(I think we have known each other long enough to drop the 'Mr.')." In 1884, Sharp dedicated his second book of poems, *Earth's Voices*: *Transcripts from Nature*: *Sospitra and other Poems*, as follows: "Dedicated in High Esteem and in Personal Regard to my Friend, Walter Pater, Fellow of Brasenose College, Oxford." Sometime in the late spring of 1885, the Sharps went "down to Oxford," according to Elizabeth, so she could "meet the Misses Pater at their brother's house" (*Memoir*, 119–120). While staying there, Sharp saw an advertisement for "a desirable cottage to be let furnished, with service, and garden stocked with vegetables" on Loch Tarbert in Scotland, and they rented it for July.

The cottage turned out to be less desirable than advertised, but Sharp described its location glowingly in a July 22 letter to Edward Dowden:

> I came here from London some weeks ago, with my wife and a young sister who lives in Glasgow. I forget, by the by, whether I ever told you that I was married late last autumn? I am always glad to get north, both loving and knowing the Western Isles and Highlands, and all places wherever broods the Celtic glamour. West Loch Tarbert is one of the loveliest of the Atlantic sea-lochs: severing Knapdale (Northern Argyll) from "wild Cantyre;" its length is about 11 miles, from its commencement east of the islands of Giglia and Islay up to the narrow Isthmus of Tarbert on the western side of Loch Fyne. From our windows we get a lovely view up the loch, looking out on the mountainous district of Knapdale and the small-islanded water towards Tarbert. To the North-east is Shobli-Ghoil — the Hill of Love — the mountain where that Celtic Achilles, Diarmid, met his death by a wound in the heel through the envy of Fingal. Behind us are endless moorlands, and only one or two cottages at wide distances.

Foreshadowing more overtly his writing as Fiona Macleod, he continued: "I have a stirring and heroic Celtic subject in my mind for poetic treatment and hope to make a start with it erelong. It will be with regret that we will leave at the end of the month — but we have two or three other places to go to in Scotland before returning to London — which we do not intend doing till the end of September." The purpose of the letter was to ask for Dowden's opinions about the placing of several sonnets in an edition of Shakespeare's poems he was working on for inclusion in the Canterbury Poets, a series of inexpensive editions of the works of well-known English poets that was to be issued by the Walter Scott Publishing House. After publishing *Shakespeare: A Critical Study of His Mind and Art* in 1875, Dowden, a Professor at Trinity College in Dublin, became a leading expert on Shakespeare, and Sharp valued his opinions.

The care Sharp exercised in arranging the poems and writing the Introduction for *Songs, Poems, and Sonnets of William Shakespeare* in the fall of 1885 led the Walter Scott Publishing House to accept his proposal for a book containing a selection of the best sonnets of the century and to appointment him, in 1886, general editor of the Canterbury Poets. The firm played a crucial role in establishing Sharp's reputation as a writer and editor. Walter Scott was a prosperous businessman in Newcastle who acquired the bankrupt Tyne Publishing Company in 1882. He

Fig. 5 Photograph of Edward Dowden Robinson (c. 1895), Wikimedia, https://commons.wikimedia.org/wiki/File:Portrait_of_Edward_Dowden.jpg, Public Domain.

named David Gordon, a dynamic Scotsman, as manager of the renamed Walter Scott Publishing House. Gordon convinced Scott he could turn the firm to profitability by speeding up the publication of inexpensive editions of major writers, separating them into several series, advertising them aggressively, and selling them for one shilling at the rate of one per month to an expanding reading public. After buying and reading one volume, readers would be motivated to acquire another. Gordon proceeded to create in short order not only the Canterbury Poets Series, but also the Camelot Classics Series (for prose works), the Great Writers Series (biographies), and the Contemporary Science Series.

Gordon turned first to Joseph Skipsey (1832–1903), who was living in Newcastle, to edit the Canterbury Poets. Son of a coal miner, Skipsey taught himself to read and matured into a well-known and highly respected poet. Under his editorship, in 1884 and 1885 the firm produced editions of Samuel Taylor Coleridge, Percy Bysshe Shelley, William Blake, Robert Burns, and Edgar Allan Poe (all edited by Skipsey), George Herbert (edited by Ernest Rhys), and Sharp's edition of Shakespeare's poems. Scott and Gordon knew little about English or any other literature; they were businessmen intent on making money. In his autobiographical *Wales England Wed*, Ernest Rhys recalled receiving in early 1886 "an unexpected call at his London home from 'two prosperous-looking men in top hats' who turned out to be Walter Scott's representatives." They were there to offer Rhys the editorship of a prose series complementing the Canterbury Poets. Rhys gradually realized the two men thought they were talking to Professor John Rhys, a well-known Celtic scholar. Nevertheless, Ernest got the job, and he described the visit more fully in *Everyman Remembers* (75–76):

> One morning two visitors were announced at an awkwardly early hour. [...] A loud knocking woke me in no state to receive strangers, clad in an old Rob Roy dressing-gown and slippers. It was too late to retreat. One of the callers, a red-haired Scotsman, was already entering. [...] These morning callers were emissaries of Walter Scott Ltd. [...] they carted me off to lunch at a City tavern and asked me to edit a prose series for a ridiculously modest stipend. Before we parted, I had sketched a chart of a dozen possible titles. So lightly was I launched on the career of editing.

After accepting the offer from the emissaries, one of whom must have been David Gordon, Rhys chose Camelot as the name of the new series, and settled on Sir Thomas Malory, "the father of English prose," for its first volume, which he edited under the title *Romance of King Arthur*. The Camelot Series was a remarkable success, as were the other three series. The volumes disappeared as fast as the Scott firm and its editors could produce them. When the Camelot Series ran its course, Ernest Rhys convinced an unknown publisher, J. M. Dent, to undertake another series of inexpensive editions of higher quality, which became the phenomenally successful Everyman's Library. Dent, its publisher, made vast sums of money, and Rhys, its first and long-time editor, became famous as "Everyman."

Shortly after returning to London in the fall of 1885, Sharp health gave way again. "Disquieting rheumatic symptoms" according to Elizabeth, but he was able to work on various writing and editing projects, chief among them an anthology of nineteenth-century sonnets for the Canterbury Poets Series. He asked many well-known poets for permission to use one or two of their works and composed the volume's introductory essay — "The Sonnet: Its History and Characteristics" — which George Meredith considered "the best exposition of the sonnet known to him" (*Memoir*, 116). Elizabeth contributed to the selection and arrangement of the poems. By late December, the volume was ready, and it was published on January 26, 1886. It sold well and was reissued several times during the year. Sharp made some revisions during the summer and fall of 1886 for a new edition in December. The anthology went through several more editions and became, after 1899, *Sonnets of the Nineteenth Century*. Though Sharp was hired by the Scott firm to prepare the book and later to revise it, he did not share in its long-term financial success, but he told Edward Dowden (February 3, 1886) the publishers had "behaved very decently" to him. No matter how decent their behavior, it paled in contrast to what Sharp would have earned had he received royalties, and that income would have eased the financial difficulties the Sharps endured for many years. Though Sharp's earnings from the volume were meager, it established his reputation as an editor.

Sharp also managed to write in the fall of 1885 a three-volume sensational novel set in Scotland and Australia called *The Sport of Chance* which was published serially in *The People's Friend* in early 1887 and as a book by Hurst and Blackett in 1888. He also began planning a biography of Shelley for Walter Scott's Great Writers Series, which was edited by his friend Eric Robertson. For this series, Sharp eventually produced, in addition to the Shelley (1887), biographies of Heinrich Heine (1888) and Robert Browning (1890). Despite his frequent illnesses in the fall of 1885, he wrote the introduction and edited for the Canterbury Poets' *Poetical Works of Sir Walter Scott*, a Walter Scott who differed significantly from the book's publisher.

When Sharp learned the Scott firm was planning a Camelot prose series with Ernest Rhys as General Editor, he saw an opportunity to make some additional money. He asked a mutual friend for an introduction to Rhys and sought him out with a proposal to edit and introduce Thomas De Quincey's *Confessions of an Opium Eater*. According to Rhys, Sharp "burst in" on him "one summer morning" as he was "having a bath." Rhys described their meeting in *Everyman Remembers* (76):

This was William Sharp, the poet, who towered up, a rosy giant, in the low-raftered room. His fine figure and exuberant contours, set forth in unusually resplendent clothes, suggested a stage Norseman. He talked very fast and excitedly, his bright yellow hair brushed up from an open brow, under which blue eyes, rosy cheeks, full red lips, and a pointed yellow beard suggested a picture by some impressionist painter. He had been editing the Canterbury Poets, in which series my George Herbert volume appeared, and had heard from the publishers of my prose argosy. Here was an opening after his own heart. In half an hour he had proposed half a dozen books which he would like to edit for me, and De Quincey's *Opium-Eater* was there and then allotted to him.

He described this meeting earlier and at greater length in a 1907 *Century Magazine* article. Sharp was

joyously and consciously exuberant. He told of adventures in Australian backwoods, and of intrigues in Italy; [...] and then he turned, with the same rapid flow of brief staccato sentences, to speak of his friend Mr. Swinburne's new volume of poems, or of the last time he walked along Cheyne Walk [where Rhys then lived] to spend an evening with Rossetti. He appeared to know everybody, to have been everywhere. [...] It is not easy to avoid extravagance in speaking of one who was in all things an illusionist. Sharp's sensations, artistic ideas, and performances were not to be counted by rule or measure. He was capable of predicting a new religion as he paced the Thames Embankment, or of devising an imaginary new theater for romantic drama — whose plays were yet to be written (by himself) — as he rode home from the Haymarket.

And again:

Thanks to his large and imposing presence, his sanguine air, his rosy faith in himself, he had a way of overwhelming editors that was beyond anything, I believe, ever heard of in London, before or since. On one occasion he went into a publisher's office and gave so alluring an account of a long-meditated book that the publisher gave him a check for 100£, although he had not written a word.

Those descriptions capture better than any others the appearance and mannerisms that made Sharp appealing — to women and to men — as he was making his way in the London publishing world in the 1880s.

Elizabeth recalled the start of 1886 as "unpropitious." It was a wet winter, and Sharp was ill and dejected. In mid-February, he sent two sonnets to his friend Eric Robertson for his birthday. One begins with following sestet:

> A little thing it is indeed to die:
> God's seal to sanctify the soul's advance —
> Or silence, and a long enfevered trance.
> But no slight thing is it — ere the last sigh
> Leaves the tired heart, ere calm and passively
> The worn face reverent grows, fades the dim glance —
> To pass away and pay no recompense
> To Life, who hath given to us so gloriously.

In a letter accompanying the sonnets, Sharp wrote, "There are two 'William Sharps' — one of them unhappy and bitter enough at heart, God knows — though he seldom shows it. This other poor devil also sends you a greeting of his own kind [the sonnet]." From childhood on, Sharp assumed to an unusual extent the guise of different people. Gradually the trait progressed to his portraying himself two people inhabiting a single body. This letter is one of the early signs of the movement toward duality. Here the duality is defined by mood; one William Sharp is happy and outgoing, the other unhappy and bitter. The notion of two people in one body was a means of explaining and coping with the intense mood swings that plagued him throughout his life. Gradually he came to define the duality as the dominance of reason and the dominance of emotion, as living in the material world and the spirit world, and finally as being both a man and a woman. That trend finally culminated in the creation of a fully functional second self in the form of the woman he called Fiona Macleod.

Of the *Opium-Eater* assignment, Rhys wrote: "But alas! before he [Sharp] had completed the copy or even written his preamble for the book, he came down with scarlet fever. Careless of infection, I spent an hour at his bedside when the fever abated, in talking over De Quincey, and then wrote the preamble myself over his name" (*Everyman Remembers*, 77). Since the volume appeared on March 26, 1886, Sharp must have been ill with scarlet fever in February, not long after his first meeting with Rhys. "In the early spring of 1886," Elizabeth wrote, "my husband was laid low with scarlet fever and phlebitis. Recovery was slow, and at the press review of the Royal Academy he caught a severe chill; the next day he was in the grip of a prolonged attack of rheumatic fever" (*Memoir*, 125–126). The catalogue of Sharp's colds and bouts of rheumatic fever in the nineteen eighties is extensive:

1. In January 1880 a bad cold while visiting Rossetti;
2. In summer and fall 1880, another cold culminating in his initial bout of rheumatic fever;
3. In fall 1883 a second attack of rheumatic fever which seriously damaged a heart valve and drew his sister Mary from Edinburgh to help Elizabeth nurse him back to health;
4. In June 1884 another cold that threatened to produce another episode of rheumatic fever, which Sharp described in a pitiful letter to Hall Caine in a hand so cold and shaky the writing is nearly illegible;
5. In fall 1885, disquieting rheumatic symptoms;
6. In February 1886 scarlet fever and another attack of rheumatic fever.

This record of illnesses contrasts markedly with the robust figure who appeared to Rhys. Sharp described the dichotomy in a letter to Caine in November 1883: "I am one day in exuberant health and the next very much the reverse."

The rheumatic fever attack in the spring of 1886 was particularly severe. "For many days, Elizabeth wrote, "his life hung in the balance." Her description of his hallucinations during the illness is especially compelling as it bears upon how his imagination worked and his later creation of the Fiona Macleod persona:

> During much of the suffering and tedium of those long weeks the sick man passed in a dream-world of his own; for he had the power at times of getting out of or beyond his normal consciousness at will. At first, he imagined himself the owner of a gypsy travelling van, in which he wandered over the to him well-known and much-loved solitudes of Argyll, resting where the whim dictated and visiting his many fisher and shepherd friends. Later, during the long crisis of the illness, though unconscious often of all material surroundings, he passed through other keen inner phases of consciousness, through psychic and dream experiences that afterward to some extent were woven into the Fiona Macleod writings, and, as he believed, were among the original shaping influences that produced them. For a time, he felt himself to be practically

> dead to the material world and acutely alive "on the other side of things" in the greater freer universe. He had no desire to return, and he rejoiced in his freedom and greater powers; but as he described it afterward, a hand suddenly restrained him: "Not yet, you must return."

He believed he had been "freshly sensitized," Elizabeth continued, he "knew he had — as I had always believed — some special work to do before he could again go free." While his illness persisted, Ernest Rhys brought him branches of a tree in early leaf, which Elizabeth placed on the windowsill. The effect of their "fluttering leaves," she wrote, helped his imagination. But they had another effect: They "awoke 'that dazzle in the brain,' as he always described the process which led him over the borderland of the physical into the 'gardens' of psychic consciousness he called 'the Green Life'."

Here Elizabeth broached the psychic experiments — enhanced by drugs — Sharp undertook in the 1890s. She discouraged those experiments because they negatively affected his overall mental health. She worried they might drive him into a state of schizophrenia from which he could not recover. Such experiments led him in the nineties into the orbit of William Butler Yeats, who enlisted both Sharp and Fiona Macleod in his efforts to obtain by psychic experiments the rituals of the Celtic Mystical Order he planned to house in an abandoned castle in the west of Ireland. Many years later Yeats recounted a story Sharp told him and commented "I did not believe him, and not because I thought the story impossible, for I knew he had a susceptibility beyond that of anyone I had ever known to symbolic or telepathic influence, but because he never told anything that was true; the facts of life disturbed him and were forgotten" (*Autobiographies*, 340).

After recovering from the worst of the 1886-episode, Sharp was unable for many months to engage in sustained writing, and that left him desperately short of money. "At the end of ten weeks," Elizabeth wrote, "he left his bed. As soon as possible I took him to Northbrook, Micheldever [in Hampshire], the country house of our kind friends Mr. and Mrs. Henryson Caird, who put it at our disposal for six weeks. Slowly his strength came back in those warm summer days, as he lay contentedly in the sunshine" (*Memoir*, 126). From Micheldever on August 14, he described his condition to Theodore Watts, who was helping him with the second edition of *Sonnets of this Century*:

> I am gaining strength very satisfactorily. My doctor ran down to see me before going off to Canada on his autumn holiday, and he told me he could now find no trace of heart-disease, though I undoubtedly inherited from the Rheumatic fevers (the recent attack & that of 5 years ago) a heart-complaint which would require my care for a year or so to come. I am not to work too hard, and never after the afternoon. This is all very well, but whether I can keep to such orders is a different matter.

In a September 7 letter to Frederick Shields, he said he was "progressing slowly but steadily." In a September 13th letter, he told Ford Madox Brown he was "nearly robust again." He had benefited from "his extended stay at this pleasant country house." He had begun to do a little work, "chiefly reviewing," but he had been instructed "to wait another month at least before getting in full sail again." He had hoped to be able to go to Manchester to see and review the frescoes Brown was painting for the Great Room of the newly constructed Town Hall, but that would have to wait until spring. His doctor thought he needed "bracing" and advised him to go to his "native air." He and Elizabeth left Micheldever in mid-September and spent two weeks in and around Edinburgh.

In mid-October, Sharp told J. Stanley Little, who would soon become a close and valued friend, he was incapacitated by a sudden illness. Elizabeth noticed "new disquieting symptoms" as "he began to assert himself. His heart proved to be severely affected, and his recovery was proportionately retarded" (*Memoir*, 126). Nevertheless, he returned to the life of Shelley he promised for the Great Writers Series. In late November he thanked Edward Dowden for sending as a gift his recently published two-volume *Life of Shelley*. He needed it for his writing and could not afford to buy it. As 1886 ended, Sharp had suffered varying degrees of illness for nine months, his health remained precarious, and money was in short supply

Chapter Four

1887–1888

In the spring of 1887, Sharp succeeded his friend Eric Robertson as editor of the "Literary Chair" in the *Young Folk's Paper*, a widely circulated weekly paper for boys. This appointment brought "steady work" and "a reliable income, a condition of security hitherto unknown to us, which proved an excellent tonic to the delicate editor" (*Memoir*, 127–128). Assisted by Elizabeth, Sharp read evaluated, and responded to "efforts in prose and verse of the 'young folk' who wished to exercise their budding literary talents." The best pieces appeared in the paper "prefaced by an article of criticism and instruction written by their editor and critic."

Though he remained weak, Sharp continued to work and travel. After resting again for a time at the Caird's country house in Hampshire, he and Elizabeth went to Paris in early May to review the Salons for the *Glasgow Herald*. On April 28, before leaving for Paris, he asked Ford Madox Brown, who was in Manchester painting frescoes in the new Town Hall, if it would be convenient for him to stay with him on May 16 or 17 when he planned to be in Manchester for the Royal Jubilee Exhibition celebrating the fiftieth year of Queen Victoria's reign. He wanted to examine a painting in the Exhibition for a review in the *Glasgow Herald*. In a January 1890 letter to Brown, he recalled and praised a framed etching of Brown's "Entombment" he had seen in the Exhibition. In his April 1887 letter to Brown, he said he had finished a "memoir of poor Philip Marston to precede his forthcoming volume of stories." That volume, which Sharp called *For a Song's Sake and other Stories*, was published by the Walter Scott firm in May 1887. Brown had known Philip and was close to the Marston family. In a July letter to

Louise Chandler Moulton, another friend of the Marston's, Sharp said the volume was selling well "almost solely on a/c" of his introductory memoir. The stories have not taken well, he continued, but the reviews were flattering; in fact, one said Philip "was at least fortunate in death to have such a biographer."

Along with his articles and editorial work on the *Young Folk's Paper* and for the Walter Scott firm, Sharp's main endeavor in 1887 was his monograph on Shelley for Scott's Great Writers Series. He continued to correspond with Shelley experts, chief among them Edward Dowden, and devoted considerable effort to the book, which was published on the first of October. It contained instead of a dedication a "special acknowledgment of indebtedness" to Dowden "whose two comprehensive volumes on Shelley form the completest and most reliable record extant, and at the same time constitute the worthiest monument wherewith the poet's memory has yet been honored." Elizabeth's description of his choice of Shelley for his first Great Writers book is telling. Shelley was the inspiring genius of his youth, she wrote, and "He was in sympathy with much of Shelley's thought: with his hatred of rigid conventionality, of the tyranny of social laws, with his antagonism to existing marriage and divorce laws, with his belief in the sanctity of passion when called forth by high and true emotion" (*Memoir*, 131). A letter Sharp wrote to a Mr. Clarke in December 1887 demonstrates the strength of his convictions regarding women's rights. He called the views of women in a poem Clarke sent him for comment "absolute lies and absurdities." In a second letter to Clarke, he affirmed the influence of Shelley: "instead of my reverence for true womanhood falling off, it is yearly growing more strengthened, till now with Shelley it is one of my cardinal faiths — the equality of the sexes." Those were the sentiments of Mona Caird and Elizabeth herself. By mentioning them here in the context of the Shelley biography, she set the stage for the events that changed the course of their lives in the following decade.

In August 1887 Sharp received a letter from Hall Caine expressing his concern about the state of Sharp's health. Sharp's response, from North Queensferry in Fife on September first, is a frank and detailed account of the heart problem that plagued him:

> I think you are the only one of my friends who has recognised what a secret enemy my ill-health is. I look so robust, and (often at a great effort)

try to be cheerful and sanguine that many think I have little to complain of. <u>You</u>, however, realise something of what I have really to endure. There are perhaps few people who know what "angina pectoris" really is, though "snake in the breast" gives them some idea it is not pleasant. If from hereditary taint it sometimes attacks the most robust natures, & is then deadliest. The agony of it is sometimes too great for conscious endurance, and over one's head always hangs the shadow of sudden death. The doctor has warned me it may come at any moment; I may stoop too suddenly, may fall, may receive startling news — anything of the kind may bring about instant death. This, added to the precariousness of the literary life and its incessant hard work, gives me many a dark hour. Sometimes I awake at night with the dull gripping pain which is ominous of attack, and as I lie by my sleeping wife I do not know if I shall ever see the morning's light. Then I think of the hard struggle of life, and what my death would mean to my wife, and — well, I needn't dilate on the subject.

He continued, revealing more about his approach to life and death:

But partly because it is my natural bias and in great part because I have trained myself to this kind of self-control, I betray nothing of all this to anyone. The other day a friend remarked to my wife that I was looking so well and was so cheerful & confident that I must surely be exceptionally well — and yet this was shortly after an attack so violent and dreadful that it was some time before I came round. If, however, I did not keep this "brave front" before the world, I would give way to the shadow that dogs me always. I <u>never</u> allow it to overcome me: if it be too appellant, I face it and as it were frown it down. I have no fear of death, which the soul in me knows to be but the gate of life. The world is so very beautiful, and full of such transcendent hints of the divine, that death should be as welcome to all as the first breath of summer to the hillslopes and meadows. Yet oh I do cling to life too! There is so much I want to do, so many dreams which I would fain should not all pass oblivion-ward unaccomplished.

Finally, he confirmed the singularity of his relationship with Caine: "You are the only one of my friends to whom I have written this — but you drew it from me by your brotherly sympathy. And now having read my words destroy and forget them." Since Caine ignored that direction, we have in this newly discovered letter Sharp's deepest thoughts powerfully expressed about life and death. Reading the letter, we can feel the pain that often gripped him and recognize the burden of knowing each day might be his last.

Improved finances enabled the Sharps to move, at the close of 1887, from a flat on Talgarth Road in West Kensington to a larger house in South Hampstead where "the air was purer and access to green fields easier." In early November, in good health and spirits, Sharp told Caine he had taken "a most delightful house" in Goldhurst Terrace, South Hampstead, and planned to move in at the end of December. He suggested Caine do the same as the neighborhood was "well sheltered from fog & east wind," healthy and not inconvenient. It would be grand to have Caine as a near neighbor. Later in the month, before the move, ill-health struck again, and Elizabeth took her husband to the Isle of Wight to recover from "inflammation of the lungs." After returning in early January, they settled into the South Hampstead house which had, according to Elizabeth, a sunny study on the ground floor so the "invalid" would not have to deal with stairs. Since its address, 17a Goldhurst Terrace, was frequently confused with 17 Goldhurst Terrace, the house in front facing the street, it needed a name, and the Sharps settled on "Wescam," a name made up of the initials the two Sharps and Mona Caird who lived near by. They began holding Sunday evening "at homes" which were attended by "all those with whom we were in sympathy," and the list of guests Elizabeth provided in the *Memoir* (140–141) includes many well-known writers and editors. As winter turned to spring Sharp's health held in the new location. His editorial work and Elizabeth's well-placed friends and her charm as a hostess solidified their position near the center of London's literary life.

Mona Allison Caird and her husband James Alexander Henryson Caird had a much larger house a few blocks north on Arkwrite Road where the Sharps were frequently entertained and met many of Mona's well-placed friends, including Thomas Hardy. She was a formidable figure who was gaining a reputation, praised by many and denigrated by more, as an advocate for women's rights, especially greater equality in marriage. The American women's rights activist Elizabeth Cady Stanton visited Mona Caird in February 1888 and recalled in 1898: "Mrs. Caird was a very graceful, pleasing woman, and so gentle in manner and appearance that no one would deem her capable of hurling such thunderbolts at the long-suffering Saxon people" (*Eighty Years and More*: *Reminiscences 1815–1897*). The Sharps shared Mona's views on marriage and women's rights, and she invariably came to their rescue when they needed help.

Fig. 6. Alice Mona (Alison) Caird (1854–1922) Engraving based on a photograph by H. S. Mendelssohn Wikipedia, https://en.wikipedia.org/wiki/Mona_Caird

Sharp's improved health enabled greater productivity. He selected poems and wrote prefaces for an anthology of odes and a book of American sonnets, both published in Scott's Canterbury Series, of which he was General Editor. He contributed reviews and critical articles to the *Academy*, the *Athenaeum*, and the *Literary World*. In April, he reviewed a Paris Salon for the *Glasgow Herald* and described it to Frederick Shields as "the resort of the evil rather than of the good spirits of art." George Meredith invited the Sharp's to spend Whitsuntide with him in Surrey, and Sharp described their visit in a May 22 letter to Richard Le Gallienne: "I have just returned from my delightful visit to the loveliest part of the loveliest county in Southern England — and with glorious weather & such a host as George Meredith I need not say that I have enjoyed the last few days immensely." From Box Hill, the Sharps walked over to Dorking to see their friend Grant Allen who was entertaining Joseph Cotton who edited the *Academy*. Sharp told Cotton he was pleased by Le Gallienne's *Academy* review of his edition of Philip Marston's poetry. Meredith and Sharp had long conversations during the day and,

Elizabeth recalled, Meredith read from his novels at night: "The reader's enjoyment seemed as great as that of his audience, and it interested me to hear how closely his methods of conversation resembled, in wittiness and brilliance, those of the characters in his novels" (*Memoir*, 145). On May 23, Sharp wrote to Theodore Watts: "What a charming fellow G. M. is — is he not? The more I see of him, the more I admire and like him."

Fig. 7 George Meredith in *Robert Louis Stevenson: A Bookman Extra Number 1913* (London: Hodder & Stoughton), p. 138, Wikimedia, https://commons.wikimedia.org/wiki/File:George_Meredith%27s_Portrait.jpg, Public Domain.

Sharp also told Watts on the 23rd that he would send him a copy of his third book of poetry — *Romantic Ballads and Poems of Phantasy* — which had just been published by Walter Scott. It was a "maturer work," and he hoped Watts would find it an improvement over his first two volumes of poetry.

> In substance, it is imaginative in the truest sense — as I do not hesitate to say. It honestly seems to me that with all its demerits there is stuff in it of the purely imaginative kind such as you will not easily find in the work of other contemporary minor poets. Of course, I shall be disappointed if no one likes it, or thinks highly of it — but for the first time in my life I am indifferent to adverse criticism: for I feel well assured that the little

booklet is sterling — and with this assured confidence a bad reception can at the worst be but unfortunate and disagreeable.

Having described the main qualities of the book, Sharp said he was not urging Watts to review it (in the *Athenaeum* where he was a poetry critic), but the letter spells out what he hoped Watts would say should he decide to do so.

Sharp intended to print only a hundred copies. Given the "unexpected and gratifying anticipatory demand," he agreed to a "larger edition" most of which was "already engaged." The high demand might encourage Watts to write or solicit a review. In the "Dedicatory Introduction" to the volume Sharp expressed his "earnest conviction" that "a Romantic revival [is] imminent in our poetic literature, a true awakening of genuine romantic sentiment." He dedicated the volume to his wife who has "a sterling appreciation of imaginative literature." She shared with him "the true Celtic passion for the weird and supernatural, and for vividly romantic sentiment and action." In predicting a turn away from realism and formalism, Sharp hoped the volume would inspire a third romantic movement in the century's poetry, the first begun by Wordsworth and Keats and the second by Rossetti and William Morris. Several poems in the volume are a decided improvement over those published earlier, but its main interest is the "Introduction" which forecasts the poetry Sharp would write as Fiona Macleod. The volume did not have the broad impact Sharp anticipated or bring him the recognition he sought.

As 1888 proceeded, Sharp developed a close friendship with Richard Le Gallienne, an aspiring poet who lived in Liverpool and would move to London in 1891 to write for *The Star*. On May 19, he thanked Le Gallienne for his friendly and sympathetic *Academy* review of his Marston book. Three days later he asked Le Gallienne to let him know when he would be in London as he looked forward to the pleasure of meeting him. When Le Gallienne came to London in early June, Sharp sent him a special invitation: "If you have not made any other arrangement could you come here on Sunday evening next? We don't 'dress' on Sunday evenings, as friends sometimes drop in then promiscuously: and indeed on Sunday next we are, I believe, to have 'high tea' in place of dinner, for the sake of domestic convenience of some kind." He asked Le Gallienne to come at six so they could have a private "hour's chat" before the other guests arrived. He had sent Le Gallienne a copy of *Romantic Ballads* and wanted to talk with him about the new Romantic movement its preface forecast. He sensed from reading Le Gallienne's poems that he might be a willing recruit for the new Romanticism and recognized his potential as a major actor in London's literary life. Sharp's interest in Le Gallienne and the attention he received when he moved to London were due in no small measure to the young man's carriage and physiognomy — indeed, his physical beauty.

Fig. 8 Richard Le Gallienne (1866–1947). Photograph by Arthur Ellis (1894). Wikimedia, https://commons.wikimedia.org/wiki/File:Richard_Le_Gallienne,_by_Alfred_Ellis.jpg, Public Domain.

Twenty years after Sharp's death, in his *Romantic Nineties* (1926), Le Gallienne painted a vivid picture of one of his dearest friends:

> When I reached London [from his native Liverpool], Sharp was already known as the biographer of Rossetti, the editor of an excellent anthology of sonnets, a popularizer of poetry. As editor of the famous "Canterbury" series, model of many such to follow, [and] something of a poet himself. [...] It was his personality that mattered most. He was probably the handsomest man in London, a large flamboyant "sun-god" sort of creature, with splendid, vital, curling gold hair and a pointed golden beard, the bluest of Northern eyes, and the complexion of a

girl. Laughing energy radiated from his robust frame, and he was all exuberance, enthusiasm, and infectious happiness, a veritable young Dionysus. [...] No one could know him without falling under the spell of his generous magnetic nature, and I was proud to count him among my dearest friends (111).

This description confirms that of Ernest Rhys in *Everyman Remembers* and differs radically from that in Sharp's 1887 letter to Hall Caine. In 1900 Le Gallienne dedicated his *Travels in England* to Sharp with affection and a brief but compelling piece of doggerel:

> Will, you have travelled far and wide
> On many a foreign country-side,
> Tell me if you have fairer found
> Than honeysuckled English ground;
> Or did you, all the journey through,
> Find such a friend, dear Will — as you?

In August 1888, the Sharps went to Scotland and stayed two and a half months visiting family and friends. In a mid-October birthday letter to Theodore Watts, Sharp said there had been only four "wholly wet days" during their visit. They had been on the west or east coast most of the time, but were also "for some weeks at a glorious spot in Strathspey, a lovely moorland farm a thousand feet above the sea, among the Grampians, in Morayshire" just northwest of Aberdeen. While in Scotland he finished his second book for Walter Scott's Great Writers Series, a study of the German poet Heinrich Heine (1897–1865). He was seldom ill during his annual visits to Scotland, and his letters were invariably cheerful. Even that to Caine from Fife in September describing bouts of illness concluded, "I have been in a strong mental and spiritual ferment lately, and I think I shall speedily write something I have long had in my mind." The fresh air and familiar surroundings, augmented by relief from the pressures and tensions of London, were restorative.

When he returned to London in the fall, Sharp asked Andrew Chatto if his firm would like to publish a novel he was writing called *Sampriel*. He compared it to his *Romantic Ballads and Poems of Phantasy* as exemplifying the "new romantic movement." Just as the poems represented a new flowering of Romanticism, the novel was "destined to revolutionize contemporary fiction." Chatto accepted the offer and published it in 1889 as *Children of Tomorrow*. The love affair at the center of the romance encompassed many of the ideas he encountered in writing the Shelley monograph for Walter Scott: Elizabeth tied the novel to the advanced views of love and marriage among their circle of friends:

> A minority of dreamers and thinkers look beyond the strictly guarded, fettered conditions of married life, to a time, when man and woman, equally shall know that to stultify or slay the spiritual inner life of another human being, through the radical misunderstanding between alien temperaments inevitably tied to one another, is one of the greatest crimes against humanity. That the author [Sharp] knew how visionary for the immediate future were these ideas which we at that time so eagerly discussed with a little group of intimate sympathetic friends is shown by the prefatory lines in the book.

> > Forlorn the way, yet with strange gleams of gladness;
> > Sad beyond words the voices far behind,
> > Yet we, perplex with our diviner madness,
> > Must heed them not — the goal is still to find:
> > What though beset by pain and fear and sorrow,
> > We must not fail, we Children of To-morrow (*Memoir*, 146–147).

In the book one character says of another whose name, H. P. Siwäamill, is an anagram of William Sharp:

> He sees, as do so many of us, that the old conventionalities, the old moralities even, are in process of rapid evolution, if not dissolution, and he perceives that now, as always heretofore, the future is foreshadowed in the present, the Tomorrow is foretold in certain vivid moments of Today (75).

This sentence appears on the book's title page attributed to none other than H. P. Siwäamill: "We, who live more intensely and suffer more acutely than others, are the Children of To-morrow, for in us the new forces of the future are already astir or even dominant." Sharp neatly inserted his advanced views of marriage into the novel; Siwäamill's opinions are his.

The renewed good health Sharp enjoyed during the summer in Scotland lasted through the fall, enabling him to continue the writing and editing that produced a reasonable income. Although these two years — 1887 and 1888 — were marked by bouts of ill health, they also included periods of work that brought improved financial circumstances and acceptance in London's literary establishment, but neither *Romantic Ballads and Poems of Phantasy* nor *Children of Tomorrow* brought the accolades and acolytes Sharp sought. The new Romanticism proclaimed in the books was undercut by the quality of the products. Oscar Wilde made that point bitingly in reviewing *Romantic Ballads*: the "Introduction" announcing the new Romanticism was the "most interesting part of the volume," but it heralded "a dawn that rose long ago," and the poems were "quite inadequate." The lack luster response to the two volumes convinced Sharp his work as an editor and critic hampered his effort to gain approval for his poetry and fiction. That belief led to his decision in 1890 to break from editing and launch a new life that culminated four years later in Fiona Macleod through whom he relaunched his "new Romanticism" pseudonymously under the umbrella of the Celtic revival.

Chapter Five

1889

The high point of 1889 for Sharp was his first visit, in late summer, to Canada and the United States. His interest in North America increased as he edited in early 1889 a collection of American sonnets for Scott's Canterbury Poets, and he came to view the States as a market for his work. In January, he offered the Century Publishing Company in New York the American rights to *Children of Tomorrow*, which was scheduled for British publication by Chatto & Windus in April. Also in January, he proposed two articles for publication in Philadelphia's *Lippincott's Magazine*. In the spring, he thanked Thomas Wentworth Higginson, the American man of letters and friend of Emily Dickinson, for a book of his poetry and said he would try to mention it favorably in print. He told Higginson, who planned to be in London shortly, that he would hold a copy of *American Sonnets* to present in person. In July, he sent copies to Frank Dempster Sherman and Clinton Scollard, both represented in the anthology. The enclosed letters praised their poems and expressed his hope to meet them in the fall when he planned "to pay a short visit to E. C. Stedman and one or two other friends in New York."

A New York banker and a poet, anthologist, and critic, Stedman was the most powerful literary figure in the United States. He exerted substantial influence over publishers and editors in New York, which had supplanted Boston as the literary center of the country. Sharp could not have chosen a better advocate in the American publishing world. His contacts with Stedman began in 1887 when, in an article on the younger British poets in the October issue of the *Century Magazine*, Stedman, relying on the Australian poems in Sharp's *The Human Inheritance*, placed him among the "Colonial" poets. Sharp knew the *Century* article was to become a supplementary chapter on young

British poets in the thirteenth (Jubilee) edition of Stedman's *Victorian Poets*, a groundbreaking study first published in 1875. When Sharp saw the *Century* article, he asked Stedman to correct the error: "Since you are so kindly going to do me the honour of mention in your forthcoming supplementary work, I should not like to be misrepresented." He was a Scotsman, not a "Colonial." Stedman replied warmly: "Something in your work made me suspect that, despite your Australian tone, etc., you did not hail (as we Yankees say) from the Colonies. So, you will find in my new vol. of Victorian Poets that I do not place you with the Colonial poets, but just preceding them, and I have a reference to your Rossetti volume" (*Memoir*, 129).

Fig. 9 An 1897 photograph of Edmund Clarence Stedman (1833–1908), an American poet, critic, essayist, banker, and scientist. Wikimedia, https://commons.wikimedia.org/wiki/File:Edmund_Clarence_Stedman_cph.3a44372.jpg, Public Domain.

This exchange "led to a life-long friendship" with Stedman who had "so genial a nature that, on becoming personally acquainted in New York two years later, the older poet declared he had adopted the younger man from across the seas as his 'English son'" (*Memoir*, 129). Elizabeth's offhand comment contains an important insight. Sharp's father, who disapproved of his son's interest in literature and his desire to become a writer, died when Sharp was twenty-one. From that point forward, he sought out older literary men, worked to gain their friendship and approval, and depended on them for advancement, not an unusual pattern for young people making their way in the world. The list of such men in Sharp's life — Dante Gabriel Rossetti, John Addington Symonds, Walter Pater, George Meredith, to name only a few of the most prominent — is unusually long, and the son/father trope pervades his correspondence with them. Of all these, his relationship with Stedman was the most consequential and long-lasting. After their initial meeting in 1889, when Sharp stayed with Stedman and his wife Laura in New York, Sharp's letters became increasingly familiar until Stedman began to function as both a father confessor and a trusted comrade. The first of the surviving Sharp letters, which is in the Pattee Library at Pennsylvania State University, is dated July 27, 1889, shortly before Sharp left for North America. Excepting the short quotation from an 1887 letter Elizabeth Sharp included in her *Memoir*, earlier correspondence between the two men has not surfaced. Sharp surely corresponded with Stedman in 1888 as he prepared his anthology of *American Sonnets*. His dedication of that volume to Stedman — "the Foremost American Critic" — was an expression of gratitude for Stedman's help in choosing the poets and poems for the volume.

In a letter dated February 16, 1889, Sharp told Theodore Watts he was staying for a fortnight or more with his friend Sir George Brisbane Scott Douglas (1856–1935), a Scottish Baronet and a poet and editor who lived in Springwood House, the family seat near Kelso in the Scottish Border Region. He was working hard and enjoying the "beautiful old place — near the junction of the Teviot and the Tweed, both of which flow through D.'s property. The Teviot is but 200 yards from my window, and some 300 yards away is the picturesque mound-set ruin of the ancient Roxburghe Castle. Last night I fell asleep to the hooting of the owls blended with the brawling undertone of the Teviot." The main purpose of the letter was to inform Watts, poetry editor of *The Athenaeum*, that the second edition of his *Romantic Ballads and Poems of Phantasy* containing "many important alterations" and a new poem would be published the following week. As described in the previous chapter, when the first edition appeared the previous May, he sent Watts a copy and spelled out what he would like to see in a review of the book while telling Watts he did not expect him — given their friendship — to write the review. Now he told Watts he was "a little hurt" that Norman MacColl, the editor of the *Athenaeum*, had not printed a review. He had also been disturbed by some negative remarks Watts reportedly made, but he had chalked that up to "misapprehension" and refused to let it interfere with their friendship. Now he asked Watts, if not inconvenient or disagreeable, to send MacColl a paragraph simply announcing the second edition with alterations and additions. The appearance of such a paragraph in the prestigious *Athenaeum* would help the book's sales.

Sharp began his February 16 letter to Watts by asking what he thought of Hall Caine's new play. "From what I hear privately (from my wife, Cotton, and others) I gather that it is a very third-rate affair though with some strong melodramatic situations." Caine's "Good Old Times" which had recently opened in London's Princess Theatre was drawing enthusiastic crowds and generating a good deal of money. Sharp and his host George Douglas had little regard for Wilson Barrett, who produced the play and acted in it. They thought Caine should be turning his attention to more serious and consequential fiction and drama. On March 4, back in London, Sharp expressed their concern in a letter to Caine. He was delighted to hear of the play's financial success, but he thought Caine should spend his time with more serious writing:

> though I honestly admit that you, with your high abilities, should be working at more enduring stuff than ordinary melodrama. We need a true dramatic writer, and you have it in you to be the man — but! I have your reputation so truly to heart that what you yourself say is good news to me. Still, it is always something to have achieved so great a financial success in these difficult days — though the financial aspect, with a man like you, ought to be — and in your case is — of secondary import... Douglas [Sir George] believes in you — but dislikes what he calls Wilson Barrettish melodrama: and he expressed an earnest hope the other day that your next play would be, in truth, a big thing. I'm delighted to hear what you say about your prospective novel and play....

In mid-month, he would try to get down to Bexley, then a village where Caine was living and now a Borough of Greater London, to talk about that and other matters. He hoped Caine, should he be in town the following Saturday, would find his way out to Wescam, the Sharp's home in South Hampstead, for a party: "Some seventy to eighty literary and artistic friends have been asked — and probably somewhere about 40 or 50 will come." Those numbers demonstrate the extent to which he and Elizabeth had immersed themselves in London's literary society.

Concern about Caine's work took a back seat in mid-month when Sharp decided to stand for election to the Chair of Literature at University College, London. The Chair was vacant following the retirement of Henry Morley (1822–1894), one of the first Professors of English Literature and a dynamic lecturer who had occupied the chair since 1865. Sharp requested and received supporting letters from Caine, Edward Dowden, and Richard Garnett, and, according to Elizabeth, his candidacy was also supported by Robert Browning, George Meredith, Walter Pater, Theodore Watts, Alfred Austin, Professor Minto, Sir George Douglas, Aubrey de Vere, and Mrs. Augusta Webster. That he sought this post despite having spent only two years studying literature at Glasgow University reflects the self-confidence he gained through his reading, editing, and reviewing. The list of his supporters reflects the extent to which his work and his forceful personality had penetrated and gained the respect of fellow authors. Despite the support of these literary luminaries and the prestige and security the post would bring, Sharp withdrew from consideration when, again according to Elizabeth, his doctor advised his heart might not withstand the strain. Whatever the reason, he was relieved when left "in possession of his freedom." For all his gregariousness, Sharp became agitated whenever he was asked to give a formal lecture or even speak informally before an audience. Realizing this deficiency and concerned about the condition of his heart, his doctors continued to advise against lecturing. From this distance the inappropriateness of Sharp's application is abundantly clear. Even his supporters must have recognized his inability to replicate the energetic lecturing and vast knowledge of the retiring Professor of English at University College.

On May 5, the Sharps left London to review the Salon in Paris. On the 9th, Sharp wrote to thank Richard Le Gallienne for his second book of poetry, *Volumes in Folio*, which he declared he would read with interest when he returned to London in a week or so. In the letter accompanying the volume, which was forwarded to Paris, Le Gallienne said he was planning to accompany the actor Wilson Barrett, for whom he served as secretary, on his tour of America in October. Setting aside his opinion of Barrett, Sharp told Le Gallienne he would also be there in October and suggested they meet. As it turned out, an attack of asthma prevented Le Gallienne from traveling. On the 10th, Elizabeth sent a short review of the sculpture exhibited in the Salon to James Mavor who printed it without attribution following her husband's unsigned review of the Salon's paintings in the June number of the *Scottish Art Review*. The Sharps left Paris on May 11 to spend a week or so in the countryside. When they returned to London, Sharp asked Mavor when he needed the manuscript for Pt. I of H. P. Siwäarmill's "Emilia Viviana" which Mavor had agreed to publish in the July number of the review. In a postscript, he asked Mavor to be sure and preserve the secret of his identity. He had used H. P. Siwäarmill for an epigraph and for a character in *Children of Tomorrow* which was published on May 10 while the Sharps were in Paris. The pseudonym demonstrates his predilection — well before he created Fiona Macleod — for disguising his identity. There is no sign of "Emilia Viviana" in the *Review* which means Sharp failed to produce it or Mavor decided not to print it.

In a mid-July letter to Louise Chandler Moulton, Sharp said he was pleased she had found something attractive in *Children of Tomorrow*, which had been "badly received by the press." He was

> vain enough to believe that with all its faults & demerits it is not altogether a book of "today." I have written it as an artist — and someday, if not now, it will gain its measure of recognition. At the same time, it is only a tentative effort, or a herald rather, of a new movement. I see the *Athenaeum* of today passes it by with "damning indifference" — and, on the other hand, *Public Opinion* has a long & sympathetic (tho' fault-finding) review beginning "a remarkable book by a remarkable man."

Mavor printed a carefully worded notice in the June issue of the *Scottish Art Review*. He recognized the novel's effort to portray in prose fiction the manifesto of the new Romantic School, whose advent Sharp had forecast in his dedicatory introduction to *Romantic Ballads*. For that reason, the novel was interesting in itself and "of no ordinary interest in the history of current literature." In portraying the complications of two married couples falling in love with each other's spouses, Sharp had constructed a "powerful drama of passion and destiny." For the details and "for information regarding the sect called Children of Tomorrow,"

Mavor referred "readers to the book itself." Despite his reservations, Mavor found a way to accommodate Sharp's request for a notice while preserving their friendship.

As described in the previous chapter, the "book itself" was quite remarkable for its time. It went further than Mona Caird in critiquing the restraints of marriage. The 'Children of Tomorrow' would be free to realize their potential and preserve their sanity by developing "romantic" relationships outside the bonds of marriage. Sharp would soon find cause to join those children, but the novel predicted a future of free love that neither reviewers nor readers could sanction. Despite their response, Sharp believed the novel would be recognized in time as a herald of things to come. The strict bonds of marriage surely relaxed as the twentieth century unfolded, but the density and excesses of Sharp's *Children of Tomorrow* and the dark improbabilities of its action render it even less readable today than when it appeared.

Sharp's plans for North America crystallized during the summer. Mona Caird asked Elizabeth to accompany her to Austria for "the Suncure at Valdes in the Carpathian mountains." After they left in mid-July (*Memoir*, 149–150). William went down to Box Hill to spend a few days with George Meredith. In a July 27 letter, he told Stedman he had been staying with Meredith in Surrey. He had been ill but had "regained [his] power to sleep." It would be good "to get away, and to see no proofs, letters, or MSS for ten days at least." Of the American trip, Elizabeth wrote, "going by himself seemed to promise chances of complete recovery of health; the unexplored and the unknown beckoned to him with promise of excitement and adventure" (*Memoir*, 150). Sharp chronicled his North American trip, as he had his 1884 Italian trip, in a series of letters to Elizabeth, and there is no mention of ill-health. The trip had its intended effect.

Word of Sharp's reputation had made its way across the Atlantic. He was warmly welcomed, first in Canada and then in the United States. Stedman's sponsorship paved the way, but Canadian and American editors and writers were familiar with Sharp's Rossetti book, his two books of poetry, his editing and writing for the Walter Scott firm, and his articles in British journals. Their desire to strengthen contacts with London's literary establishment — augmented by Sharp's handsome appearance and Scottish charm — resulted in his treatment as a celebrity by prominent literary figures in Canada, Boston, and New York.

The course of his visit can be traced in the portions of letters Elizabeth printed in the *Memoir*. Charles G. D. Roberts — a well-known poet and a Professor of English Literature at King's College in Windsor, Nova Scotia — met him when he arrived in Halifax. In a letter to Stedman on August 17, he said he was leaving at once on a trip to Prince Edward Island and elsewhere with Roberts, Bliss Carman — Roberts' brother-in-law and an aspiring poet and editor — and James Longley, the Attorney General of Canada. He expected to be back in Windsor on August 25 or 26, and he would reach New York in early October where he planned to stay with the Stedmans. After returning from what turned out to be an extensive excursion with Roberts, he described it enthusiastically for Elizabeth:

> Prof. Roberts and I, accompanied for the first 100 miles by Mr. Longley, started for Pictou, which we reached after 5 hours most interesting journey. The Attorney General has kindly asked me to go on a three days' trip with him (some 10 days hence) through the famous Cape Breton district, with the lovely Bras D'Or lakes: and later on, he has arranged for a three days' moose-hunt among the forests of Southern Acadia, where we shall camp out in tents, and be rowed by Indian guides.... I went with Charles Roberts and Bliss Carman through Evangeline's country. En route I traveled on the engine of the train and enjoyed the experience. Grand Pré delighted me immensely — vast meadows, with lumbering wains and the simple old Acadian life. The orchards were in their glory — and the apples delicious! At one farmhouse we put up, how you would have enjoyed our lunch of sweet milk, hot cakes, great bowls of huckleberries and cream, tea, apples, etc.! We then went through the forest belt and came upon the great ocean inlet known as the 'Basin of Minas,' and leagues away the vast bulk of Blomidon shelving bough-like into the Sea....

This trip with Roberts was the first of many adventures during his remaining four weeks in Canada. After returning to Halifax, he stayed with the family of Attorney General Longley who took him on the two excursions described above and introduced him to many of the "leading people."

On September 12, his birthday, he told Elizabeth he was now alone for the first time. There was nothing definite about him in the newspapers "save that I 'abruptly left St. John' (the capital of New Brunswick) and that I am to arrive in Quebec tomorrow." He was glad to leave New

Brunswick with its "oven-like heat," endless forests of living and dead trees, and forest fires that nearly scorched him. After reaching the St. Lawrence River he "made a side excursion up the Saguenay River for 100 miles to Ha! Ha! Bay" and then resumed his trip up the St. Lawrence to Quebec where he was the guest of George Stewart, editor of the *Daily Chronicle*. On September 16 he traveled further up the St. Lawrence to Montreal and wrote to ask Grant Allen's father, Joel Asaph Allen, if he could visit him on September 21 in Alwington, an area of Kingston, Ontario and the name of Allen's house. He did not make it to Alwington as he wrote again to Stedman on the 17th to say he was leaving Montreal for Boston on the 22nd and hoped to reach New York on the 24th where he would spend 12 or 14 days before sailing home on October 6 or 8. Stedman expressed some annoyance at Sharp's "bewildering changes of plans" as he wanted to settle his plans for the fall. Sharp apologized in a letter of September 22 and asked Stedman when he wanted him and for how long. He had other friends in New York and may have to advance his date for sailing home.

After leaving Montreal on the 22nd, a Friday, he traveled "through the States of Vermont, Connecticut, and Massachusetts" to Boston where he spent the weekend with Arthur Sherburne Hardy (1847–1930), a well-known engineer, novelist, poet, and a Professor of Mathematics at Dartmouth College. Boston was "a beautiful place — an exceedingly fine city with lovely environs" (*Memoir*, 153). Hardy introduced Sharp to members of the Harvard faculty and took him to Belmont to visit the novelist W. D. Howells whom he had met in Italy in 1883. He arrived in New York on Monday, September 25, where the Stedmans' house became his base for ten days. In the city, he met — among others — Richard Watson Gilder, editor of the *Century Magazine*; Henry Chandler Bowen, editor of the *Independent*; and Richard Henry Stoddard, whom he christened the "father" of recent American letters. He was elected an honorary member of the "two most exclusive clubs" in New York — the Century and the Players — and he attended a special meeting of the Author's Club where he was "guest of the evening." He spent the weekend of the 29th with Henry Mills Alden, editor of *Harper's Magazine*, in Metuchen, New Jersey, a visit that cemented his friendship with Alden and his family. Before sailing from New York on October 4, he left instructions with a florist to deliver on Stedman's birthday (October 6) both a bouquet and a letter, which was the first of many annual birthday letters to Stedman. During the seven weeks of his Canadian and American trip Sharp was entertained, feted, and, through the good offices of Stedman, introduced to editors of the principal literary magazines.

In an October 1 letter, Sharp told Elizabeth about a couple he met in New York: Thomas Allibone Janvier — a journalist and native of New Orleans — and his wife Catherine Ann Janvier, a member of the prominent Drinker family of Philadelphia and an aunt of the twentieth-century novelist Catherine Drinker Bowen. "They are true Bohemians and most delightful," Sharp wrote, "He is a writer and she an artist… . We dined together at a Cuban Cafe last night. He gave me his vol. of stories called "Colour Studies" and she a little sketch of a Mexican haunted house — both addressed to "William Sharp. Recuerdo di Amistad y carimo." Soon the Janviers began stopping in London on their way to and from southern France where they spent winters. The Sharps, in turn, visited them often in Southern France. Catherine and William developed a special bond. She would be the first person other than family to recognize the writings of Fiona Macleod as the work of William Sharp.

Sharp landed in Liverpool in mid-October and went on to Germany at the end of the month to accompany Elizabeth home. Buoyed by his reception in Canada and the United States, he set to work with renewed vigor. Following Robert Browning's death in Venice on December 12, he wrote a long elegiac poem that appeared in the February 1890 number of the *Art Review*, and he began a biographical/critical study for the Great Writers Series. He also began a series of prose "Imaginary Journals" modeled after Browning's dramatic monologues in poetry. One of the projected stories was to be called "The Crime of Andrea dal Castagno" which Sharp described as "A fragment from the Journal of this murderer painter and successful hypocrite, written not long before his death." He described his plans for the "Imaginary Journals" in a December 18 letter to Richard Watson Gilder, who decided against publishing them. When he heard Sharp had begun a book on Browning, Oscar Wilde, recalling the Rossetti book, remarked, "When a great man dies, Sharp and Caine go in with the undertaker."

Chapter Six

1890

After spending Christmas with the painter Keeley Halswelle and his wife Helena near Petersfield in Hampshire, the Sharps entertained friends for dinner at their South Hampstead home on New Year's Day. A good deal of alcohol was consumed, or so he told Ford Madox Brown in a letter thanking him for his New Year's card, a proof of his Samson and Delilah etching. In the first two months of 1890, Sharp recorded his activities in a diary, parts of which his wife preserved in the *Memoir*. In early January, he was working on the Browning monograph and beginning a novel, "The Ordeal of Basil Hope," which he never finished. He was also writing articles for the *Scottish Leader* and "London Letters" for the *Glasgow Herald*. In mid-January, to escape the distractions of London, he went to Hastings where he worked steadily on the Browning biography and enjoyed long walks with the poet Coventry Patmore. After returning to London in February, he continued work on the Browning manuscript and "Basil Hope." In mid-March, he congratulated Bliss Carman, the Canadian poet he met the previous summer in Canada, on his appointment as an editorial writer for the *New York Independent*. The letter was written in Edinburgh where he was visiting his mother and resting his eyes and head after intense work on the Browning book. In an April 7 letter to Frank Marzials, general editor of Walter Scott's Great Writers Series, he said he had nearly finished reviewing and revising proofs of the Browning book and would return them in the morning. The half-dozen advanced copies which were printed several days later must not have contained Sharp's corrections as he sent an "Errata and Addenda" slip to potential reviewers. On April 16, he told J. Stanley Little his life of Browning was "going splendidly — already about 10,000 copies disposed of."

While working on the Browning biography, Sharp also wrote the Browningesque prose piece "Fragments from the Lost Journal of Piero di Cosimo" which appeared in two parts in the January and April issues of the *Art Review*, the short-lived successor to the *Scottish Art Review*. Both journals were edited by Sharp's friend James Mavor and published by Walter Scott. He also selected the poems and wrote the introduction for *Great Odes: English and American*, a Canterbury volume that appeared in April. He wrote a play, "The Northern Night," that was included in an 1894 collection of short dramas called *Vistas*. He produced an article on D'Annunzio for the *Fortnightly Review* and an article on American literature for the *National Review*. In early May, he went to Paris to review the Salons for the *Glasgow Herald*. He wrote a "Critical Memoir" for an English translation of Sainte-Beuve's *Essays on Men and Women* which Walter Scott published in September in David Stott's "Masterpieces of Foreign Authors" series. He was also reading extensively in contemporary French, Belgian, and Italian literature. His interests ranged widely, and his relatively good health in 1889 and the first half of 1890 enabled him to focus on writing projects that produced income.

In May, he sent Bliss Carman a poem, "The Coves of Crail," which stands out for its stark imagery and what it portends. It was included in the second (1889) edition of Sharp's third book of poems, *Romantic Ballads and Poems of Phantasy*, but that book was not published in the United States which freed Carman to publish it in the July issue of the *New York Independent*.

> The Coves of Crail
> The moon-white waters wash and leap,
> The dark tide floods the Coves of Crail;
> Sound, sound he lies in dreamless sleep
> Nor hears the sea-wind wail.
>
> The pale gold of his oozy locks,
> Doth hither drift and wave;
> His thin hands plash against the rocks,
> His white lips nothing crave.
>
> Afar away she laughs and sings —
> A song he loved, a wild sea-strain —
> Of how the mermen weave their rings
> Upon the reef-set main.

> Sound, sound he lies in dreamless sleep,
> Nor hears the sea-wind wail,
> Tho' with the tide his white hands creep
> Amid the Coves of Crail.

Crail is both a small village on the rocky east coast of Scotland, and the name of the harbor the village overlooks. The handsome man in the poem who now moves only with the waves was lured to the sea by the song of a mermaid and drowned in his attempt to reach her. The poem's subject, tone, and form anticipate the poetry Sharp would attribute to Fiona Macleod. He heard many versions of its story from men and women he encountered in the Hebrides. It reflects the dangers of life on the sea for fishermen and other sailors as well as the danger of trying to cross the boundary between the world we know and the spirit world we would like to know. A common theme in fairy tales of all languages, it became a frequent motif in the writings Sharp published as Fiona Macleod.

Sharp's burst of writing and editing in the winter and spring of 1890 finally produced enough money for a break from editing, reviewing, and the pressures of life in London. In a January 23, 1889 letter, he told Hall Caine he hoped to be settled in Rome the next winter: "I am tired of living in this abominable climate, and of so much pot-boiling. I want to retire for a year and devote myself to original work." On February 22 he wrote to Richard Watson Gilder:

> Next October I am going to leave England for six months at any rate, and perhaps for 18, and return to my well-loved Italy. I am sick of pot-boiling and wish to get on with purely original work. The Drawback is — heavy pecuniary loss. However, I feel I must do it, now or never.

On June 17, he announced his decision to "begin *literary life anew*" in a long letter to Stedman:

> As for us, we are both at heart Bohemians — and are well-content if we can have good shelter, enough to eat, books, music, friends, sunshine, and free nature — all of which we can have with the scantiest of purses. Perhaps I shd be less light-hearted in the matter if I thought that our coming Bohemian life might involve my wife in hard poverty when my hour comes — but fortunately her 'future' is well assured.

The Sharps divested themselves of some of their writing and editing obligations, stored their furniture, and vacated their South Hampstead house on June 24. They would travel while Sharp devoted himself to serious literary work. Their financial circumstances precluded a complete break. Sharp transferred to Elizabeth the post of London art critic for the *Glasgow Herald* and resigned his lucrative though time-consuming position with the *Young Folks' Paper*, but he retained his Canterbury Poets editorship. After leaving Wescam, the Sharps spent a week in the Caird's Northbrook House in Micheldever, Hampshire, which he described in a June 17 letter to Stedman as "a friend's place 7 miles across the downs north of Winchester." When they returned to London, they stayed with the Cairds in their large South Hampstead house and decamped to Scotland at the end of the month.

In the summer of 1887 or 1888 the Sharps spent a weekend in Surrey with Sir Walter and Lady Hughes, friends of Elizabeth's mother. While there they met Walter Severn, a well-known painter who was familiar with Sharp's book on Rossetti. He asked Sharp if he would like to undertake a biography of his father, Joseph Severn, also a painter, who accompanied John Keats to Rome and cared for him there as tuberculosis took his life. Sharp agreed to undertake the project, and Severn gave him a large quantity of unpublished manuscripts written by and related to his father. Sharp began working intermittently on this project in the Spring of 1890. On July 15, he wrote to William Wetmore Story asking if he had known Severn, who spent the winter months in Rome and eventually served as British Ambassador to Italy. Elizabeth reproduced a portion of Story's reply:

> I knew Mr. Severn in Rome and frequently met and saw him, but I can recall nothing which would be of value to you. He was, as you may know, a most pleasant man — and in the minds of all is associated with the memory of Keats by whose side he lies in the Protestant Cemetery in Rome. When the bodies were removed, as they were several years ago, and laid side by side, there was a little funeral ceremony, and I made an address on the occasion in honor and commemoration of the two friends (*Memoir*, 169).

An American lawyer, sculptor, poet, and novelist, Story (1819–1895) moved to Rome in 1850. His apartment became a gathering place for British and American artists and writers, among them Elizabeth and Robert Browning, Nathaniel Hawthorne, and Henry James (who wrote his biography). His monumental sculptures, mostly of Biblical and Classical figures, are displayed in museums in the United States and Britain. Sharp met Story when he was in Rome in 1883. His July 15 letter had the secondary purpose of reestablishing contact so Story might welcome him into his social network when he reached Rome in December.

In early August, the Sharps learned Eric Sutherland Robertson had returned briefly to London from Lahore where he held the chair of literature and logic in the University. Robertson and Sharp were good friends before he left for Lahore in 1887. A graduate of Edinburgh University, he edited the Great Writers Series for the Walter Scott firm, and he served as Sharp's best man when he and Elizabeth married in 1884. Before leaving for Lahore, he arranged for Sharp to succeed him as editor of the "Literary Chair" in the *Young Folk's Paper*, a position that provided a regular income and increased Sharp's visibility in the London literary scene. Sharp wrote to Robertson on August 15: "I have often missed you for, as you know, I was strongly drawn to you from the first, and look upon you as one of my very few "deep" friends. My most intimate friend since you left is Theodore Roussel, the French painter, who now lives in London."

Fig. 10 A self portrait of Theodore Roussel (1847–1926) a French painter, who moved to London in 1878 and two years later married the widow Frances Amelia Smithson Bull (1844–1909). A close friend of James McNeill, he was William Sharp's "most intimate friend" in 1890. Wikipedia: https://commons.wikimedia.org/wiki/File:Theodore_Roussel_(autorretrato)_(1).jpg

In case Robertson could meet them in Scotland, Sharp gave him their Scottish itinerary. On the next day they were leaving for the West Highlands — Tarbert on Loch Fyne in Argyll — where they would spend three weeks. From September 8 to 12, Sharp would be in Glasgow while Elizabeth was visiting a friend, Mary Georgina Wade Wilson, in South Bantaskine. From the 12th to the 17th both Sharps would be in North Queensferry, a village across the Firth just northwest of Edinburgh. They planned to go north to Aberdeen for a few days on the 17th, and on the 22nd they would be back in Edinburgh staying with Sharp's mother. They followed that itinerary and returned to London at the end of September where they stayed with Elizabeth's mother at 72 Inverness Terrace in Bayswater. Robertson did not make it to Scotland, but they met in London. In a letter of October 1, Sharp told Theodore Watts that Elizabeth intended to invite him for afternoon tea on October 4 with Eric Robertson and George Meredith.

The letter to Watts conveyed Dr. Donald Macleod's willingness to speak with him about the possible serial publication of Watts' novel — *Alwyn* — in *Good Words*. While Sharp was in Tarbert in late August and early September, he spent a good deal of time with Macleod, an eminent Presbyterian clergyman, a respected theologian, and a talented and prominent minister who served in Park Church, Glasgow from 1869 until 1901. He also edited from 1872 until 1907 the evangelical journal *Good Words*. Under his editorship, the journal began to branch out from it purely religious base to include non-religious essays and works of fiction. Macleod was also a repository of Celtic myth and the source of many of the Fiona tales. Sharp indirectly acknowledged his debt by adopting Macleod's surname to provide a measure of authenticity and prestige for Fiona. During this visit, Elizabeth recalled, Macleod sang to Sharp "with joyous abandonment a Neapolitan song" and asked him to send him from Italy an article for *Good Words*. Sharp's "Reminiscences of the Marble Quarries of Carrara," which appeared in *Good Words* late in 1890, must have derived from a visit to the quarries during Sharp's first trip to Italy in 1883 since the Sharps did not reach Tuscany on their way to Rome until December 1890, too late for that month's *Good Words*.

On October 11, Sharp told Stedman he and Elizabeth were leaving the next day for Germany where they planned to stay through November. He asked Stedman for a "line of introduction" to Blanche Willis Howard, an American novelist who had recently married Dr. Julius von Teuffel, the court physician of Württemberg. The Sharps went first to Antwerp, stopped in Bonn, and went on to Heidelberg where, he told James Mavor, they were "very comfortably settled in a romantic old house adjoining the Castle grounds — and with interesting literary associations. Goethe himself wrote one of his poems in the balcony of the quaint, picturesque room I occupy." According to Elizabeth, her husband was disappointed with the Rhine, and he expressed some surprising anti-German, pro-French sentiments in a letter to an unknown friend: "The real charm of the Rhine, beyond the fascination that all rivers and riverine scenery have for most people, is that of literary and historical romance. The Rhine is in this respect the Nile of Europe." He thought it should be the boundary between Germany and France.

> Germany has much to gain from a true communion with its more charming neighbor. The world would jog on just the same if Germany were annihilated by France, Russia, and Italy: but the disappearance of brilliant, vivacious, intellectual France would be almost as serious a loss to intellectual Europe, as would be to the people at large the disappearance of the Moon.

Sharp wrote again to Stedman on November 4 to thank him for the introduction to Blanch Willis Howard. He had forwarded it and asked to see her in the following week. In sending the introduction, Stedman asked Sharp if he had a hidden motive in wishing to meet her, and thus began the repartee that continued for many years regarding possible extramarital affairs. Sharp replied he was indeed going to Stuttgart alone, but only because Elizabeth was otherwise occupied in Heidelberg. He did plan "to cut about a bit" on his own, visiting "Karlsruhe, Mannheim, the Neckar, and so forth" and he was going alone to Frankfurt at the end of the week to hear Wagner's "Rienzi." There followed another complaint about Germany: "*Mon Ami*, it is only too easy to be virtuous here. The women — ah, 'let us proceed!'"

The Sharps left Heidelberg on November 25 and reached Tuscany, "flooded in sunshine and glowing colour," in the second week of December. After a few days with Elizabeth's aunt in Florence, they went on to Rome and settled in rooms on Via delle Quattro Fontane, near the summit of the Quirinal Hill. Shortly after arriving, Sharp conveyed his opinion of Germany to Catherine Janvier:

> Well, we were glad to leave Germany. Broadly, it is a joyless place for Bohemians. It is all beer, coarse jokes, coarse living, and domestic tyranny on the man's part, subjection on the woman's — on the one side: pedantic learning, scientific pedagogism, and mental *ennui*; on the other: with, of course, a fine leavening *somewhere* of the salt of life.

He described their six weeks in Heidelberg as "wet," but admitted it was "only fair to say we were not there at the best season." Stuttgart was his favorite German city. "Wonderfully animated and pleasing for a German town," it had a charming double attraction both as a medieval city and as a modern capital." He now had a friend there in Blanche Willis Howard, who was rejoicing in the title "Frau Hof-Arzt von Teuffel." Her husband, Doctor von Teuffel, was "one of the few Germans who seem to regard women as equals." Sharp's visit to the von Teuffels had a curious result: an epistolary novel called *A Fellow and his Wife* in which Howard wrote the letters of a male aristocrat who stayed home in Germany while Sharp wrote the letters of his wife who had taken off for an extended stay in Rome. This tour de force became the first instance of Sharp adopting and sustaining with remarkable consistency the persona of a woman.

He described for Catherine Janvier his writing plans, but Rome soon eclipsed them. The many "schemes he planned mentally," Elizabeth wrote, "were never realized.... A new impulse came, new work grew out of the impressions of that Roman winter which swept out of his mind all other cartooned work." Under the spell of the warmth and beauty of Rome and its surroundings, Sharp in his mid-thirties fell in love with a beautiful woman ten years his junior, a woman he knew in London who took on a compelling new radiance in Rome where she changed the course of Sharp's life and the trajectory of his work.

Chapter Seven

1891

When the Sharps reached Rome in early December of 1890, they settled in for the winter. Elizabeth recalled those months as "one long delight" for her husband; they "amply fulfilled even his optimistic anticipation. He reveled in the sunshine and the beauty; he was in perfect health; his imagination was quickened and worked with great activity" (*Memoir*, 173). In mid-December Edith Wingate Rinder came from London to spend three weeks with Mona Caird who was wintering in Rome "for her health." A beautiful and intelligent young woman of twenty-six, Edith had married Mona's first cousin, Frank Rinder, less than a year earlier, on February 17, 1890. Edith and Frank were childhood sweethearts who had grown up as landed gentry on neighboring farms in the north of England. Educated at home and locally, Edith spent a year studying in Germany and worked for a time as a governess in Lincolnshire after returning home. Frank was also educated in Lincolnshire before his parents sent him to Fettes College, an established boarding school in Edinburgh. During his first year — 1883–1884 — he became ill with cerebral meningitis which left him somewhat crippled for the rest of his life. Back in Lincolnshire, Edith and Frank felt isolated. Deprived of culture, without prospects, and unable to overcome their parents' opposition to their marrying, they set their sights on London and Frank's first cousin Mona Caird.

Alice Mona Alison was the daughter of John Alison of Midlothian, Scotland, who invented the vertical boiler. As a girl she lived with her family in a substantial house on Bayswater Road in London, close to Elizabeth Sharp's family home in Inverness Terrace, and the two girls became life-long friends. In 1887 Mona married James Alexander Henryson-Caird (1847–1921) of Cassenary, Creeton, Kirkendbrighten.

A member of Parliament and a determined agrarian, he spent most of his time on his farm in Scotland and his country house in Micheldever, a village in Hampshire. His wife, on the other hand, spent most of her time in their large South Hampstead house where she entertained many of the day's luminaries. An early advocate of freedom from the stultifying restraints of high Victorianism, Mona, in 1888 invited her cousin Frank Rinder and Edith Wingate to London and welcomed them into her household. Two years later, against the wishes of their parents, she facilitated their marriage, which took place not at a church, as was customary, but at a London Registry Office.

Wescam, the Sharp's South Hampton house, was only a few blocks from the Caird's house, and there was frequent entertaining back and forth. The Sharps were well-acquainted with the Rinders, but we do not know if William and Edith were attracted to each other before Edith arrived in Rome. By December 1890, Edith and Frank had been living with each other for at least three years, and the glow had worn off their relationship. Sharp's relationship with Elizabeth, which also began as a youthful friendship, had devolved into that of a mother overseeing her frequently ill child whom she called "my poet." In any case, the friendship between the handsome William Sharp, free of pressing obligations and revitalized at the age of thirty-five, and the strikingly beautiful Edith Rinder, who was twenty-six, blossomed under the warm Italian sun. Edith would become the mysterious unnamed friend Sharp frequently alluded to in letters and conversations and the principal catalyst for the Fiona Macleod phase of his literary career. In an 1896 letter to his wife, Sharp said he owed to Edith his "development as 'Fiona Macleod' though, in a sense of course, that began long before I knew her, and indeed while I was still a child." "Without her," Sharp continued, "there would have been no 'Fiona Macleod'." After quoting from this letter (*Memoir*, 222), Elizabeth continued, with remarkable generosity,

> Because of her beauty, her strong sense of life and the joy of life; because of her keen intuitions and mental alertness, her personality stood for him as a symbol of the heroic women of Greek and Celtic days, a symbol that, as he expressed it, unlocked new doors in his mind and put him "in touch with ancestral memories" of his race.

When the first Fiona Macleod book, *Pharais: A Romance of the Isles*, was published in 1894, it was dedicated to "E. W. R." — Edith Wingate Rinder.

Sharp and Edith took long walks together in the Roman Campagna in late December and early January. The beauty of the countryside and the joy of his newfound love moved Sharp to compose in February a sequence of exuberant poems that were privately printed in March 1891 as *Sospiri di Roma* which translates as sighs or whispers of Rome. Of that volume and Edith Rinder's role in its genesis, Elizabeth wrote

> The "Sospiri di Roma" was the turning point. Those unrhymed poems of irregular meter are filled not only with the passionate delight in life, with the sheer joy of existence, but also with the ecstatic worship of beauty that possessed him during those spring months we spent in Rome when he had cut himself adrift for the time from the usual routine of our life, and touched a high point of health and exuberant spirits. There, at last, he found the desired incentive towards a true expression of himself, in the stimulus and sympathetic understanding of the friend to whom he dedicated the first of the books published under his pseudonym. This friendship began in Rome and lasted throughout the remainder of his life (*Memoir*, 222).

Elizabeth included in the *Memoir* excerpts from Sharp's diary that detail his activities and his writing during January and February. On January 3, he and Edith traveled by train to the village of Albano south of Rome and walked from there to Genzano where they looked down into Lake Nemi, which was "lovely in its grey-blue stillness, with all the sunlit but yet somber winterliness around. Nemi, itself, lay apparently silent and lifeless, 'a city of dream,' on a height across the lake." He continued, "One could imagine that Nemi and Genzano had once been the same town, and had been riven asunder by a volcano. The lake-filled crater now divides these two little hill-set towns."

This excursion stands out among others Sharp described because he used it to define his relationship with Edith Rinder and his creation of Fiona Macleod. On February 8, after Edith had returned to London, he wrote a poem about the experience:

The Swimmer of Nemi
(The Lake of Nemi: September)

White through the azure,
The purple blueness,
Of Nemi's waters
The swimmer goeth.
Ivory-white, or wan white as roses
Yellowed and tanned by the suns of the Orient,
His strong limbs sever the violet hollows;
A shimmer of white fantastic motions
Wavering deep through the lake as he swimmeth.
Like gorse in the sunlight the gold of his yellow hair,
Yellow with sunshine and bright as with dew-drops,
Spray of the waters flung back as he tosseth
His head i' the sunlight in the midst of his laughter;
Red o'er his body, blossom-white 'mid the blueness,
And trailing behind him in glory of scarlet,
A branch of red-berried ash of the mountains.
White as a moonbeam
Drifting athwart
The purple twilight,
The swimmer goeth —
Joyously laughing,
With o'er his shoulders,
Agleam in the sunshine
The trailing branch
With the scarlet berries.
Green are the leaves, and scarlet the berries,
White are the limbs of the swimmer beyond them
Blue the deep heart in the haze of September,
The high Alban hills in their silence and beauty,
Purple the depths of the windless heaven
Curv'd like a flower o'er the waters of Nemi.

In his diary, Sharp followed the poem's title with "(Red and White) 42 lines" though it was shortened to thirty-one lines when it appeared in *Sospiri di Roma*. The free verse of this poem and others in the volume is a deliberate departure from the rigid formalism of "Victorian" poetry. Rather than describing a place in detail, the poems use color and partial glances to create an impression of a place. From Rossetti and other Pre-Raphaelites, Sharp inherited an interest in the relationship between painting and poetry. In Rome, he created with words what the

French impressionists were creating in painting. That effort reemerged in the poetry he wrote as Fiona Macleod, especially in the prose poems, or what Sharp preferred to call "prose rhythms," in "The Silence of Amor" section of *From the Hills of Dream* (1896) which Thomas Mosher published separately, with a "Foreword" in 1902.

> More can be said about the Nemi poem. Sharp may have seen paintings of the lake by John Robert Cozens (1777) and George Inness (1857); he surely knew J. M. W. Turner's many depictions of the lake and its surroundings. He must also have known the lake was associated with the Roman Goddess Diana Nemorensis ("Diana of the Wood") who was the goddess of wild animals and the hunt. She derived from the Greek goddess Artemis who was also goddess of the hunt, the wilderness, and wild animals. The sister of Apollo, Artemis was also a goddess of the moon and fertility. Sharp must also have been aware of the myth central to James Fraser's ground-breaking *Golden Bough*, which appeared in 1890. Therein the King of the Woods — Rex Nemorensis — guards the temple of Diana Nemorensis, Diana of the Wood, with a golden bough that symbolizes his power. Annually, reflecting the progress of the seasons and the harvest, a man plucks a bough from the golden tree, swims Lake Nemi, kills the King, assumes his powers, and guards Diana's temple. In his poem, Sharp idealizes himself as the handsome and powerful swimmer who carries the red-berried ash bough, a symbol of dynamic life, to lay at the feet of Diana's reincarnation as the beautiful Edith Rinder.

Fig. 11 John Robert Cozens, *Lake Nemi* (1777). © Tate, https://www.tate.org.uk/art/artworks/cozens-lake-nemi-t00982, CC-BY-NC-ND 3.0.

Fig. 12 Joseph Mallord William Turner, *Lake Nemi* (c. 1827–1828). Turner visited Lake Nemi in 1819 and painted this sketch from memory in Rome in 1828. © Tate, https://www.tate.org.uk/art/artworks/turner-lake-nemi-n03027, CC-BY-NC-ND 3.0.

Fig. 13 Lake Nemi, Engraved by Middiman and Pye in 1819 after a sketch by Joseph Mallord William Turner. Transferred from the British Museum to Tate Britain in 1988, CC-BY-NC-ND (3.0 Unported), https://www.tate.org.uk/art/artworks/turner-lake-of-nemi-engraved-by-middiman-and-pye-t06023

Sharp's fascination with Lake Nemi, its renewal myth, and the day — January 3, 1891 — he visited Nemi with Edith Rinder did not end with the poem. Years later he cast the day in a different guise, but with the same significance. He transformed the poem's handsome male swimmer into a beautiful woman. Ernest Rhys, in his *Everyman Remembers*, recalled Sharp telling him that

> His first meeting with Fiona was on the banks of Lake Nemi when she was enjoying a sun-bath in what she deemed was virgin solitude, after swimming the lake. "That moment began," he declared, "my spiritual regeneration. I was a New Man, a mystic, where before I had been only a mechanic-in-art. Carried away by my passion, my pen wrote as if dipped in fire, and when I sat down to write prose, a spirit-hand would seize the pen and guide it into inspired verse. We found we had many common friends: we traveled on thro' Italy and went to Rome, and there I wrote my haunting *Sospiri di Roma*."

Rhys took Sharp's words to mean there was "an objective Fiona Macleod," and "the passion she inspired gave Sharp a new deliverance, a new impetus." Though Rhys did not know who she was, he was correct. A real woman figured crucially in Sharp's creation of Fiona Macleod. The male swimmer in Sharp's Nemi poem, "Ivory-white, or wan white as roses | Yellowed and tanned by the suns of the Orient," was initially an idealized self-portrait. Years later, he had become Fiona "enjoying a sun-bath in what she deemed was virgin solitude, after swimming the lake." The lengthy diary account of his first day-long walk with Edith Rinder and the importance he placed on their visit to Nemi suggest that may have been the day their relationship deepened. It was she, not the imaginary Fiona, who was responsible for his "spiritual regeneration," for his becoming a "New Man, a mystic," where before he "had been only a mechanic-in-art." She was responsible for the burst of creativity that produced the poems of *Sospiri di Roma* and later for the emergence of Fiona Macleod

On February 8, Sharp wrote "A Winter Evening" which describes his walk through a heavy snowstorm on January 17. His diary entry for the 17th begins "Winter with a vengeance. Rome might be St. Petersburg." In the late afternoon, he had gone alone for a walk on the Pincio Terrace in the whirling snow.

> Returning by the Pincian Gate, about 5:45 there was a strange sight. Perfectly still in the sombre Via di Mura, with high walls to the right, but the upper pines and cypresses swaying in a sudden rush of wind: to the left a drifting snow-storm: to the right wintry moonshine: vivid sweeping pulsations of lightening from the Compagna, and long low muttering growls of thunder. (The red light from a window in the wall) (*Memoir*, 176–177).

When he formed this experience into a poem on February 8, the same day he wrote "The Swimmer of Nemi," he focused on that red light:

A Winter Evening
(An hour after Nightfall, on Saturday, January 17, 1891)
[To E. W. R.],

> Here all the snow-drift lies thick and untrodden,
> Cold, white, and desolate save where the red light
> Gleams from a window in yonder high turret

And the poem ends:

> Here in the dim, gloomy Via dell'Mura,
> Nought but the peace of the snow-drift unruffled,
> Whitely obscure, save where from the window
> High in the walls of the Medici Gardens
> Glows a red shining, fierily bloodred.
> What lies in the heart of thee, Night, thus so ominous?
> What is they secret, strange joy or strange sorrow?

Why he chose this poem to dedicate to Edith we cannot know, but it is tempting to speculate. Walking home, he observed the contrast between the sweeping winds above and the relative peace below as the lightning and thunder approached the city, the rush of wind and snow on one side and wintry moonshine on the other. He was walking alone, and the dedication to Edith suggests the poem was meant to describe the experience for her. If so, he may intended the red light high in the dark wall to represent Edith — a steady, though now remote, beacon of warmth and contentment for the poet who, Edith having returned to London, was alone and buffeted between periods of moonlit joy and stormy depression.

In mid-January, the Sharps became more active in the literary and artistic life of Rome, attending lectures and visiting art studios. Sharp's diary shows he was sampling a remarkable array of writers: Élie Reclus, Pierre Loti, George Meredith, Robert Browning, Charles Swinburne, Coventry Patmore, Antonio Fogazzaro, Gabriele D'Annunzio, Henrik Ibsen, Edgar Allan Poe, Honoré de Balzac , and Charles Augustin Sainte-Beuve. He wrote articles for the *New York Independent* and the *British National Review* and a poem for *Belford's Magazine*. He met Elihu Vedder who wanted to know what the British press had written about his illustrations for *Omar Khayam*. On January 10, Sharp thanked Bliss Carman, literary editor of the *New York Independent*, for sending the issue of December 25 that printed his poem, "Paris Nocturne," an unrhymed impressionistic poem that anticipated those he was writing in Italy.

On January 30, Sharp turned in earnest to the poems that would become *Sospiri di Roma*. By February 2, he had written fourteen and remarked in his diary, "Such bursts of uncontrollable poetic impulse as came to me today, and the last three days, only come rarely in each year." The next day, February 3, he sent several poems to Bliss Carman and asked him to consider publishing them or send them to other American editors for consideration. If accepted they should appear before the volume of poems he planned to publish in March. On February 10 and 11, Sharp sat for a drawing by Charles Holroyd that became the etched portrait Sharp used to face the title page of *Sospiri di Roma*. In late February, Charles Ross, a Norwegian painter, asked Sharp to sit for him and produced a pastel portrait that Elizabeth reproduced in the *Memoir* (180). The many surviving portraits of Sharp suggest painters and photographers considered him a handsome and imposing figure.

Fig. 14 Sir Charles Holroyd's etching of William Sharp, which Sharp reproduced for insertion opposite the title page of *Sospiri di Roma*, the book of poems he wrote in Rome in January/February 1891 and published privately in Tivoli in March 1891, https://www.google.co.uk/books/edition/Sospiri_di_Roma/jT9DAQAAMAAJ?hl=en&gbpv=1

Fig. 15 A pastel painting of William Sharp by the Norwegian painter Charles M. Ross. Sharp sat for this portrait in Rome in early March 1891. This is a photograph of the copy Elizabeth Sharp reproduced in her *Memoir*, taken by William Halloran (2021).

Sharp arranged to have the poems printed by the Societa Laziale's press in Tivoli and continued writing and revising until mid-March when Elizabeth left for Florence to spend more time with her aunt. Sharp went to Tivoli for a few days to put the poems in final shape and oversee their type setting. Julian Corbett, a prominent British naval historian who had just published a biography of Sir Francis Drake, accompanied him, and the two men spent mornings working and afternoons exploring Tivoli and the surrounding hills. During a visit to the castle of San Poli dei Cavalieri, they met a "comely woman" who gave them some wine. She also told a tale that found its way, along with the town and surrounding scenery, into Sharp's "The Rape of the Sabines," a convoluted story that appeared the following year in the first and only issue of Sharp's *Pagan Review*.

Towards the end of the month Sharp joined Elizabeth in Pisa, and from there they went to Arles in the south of France. On March 30, Sharp sent Catherine Janvier a letter from Provence in which he told her his *Sospiri di Roma* was being printed that very day to the sound of the Cascades of the Anio at Tivoli, in the Sabines — one of which turns the machinery of the Socièta Laziale's printing-works. I do hope the book will appeal to you, as there is so much of myself in it. No doubt it will be too frankly impressionistic to suit some people, and its unconventionality in form as well as in matter will be a cause of offense here and there. You shall have one of the earliest copies (*Memoir*, 182–183).

About seventy-five copies were printed and sent to Sharp who sent them to his friends and to newspapers and periodicals where they were most likely to be well received. He told Catherine Janvier that Marseilles was unattractive compared to Rome. He and Elizabeth preferred Arles, but it paled in comparison to the hill towns of the Apennine and the Sabines:

When I think of happy days at the Lake of Nemi, high up in the Albans, of Albano, and L'Ariccia, and Castel Gandolfo — of Tivoli, and the lonely Montecelli, and S. Polo dei Cavalieri, and Castel Madamo and Anticoli Corrado, etc., among the Sabines — of the ever new, mysterious, fascinating Campagna, from the Maremma on the North to the Pontine Marches, my heart is full of longing.... You will find something of my passion for it, and of that still deeper longing and passion for the Beautiful, in my "Sospiri di Roma," which ought to reach you before the end of April, or at any rate early in May.

Sharp was in Scotland on May 1 when he wrote again to Catherine Janvier, this time about the critical response to *Sospiri di Roma*:

It is no good to any one or to me to say that I am a Pagan — that I am "an artist beyond doubt, but one without heed to the cravings of the human heart: a worshipper of the Beautiful, but, without religion, without an ethical message, with nothing but a vain cry for the return, or it may be the advent, of an impossible ideal." Equally absurd to complain that in these "impressions" I give no direct "blood and bones" for the mind to gnaw at and worry over. Cannot they see that all I attempt to do is to fashion anew something of the lovely vision I have seen, and that I would as soon commit forgery (as I told someone recently) as add an unnecessary line, or "play" to this or that taste, this or that critical opinion. The chief paper here in Scotland shakes its head over "the nude sensuousness of 'The Swimmer of Nemi', 'The Naked Rider', 'The Bather', 'Foir di Memoria', 'The Wild Mare' (whose 'fiery and almost savage realism!' it depreciates — tho' this is the poem which [George] Meredith says is 'bound to live') and evidently thinks artists and poets who see beautiful things and try to fashion them anew beautifully, should be stamped out, or at any rate left severely alone (*Memoir*, 185–186).

Sharp objected to being called a "Pagan" if it connoted only unrestrained sensuality and the absence of ethical messages and religious beliefs, but the more he thought about the term, the more he warmed to it. The unclothed statues he saw in and about Rome were certainly pre-Christian and therefore Pagan. His descriptions of them in the *Sospiri* poems reflect his renewed energy, sexual and artistic, his reawakened appreciation of the beauty of the naked human form, and his incorporation of sensuality into a wholistic view of human life. Those were the very qualities that bothered the unnamed reviewer in Scotland's chief paper, the Edinburgh *Scotsman* (April 20, 1891, 3). Soon, as if to flaunt the reviewer, he would appropriate the term and write under various pseudonyms the essays, stories, and poems in his *Pagan Review*.

It is no wonder the conservative papers and journals that received copies of the book were put off by its "nude sensuousness." The male swimmer in the Nemi poem is one of several white nudes — men and women and even a white mare pursued and mounted by a dark stallion — that populate the volume. Shortly after his previous volume of poems — *Romantic Ballads and Poems of Phantasy* — appeared in 1888, Sharp wrote to a "friend:"

> I am tortured by the passionate desire to create beauty, to sing something of the "impossible songs" I have heard, to utter something of the rhythm of life that has touched me. The next volume of romantic poems will be daringly of the moment, vital with the life and passion of today.

Three years later he fulfilled that promise in a month-long burst of creativity in Rome. He saw himself as part of a wider effort to break through the constraints of late Victorianism, but the assault on poetic forms and sexual norms that resulted from his "passionate desire to create beauty" in *Sospiri di Roma* met resistance or avoidance among all but a few close friends who shared his goals. George Meredith was one of those friends. In a letter to Sharp, he praised the volume with some reservations: "Impressionistic work where the heart is hot surpasses all but highest verse.... It can be of that heat only at intervals. In 'The Wild Mare' you have hit the mark." That was the poem the reviewer in the *Scotsman* criticized for its "fiery and almost savage realism."

The Sharps stayed in Provence until the end of April. In early May Sharp went to London and intended to go back to France where they would spend the summer in the forest of Fontainebleau. While he was away, Elizabeth became ill with an "insidious form of low fever" and returned to England for treatment. Along with medication, she needed rest so they went to Eastbourne on the Sussex coast for two weeks where she could have the fresh sea air, and he could work undisturbed on the Severn book. After several weeks Sharp went to see his mother in Edinburgh while Elizabeth, restored to health, stayed with her mother in London. In mid-July they met in York and went to Whitby on the Yorkshire coast for six weeks. On August 21, back in London, Sharp asked the editor of *Blackwood's Magazine* if he might be interested in publishing a story curiously entitled "The Second Shadow: Being the Narrative of Jose Maria Santos y Bazan, Spanish Physician in Rome." *Blackwood's* declined, but Bliss Carman published it on August 25, 1892 in the *New York Independent*. From May until mid-August, Sharp spent most of his working hours on his biography of Joseph Severn. Having finished the last revisions on August 28, he and Elizabeth left for Stuttgart where Sharp and Blanche Willis Howard would execute their collaboration.

For a title, the two writers adapted a line from Shakespeare's *Othello* — "A fellowe almost damned in a faire wife." The main characters of *A Fellowe and His Wife* would be a German Count and his beautiful young Countess who goes to Rome to become a sculptor. Sharp drew upon his experience in Rome to write the letters of the "faire wife" while Howard drew upon hers in the German court to write the Count's replies. In Rome, the wife falls under the spell of a famous sculptor who seduces and then betrays her. Though it takes a great deal of heightened prose, especially on the wife's part, the husband finally goes to Rome, confronts the sculptor, forgives his wife, and takes her back to Germany. Sharp's decision to play the part of the Countess was logical enough given his recent immersion in Rome. His easy adoption of the role and his obvious pleasure in molding the female character through her writing foreshadowed his decision to adopt a female authorial voice and pseudonym for his first Fiona Macleod romance in 1894. Published in both America and Britain in 1892, *A Fellowe and His Wife* contained a good deal of Sharp's enchantment with the beauty and culture of Rome and Howard's with the German aristocracy she recently joined.

Fig. 16 Blanche Willis Howard, in F. E. Willard, *A Woman of the Century: Fourteen Hundred-Seventy Biographical Sketches Accompanied by Portraits of Leading American Women in All Walks of Life* (Buffalo, N. Y.: Moulton, 1893), 735. Wikipedia, https://commons.wikimedia.org/wiki/File:BLANCHE_WILLIS_HOWARD_VON_TEUFFEL._A_woman_of_the_century_(page_745_crop).jpg, Public Domain.

Sharp was energized by the warm fall weather in southern Germany and by his relationship with Howard, who enjoyed being called the Frau Hof-Arzt von Teuffel. In a letter to Catherine Janvier on September 3, he said he was "electrified in mind and body:"

> The sun flood intoxicated me. But the beauty of the world is always bracing — all beauty is. I seemed to inhale it — to drink it in — to absorb it at every pore — to become it — to become the heart and soul within it. And then in the midst of it all came my old savage longing for a vagrant life: for freedom from the bondage we have involved ourselves in. I suppose I was a gypsy once — and before that 'a wild man o' the woods.

He also wrote excitedly to Bliss Carman on September 3:

> How strangely one drifts about in this world. Not many days ago I was on the Yorkshire moors or along the seacoast by Whitby: a few days ago I was in Holland, and rejoicing in the animated life of that pleasant 'waterland': last Sunday I was strolling by the Rhine or listening to the music in Cologne Cathedral. And now we are temporarily settled down in this

beautiful Vine-land — in Stuttgart, the loveliest of all German capitals. It is glorious here just now. The heat is very great, but I delight in it. These deep blue skies, these vine clad hills all aglimmer with green-gold, this hot joyous life of the South enthralls me — while this glorious flooding sunshine seems to get into the heart and the brain.

He concluded the letter to Catherine Janvier on that high note:

I have had a very varied, and, to use a much-abused word, a very romantic life in its external as well as in its internal aspects. Life is so unutterably precious that I cannot but rejoice daily that I am alive: and yet I have no fear of or even regret at the thought of death. There are many things far worse than death. When it comes, it comes. But meanwhile we are alive. The Death of the power to live is the only death to be dreaded.

With the Severn biography finally behind him, Sharp experienced in Germany in September and October 1891 a joy that came powerfully, seldom. Soon after arriving in Stuttgart, he confided in his diary, "What a year this has been for me: the richest and most wonderful I have known. Were I as superstitious as Polycrates I should surely sacrifice some precious thing lest the vengeful gods should say, 'Thou hast lived too fully: Come!'"

In his diary on September 6, Sharp called Howard a "charming woman." He "liked her better than ever" and had to remind himself he was there to collaborate with her on a novel. Conscious of his propensity to fall in love with attractive women, he wrote, "I must be on guard against my too susceptible self." In his late September annual birthday letter to E. C. Stedman, he wrote more expansively:

I am here for a literary purpose — though please keep this news to yourself meanwhile i.e., collaborating with our charming friend Blanche Willis Howard (von Teuffel) in a novel. It is on perfectly fresh and striking lines, and will I think attract attention. We are more than half through with it already. She is a most interesting woman and is of that vigorous blond race of women whom Titian and the Palmas loved to paint, and whom we can see now in perfection not in Venice but at Chioggia, further down the Adriatic. But if I fall too deeply in love, it will be your fault — for it was you who introduced me to her! I told her about your birthday, and I think she is going to send you a line of greeting. We see each other for several hours daily, or nightly, and — well, literary life has its compensations! But our affectionate camaraderie is as Platonic as — say, as yours would be in a like instance: so don't drag from its mouldy tomb that cynic smile which lies awaiting the possible resurrection of the Old Adam! Your ears must sometimes tingle as your inner sense overhears our praises of you as man and writer.

He proceeded to tell Stedman he planned to visit America in early 1892 and give a series of public lectures in Boston, Philadelphia, Baltimore, Cincinnati, Chicago, Buffalo, Albany, & perhaps elsewhere. He listed fourteen topics ranging from the Pre-Raphaelites to "Poets and Poetry Today" and asked Stedman for advice and assistance in making the arrangements. More immediately, he and Elizabeth left Germany in mid-October and returned to England via Amsterdam on October 20.

The extreme high Sharp experienced in Germany collapsed into physical illness and a deep depression in London. Elizabeth wrote, "The brilliant summer was followed by a damp and foggy autumn. My husband's depression increased with the varying of the year." On November 9 he spent all day at his London club — the Grosvenor — and wrote as follows in a note to Elizabeth who was spending the day with her mother.

> I have been here all day and have enjoyed the bodily rest, the inner quietude, and, latterly, a certain mental uplifting. But at first I was deep down in the blues. Anything like the appalling gloom between two and three-thirty! I could scarcely read or do anything but watch it with a kind of fascinated horror. It is going down to the grave indeed to be submerged in that hideous pall. As soon as I can make enough by fiction or the drama to depend thereon, we'll leave this atmosphere of fog and this environment of deadening, crushing, paralysing death-in-life respectability. Circumstances make London thus for us: for me at least — for of course we carry our true atmosphere in ourselves — and places and towns are, in a general sense, mere accidents (*Memoir*, 192).

In a December letter to Catherine Janvier he asked, "Do you not long for the warm days — for the beautiful living pulsing South? This fierce cold and gloom is mentally benumbing." He looked forward to seeing her in New York in three weeks and reading for her one of the pieces of "intense dramatic prose" he had written in Germany.

While dealing with his depression and proceeding with his "Dramatic Interludes," Sharp had to return to his Severn biography. The publisher — Sampson Lowe, Marston & Company — decided to issue the work as one volume rather than two. He was forced to condense the first volume and eliminate most of the second which chronicled

Severn's life after Keats died, including the twenty years he spent as British Counsel in Rome. He fashioned an article, "Joseph Severn and His Correspondents," to make use of some of the material he was forced to eliminate from the biography. Horace Scudder published it in the December 1891 issue of the *Atlantic Monthly*. In early December he wrote to Scudder:

> If *practicable*, within the next fortnight or 3 weeks I shall send you the promised "Unpublished Incidents in the Life of Joseph Severn" (or such title as you prefer). I am glad there is a chance of these reminiscences appearing in a conspicuous place — for it appears that many people both in America and here are mainly anticipating the record of Severn's *consular life* (partly, no doubt, after Ruskin's splendid eulogium of him in *Praeterita*) — which is, so far as the book is concerned, regrettable.

Scudder published that article as "Severn's Roman Journals" in the May 1892 issue of the *Atlantic*.

On December 8 Sharp informed Bliss Carman he had booked passage on the Teutonic which would sail from Liverpool on January 6 and arrive in New York on January 12 or 13. He had been forced to postpone all lecturing.

> I am going out partly to attend to some private literary business, best seen to on the spot; partly to arrange for the bringing out in America of a play of mine which is to be produced here; and partly to get a glimpse of the many valued friends and acquaintances I have in N.Y. and Boston. I shall be in N.Y. for three weeks at any rate. Perhaps later on, say in your issue for the first week in January, you will be able to oblige me by inserting in the Independent a para to the above effect: as this would save me letting a lot of people know, and enable me to economize my limited time.

According to Elizabeth, Sharp's doctor had "strictly prohibited" him from giving lectures in the United States. Once in New York, he used that excuse to decline a request from a Harvard faculty member to lecture there "upon a subject of contemporary literature." His doctor may have warned Sharp to avoid stress, but the fact that no lectures were prepared followed a pattern of planning and then canceling. That pattern, I believe, was rooted in a deep insecurity about the depth of his knowledge which caused his weak heart to race uncontrollably before and during any presentation to a potentially critical audience.

Chapter Eight

January–June 1892

Sharp left for America on January 6th aboard the *Teutonic* and arrived in New York a week later where he stayed initially with the Stedmans at 173 West 78th Street. Through his friendship with the Stedmans and others he met during his first visit to New York in 1889, he had immediate access to the literary and publishing elite of the city. Chief among them was Richard Henry Stoddard, a poet and man of letters who with Stedman presided over the literary life of the city. Stedman also arranged for Sharp to meet J. M. Stoddart who edited the prestigious *Lippincott's Monthly Magazine* in Philadelphia. When Sharp wondered if it might be possible to meet Walt Whitman, who lived in Camden, New Jersey across the Delaware River from Philadelphia, Stedman's son Arthur, who knew Whitman, offered to write a letter of introduction. Whitman was a revered figure in the literary circles Sharp frequented in London, and the possibility of meeting him was enormously attractive. After arriving on Wednesday, January 13th Sharp went by train to Philadelphia on the fifteenth and the next morning he called on Stoddart to discuss articles he might write for publication in Lippincott's. When Sharp said he hoped to meet Whitman, Stoddart immediately contacted Horace Traubel who clerked in a nearby bank.

A handsome man of thirty-four who was himself a poet, Traubel was Whitman's principal caretaker and would be his literary executor and biographer. He is best known for transcribing and compiling nine volumes of daily conversations entitled *With Walt Whitman in Camden*. His main concern in 1892 was keeping Whitman in good health and good spirits. Unable to get his letter of introduction to Sharp before he left New York, Stedman sent it to a Philadelphia bookseller for Sharp to retrieve. Traubel said a letter of introduction was unnecessary and offered to take Sharp to Camden that afternoon to meet Whitman who was bedridden, but able to receive guests. Sharp described the visit in a letter to his wife. Whitman was lying in "his narrow bed, with his white beard, white locks, and ashy-gray face in vague relief, in the afternoon light, against the white pillows and coverlet." They discussed the London literary scene, and Sharp assured the ailing poet he was revered by many British writers. In his parting words, Whitman gave Sharp a mission:

> William Sharp when you go back to England, tell those friends of whom you have been speaking, and all others whom you may know and I do not, that words fail me to express my deep gratitude to them for sympathy and aid truly enough beyond acknowledgment. Good-bye to you and to them — the last greetings of a tired old poet.

Two months after Sharp's visit, Whitman died.

Fig. 17 Photograph of Walt Whitman and his nurse Fritzenger (1890). Wikimedia, https://commons.wikimedia.org/wiki/File:Whitman,_Walt_(1819-1892)_ and_his_male_nurse_Fritzenger.JPG, Public Domain.

Fig. 18 Photograph of Horace Traubel (c. 1912). Wikimedia, https://commons.wikimedia.org/wiki/File:Portrait_of_Horace_Traubel.jpg, Public Domain.

After returning to New York, Sharp continued meeting with publishers and friends. On Friday, he crossed the Hudson River with Henry Mills Alden, editor of *Harper's Magazine*, and spent the weekend with Alden's family in Metuchen, New Jersey. On Monday, he returned to the city with Alden and boarded a train to Boston to meet Horace Scudder, editor of the *Atlantic Monthly*, and visit Louise Chandler Moulton who was frequently in London and shared Sharp's affection for the Marston family. He had considered extending his stay in America to talk with more editors and publishers, but shortly after arriving in Boston he received word of his younger brother Edward's unexpected death and decided to sail for home as planned the following Wednesday, February 3. He returned to New York on Thursday and spent the night with Arthur Stedman. On Friday he moved to E. C. Stedman's house, and on

Saturday evening had dinner with Mrs. Thomas Harland, the mother of Henry Harland, an American writer and a good friend who was living in London. During the weekend he met again with Alden and, in a letter thanking Scudder for his hospitality, reported Mrs. Alden's health was deteriorating. Scudder and Alden met as undergraduates at Williams College and remained life-long friends. On Tuesday he moved to a midtown hotel and boarded the Majestic early the next morning.

The eighteen-day visit in the United States was pleasant and productive. Sharp solidified his friendships with the editors of *Harper's Magazine*, the *Atlantic Monthly*, and the *New York Independent* and met the editor of *Lippincott's Monthly Magazine*. He gained a better idea of the kind of articles and poems they would publish and discussed various writing projects. Like so many British writers Sharp wanted to take advantage of the growing American market. He received an offer from a leading American theatrical manager to buy the rights to the play he was writing based on *A Fellowe and His Wife*. Through Arthur Stedman, he negotiated successfully with Charles Webster and Company for the American publication of *Romantic Ballads* and *Sospiri di Roma* in a single volume that appeared in the latter part of 1892 as *Flower o' the Vine*. Sharp wanted his friend Bliss Carman, a fellow poet, to write the introduction to the volume, but Stedman preferred another friend of Sharp's, Thomas Janvier, a short story writer, not a poet, but better known than Carman. Sharp relented and informed Stedman that Janvier would write the introduction if properly compensated. A deal was struck, and Janvier produced a glowing introduction for which Sharp was grateful.

After a rough mid-winter crossing, the Majestic arrived in Liverpool on February 10. Sharp spent a few days recuperating in London before going north on February 14 to comfort his mother. In Edinburgh, he explained in a letter to Arthur Stedman why he was not enthusiastic about giving his next book, which he now called "Dramatic Vistas," to Charles Webster as a follow-up publication to *Flower o' the Vine*. Acting as an agent for Webster and Company, Arthur had written to say Sharp's reluctance in this regard was "shabby." Sharp said he did not wish to issue these "new things in a new dramatic form" in an ordinary way, but pseudonymously in a small privately printed edition. He believed his reputation as an editor and enemies he made as a reviewer were responsible for the lukewarm reception of his *Romantic Ballads* and *Sospiri di Roma*.

> I have my own reasons for wishing to issue them in this way in the first instance. They are new in method and manner, and are, I believe, the best work of the kind I can do. Work of this kind is so dear to me that I am relatively indifferent to its financial success: and, in addition, I am particularly curious to see how these "Dramatic Vistas" will be received, without any of the bias for or against involved in the attachment of my name to them.

The Webster firm might publish a trade edition of the book as by Sharp, but only after he issued a small private edition for friends and reviewers under the pseudonym H. P. Siwäarmill, his anagram for William Sharp. When he was in Germany working with Blanch Willis Howard on *A Fellowe and His Wife* in October 1891, he purchased Maurice Maeterlinck's *La Princess Maleine* and *Les Aveugles*, read straight through them, and, in his diary, called their author a "writer of singular genius." According to the diary, he produced over the next two days, under the influence of Maeterlinck, five "Dramatic Interludes" which he intended to publish pseudonymously. In late February 1892, the five interludes had grown to eight entitled *Dramatic Vistas*. When the book finally appeared in 1894, Sharp claimed authorship and dropped *Dramatic*, leaving just *Vistas*.

Back in London from Edinburgh by February 19, Sharp thanked Thomas Janvier for a copy of his recently published *The Uncle of an Angel and Other Stories* and said he was planning to settle down in London for a period of intense writing. He had finished "Dramatic Vistas," two or three of which he read to Catherine Janvier in New York. In a letter of February 23, he told Laura Stedman he had rented rooms at 11 Bedford Gardens, near Campden Hill in Kensington which had a studio where Elizabeth, who had many friends in the area, was doing some painting. They took the rooms for only a brief period because they planned to rent "a cottage or small house somewhere in the country — probably at a place a few miles north of Cookham Dene and the Woods of Waldegrave." They would remove all their books and furniture from storage, and "either live in it for weeks at a time, or for a day or two as the humour takes us." The house would provide a retreat where Sharp could focus on "more serious and lasting work," but it would have to be near London so both Sharps could continue writing and reviewing for the periodicals and papers.

Sharp's *Life and Letters of Joseph Severn* finally appeared in late February or early March, and in March, *A Fellowe and His Wife* was published by Osgood, McIlvaine & Company in London and Houghton and Mifflin & Company in Boston. It was issued simultaneously in Germany in the Tauchnitz Collection of British Authors. In early March Sharp visited Thomas Hardy in Dorset and produced an article on Hardy that appeared in the July *Forum*. On March 9, he wrote a letter to a new friend, J. Stanley Little, an art critic who lived with his brother George Leon Little, a painter, in Bucks Green, a small village in Sussex. He asked Little if he knew of any cottages or small houses (two sitting rooms, four bedrooms, and near a station) available for a modest rental. He would come down and see anything that might be suitable.

By mid-April, the Sharps had given up their rented rooms in Kensington. The return address on his April 13 letter to E. C. Stedman — 16 Winchester Road | Swiss Cottage — was the home of Edith and Frank Rinder. He told Stedman he was about to go to France for some weeks and continued: "The 'Old Adam' calls me, and alas I am weak." Elizabeth, he said, had gone with friends to the Isle of Wight for a week or so and would join him in Paris "three weeks hence." He added this passage: "My love to Mrs. Stedman — but do not let her know that I am a backslider, as she already has but an indifferent opinion of my much-tried virtue. I really am going to reform — but 'owing to unavoidable circumstances' must not begin all at once or too hurriedly!" It is hard to read such a passage without speculating that Elizabeth and William, in all their moving about and absences from each other, were attempting to adjust to the presence of Edith Rinder in their lives, trying to find spaces and places for Edith and William to be together. Some of his letters from France imply Edith was with him for at least part of his first two weeks there. His desire to be alone for periods of time with Edith, which Elizabeth seems to have accepted, may have been a factor in the plans for a house in Sussex.

Before he left for Paris Sharp returned the proofs of the "Sospiri di Roma" section of *Flower o' the Vine* to Charles Webster along with the manuscript of a new poem entitled "Epilogue | Il Bosco Sacro | To _____." In the letter accompanying the proofs, he said he would not "let Sospiri appear again without the 'Epilogue' — which, to my mind, is one of the most essential things in the book." It is a love poem in which the speaker, Sharp, is alone in a sacred grove [*Il Bosco Sacro*] on the Campagna where

> The Dusk, as a dream;
> Steals slowly, slowly,
> With shadowy feet
> Under the branches
> Here, in the woodland,
> Hushfully seeking
> the Night, her lover.

As dusk slowly turns into darkness there is silence, "Rest, utter rest | Utter peace." Then, suddenly, the speaker hears "thrilling | Long-drawn vibrations! | Passionate preludes | Of passionate song!" But the "wild music" and the "sweet song" are only a memory that soon fades. The speaker recalls a day of rapture in the sacred grove:

> Here, where we gather'd
> The snow-pure blossoms,
> The Flowers of Dream:
> Here, when the sunlight
> On that glad day
> Flooded the mosses
> With golden wine
> And deep in the forest,
> Joy passed us, laughing,
> Laughing low,
> While ever behind her
> Rose lovely, delicate.
> Beautiful, beautiful,
> The fadeless blossoms,
> The Flowers of Dream.

He asks his beating, yearning heart to be sill as now there is only silence.

> Here, where the moonlight,
> Lies like white foam on
> The dark tides of night.
> Here is one only,
> Longing forever,
> Longing, longing
> With passion and pain.

He cries out to his "beloved," but there is no answer, only silence. Still, he retains the memory of the rapture, the glad voice of his passion sings there "Out of the heart of | The fragrant darkness." His "soul's desire" is "never| Lost though afar, | My Joy, my Dreams." The poem ends:

Too deep the rapture
Of this sweet sorrow,
Of this glad pain:
O heart, still thy beating
O bird, thy song!

The Dusk, as a dream; The dedicatee following the title was left blank, but the poem was intended for Edith Rinder who, after she returned to London, was "afar," but "never lost." All the poems in the volume were written after Edith left Rome, but they were inspired by his recollections of their time together on the Campagna and reflect Sharp's joy in the love they shared and his sorrow after her departure. He insisted the poem be included as an epilogue to the Sospiri poems because it neatly summarizes the central theme of the entire volume.

Sharp's insistence on adding the "Epilogue" while omitting the "Preface" to the 1888 *Romantic Ballads and Poems of Phantasy* is significant. The "Preface" announced the dawn of a new Romanticism in which imagination would take precedence over formal perfection in poetry. The poems in that volume initiated the dawning age, but his next volume would reflect its full glory. "I am tortured by the passionate desire to create beauty, to sing something of the 'impossible songs' I have heard, to utter something of the rhythm of life that has most touched me." The next poems "will be daringly of the moment, vital with the life and passion of today, yet not a whit less romantic." Three years passed before he was able to realize that objective in a burst of creativity. The "Epilogue" added to the sospiri section of *Flower o' the Vine* typifies the sensuousness that infused those poems but was absent in the "romantic ballads" of the 1888 volume. Influenced by the nude statuary in and around Rome and by the frank sexuality he experienced or imagined during his walks on the Roman Campagna, the "beauty" he sought in the sospiri poems included that of the human body framed by the beauty of the natural world. The two sections of *Flower o' the Vine* reflect what Sharp viewed as a progression from the elusive romanticism announced as a "new movement" in the 1888 "Preface" to the sensuality of the "Epilogue": "daringly of the moment and vital with life and passion." The very title of the volume, *Flower o' the Vine*, evokes Bacchus, who frequents the sospiri poems in various guises. By mid-1892, Sharp had found a name for the transformation he experienced in Rome in 1891.

The sospiri poems were an initial expression of the Paganism he would soon proclaim more directly in his *Pagan Review*.

On April 23, Sharp thanked Thomas Janvier for his over-generous introduction to *Flower o' the Vine*, which he read in proofs from the Webster firm:

> I thank you most heartily for what you say there, which seems to me, moreover, if I may say so, at once generous, fittingly reserved, and likely to win attention. You yourself occupy such a high place in Letters oversea that such a recommendation of my verse cannot but result to my weal.

He told Janvier he was trying to keep down his "too cosmopolitan acquaintanceship" in Paris and assured him that "after the second of May" he was "going to reform and remain reformed." In the meantime, "after a week or so of the somewhat feverish Bohemianism of literary and artistic Paris, we shall be happy at our 'gypsy' encampment in the Forest of Fontainebleau." The "we" implies Edith Rinder was with him both in Paris and at the "encampment." If so, she must have returned home by May 2 when Elizabeth, having succeeded her husband as the paper's London art critic, arrived to review the Salons for the *Glasgow Herald*. Sharp described for Janvier the beauty of Paris in the spring, mentioned a chance meeting with Paul Verlaine, and listed some of the writers and artists he was meeting:

> I went round to Leon Vanier's, where there were many of les Jeunes — Jean Moréas, Maurice Barrés, Cazalis, Renard, Eugène Holland, and others (including your namesake, Janvier). To-night I ought to go to the weekly gathering of a large number of les Jeunes at the Café du Soleil d'Or, that favourite meeting place now of les decadents, les ymbolists, and les everything else.

He concluded by listing his plans for the rest of the year:

> (1) Lill joins me in Paris about 10 days hence and remains to see the two Salons, etc.
> (2) From the middle of May till the middle (14th) of July we shall be in London.
> (3) Then Lill goes with friends to Germany, to Bayreuth (for Wagnerian joys) and I go afoot and aboat among the lochs and isles and hills of the western Scottish Highlands.
> (4) We meet again in Stirling or Edinburgh, early in August — and then, having purchased or hired a serviceable if not a prancing steed, we go off

for three weeks vagabondage. The steed is for Lill and our small baggage and a little tent. We'll sometimes sleep out: sometimes at inns, or in the fern in Highlander's cottages. Thereafter I shall again go off by myself to the extreme west "where joy and melancholy are one, and where youth and age are twins" as the Gaelic poet says.

(5) The rest of September visiting in Scotland.

(6) Part of October in London then (O Glad Tidings).

(7) Off for 6 months to the South: first to the Greek side of Sicily: then to Rome (about Xmas) for the Spring. Finally: a Poor-House in London.

Few of these plans materialized because J. Stanley Little found a house available for leasing in Bucks Green, a small hamlet in Sussex. The Sharps planned to visit it in the first weekend of June, but Elizabeth, on June 3, developed an extremely high fever, a relapse of the malaria she contracted in France in the spring. Sharp went alone to Bucks Green on June 7, liked the house, and signed a three-year lease. When Elizabeth recovered, she visited the house and described it in the *Memoir* (200) as

> a little eight-roomed cottage, near Rudgwick, with a little porch, an orchard and garden, and small lawn with a chestnut tree in its midst... . [It] stood at the edge of a little hamlet called Bucks Green, and across the road from our garden gate stood the one shop flanked by a magnificent poplar tree, that made a landmark however far we might wander. It was a perpetual delight to us.

In a history of Bucks Green, Roger Nash of the Rudgwick Preservation Society identified the house leased by the Sharps as the Toll House which

> was built in the curtilage of the smithy, first called Arun Villas, then The Laurels, then Phenice Croft, before its present post-war name [Toll House]. The name Phenice Croft (a place in Crete, referred to in the Bible) was given by William Sharp about 1892, who lived there somewhat secretly, for 2 years. He was a much-travelled Scottish writer of a troubled disposition who invented his pseudonym 'Fiona McCloud' whilst writing a book titled *Pharais* in Bucks Green. He was a friend of another literati, Stanley Little, who lived in Rudgwick rather longer, and at the time was lodging at Bucks Green Place. Both, I think, were drawn to the area by its Shelley connections.

Chapter Eight: January–June 1892

Fig. 19 Early twentieth-century photograph of the house across the road from the Sharp's Phenice Croft in Bucks Green, Rudgwick Sussex. © Rudgwick Preservation Society. Courtesy of Roger Nash, Chair, Rudgwick Preservation Society, https://www.rudgwick-rps.org.uk

Fig. 20 Mid-twentieth-century photograph of Bucks Green, Rudgwick, Sussex. Phenice Croft, now the Toll House, is across the road from the building, now white, which housed the shop. © The Francis Frith Collection, https://www.francisfrith.com/bucks-green/bucks-green-the-village-c1965_b587001

According to Nash,

> In 1890 James Stanley Little and his brother George Leon Little lived in Bucks Green at The Kraal, a house in Lynwick St, now called The Old School House. In 1891, J Stanley Little lived at Bucks Green Place with William Kensett, a dairy farmer who was a near neighbor of the Sharps.

The Sharps would not have become residents of Bucks Green if Stanley Little had not found them a house they liked.

For the remainder of June Sharp corresponded regularly with Little about the house. On the twenty-second, he asked Little to tell a man named Napper that "Mr. Sharp says he has nothing to do with any extra labour unauthorised by him, and that this engaging extra assistance without consulting him first, is a thing he will not tolerate again." He also passed on specific instructions from Elizabeth:

> She would like (if nothing has yet been done) if the paint of the stairway, landing, and doors belonging thereto be done in a dark red (Pompeian red) — of one colour only, instead of the two shades already approved to match the paper. The doors in the Hotel at Littlehampton are responsible for this change of view. Again, if the drawing room has not been gone on with, we would now like if the painting of the skirting, doors, and mantel piece be uniformly of the pale tint of yellow, instead of the pale and yellow, as first arranged — but the inside of the doorless cupboard to be entirely of the deeper shade of yellow.

Sharp expected to "enter the house with the furniture about the 13th or 14th of July — just when E. goes away for a fortnight to Germany." At the close of June 1892, the Sharps were set for a new phase of their lives in a house in rural Sussex called "The Laurels." They rechristened it first "Kingscroft" in recognition of a former resident named King and then settled on "Phenice Croft" which combined the Greek name for the Phoenix, a unique bird that burned itself on a funeral pyre and rose from the ashes with renewed youth to live through another cycle, and the Scottish name for a rural cottage (croft). The stage was set for their "renewal," a period of concentrated writing in which Sharp produced first the *Pagan Review* and the early writings of Fiona Macleod.

When my wife and I drove south from London and found Phenice Croft in 1965, it was called the Toll House and occupied by a gracious couple who welcomed us into the house and introduced us to guests they were entertaining on the rear patio. They were interested in what we were able to tell them about the Sharps and their occupancy of the house in 1890s. Only recently, thanks to Roger Nash, have we learned what a distinguished occupancy the former Phenice Croft enjoyed in the 1960s. Our hosts that day were Admiral Sir Randolph Stewart Gresham Nicholson and his wife Cecilia. Nicholson commanded ships that survived several encounters with the enemy in the first and second World Wars. Promoted to Admiral in 1943, he became Deputy to the Commander-in Chief of the Eastern Fleet in 1944. Following the war, he was appointed Admiral Commander of Her Majesty's Dockyard in Devonport. Upon his retirement in 1950, he was granted a knighthood (KCB), and between 1953 and 1958 he served as Lieutenant Governor of Jersey. The Nicholsons acquired the Toll House in 1950 and refurbished it in a style befitting a distinguished Admiral. After a life of accomplishments, Nicholson died in 1975 at the age of eighty-two, and his wife died in 1980. Since they vacated the house, its residents have been uninterested in its history and less gracious in welcoming those who are.

Chapter Nine

July–December 1892

On July 8, Sharp apologized to Julia Ward Howe's daughter, Maud Howe Elliott, for being unable to entertain her since he had no residence in London. His wife, moreover, was leaving in a few days for the Wagner festival in Bayreuth, and he was "going into Sussex to superintend the arrival of our furniture at a country place I have taken there." Elizabeth left for Germany on July 11, and the next day Sharp went down to Bucks Green, Sussex, where he stayed with Stanley Little until the furniture arrived. When Elizabeth returned from Bayreuth in the third week of July she joined her husband, and they settled into the old stone house that would be their home for two years.

On July 10 Sharp wrote a letter that includes his response to Little's request that he give the main address at an early August celebration Little was organizing to commemorate the centennial of Percy Bysshe Shelley's birth. The letter contains details about the state of his health and his opinions about several contemporary writers.

> And now about the Shelley address. For several reasons it would be a pleasure as well as an honour — but the truth is that I dare not venture just now on anything of the kind, for physiological reasons. My doctor has just warned me of this vein-trouble that I have not yet satisfactorily got under. The least thing may bring it back — and this must not be, as it might easily become dangerous ("clotting"). One requisite is — not to stand. Walking does not now hurt me if in moderation: but even a short stand involves pain and discomfiture. And though I may be all right again by the end of the month I really must not risk the danger involved in the fatigue of standing to address.

In 1892, when he was thirty-seven, Sharp developed symptoms of diabetes; and his heart, weakened by rheumatic fever in 1884, was not moving blood through his veins with sufficient strength. Standing without moving risked the possibility of serious blood clots in his legs. He told Little he could write an address for him or someone else to read, but it would be far better to have a prominent Shelleyan give the address. He thought the best choice would be Stopford Brooke, next Edward Dowden (two Irishmen), next Roden Noel, next John Nichol (two Scotsmen), next Sir George Douglas, or why not Little himself who was organizing the event. Richard Garnett, Sharp warned, was "not a good speaker and has not the right manner," and surely not H. Buxton Forman who was "a jellyfish" and "a Philistine of the Philistines in manner and address."

Shelley was born in Horsham, Sussex on August 4, 1792, and the commemoratory event took place there on August 4, 1892. It was described in an article in the August 11 issue of the *West Sussex Gazette* which may have been written by Stanley Little. The venue was the stately home of Mr. Hurst of Horsham Park "with its beautiful gardens laughing in the sunlight of a lovely summer day" and affording "to visitors no untrue glimpse of the surroundings amid which Shelley as the son of an English squire was brought up." Many literary luminaries attended; and "The hall was crowded; all classes were represented, and Horsham, the county, and London, divided the audience fairly amongst them." Following Sharp's advice and with his help, Little engaged as the principal speaker Professor John Nichol with whom Sharp studied at Glasgow University. The September issue of *The Artist* reported "What Nichol said about Shelley, at Horsham, was the very thing that needs to be said." He "completely carried his audience." The organizers, principally Little, were "brilliantly successful in their arrangements." With Sharp as his adviser, Little gathered a committee and many illustrious sponsors to raise money for a Shelley Museum in Horsham, and their efforts survive today as a substantial collection of books, manuscripts, portraits, and sculptures in the Shelley Gallery of the Horsham Museum.

Sharp's July 10 letter to Little asked him to tell the Bucks Green postman the house formerly called the Laurels was now Phenice Croft. All mail addressed to the Sharps and all mail addressed to Mr. W. H. Brooks at Bucks Green, Rudgwick was to be placed in a post bag to be picked up by a boy in the forenoons. Sharp had settled on the *Pagan Review* as the name of the quarterly he would produce at Phenice Croft, and it would be edited by W. H. Brooks, a pseudonym for Sharp and

Fig. 21 Park House, Horsham, Sussex. Photograph by Whn64 (2013), Wikimedia, https://commons.wikimedia.org/wiki/File:Horsham_-_horsham_park.jpg, CC BY-SA 3.0.

a nod to his maternal grandfather, William Brooks, the Swedish Vice-Counsel in Glasgow and the last person in all of Scotland to edit — or to read — a *Pagan Review*. Sharp would write the entire content of the first issue under various pseudonyms. He began working on the content when he and Elizabeth were staying in the Cairds' house in Northbrook, Micheldever in early June. His diary entry for June 2 begins: "In the early forenoon, after some pleasant dawdling, began to write the Italian story, 'The Rape of the Sabines,' which I shall print in the first instance in my projected White Review as by James Marazion." The color white had figured prominently in the poems of *Sospiri di Roma*, white marble statues, white flowers, white statues, and white human bodies, but as the content of the review evolved "pagan" supplemented "white" in the magazine's title. In an April 23 letter from Paris Sharp addressed the Janviers as "fellow Pagans." He was drawn to the "feverish Bohemianism of literary and artistic Paris," and it may have been in Paris that he settled on the term "Paganism" to define his encounter with the remnants of the Roman past in Italy and his desire to join the decadents in breaching the restraints of high Victorianism.

Dennis Denisoff and Loraine Kooistra in *Yellow Nineties Online* describe the "Foreword" to the *Pagan Review* as having "the urgency of a manifesto [...] declaring on behalf of the 'younger generation' that the magazine's contributors challenged both the religion and the ideals of their forefathers."

> The editor's apparent preference for authors with French names, the foreword's discussion of art for art's sake, and the publication's references to Charles Baudelaire, Theophile Gautier, Oscar Wilde [...] signal Sharp's wish to have his readers associate the magazine with aestheticism. By 1892, the Aesthetic Movement had already had a lengthy run of popularity and was shifting into its final, decadent phase [...] To this phase of the Aesthetic Movement, the *Pagan Review* offers a notable contribution.

"Its emphasis," they continue, is "on the dissident, mythic, and obscure. Its tendency toward overwrought descriptions and archaic dialogue are reminiscent of decadent authors and artists, [...] and its mystical depictions of alternative gods and spiritualities aligns it with paganism in a more earnest and disconcerting way than many other British contributions to the decadent movement."

Having announced in the preface to *Romantic Ballads* in 1888 the advent of a new Romanticism, Sharp added to that initiative in 1891 the sensuality and escape from rhyme in *Sospiri di Roma*. By the summer of 1892, he had settled on "New Paganism" as the name of the movement he was trying to launch and for which the *Pagan Review* served as a manifesto. Its "first number," dated August 15, 1892, contained:

> A lengthy unsigned "Foreward."
> Two poems: "The Coming of Love" by W. S. Fanshaw
>   "An Untold Story" by Lionel Wingrave
> Three stories: "The Pagans: A Memory" by Willand Dreeme
>   "The Rape of the Sabines" by James Marazion
>   "The Oread: A Fragment," by Charles Verlaine
> A Fragment of a Lyrical Drama: "Dionysos in India" by Wm. Windover
> A "dramatic interlude": "The Black Madonna" by W. S. Fanshaw
> A review by "S" of Stuart Merrill's *Pastels in Prose* (Harper & Brothers, New York, 1890).

All that was followed by a series of comments by the editor (signed W. H. B.) on recently published works of literature by well-known writers, many Sharp's friends, including Swinburne, Hardy, Meredith, Hall Caine, and Stuart Merrill. And finally, an advertisement that the next issue of the *Review* would include an article titled "The New Paganism" by H. P. Siwäarmill, the anagram of William Sharp, he invented the previous fall in Germany for the author of the "Dramatic Interludes." In the *Pagan Review* one such interlude, "The Black Madonna," is attributed to W. S. Fanshawe. When the dramatic interludes were published in 1894 as *Vistas*, their author was William Sharp. The back cover of the *Pagan Review* contained an advertisement which combined the two titles: *Vistas: Dramatic Interludes* by W. S. Fanshawe which would soon be printed privately. Each of these items merits discussion for what they reveal about Sharp's state of mind, what he hoped to accomplish as a writer, and his method of composition. Two stand out because they are directly traceable to his April/May experience in Paris.

First, the review of Stuart Merrill's *Pastels in Prose* which contains Merrill's translations of "prose poems" by contemporary French writers. The review associates the *Pagan Review* with the symbolist poets and the decadence infusing literature in Paris and London. It also reflects Sharp's genuine interest in alternatives to rhymed and cadenced poetry. The prose poem differs, he wrote in the review, from a "quoted specimen of poetic prose." It must be brief and complete in itself, the equivalent of a pastel in the art of painting. The pastel artist must be "what is somewhat too vaguely called an impressionist" whose aim is "suggestion, not imitation." The prose poem is "a consciously-conceived and definitely-executed poetic form." Sharp concluded the review by quoting from William Dean Howells's description of the form in his introduction to Merrill's book: "The very life of the form is its aerial delicacy: its soul is that perfume of thought, of emotion, which these masters here have never suffered to become an argument. They must be appreciated with sympathy by whoever would get all their lovely grace, their charm that comes and goes like the light in beautiful eyes." Sharp experimented with this form in the writings of Fiona Macleod.

Second, "The Pagans: A Memory" by Willand Dreeme, which is identified as "Book One" and, at the end, "To be Continued." As with the poems of *Sospiri di Roma*, the story recounts Sharp's personal experience overlaid by dreams and imaginings. Unlike the sospiri, a pseudonym removes the possibility of identifying the true source of the experiences. The appendage to the title ("A Memory") and the name of the author (Willand Dreeme) invite the reader to wonder if the content is Willand's memory or his dream. It is impossible to divorce the real author of the story, William Sharp, from its supposed author, Willand Dreeme, and equally impossible to separate its real author and supposed author from the story's narrator and main character, Wilfred Traquair, who is called Will. As might be expected, Sharp's relatives and close friends called him Will. The title signals the story as the most pagan of the contributions to the *Pagan Review*, and the three quotations of its preface — from George Eeckhoud's *Kermesses*, from "The Song of Solomon," and from Oscar Wilde — associate it with the Belgium/French/English decadence.

Sharp wrote the story on June 3 and 4, less than a month after returning from France. The story's narrator, Wilfred Traquair, recalls walking with Clair, his beloved, in a warm Italian landscape among the trees 'under the deep blue wind-swept sky" where they "first realized each had won from the other a lifetime of joy." His recollection is Sharp's recollection of his walks with Edith Rinder on the Roman Campagna fifteen months earlier.

> The snow lay deep by the hedges, and we had to slip through many a drift before we reached the lonely woodland height whither we were bound. But was there ever snow so livingly white, so lit with golden glow? Was ever summer sky more gloriously blue? Was ever spring music sweeter than that exquisite midwinter hush, than that deep suspension of breath before the flood of our joy?

Eventually Clair returned to Paris and the narrator, Will Traquair, to the London he "hated so much, there to write things about which I cared not a straw, while my heart was full of you, and my eyes saw you everywhere, and my ears were haunted day and night by echoes of your voice." When he accumulated enough money to be independent of London, he went to Paris to meet Clair. Shifting effortlessly between directly addressing his beloved and third-person narration, he recalls his joy in finding "we loved each other more than ever":

> Those hours at twilight, in the Luxembourg Gardens, when the thrush would sing as, we were sure, never nightingale sang in forest-glade, or Wood of Broceliande: those hours in the galleries, above all before our beloved Venus in the Louvre; ah, beautiful hours, gone forever, and yet immortal, because of the joy that they knew and whereby they live and are even now fresh and young and sweet with their exquisite romance.

They were even happier when they left Paris behind and went away together, "as light-hearted as the April birds, as free as the wind itself."

Letters Sharp wrote from Paris in April to E. C. Stedman, Thomas Janvier, and J. Stanley Little, implied the woman he loved was with him in Paris for the last two weeks of April after which he intended to "reform." Though details differ, this story about the two Pagans parallels the experiences of Sharp and Edith: their meeting in Rome in December 1890, their parting when she returned to London in early January, and Sharp's recent escape from London to Paris where the April birds were singing. Sharp may have been recounting only what he imagined it would have been like to have Edith with him in Paris, but the innuendos are so telling, the parallels so obvious, and the writing so impassioned it is hard to avoid concluding she was there. As in the *Sospiri* poems after Edith left Rome, so in this story, Sharp's intense feelings begged for release. The adolescent tinge to the writing suggests Sharp was recounting his first experience of falling passionately in love. William and Elizabeth were first cousins who became engaged as teenagers. Their relationship, while close, was from the start a meeting of minds and a matter of convenience. It developed over time into a deep friendship in which Elizabeth functioned as a protector, nurse, and enabler overseeing the well-being of her "poet." It was only after Sharp's experience with Edith in Rome that impassioned love affairs became a prominent theme of his writings.

The body of "The Pagans: A Memory" contains a long and detailed description of the beautiful Clair. She is a painter living with her brother, also a painter, who is hyper-concerned about his reputation and status. Clair's skin was "pale as ivory, but "touched with a delicious brown, the kiss of sunshine and fresh air." It was "in keeping with the rich dark of her hair and sweeping eyebrows and long lashes." The description mirrors a portrait of Edith Rinder known as the "Lady Green Sleeves," reflecting the green velvet dress she wore for the sitting and referencing both the sixteenth century English folk song "A Newe Northen Dittye of ye Ladye Greene Sleves" and Daniel Gabriel Rossetti's painting of that mythical woman of great beauty.

Clair's brother disapproves of her relationship with Wilfred and threatens to take away her inheritance, as is his right, if she persists, but persist she does. She leaves her brother and goes off with Will, flouting

Fig. 22 Photograph of Edith Wingate Rinder known as "My Lady Greensleeves" reflecting the green velvet dress she wore for the sitting (c. 1894). The pose mirrors many of the paintings of the Pre-Raphaelite Brotherhood, especially those of Dante Gabriel Rossetti. Photographer unknown. Courtesy of Fig the Rinder family.

Fig. 23 Daniel Gabriel Rossetti, *My Lady Greensleeves* (1872). Oil on panel, 33 x 27.3 cm. Harvard Art Museums, Fogg Museum. Wikimedia, https://commons.wikimedia.org/wiki/File:Dante_Gabriel_Rossetti_-_My_Lady_Greensleeves_-_1943.203_-_Fogg_Museum.jpg, Public Domain.

her brother's standards of acceptable behavior and his beliefs about the subservience of women to men. As they leave, the brother gives Wilfred a letter addressed to a "Vagrant, of God-knows where" which reads:

> That my sister has chosen to unite herself with **a beggarly Scot** [emphasis added] is her pitiable misfortune: that she has done so without the decent veil of marriage is her enormity and my disgrace. [...] neither you nor the young woman need ever expect the slightest tolerance, much less practical countenance from me. You are both at liberty to hold, and carry out, the atrocious opinions (for I will not flatter you by calling them convictions) upon marriage which you entertain or profess to entertain. I, equally, am at liberty to abstain from contagion of such unpleasant company, and to insist henceforth upon an unsurmountable barrier between it and myself.

It is pleasantly ironic that Sharp's extensive and bitter expression of the conservative of marriage he opposed is directed against a "beggarly Scot" named Will. The story ends: "Outcasts we were, but two more joyous pagans never laughed in the sunlight, two happier waifs never more fearlessly and blithely went forth into the green world." Though the story was "To be continued" it was not, but it would be told over and over again with different characters in the stories Sharp would tell as Fiona Macleod. The beginning sentences of "The Pagans" speaks of Clair Auriol in the past tense. The wonderful relationship has ended with no reason given. A true romantic, Sharp focused on the beginnings of passionate relationships not their inevitably sad endings. This story is the first of many renditions of the impossibility of permanence in his relationship with Edith since neither could sever their marital ties, she to Frank Rinder and he to Elizabeth Sharp.

Sharp sent copies of his *Pagan Review* to friends and editors of periodicals where it might warrant notice. He sought subscribers at twelve shillings a year, and he welcomed contributions of short stories and poems that conformed to the purposes described in the first number's Foreword. On August 13 Sharp wrote to E. C. Stedman from Selsey Bill on the Sussex Coast, where he and Elizabeth had gone to escape the "extreme heat" of Bucks Green. He was sending a copy of the *Pagan Review*, and he confessed he was responsible for all its contents. It was to be the voice of "Neo-Paganism," a "new movement in letters [...] unlike any that has taken place in England before, in the Victorian Age at any rate: though indeed it is a movement that is at hand rather than really forward." Sharp was initiating yet another "movement."

Stedman subscribed, but must have expressed reservations since Sharp's letter to him on September 28 contained the following passage:

> I thank you for your lovely & friendly letter. I feel there is a good leaven of truth, to say the least, in what you say about the "Pagan Review." But set your mind at rest: the poor thing is dead. There is a possible resurrection for it next year as a quarterly, but this is still in nubibus. It has, however, so far accomplished its aim of stimulus among the younger people, and that is good. I return herewith your subscription, with sincerest thanks. Have mislaid it. No time to hunt for it now. Hope to send it by next post. By the way, keep your P/R. It is already being sought by collectors. I can send you another if you wish.

Elizabeth said the *Pagan Review* was born of Sharp's "mental attitude at that moment, … a sheer reveling in the beauty of objective life and nature, while he rode the crest of the wave of health and exuberant spirits that had come to him in Italy after his prolonged illness and convalescence" (*Memoir*, 204–207). He soon realized he could not continue the *Review* as it would be hard to repeat the tour de force, and he had other projects in mind. Elizabeth agreed the one number had served its purpose "for by means of it he had exhausted a transition phase that had passed to give way to the expression of his more permanent self." In other words, the *Review* was a step toward the writings of Fiona Macleod.

Sharp returned all the subscriptions and submissions with the following memorial card:

> On the 15th of September, still-born *The Pagan Review*.

> Regretted by none, save the affectionate parents and a few forlorn friends, *The Pagan Review* has returned to the void whence it came. The progenitors, more hopeful than reasonable, look for an unglorious but robust resurrection at some more fortunate date. "For of such is the Kingdom of Paganism."

In a "solemn ceremony," with Sharp's sister Mary and Stanley Little as "mourners," they buried the *Review* in a corner of the garden at Phenice Croft and marked the spot with a framed inscription.

Robert Murray Gilchrist, a writer Sharp corresponded with when he edited the "Literary Chair" of *Young Folk's Papers*, submitted a story for the *Pagan Review* called "The Noble Courtesan," which Sharp read with interest. Writing first as W. H. Brooks in early October, Sharp said he thought it would be much improved "by less — or more hidden — emphasis on the mysterious aspect of the woman's nature. She is too much the 'principle of Evil,' the 'modern Lilith.'" Then on October 22, he wrote again, this time as William Sharp, to thank Gilchrist for his "friendly and cordial article" about the *Pagan Review* in *The Library*. When the *Review* is revived next year as a quarterly, Sharp wrote, he would look to Gilchrist "as one of the younger men of notable talent to give a helping hand." Born in Sheffield in 1867, Gilchrist was apprenticed to a manufacturer of cutlery after attending grammar school. In 1888 he decided to become a writer, left the apprenticeship, and moved to Highcliffe Farm, near the village of Eyam several miles southwest of Sheffield in Derbyshire. He was soon joined there by George Alfred Garfitt, who was also born and educated in Sheffield. Five years older than Gilchrist, Garfitt may have been a fellow apprentice. In any case, he became a manufacturer of cutlery, an amateur historian, and Gilchrist's life-long partner. Sharp concluded his letter to Gilchrist by asking him to visit Phenice Croft when he next came south. "I can offer you a lovely country fare, a bed, and a cordial welcome." As it happened, Gilchrist and Garfitt did not visit Phenice Croft until 1894, but Sharp visited them in Eyam in September 1893. At this first meeting, the three men formed a close friendship that lasted many years and impacted the course of Sharp's publications.

It is a matter of some interest that when John Lauritsen established his Pagan Press in 1982 to publish "books of interest to the intelligent gay man" the first book he published was Edward Carpenter's *Iolāus, An Anthology of Friendship* which had been out of print for many years. In 1891, when Carpenter was teaching in Sheffield, he met and formed a relationship with George Merrill, a working-class man twenty-two years his junior. In 1898 they began living together in rural Millthorpe, Derbyshire only a few miles from Holmesfield, Derbyshire where Gilchrist and Garfitt had moved into the family's large manor house they shared with Gilchrist's mother and sisters. The two couples became close friends. Both chose, quite sensibly, to live quiet lives miles away from the uproar caused by the Oscar Wilde trial in London. Paganism, a fascination with pre-Christian Roman and Greek civilizations, has a long history preceding and following Sharp's "New Paganism." By necessity if not by choice, Sharp's paganism was heterosexual, but he had many homosexual friends, and he was comfortable with love and desire no matter its form. He would be amused by the coincidental linkage a century later of his "New Paganism" with the first product of Lauritsen's Pagan Press by a writer, Edward Carpenter, who, with his same-sex partner, was a near neighbor and close friend of Sharp's close friend, Robert Murray Gilchrist, and his same-sex partner, in remote Derbyshire.

In Sharp's August 13 letter to Stedman, he objected to Stedman classifying him as "an Australian poet" in the latest edition of his study of Victorian poets and asked him to remedy that error in the volume's next edition. After describing the *Pagan Review* and asking Stedman what he thought of it, Sharp continued:

> By the time you get this — no, a week later — I shall be in Scotland, I hope. My wife cannot go north this year. If all goes well — this ought to be one of the happiest experiences of a happy life. I cannot be more explicit: but perhaps you will understand. But even to be in the Western Highlands alone is a joy. Then I am going to reform and work hard all winter. I rather doubt if we'll get away to Greece after all: funds are villainously low for such exploits.

He implies he and Edith Rinder would be together in the Western Highlands where the Rinders usually rented a house for the month of September. The implication is strengthened by a passage in a letter to Bliss Carman, also in August: "Think of me early in September (from August 30th) in the loveliest of the West Highlands — & in one of the happiest experiences of my life. I can't be more explicit — but you will understand! Thereafter I am going to reform — definitely."

When Alfred, Lord Tennyson died in early October, some began to question the need to appoint a successor Poet Laureate. Sharp considered joining those who opposed the appointment of another laureate, but on October 9 he told Stanley Little he had decided not to take any initiative in the "abolishment scheme." After attending Tennyson's funeral in Westminster Abbey on the twelfth, Sharp sent a letter to the poet Alfred Austin saying he was pleased to have seen him at the funeral. After describing his removal to "a small house in a remote part of Sussex" where the rent was cheaper than in London, he turned to the Laureateship. "If you, as many think, are to be the heritor, the laurel will go to one who will sustain the high honor with dignity and beauty." Austin did inherit the title, and he may have recalled this letter in 1902 when Sharp was desperately in need of money. A Civil List Pension was out of the question because Sharp refused to reveal to members of Parliament his authorship of Fiona Macleod's popular writings. His friend Alexander Nelson Hood, who was the Duke of Bronte, and Alfred Austin, the Poet Laureate, were the principals in the effort to obtain the pension. They were supported by George Meredith, Thomas Hardy, and Theodore Watts-Dunton. Finally, Sharp agreed to Austin and Hood telling Arthur Balfour, the recently elected Prime Minister, in strict confidence Sharp was the author of the writings of Fiona Macleod, whereupon Balfour found the money for a grant that provided needed relief.

Concluding his August 13 letter to Stedman, Sharp doubted he and Elizabeth would be able to go to Greece during the winter as funds were "villainously low for such exploits." He hoped to continue with his creative work in the fall, but Elizabeth's health intervened. She had not fully recovered from the malaria she contacted in Italy in the spring of 1891. In her words (*Memoir*, 208), "The prolonged rains in the hot autumn, the dampness of the clay soil on which lay the hamlet of Bucks Green, made me very ill again with intermittent low fever." It was imperative, her doctor said, for her to spend at least part of the winter in a dry climate. Since they lacked the funds for traveling south, Sharp put aside his "dream work" and wrote between October and December two boys' adventure stories. "The Red Rider: A Romance of the Garibaldian Campaign in the Two Sicilies," appeared serially in the *Weekly Budget* in late 1892, and "The Last of the Vikings: Being the Adventures in the East and West of Sigurd, the Boy King of Norway" was accepted by *Old and Young* and published in 1893. Both appeared subsequently in book form from James Henderson and Sons, Ltd. These efforts and others by both Sharps enabled them to go south for the first two months of 1893. In early December Sharp told Stanley Little they were planning to go to Florence via Switzerland and the Gothard Pass and then on to Sicily and North Africa. He urged Little to accompany them as far as Florence or Rome. Little needed a break from work, and he would find wonderful paintings to view and assess. By mid-December, they had decided to go to the Mediterranean by ship "as it is at once considerably less expensive, & more restorative for E."

In a letter to Arthur Stedman at the end of November, Sharp said he had just "finished reviewing for the *Academy* the book of the season in literary circles here — the late Wm. Bell Scott's Autobiography." A Pre-Raphaelite poet and painter, Scott left a large body of reminiscences when he died in 1890, and the Scottish critic and novelist William Minto set about editing them. His *Autobiographical Notes of the Life of William Bell Scott and Notices of his Artistic and Poetic Circle of Friends 1830 to 1882, Illustrated by Etchings by Himself and Reproductions of Sketches by Himself and Friends* was published in 1892 in two substantial volumes by James R. Osgood, McIlvaine & Co. in London and by Harper Brothers in New York. Though "full of misstatements and ill-intentioned half-statements," Sharp wrote to Stedman, it was a fascinating book because of its letters and anecdotes. Algernon Charles Swinburne, he continued, had a different opinion. When dining at his house in Putney a few days ago, Sharp found Swinburne "excited over 'The Monster' [Scott] to whom he has paid so many affectionate tributes in verse!" He was going to "slate the book unmercifully (and very foolishly) in the December *Fortnightly*." Titled "The New Terror," Swinburne's review appeared in the December issue of *The Fortnightly Review*, and Sharp's in the December issue of *The Academy*.

In mid-November, Sharp's opinion of the *Autobiographical Notes* was less balanced. Theodore Watts [not yet Dunton] asked Sharp to review the book. Perhaps influenced by Swinburne's anger, Sharp had nothing good to say about the book in a November 14 letter to Watts. He recoiled at Scott's treatment of Watts: he "persistently pooh-poohed your good & gracious service to" Rossetti and portrayed himself as Rossetti's only true "nurse & friend". He continued:

> As to the lies current that you, and others including myself, assisted rather than deplored D. G. R.'s chloral habit, & made out that he was much worse than he was, will gain some colour by the implication in the second allusion to yourself. I think you know how I love and reverence Gabriel Rossetti's memory. I am not blind, of course, & I know his faults & weaknesses — but he was a great genius, & as man he won my love, & shall have it till I die. I have glanced thro' the D. G. R. passages since I wrote to you last, & with deepest pain.

Next, Sharp complained about Scott's "insultingly cruel epithet to Ruskin" and expressed his amazement that Minto, the editor, had "let pass uncorrected (if he could not suppress, as he ought to have done) so much that ought not to have seen the light." He was outraged by

> the remarks about Swinburne — one of the greatest poets of our century. The more one knows & rereads his work, & critically & comparatively, the more one admires it & his high attitude throughout. He was my idol in old days, & now again I realise how great a poet he is. And just as the public mind is slowly veering towards that high acceptation of him which is his due — out comes this foolish & spiteful nonsense, which will spread abroad to his detriment! Well, W. B. S. can't hurt A. C. Swinburne, nor a thousand W. B. S.'s.

Sharp said he would send his review for Watts and Swinburne to read and suggest revisions.

Several days later, in a November 18 letter to Watts, Sharp said he was having trouble writing the review and had decided to start over from scratch.

> Now that I have finished the book & gone carefully into it, I not only more than ever regret Swinburne's article but think we have all underestimated the good in the book. There is a great deal of interesting matter, particularly in the letters introduced: and I do not see how the book is to be killed, or that it should be killed. [...] Once pruned of its misstatements and otherwise carefully revised, it would be extremely entertaining and to future students of the period profoundly interesting & even valuable. One must be fair all round. It is a damnably difficult thing to do in this instance: but I'll have one more shot anyway!

Since a deadline for the December *Academy* was approaching, Sharp said he would stay up all night writing if necessary. The next morning he sent Watts a portion of the article with a note: "It has been an infernally difficult review to write. I began, after a third trial, in this more moderate & advisable fashion." He asked Watts to "rectify" him if necessary and added "Please do not cut out or alter in any way my MS, but jot any suggestions in pencil on a separate slip."

He finished the article in time for it to appear in the December 3 *Academy* and wrote again to Watts on December 7 to thank him for his

> generous appreciation, though I'm bound to say I don't see anything particular in the review, except tact — for it was infernally difficult to be

just to what is good in the book and yet to blow the counterblast. From what I hear, it has been a good deal noted in the very quarters I wanted it to be — namely among those who bear neither you nor me any good will: and it is admitted that my frank outspokenness knocks the ground from under "Scott's" feet as regards D. G. R., your relations to him and so forth.

He knew there will be one or two American critics "who will hold up W. B. S. as a trustworthy authority to show how poor a fellow D. G. R. was, how deserted by his worthiest friends, and how you were only "a minor newcomer," & so forth." He planned to go out of his way to have his review reproduced in one or two influential American journals to set the record straight. Despite the difficulty of writing the review, he thought he had reached the right balance, and the review appears to have been well-received.

On November 18 Sharp wrote to Kineton Parkes to propose for the December issue of the *Library Review* a review of a" remarkable book" by E. C. Stedman — *The Nature and Elements of Poetry* — which was a revised reprint of his "much-noted essays on Imagination, Truth, Beauty, Melancholia, etc. which have been appearing in *The Century*." The next day he wrote again to Parkes to say he was too busy to write an adequate review as he wanted to do more than a mere notice. He could, though, send Parkes an article on Scott's "'Reminiscences' with its wealth of addenda concerning the poet-painters and painter-poets of the Pre-Raphaelites." On November 28 he wrote to the editor of *Blackwood's Magazine* in Edinburgh to say he would be able to submit an article about William Bell Scott's relations with other painters and poets in the Rossetti circle by the end of the week. Writing again on December 5, he said he was too busy with commissioned articles and other literary work to finish the Scott article for the January number. The promises and retractions indicate the extent to which he was overextending himself trying to acquire funds for the impending trip.

He did, however, accomplish a good deal of writing in the first half of 1892, and there were a sizeable number of publications. His *Life and Letters of Joseph Severn* appeared in February, and *A Fellowe and His Wife* appeared in the spring in England, America, and Germany. He published articles on Philip Marston and Maeterlinck in *The Academy* and on Thomas Hardy in *The Forum*. *Flower o' the Vine* containing poems from his *Romantic Ballads* and *Sospiri di Roma* was published in the United States. "Second Shadow: Being the narrative of Jose Maria Santos y Bazan, Spanish Physician in Rome" was published in the *Independent* in New York, and an article titled, "Severn's Roman Journals" appeared in Boston's *Atlantic Monthly*. He completed and submitted *Vistas*, the Maeterlinckean short dramas or interludes he started writing in Germany in the fall of 1891, to Elkin Mathews in England and Charles Webster in America. They decided not to publish it, but the volume would find a publisher in 1894. In mid-1892 the Sharps had settled into Phenice Croft where they hoped to experience a Phoenix-like rebirth, but the need to generate money forced a delay in their plans for creative work.

Chapter Ten

1893

The Sharps boarded a ship bound for North Africa on January 7, 1893 and arrived a week later in Algiers. On January 16, Sharp sent a card to Arthur Stedman and asked him to share it with his father:

> We have enjoyed our first week in North Africa immensely. Even apart from the Moorish and oriental life, everything is charming to the eyes after London fogs — the greenness, the palms, the orange and lemon trees, the roses and brilliant creepers, the blue of the sea and the deeper blue of the sky.

The next day they headed west, mostly by train, and in a letter to Stanley Little dated January 22 Sharp said they were in Blida at the base of the Atlas Mountains. They were headed to Tlemcen and planned to push on "across the frontier of Morocco to the city of Oujda" if the tribes were not up. The landscape was "strange & beautiful: miles of orange and tangerine trees in full fruit à terre, and on high the grand heights and fantastic peaks of the Atlas range." They made it into Morocco for a few days before returning to Algiers and heading south across the mountains and into the desert.

On February 2, they were in Biskra, the City of Palms, where Sharp wrote to an unidentified friend a lengthy letter Elizabeth reproduced in the *Memoir* (208–212). The letter's familiar tone and level of detail suggests the friend was Edith Rinder. "Here we are in the Sahara at last! I find it quite hopeless to attempt to give you any adequate idea of the beauty and strangeness and the extraordinary fascination of it all." He proceeded, nonetheless, to a vivid description of their arrival the previous night. The sun was setting, and the hills became a deep purple:

> For the rest, all was orange-gold, yellow-gold, green-gold, with, high over the desert, a vast effulgence of a marvelous roseate flush. Then came

> the moment of scarlet and rose, saffron, and deepening gold, and purple. In the distance, underneath the dropping sparkle of the Evening Star, we could discern the first palms of the oasis of Biskra. There was nothing more to experience till arrival, we thought: but just then we saw the full moon rise out of the Eastern gloom. And what a moon it was! Never did I see such a splendour of living gold. It seemed incredibly large, and whatever it illumined became strange and beautiful beyond words.

Given the precision and beauty of this description, it is not surprising Sharp turned eventually to travel writing or that editors — British and American — welcomed his articles.

From Biskra the Sharps pressed further into the desert to the oasis of Sidi-Okba ("with its 5,000 swarming Arab population") where they spent a few days before traveling north to Constantine. There on February 12, he wrote again to "a friend" to say he had plunged into the "Barbaric East." Like so many nineteenth-century travelers from northern Europe, Sharp was fascinated by the availability of drugs and sex on the streets of North African cities. On the night of February 11, he wandered through the narrow, crowded streets of Constantine observing

> the strange haunts of the dancing girls: the terrible street of the caged women — like wild beasts exposed for sale: and the crowded dens of the hashish-eaters, with the smoke and din of barbaric lutes, tam-tams, and nameless instruments, and the strange wild haunting chanting of the ecstatics and fanatics.
>
> I went at last where I saw not a single European: and though at some risk, I met with no active unpleasantness, save in one Haschisch place where, by a sudden impulse, some forty or fifty Moors suddenly swung round, as the shriek of an Arab fanatic, and with outstretched hands and arms cursed the Gaiour-kelb (dog of an infidel!): and here I had to act quickly and resolutely.
>
> Thereafter one of my reckless fits came on, and I plunged right into the midst of the whole extraordinary vision — for a kind of visionary Inferno it seemed. From Haschisch-den to Haschisch-den I wandered, from strange vaulted rooms of the gorgeously jeweled and splendidly dressed prostitutes to the alcoves where lay or sat or moved to and fro, behind iron bars, the caged beauties whom none could reach save by gold, and even then at risk; from there to the dark low rooms or open pillared places where semi-nude dancing girls moved to and fro to a wild barbaric music... .

> I wandered to and fro in that bewildering Moorish maze, till at last, I could stand no more impressions. So I found my way to the western ramparts, and looked out upon the marvelous nocturnal landscape of mountain and valley — and thought of all that Constantine had been (*Memoir*, 213).

Seeking an authentic taste of Arab culture, a late-nineteenth-century Scot wandered into the exotic night life of a North African city and, so the passage implies, sampled the hashish. It may have been his first use of the drug, which, despite his wife's disapproval, he used later to obtain rituals for W. B. Yeats' Celtic Mystical Order.

Fig. 24 The Great Bridge in Constantine Algeria 1899.jpg Silverbanks Pictures Image Archive, Photographer unknown. Wikimedia Commons, https://www.flickr.com/photos/159714170@N02/48311372867/

From Constantine, the Sharps went north and east to Tunis where William visited the ruins of ancient Carthage, the "London of 2000 years ago," and described it in a third letter to a friend:

> The sea breaks at my feet, blue as a turquoise here, but, beyond, a sheet of marvelous pale green, exquisite beyond words. To the right are the inland waters where the Carthaginian galleys found haven: above, to the right, was the temple of Baal: right above, the temple of Tanit, the famous Astarte, otherwise "The Abomination of the Sidonians." Where the Carthaginians lived in magnificent luxury, a little out the city itself, is now the Arab town of Sidi-ban-Said — like a huge magnolia-bloom

on the sun swept hill-side. There is nothing of the life of to-day visible, save a white-robed Bedouin herding goats and camels, and, on the sea, a few felucca-rigged fisher boats making for distant Tunis by the Strait of Goleta. But there is life and movement in the play of the wind among the grasses and lentisks, in the hum of insects, in the whisper of the warm earth, in the glow of the burning sunshine that floods downward from a sky of glorious blue. Carthage — I can hardly believe it (*Memoir*, 214).

After a few days in and around Tunis, the Sharps crossed to Sicily and made their first of many visits to Taormina, the town set high above the Bay of Naxos on the island's eastern shore.

Fig. 25 Ruins of the Baths of Antonius Pius, Carthage, Algeria. Photograph by BishkekRocks (2004), Wikimedia, https://commons.wikimedia.org/wiki/File:Karthago_Antoninus-Pius-Thermen.JPG, Public Domain.

A recently discovered undated and unpublished manuscript poem in Sharp's handwriting (blue ink on a folded piece of onion skin paper) must have written during or soon after the North African trip. It is another result of his "plunge into the Barbaric East."

The Sheik
(A Portrait from Life)

With heavy Turban o'er his brows
And white robe folded close to him,

Ismail, the Sheik, with aspect grim
Looks towards the desert's burning rim.

Before his tent the camels drowse
In the fierce heat: within. A shade
Is cast by curtains, rich with braid
Of gold, with jewels inlaid.

All round the sloping canvas walls
Bright cloths are placed; gay Syrian hues
Of crimson, green, and purple-blues
With which stray sunbeams interfuse.

Adown their midst a striped skin falls,
Against whose fur sharp weapons lean
Ablaze with steely light, and keen
As any deadly Damascene.

Beside the Sheik a table stands
With fragrant coffee, spices rare,
Dates that have known the desert-air
The wild fig and the prickly pear.

Beyond him stretch the burning sands:
Behind him pale Iskandra lies,
Nude, and with drowsy half-closed eyes
Still dreaming of Circassian skies.

A lithe brown boy close to his feet
Upon a reed a soft low tune
Doth make, and sings an Arab rune
Of love beneath the Desert-moon.

Still grows the blazing, burning heat:
Yet ever toward the sand-wastes rim
Looks forth, with gaze no glare makes dim,
Ismail, the Sheik, with aspect grim.

El Ah'br'a.   William Sharp
Morocco

The Sheik's name, Ismail, is a variant of Ishmael, Abraham's and Hagar's son in the *Book of Genesis*. Shah Ismail I (1487–1524) ruled a vast Persian Empire from 1501 until his death. Iskandra, the nude boy in the background dreaming of his Circassian home, is a variant of Alexander and calls to mind Alexander the Great (356–323 BC), the Macedonian who ruled another vast empire, and his supposed homosexual relationship with his companion Hephaestion. Sheik Ismail is pleased to have the "lithe brown boy close to his feet" singing "an Arab rune of love beneath the Desert-moon." The poem asks if the Sheik captured or lured for his pleasure the drowsy nude Iskandra lying half asleep dreaming of his homeland on the eastern bank of the Black Sea, another allusion to Alexander the Great and to the more recent subjugation of Circassia and its absorption into the Ottoman Empire. The poem's sensual and suggestive overtones account for it not being published. That Sharp wrote and carefully copied it signals his associating Arabic North Africa with "pagan" sexual practices and demonstrates his interest in sexual fluidity.

The Sharps returned to England at the end of February. On March 23 he told Charles Webster, in a letter proposing the publication of *Vistas*, he was just back from North Africa and had not returned to his house in the country. By March 29, both Sharps were in Phenice Croft wondering why Stanley Little was staying in Kensington. "It is glorious weather, & the Rudgwickian country, Bucks Green, and Phenice Croft are all looking their best." According to Elizabeth, it was "the finest English Spring in a quarter century." She listed some of the guests who visited them: Richard Whiteing, Mona Caird, Alice Corkran, George Cotterell, Richard and Edith Le Gallienne, Roden Noel, Percy White, Dr. Byres Moir, Frank and Edith Rinder, Laurence Binyon, Agnes Farquharson Sharp (Elizabeth's mother), Robert Farquharson Sharp (Elizabeth's brother), and Mary Sharp (William's sister), whose handwriting would soon become that of Fiona Macleod.

At Phenice Croft, Sharp began working on a series of articles about North Africa: "French African Health Resorts" appeared in the December 1893 *Nineteenth Century*; "The New Winterland of French Africa" in the January 1894 *Nineteenth Century*; "Tclemcen and Its Vicinage" in the February 1894 *Art Journal*; "Cardinal Lavigerie's Work in North Africa" in the August 1894 *Atlantic Monthly*; and "Rome in Africa" in the *Harper's Monthly* of June 1895. His travel writing had begun in earnest. He also began a new life of Rossetti which William Swan Sonnenschein commissioned for his publishing firm. According to Elizabeth, Sharp had become dissatisfied with his 1882 Rossetti book; he "considered his judgment to have been immature." He wrote only a few sentences of the new biography and a "Dedicatory Chapter" to Walter Pater. The paragraphs Elizabeth reproduced in the *Memoir* (69–72) are all that survive of that dedication. They praise Rossetti and Pater and Pater's essay on Rossetti. "Of all that has been written of Rossetti's genius and achievement in poetry nothing shows more essential insight, is of more striking and enduring worth, than the essay by yourself included in your stimulating and always delightful *Appreciations*."

In an April 19 letter to his friend Henry Mills Alden, editor of *Harper's Magazine*, Sharp said he was busy "more maturely, more serenely, more hopefully, if with more mental & spiritual stress than heretofore. I shall write sometime & tell you more." What, we may wonder, caused his mental and spiritual stress? Elizabeth said her husband "was happy once more to be resident in the country, although the surroundings were not a type of scenery that appealed to him." She then touched on the stress:

> At Phenice Croft his imagination was in a perpetual ferment.... Once again he saw visions and dreamed dreams; the psychic subjective side of his dual nature predominated. He was in an acutely creative condition; and, moreover, he was passing from one phase of literary work to another, deeper, more intimate, more permanent. (*Memoir*, 221–222).

His stress was due in part to what Elizabeth called his "psychic experiments," his efforts, some aided by drugs, to invoke visions.

Elizabeth went to Paris in early May to review the salons for the *Glasgow Herald*. On the seventh Sharp wrote a card to Stanley Little while waiting in Horsham station for the train that would take him to the coast to board a ferry to the Isle of Wight. He had expected Little to drop in the previous night. He had stayed up waiting until two in the morning and finally went to the house where Little was staying, found it dark, and returned to Phenice Croft. He could forgive Little only because he was leaving to spend a week leading a "virtuous life" on the Isle of Wight. On the tenth, he responded from "somewhere or other near Freshwater" to Little's letter of apology. He understood, of course, that Little was preoccupied with his guests, one of whom must have been a young woman. Sharp would not have gone looking for Little at two in the morning if a "young charmer" had been sitting up with him discussing "debatable subjects." He expanded, "It is glorious here. By

Jove, Life is well worth living!" He and Little will "have a chat over sins and sinners" when he returns to Rudgwick. With Elizabeth in France, Sharp may have arranged a week on the Isle of Wight with Edith Rinder.

In late June Sharp told Louise Chandler Moulton, who visited London annually, he was working hard, "making the wherewithal for 'daily bread' but not omitting dreaming and the weaving of dreams." He was also enjoying life in rural Sussex during an "unparalleled Spring & Summer! Here, in Sussex, we have had no rain (save 3 brief showers, 2 nocturnal) for 3 ½ months, & an almost unbroken succession of blue skies." He wrote again to Moulton in mid-July to apologize for not arranging to see her before she returned to America.

> Alas, I have been so overwhelmed with work requiring the closest continuous attention that I have postponed and postponed and postponed. Besides this, I have purposely withdrawn from everything this year — having realized that my paramount need at present is isolation — or as much as can be had even at this distance from town. Each finds at last what he needs in order to do his best work. I do not know if I have found it yet: I doubt if I shall ever find it in England: but I am nearer to what I want than I have yet been.

He hoped to be able to call on her before the end of the month, when he and Elizabeth were going to Scotland for two months.

In a letter written the previous October, Sharp asked Robert Murray Gilchrist to visit him in Bucks Green when he came to London from his home in Derbyshire. Gilchrist did not accept Sharp's invitation until the Spring of 1894, but he invited Sharp to visit him in Derbyshire on his way to and from Edinburgh. He also mentioned Frank Murray, a bookseller in Derby, who had agreed to publish his novel, *Frangipani*, as the first in a projected Regent's Library series. He suggested Murray might consider a book by Sharp for the series whereupon Sharp, in early summer, asked Murray if he would like to publish a romance he had in mind. Murray responded favorably but said he could offer only ten pounds. In a July letter, Sharp said the terms for the projected romance were insufficient, but he would accept ten pounds for another book he had on hand. It was his "most individual imaginative work — a series of psychological problems or reveries wrought in a new form, nominally dramatic, [...] a series of seven studies collectively entitled 'Vistas'." Having offered that volume unsuccessfully to Elkin Mathews in London and Charles Webster in America, he was anxious for someone to accept it.

Chapter Ten: 1893

At the end of July, the Sharps went to Scotland where they spent three weeks in St. Andrews, stayed for a time with Marian Glassford Bell at Tirinie, near Aberfeldy in Perthshire, and then went to Corrie on the Island of Arran for a fortnight. In mid-September, Elizabeth left to visit friends, and William went to Arrochar and other places in the West. An early-August letter to Little from St. Andrews described his writing: "my 'Rossetti,' my new one-vol. novel, my vol. of short stories, & my French studies, fully occupy my mind here — when I am not swimming or walking, eating or sleeping or 'dreaming'." He described the new "one-vol. Novel" as the most "consequential" work he had in progress. It had no title, but it eventually became Fiona Macleod's *Pharais*. He planned to call the "vol. of short stories" *Comedy of Woman*. It became the volume of short stories published in 1895 by Stone and Kimball in Chicago as *The Gipsy Christ and Other Tales* and in 1896 by Archibald Constable in London as *Madge o' the Pool: The Gipsy Christ and Other Tales*.

On August 18, 1893 he asked Gilchrist if it would be convenient to spend a night with him in Derbyshire on his way back to London, on September 24. He looked forward to meeting Gilchrist, and he wanted to visit Frank Murray, the Derby bookseller, to discuss arrangements for the publication of *Vistas*. On September 30, after two months in Scotland, the Sharps left Edinburgh; Elizabeth went straight to London, and Sharp — by a complicated series of branch trains — to Eyam, Gilchrist's village in Derbyshire. After spending two nights with Gilchrist, he stopped in Derby to meet Frank Murray on his way to London. By October 7 he was back in Phenice Croft where he thanked Gilchrist for the lovely day they had on Sunday (October 1) walking on the moors. He was sending Gilchrist a copy of the etched portrait Charles Holroyd made of him in Rome and, for George Garfitt, Gilchrist's partner, a copy of the *Pagan Review*. The first meeting between Sharp and Gilchrist went well, and Sharp told Gilchrist he found Frank Murray "a decent sort of chap." Betraying his class consciousness, he added, Murray "dropped his h's" occasionally, and in certain small matters was oblivious of what some of us consider to be good breeding." Nonetheless, he thought Murray had "a genuine love of literature."

In an August 12 letter to Catherine Janvier, he described "a scene in a strange Celtic tale I am writing called Pharais, wherein the weird charm and terror of a night of tragic significance is brought home to the reader... by a stretch of dew-wet moonflowers glimmering through the murk of a dusk laden with sea mists." He continued: "I was writing in pencil in Pharais of death by the sea — and almost at my feet a drowned corpse was washed in by the tide and the slackening urgency of the previous night's gale." This is Sharp's first mention of "Pharais" as the title of the novel that would become the first publication by Fiona Macleod. It was the "romance" he had in mind when he told Frank Murray in mid-July that the terms he offered were unacceptable. He wrote sometime in November to Richard Stoddart proposing for serial publication in *Lippincott's Magazine* a romance he called Nostalgia, which never materialized, and "another story, Pharais," which he described as "written deeply in the Celtic spirit and from the Celtic standpoint" (*Memoir*, 225). Neither proposal was accepted. A December diary entry indicates he had done "the first part of a Celtic romance called Pharais;" it was one of the things he needed to finish (*Memoir*, 216). In his December 20 Christmas greetings to Murray Gilchrist, he wrote: "Today I write 'finis' to my Celtic Romance — long dreamed of — I wish I could read some of it to you. It is out of my inmost heart and brain." That Celtic Romance was *Pharais: A Romance of the Isles*.

Where, we may wonder, did Sharp find that name and what did he mean it to convey. He said pharais is a "slightly anglicized lection of the Gaelic word Pàras = Paradise, Heaven. 'Pharais' properly is the genitive and dative case of Pàras, as in the line from Muireadhach Albannach which Sharp produced on the page following the title page, 'Mithich domh triall gu tigh Pharais' — 'It is time for me to go up unto the House of Paradise.'" Muireadhach Albannach, spelled variously, was a Gaelic poet later known as Murdoch of Scotland. A portion of the poem from which Sharp quoted a line is found in the *Dean of Lismore's Book*.

When he visited Murray's Derby bookshop in September and saw the high quality of the paper, boards, and designs he was using for his Regent's Library Series, Sharp decided Murray should publish *Pharais* as well as *Vistas* despite his inability to pay more than ten pounds for each. In describing *Pharais* as a work in progress to Catherine Janvier in August and offering it as a story to Richard Stoddart in November, they naturally assumed it was the work of William Sharp. His December 20 Christmas greeting to Murray Gilchrist claimed the Celtic Romance as his own. The first recorded indication of his intention to publish it pseudonymously occurs in a late December letter to Frank Murray. Sometime before that date Sharp told Murray he wanted the book issued not only pseudonymously, not only by a woman, but specifically by Fiona Macleod.

> You will be interested to hear that last week I wrote "finis" to Pharais: and have not only finished it but think it the strongest & most individual thing I have done. For several reasons, however, I wish to adhere rigidly to the 'Fiona Macleod' authorship. I think the book will attract a good deal of notice, on account of the remarkable Celtic renaissance which has set in & will inevitably gather weight: it touches, too, new ground — and, I think, in a new way. What is perhaps best of all is that it is written literally out of my heart — and indeed, though the central incident has nothing to do with me, most else is reminiscent.
>
> It is, in fact, your agreement to accept my two most paramount conditions — pseudonymity and publication by the end of March — that weighed with me against a letter from the Editor of one of the leading magazines in America, offering me high terms for a romance written not 'to order' but really con amore. However, for reasons into which I need not enter at present, I prefer to lose at the moment so as to gain in every way later.

Sharp enclosed with this letter the "opening section" of *Pharais*; his copyist had the rest and was more than halfway through the book. There is no evidence of an offer from an American publisher.

Sharp sent as a frontispiece for *Vistas* a rare etching by William Bell Scott of a William Blake design for Milton's *Paradise Lost* that portrays Adam and Eve before the fall. Sharp thought the depiction of Adam and Eve in each other's arms with a serpent hovering above would foreshadow the danger lurking above sexual pleasure depicted in the book's "vistas." If Murray objected to the nudity, he might ask the artist who produced the design for Gilchrist's *Frangipani*, the first book in Murray's Regent's Library, to "do something satisfactory." If neither alternative was acceptable, Sharp's friend Theodore Roussel might do something. Murray did not object and used the Bell Scott etching for the special edition of seventy-five numbered and signed copies. For the frontispiece of the special edition of *Pharais*, Sharp could ask his friend William Strang to do an etching. Murray decided to use a photograph of a cold northern sea with its waves breaching the shore, a scene that reflected the book's atmosphere and content. In addition to the special editions on larger and on fine paper with white board covers and white jackets, Murray printed using the same type setting smaller trade editions of *Vistas* and *Pharais* with nicely designed green covers and without frontispieces.

Sharp's decision to publish *Pharais* pseudonymously is not surprising. Experimenting with pseudonyms during the previous two years, he came to like the mystery of disguise. More important, he believed creative work published under his name would generate skepticism or outright disdain due to his reputation as an editor and the enemies he made as a reviewer. His decision to publish under a woman's name was unusual, but predictable. His 1881 poem "Motherhood" describing a tigress, a primitive woman, and a contemporary woman giving birth was an early sign of his empathy with women. In writing the wife's letters in the 1892 epistolary novel, *A Fellowe and His Wife*, he had no trouble adopting the persona of a woman. "During the writing of *Pharais*," Elizabeth wrote, "the author began to realize how much the feminine element dominated in the book, that it grew out of the subjective, or feminine side of his nature. He, therefore, decided to issue the book under the name of *Fiona Macleod*" (*Memoir*, 226–227). The name she continued, "flashed ready-made" into his mind. Sharp said "Macleod" was born naturally from his friendship with Seamus Macleod, an older man from whom he learned Celtic lore as a young boy during summer holidays in the Hebrides. Fiona, on the other hand, was "very rare now. Most Highlanders would tell you it was extinct — even as a diminutive of Fionaghal (Flora). But it is not. It is an old Celtic name (meaning 'a fair maid') still occasionally to be found."

More than a recognition of his feminine qualities descended on Sharp at Phenice Croft in the summer of 1893. Elizabeth wrote: "So far, he had found no adequate method for the expression of his 'second self' though the way was led thereto by *Sospiri di Roma* and *Vistas*" (*Memoir*, 221–222). In 1877, when he was twenty-one, Sharp confided in a letter to Elizabeth: "I feel another self within me now more than ever; it is as if I were possessed by a spirit who must speak out" (*Memoir*, 25). At Phenice Croft, he began to entertain seriously the possibility not only that he had both masculine and feminine qualities, but that he was two people in one, both a man and a woman. The emergence of her husband's 'second self' began, Elizabeth said, in Rome in the winter/spring of 1890–1891.

There, at last, he had found the desired incentive towards a true expression of himself, in the stimulus and sympathetic understanding of the friend to whom he dedicated the first of the books published under his pseudonym. This friendship began in Rome and lasted for the remainder of his life.

This friend was E. W. R. — Edith Wingate Rinder — to whom he dedicated *Pharais*. In that dedication he was writing as a woman to another woman, and the disguise released him to speak with sincerity about their relationship, which was one of deep affection and commonality.

In the first sentences of the dedication, we hear the voice Sharp adopted for Fiona. "In the *Domham-Toir* there are resting places where all barriers of race, training, and circumstance fall away in the dust. At one of those places of peace we met, a long while ago, and found that we loved the same things, and in the same way." Most love the West of Scotland only "in the magic of sunshine and cloud," but Fiona (Sharp) and Edith love the land "when the rain and the black wind make a gloom upon every loch and fill with the dusk of storm every strath, and glen, and corrie. Not otherwise can one love it aright." Like Fiona, Edith worships at the fane of Keithoir, the Celtic god of the earth: "It is because you and I are of the children of Keithoir that I wished to grace my book with your name." We believe "the Celtic Dream" is not doomed to become "a memory merely." A few writers, Fiona among them, will revive Anima Celtica. They will lead readers to Pharais, "that Land of Promise whose borders shine with the loveliness of all forfeited, or lost, or banished dreams and realities of Beauty." Again Sharp conflated the word Pharais with Paradise. He associated Fiona's objectives with those of William Butler Yeats and the Irish Renaissance: "The sweetest-voiced of the younger Irish singers of to-day [Yeats] has spoken of the Celtic Twilight. A twilight it is; but, if night follow gloaming, so also does dawn succeed night. Meanwhile, twilight voices are sweet, if faint and far, and linger lovingly in the ear." The final paragraph returns to Edith by asserting a Paradise of Friendship wherein "we both have seen beautiful visions and dreamed dreams. Take, then, out of my heart, this book of vision and dream." By having Fiona identify with her dedicate, Edith Wingate Rinder, Sharp found a voice for his "second self" and a means of expressing his love for the beautiful and accomplished E. W. R.

In a letter of instructions to Elizabeth in the event of his death, written before a trip to the United States in 1896, Sharp said he owed his development as Fiona to Edith Rinder; "without her there would have been no 'Fiona Macleod.'" After reproducing this statement in the *Memoir* (222) and without identifying Edith, Elizabeth commented with remarkable candor and generosity:

> Because of her beauty, her strong sense of life and the joy of life; because of her keen intuitions and mental alertness, her personality stood for him as a symbol of the heroic women of Greek and Celtic days, a symbol that, as he expressed it, unlocked new doors in his mind and put him 'in touch with ancestral memories' of his race. So, for a time, he stilled the critical, intellectual mood of William Sharp to give play to the development of this new found expression of subtler emotions, towards which he had been moving with all the ardor of his nature.

Her husband's two natures were frequently at odds. They required different conditions, different environments, and different stimuli. That requirement "produced a tremendous strain on his physical and mental resources; and at one time between 1897–1898 threatened him with a complete nervous collapse." Gradually the two sides of his nature developed into two distinct personalities "which were equally imperative in their demands on him." He preferred the dreaming creative feminine existence, facilitated by the presence of Edith, in which he could produce the writings of Fiona Macleod. "The exigencies of life, his dependence on his pen for his livelihood… required of him a great amount of applied study and work." He came to associate Elizabeth — his first cousin, ever-supportive wife, and breadwinning critic and editor — with the mundane, practical side of his nature and Edith with the imaginative, creative, visionary, indeed romantic side.

Phenice Croft was linked by Sharp and his wife with the birth of Fiona Macleod and thus with Edith Rinder. Sharp "always looked back with deep thankfulness" to the two years at Phenice Croft. Initially, Elizabeth shared her husband's enthusiasm. "The summer of 1893," she wrote, "was hot and sunny; and we delighted in our little garden with its miniature lawns, its espalier fruit trees framing the vegetable garden, and its juvenile but to me fascinating flowers beds." Things began to change in the fall. She became ill again with the lingering effects of malaria. She attributed her continuing health problems to the moist air and clay soil of Rudgwick, and she began spending more time with her mother in London. During those periods of absence, Edith Rinder was often a guest at Phenice Croft, and her presence may have been a factor in Elizabeth's change of heart. Her comments about Phenice Croft and Rudgwick in the *Memoir* were as close as she came to suggesting her relationship with her husband was strained.

There was another reason for her feelings about Phenice Croft. There, she said, Sharp was "testing his new powers, living his new life, and delighting in the opportunity for psychic experimentation". For such experimentation, Elizabeth wrote, "the place seemed to him to be peculiarly suited." To her, it seemed "uncanny" and "to have a haunted atmosphere — created unquestionably by my husband that I found difficult to live in unless the sun was shining" (*Memoir*, 223). Edith may have been cooperating in the experiments, which were widespread at the time. Indeed, Elizabeth went to mediums after her husband died in 1905 and left a record of her communications with his spirit. In 1893, however, she recognized the disturbing impact of the "psychic experiments" on her husband's mental balance. As we shall see, a crisis befell Sharp in the summer of 1894 which, coupled with Elizabeth's ill health and growing distaste for the place, caused them to leave Phenice Croft and resettle in London.

Chapter Eleven

1894

In the fall of 1893 Elizabeth Sharp became increasingly uncomfortable at Phenice Croft:

> The damp, autumnal days in the little cottage on its clay soil, and the fatigue of constantly going up and down to town in order to do the work of the Art Critic for the *Glasgow Herald* — which I for some time had undertaken — proved too severe a strain on me. And I found that in the winter months I could not remain at Phenice Croft without being seriously ill (*Memoir*, 233).

The Sharps rented a flat in January 1894 — number seven in Kensington Court Gardens, then a new mansion block south of the Kensington High Street — where Elizabeth would live through the winter while her husband traveled back and forth from Phenice Croft. At the end of the month, the Sharps tried to revive the "Sunday evening informal gatherings" they held in the late eighties in South Hampstead. For the first, on February 4, Sharp invited Grant Richards for dinner. Edith and Frank Rinder would be there, and others — including the publisher John Lane would drop by later for a cup of coffee and to smoke a cigarette. Back in Phenice Croft on the ninth and hoping for a positive review, he sent Richard Le Gallienne an advance copy of *Vistas*, which Frank Murray would publish on the fifteenth. On Saturday, the tenth he was back in London writing to Stanley Little. Elizabeth was "better on the whole." He would be back in Phenice Croft the next day and in London again at the Grosvenor Club the following Saturday. He hoped Little would meet him there. Before the month was out, traveling to and from London in the mid-winter gloom affected his health.

In an early December letter, Sharp told Murray Gilchrist he could not visit him in Derbyshire in January, but he hoped Gilchrist would visit him in Bucks Green. In his Christmas greeting to Gilchrist, he wrote, "You are to come here in the early Spring, remember!" Correspondence and the pattern of events indicate Gilchrist accepted Sharp's invitation in mid-February. In a letter dated only "Wendy," either February 14 or 21, he told Gilchrist he would be happy to welcome him and his partner Garfitt at Phenice Croft the following Friday. This visit deserves attention for what it reveals about the atmosphere Sharp created in Bucks Green and the state of his mental and physical health.

More than a year later, on September 26, 1895, Sharp drew Gilchrist's attention to a section of Fiona Macleod's *The Sin Eater* called "Tragic Landscapes." That section contains three "prose poems" which Sharp described in his *Pagan Review* as impressionist word paintings, "a consciously-conceived and definitely-executed poetic form." In Sharp's letter to Gilchrist, who knew Fiona was Sharp, he described the first of the three, called "The Tempest," as a detailed word painting of a natural setting in which an approaching storm threatens to sweep away the natural world and all living inhabitants. The second "Tragic Landscape," called simply "Mist," portrays the post-apocalyptic natural world:

> A dense white mist lay upon the hills, clothing them from summit to base in a dripping shroud. The damp, spongy peat everywhere sweated forth its over-welling ooze. [...] There was neither day nor night, but only the lifeless gloom of the endless weary rain: thin soaking, full of the chill and silence of the grave.

Eventually, a shadow appears in the gloom, a slow-moving man who "stood beside a tarn. And was looking into it, as the damned in hell look into their souls." A stag appears on an overhanging rock and vanquishes his rival whereupon: "Night crept up from the glen and strath — the veil of mist grew more and more obscure, more dark. [...] there was a uniform pall of blackness. In the chill, soaking silence not a thing stirred, not a sound was audible."

The third "Tragic Landscape," called "Summer-sleep" portrays a hot, dry vista that is peaceful and drowsy with some signs of life:

> The high-road sinuated like a snake along the steeper slope of the valley. [...] The gloom of July was on the trees. The oaks dreamed of green water. The limes were already displaying fugitive yellow banners. A red flush dusked the green-gloom of the sycamores. [...] The sky was of a vivid blue, up whose invisible azure ledges a few rounded clouds,

dazzling white or grey as swans-down, climbed imperceptibly. […] The wild-bee and the wasp, the dragonfly and the gnat, wrought everywhere a humming undertone.

The landscape is descending into a dreamy sleep:

Peace was upon the land and beauty. The languor of dream gave the late summer a loveliness that was all its own, as of a fair woman asleep, dreaming of the lover who has not long left her, and the touch of whose lips is still upon her mouth and hair.

Through this personified natural world, which differs markedly from that of "The Tempest" and "Mist," three men are walking. Two were "tall and fair; one dark, loosely built, and of a smaller and slighter build."

In his September 1895 letter to Gilchrist, Sharp wrote: "You will read the third piece, 'Summer-sleep,' with mingled feelings, when you know it is an exact transcript of Phenice Croft at Rudgwick and that the three men are you, Garfitt, and myself." The two tall, fair men are Sharp and Gilchrist, and the shorter Garfitt. They approach "a small hamlet of thatched, white-walled cottages" which is Bucks Green. Sharp, the tallest wayfarer, points "to a small square house set among orchard-trees, a stone's throw from the hamlet," which is Phenice Croft, and says: "There is my home." His "comrade," Gilchrist, replies slowly, "It is a beautiful place, and I envy you." Garfitt agrees, and the owner replies "I am glad you think so." At that, the shadows of the three men "leapt to one side, moved with fantastic steps, and seemed convulsed with laughter." Perhaps the grass on the side of the road understood the speech of the shadows. If so, it would know Gilchrist said in his heart: "There is something of awe, of terror, about that house; nay, the whole land here is under a tragic gloom. I should die here, stifled. I am glad I go on the morrow." Then Garfitt said in his heart "It may all be beautiful and peaceful, but something tragic hides behind this flooding sunlight, behind these dark woodlands, down by the water-course there, past the water-mill, up by that house among the orchard-trees." If the grass understood the shadows, "It would know that the tallest man [Sharp] who lived in that square cottage by the pleasant hamlet, said in his heart: 'It may be that the gate of hell is hidden there among the grass, or beneath the foundations of my house. Would God I were free! O my God, madness and death!'" The three men know the placid landscape overlays a natural world that is "red in tooth and claw." They also know what only their shadows express: the placidity of human life overlays a chaotic darkness of tragic impulses and fear of obliteration.

Following that shadowy experience of fear and horror, the final paragraph restores the peacefulness of the land and of everyday life:

> After another long silence, as the three wayfarers drew near, the dark man murmured his pleasure at the comely hamlet, at the quiet land lying warm in the afternoon glow. And his companion said that rest and coolness would be welcome, and doubly so in so fair and peaceful a home. And the tallest of the three, he who owned the house in the orchard, laughed blithely. And all three moved onward with quickened steps, through the hot, sweet, dusty afternoon, golden now with the waning sun-glow.

After drawing Gilchrist's attention to the third "Tragic Landscape," Sharp wrote, "I cannot explain aright: you must read into what you read." We recall Elizabeth Sharp wrote of their residence in Bucks Green:

> The quiet and leisure at Phenice Croft, the peace, the "green life" around were unspeakably welcome to my husband. Once again, he saw visions and dreamed dreams; the psychic subjective side of his dual nature predominated. He was in an acutely creative condition; and, moreover, he was passing from one phase of literary work to another, deeper, more intimate, more permanent. (*Memoir*, 221)

The transition was from the work of William Sharp to that of Fiona Macleod, which Elizabeth, reflecting no doubt the opinion of her husband, thought "deeper, more intimate, more permanent." At Phenice Croft, she continued,

> he was testing his new powers, living his new life, and delighting in the opportunity for psychic experimentation And for such experimentation, the place seemed to him to be peculiarly suited. To me it seemed "uncanny," and to have a haunted atmosphere — created unquestionably by him — that I found difficult to live in unless the sun was shining. This uncanny effect was felt by more than one friend; by Mr. Murray Gilchrist, for instance, whose impressions were described by his host in one of the short "Tragic Landscapes" (*Memoir*, 223).

In his September 1895 letter to Gilchrist, Sharp wrote ominously, "The most tragic & momentous epoch of my life followed that visit of yours to Phenice Croft, & is, so far, indissolubly linked with that day I met you, and that time." What, we must wonder, happened following the Gilchrist visit that so affected Sharp? His letters, beginning in late February 1894, suggest the probable answer.

On February 26, Sharp sent Edward Dowden a copy of *Vistas* and asked him to "excuse so brief a note as I have been ill & am still debarred from much use of the pen." On March 1, in a letter thanking Stanley Little for his positive notices of *Vistas*, Sharp wrote: "I should have written to you before this, but I have not been well: & yesterday had to telegraph to a friend. I am now, however, pulling round all right. Please say nothing of this to Elizabeth. Tomorrow [Friday, March 2] I shall go up to town, & come down with her on Saty, till Monday [March 3–5]. On that weekend [March 9–11] some friends are coming for a fortnight, of which I am glad." On March 5 he wrote again to Little:

> Did I tell you how unwell I have been? I have had to "cave in" completely. I am now nearly better — but for some time to come must write only for 2 or 3 hours daily at most: and, moreover, am not to be alone at all. Elizabeth (who is steadily gaining ground) returns to town in a couple of days: & then Mr. and Mrs. Rinder come here on "a working visit" to keep me company for a fortnight. [...] I must not write more.

Elizabeth, herself unwell, but improving, was with him until at least Wednesday, March 7, and the friends, Edith and Frank Rinder, came on that weekend to stay for two weeks.

The psychic experimentations that gave Phenice Croft an "uncanny" and "haunted atmosphere" led Sharp to the "gate of hell... hidden there among the grass, or beneath the foundations" of his house and to exclaiming "Would God I were free! O my God, madness and death!" Shortly after Gilchrist and Garfitt visited Phenice Croft, Sharp suffered a nervous collapse that produced a state of depression so serious that his wife and Edith Rinder decided he should not be left alone. He was advised to stop his psychic experimentations, drastically reduce his imaginative work, and not write at all more than two or three hours a day. It must have been this collapse Sharp described in his September 1895 letter to Gilchrist as "the most tragic & momentous epoch" of his life. It recalls a letter he wrote to Hall Caine ten years earlier — on June 15, 1884 — in which he described a "sharp and sudden attack" that left his hands so chilled and pained he could hardly hold a pen. The mental collapse at Phenice Croft may well have been accompanied by a physical collapse that endangered his weakened heart. He concluded his March 5 letter to Little as follows: "This is an unusual break-down for me. But, for one thing, I have been living the life of Imagination too fiercely of late. I think you will be surprised when you learn what I have done." These sentences connect his breakdown with his writing as Fiona Macleod and suggest that work, yet unknown to Little, was initiating a splitting of self — masculine versus feminine — that contributed to his collapse.

In a March 27 letter to Gilchrist, Sharp apologized for being too unwell to write sooner and announced he was leaving Bucks Green:

> My wife's health… has long been troubling me: and we have just decided that (greatly to my disappointment) we must return to Hampstead to live. Personally, I regret the return to town (or half town) more than I can say: but the matter is one of paramount importance, so there is nothing else to be done. We leave at midsummer.

Elizabeth's illness in the fall and continuing into the winter, her dislike of the atmosphere Sharp had created in Bucks Green, and her work as London art reviewer for the *Glasgow Herald* had forced her to let the Kensington flat. Her husband's mental and physical breakdown was the last straw. He could not be left alone. Fortunately, they found someone to sublet the house, which they vacated on June 21. Sharp described his actions of the previous night:

> I took up a handful of grassy turf and kissed it three times, and then threw it to the four quarters — so that the Beauty of the Earth might be seen by me wherever I went and that no beauty I had seen or known there should be forgotten. Then I kissed the chestnut tree on the side lawn where I have seen or heard so much: from the springing of the dream flowers to the surge of the sea in *Pharais* (*Memoir*, 236).

Elizabeth understood his reluctance to leave: "Phenice Croft had seen the birth of Fiona Macleod; he had lived there with an intensity of inner life beyond anything he had ever experienced" (*Memoir* 233).

After describing their decision to give up rural living in his March 27 letter to Gilchrist, Sharp demonstrated what many of his close friends found remarkable, his ability to recover quickly no matter how debilitating the illness:

> As for me, one of my wander-fits has come upon me: the Spring-madness has got into the blood: the sight of green hedgerows and budding leaves

and the blue smoke rising here and there in the woodlands has wrought some chemic furor in my brain. Before the week is out, I hope to be in Normandy — and after a day or two by the sea at Dieppe, and then at beautiful and romantic Rouen, to get to the green lanes and open places, and tramp "towards the sun." I'll send you a line from somewhere if you care to hear.

He turned to Gilchrist's relative isolation in Derbyshire:

I think you should see more of actual life: and not dwell so continually in an atmosphere charged with your own imaginings. [...] part of the year should be spent otherwise — say in a town like London, or Paris, or in tramping through alien lands, France or Belgium, Scandinavia, or Germany or Italy, or Spain: if not, in Scotland, or Ireland, or upon our Isles, or remote counties. [...] Take your pen and paper, a satchel, and go forth with a light heart. The gods will guide *you* to strange things, and strange things to you. You ought to *see* more, to *feel* more, to *know* more, at first hand. Be not afraid of excess. "The road of excess leads to the palace of wisdom," says Blake.

Gilchrist must have told Sharp he also suffered from depression:

To be alive and young and in health is a boon so inestimable that you ought to fall on your knees among your moorland heather and thank the gods. Dejection is a demon to be ruled. We cannot always resist his tyranny, but we can always refuse to become bondagers to his usurpation. Look upon him as an Afreet to be exorcised with a cross of red-hot iron. He is a coward weakling, after all: take him by the tail and swing him across the moor or down the valley. Swing up into your best. Be brave, strong, self-reliant. Then you live.

In advising Gilchrist, who was ten years younger, to take the demon of dejection "by the tail and swing him across the moor or down the valley," Sharp drew on his own experience.

Sharp did not escape to France before the week was out. On April 3 he wrote a long letter to Herbert Stone, a Harvard undergraduate who, with his friend and classmate Hannibal Ingalls Kimball, had established a publishing firm, Stone and Kimball, which would "accept only manuscripts of literary merit and publish them in an artistic form." In August 1894, the firm relocated from Cambridge to Chicago where Stone's wealthy father, Melville Elijah Stone, edited the *Chicago Daily News*. When Louise Chandler Moulton drew Sharp's attention to the enterprise, he saw an opening. He proposed to Stone a volume of seven short stories titled "The Rape of the Sabines," after one of its stories he had included in the *Pagan Review*. As it turned out, Stone and Kimball published an American edition of *Vistas* late in 1894, and the volume of short stories in 1895 under the less provocative title *The Gypsy Christ and Other Tales*. Stone and Kimball also published the early works of Fiona Macleod, which began to establish her reputation among America's literary elite. At the suggestion of Arthur Stedman, Sharp asked Stone to negotiate for the plates and stock of his *Flower o' the Vine* from Charles Webster and Company as the firm was being liquidated. If Stone took up the suggestion, the negotiations failed since there were no further printings of that volume.

On April 8 Sharp told Arthur Stedman in a letter from Phenice Croft, "I am better, though not right yet." When he went to France is uncertain, but on April 22 he sent a card to Murray Gilchrist from Paris that promised a letter and declared "Here summer is come," and concluded "Some strange things happen in this world! Well — no more just now." Elizabeth joined him in Paris on April 30, and they both returned to London on May 3. Recalling that Elizabeth and Edith Rinder decided Sharp should not be left alone, Edith may have accompanied Sharp to Normandy in mid-April and their time together in Dieppe and Rouen may have been the "strange thing" Sharp would share with Gilchrist when they next met.

The public aspect of the Fiona Macleod phase of Sharp's literary career began in May when Frank Murray published *Pharais, a Romance of the Isles* from his Moray Press in Derby. In a May 4 letter, Sharp told Stanley Little he had asked Murray to send him a pre-publication copy of a Celtic romance written by a friend, a Miss Fiona Macleod. It was a successor to his *Vistas* in Murray's Regent's Library Series, and he was "specially interested not only in its author but in the book," which dealt with "the almost unknown life of the remoter isles of the Atlantic seaboard." Only three copies had been issued, one for him and two for Miss Macleod. He hoped Little would like the book and write a notice or review for the *Academy* or the *Literary World*. Prior to the formal publication of *Pharais*, Sharp had decided to create a separate identity for the female author and present her to the world as a real person.

As described in the previous chapter, Sharp told Catherine Ann Janvier in August 1893 he was writing "a strange Celtic tale" he planned to call *Pharais*, a Celtic word for paradise. So, we know he began writing passages in 1893 or even earlier for what became Fiona Macleod's *Pharais*. Shortly after the release of creativity he experienced in Rome in 1891, he began looking for a means of capitalizing on his knowledge of the Hebridean landscape and Celtic lore. Finally, he was able to tell Murray Gilchrist in a letter of December 20, 1893, his "long dreamed of Celtic Romance" was finished. A week later he told Frank Murray, the Derby publisher, he wished "to adhere rigidly to the 'Fiona Macleod' authorship." That decision meant Sharp's main contribution to the Celtic Renaissance would be attributed to a woman named Macleod.

Sometime between December 1893 and May 1894, Sharp realized he would have to find a means for the fictitious author to communicate with publishers and readers. His sister Mary, who lived with their mother in Edinburgh, was an intelligent woman with time on her hands. He enlisted her to copy his Fiona letters and mail them in Scotland. Mary's distinctive handwriting became an essential feature of the deception. It was frequently cited as proof the writings were not the

Fig. 26 Portrait of Mary Beatrice Sharp, William Sharp's youngest sister taken in the Davis Studios in Edinburgh in 1906. Mary provided the handwriting for Fiona Macleod's extensive correspondence. Courtesy of the Department of Rare Books and Special Collections, Dulles Reading Room, Firestone Library, Princeton University.

product of William Sharp, and it was principally through the letters that he conveyed Fiona's distinctive personality and established the fiction of her separate identity. Discreet, efficient, and available, Mary was a vital link in the two-step transmissions that contributed to the remarkable success of Sharp's covert literary career.

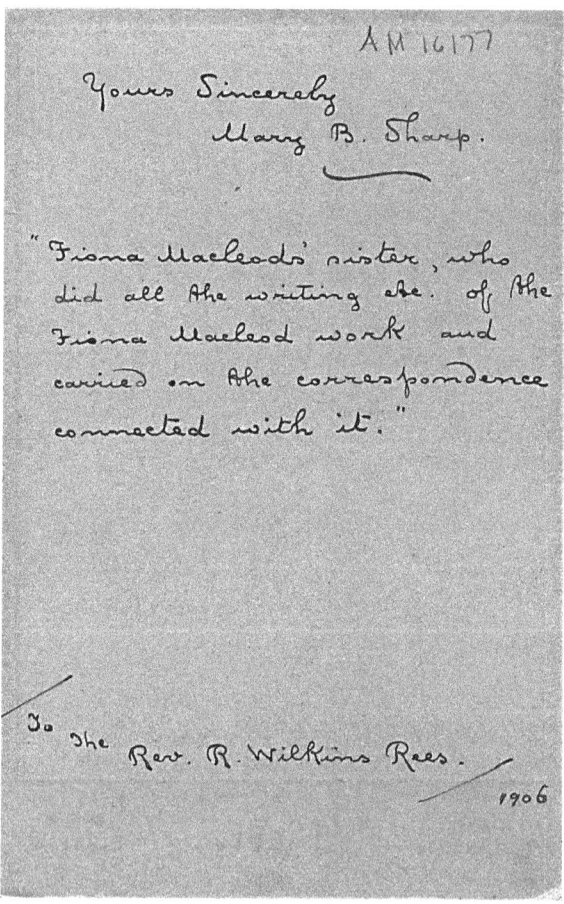

Fig. 27 Verso of Fig. 23 in Mary Sharp's handwriting (the handwriting of Fiona Macleod). The photograph is inscribed "To the Reverend R. Wilkins Rees. Yours Sincerely, Mary B. Sharp. Fiona Macleod's sister, who did all the writing of the Fiona Macleod work and carried on the correspondence connected with it." Reverend R. Wilkins Rees was the author of ghost stories, among them "Ghost-Layers and Ghost-Laying," in *The Church Treasury of History, Custom, Folk-lore, Etc.*, ed. William Andrews (London: William Andrews & Co., 1898), 241–274.) Courtesy of the Department of Rare Books and Special Collections, Dulles Reading Room, Firestone Library, Princeton University.

Sharp bolstered the deception by sharing details about the reclusive writer with friends, critics, and publishers. She was his cousin, married to a peripatetic Scottish laird who owned a yacht that could whisk her away to avoid detection. Sharp regarded her highly, provided advice and assistance as needed, and respected her desire for privacy. He sometimes floated the impression that he and Fiona were more than close friends as they would go to remote locations together. In those instances, he conflated Fiona with Edith Rinder. He often claimed he was unaware of Fiona's location so he could decline requests to meet her. When avid readers did turn up at her Edinburgh return address, she had just left to sail among the Hebrides. It was on those islands she heard the tales and absorbed the atmosphere of her stories and poems.

The first known Fiona letter was written in mid-May to Grant Allen, a well-known writer and Sharp's friend:

C/o Mrs. B. etc.
> Dear Sir,
> I have only now ascertained that you are in England. I was informed you were in the South of France. Some short time ago I asked Mr. Frank Murray of Derby to forward to you a copy of my just published romance *Pharais*. I now write to ask if you will accept it as a slight token of homage from the youngest and latest of Celtic writers to the most brilliant champion of the Celtic genius now living. I do not, however, send it by way of inveigling you to write about it, much as any word of yours would mean to me both in service and honour: but primarily because of your deep and vivid sympathy not only with nature but with the Celtic vision of nature — and, also, let me add, because of the many delightful hours I have enjoyed with your writings.
> Believe me, | Faithfully yours,
> Fiona Macleod

This letter in William Sharp's handwriting and preserved in New York's Pierpont Morgan Library was sent to Mary Sharp in Edinburgh for her to copy and send to Allen.

Fig. 28 Photograph of Grant Allen (1848–1899) by Elliott & Fry (c. 1899), Wikimedia, https://commons.wikimedia.org/wiki/File:Portrait_of_Grant_Allen.jpg, Public Domain.

The letter elicited a positive reply from Allen: *Pharais*, he wrote to Fiona "strikes me as a beautiful and poetical piece of work." He tempered his praise with a few words of criticism from an experienced writer to a novice. Interlarding English with Gaelic words was a trifle distracting. She should strive for a little more story and less pure poetry. "Perfection in literature lies in avoiding excess in any direction." He asked Fiona for some details about her life and expressed hope she would visit him and his wife who was much taken by *Pharais* (*Memoir*, 228–229). Allen accepted the fiction Sharp was creating, but according to Elizabeth "Questions as to the identity of the author were already 'in the air'" (*Memoir*, 230). In a June Fiona letter to the publisher John Lane, Sharp had Fiona raise the issue directly: "You asked me in your note who told me to apply to you with *The Mountain Lovers*. It was my cousin, Mr. William Sharp. I hear that some paper says *he* wrote *Pharais*: and I sent a disclaimer at once to the *Westminster Gazette*." Something in that periodical touched on the possibility that Sharp was the author. Even Grant Allen expressed some skepticism in a July 12 letter to Sharp:

> As to *Pharais*, I will confess I read it with some doubt as to whether it was not your own production; and after I had written my letter to Miss Macleod, I took it to my wife and said "Now, if this is William Sharp, what a laugh and a crow he will have over me! Le Gallienne, who is stopping with us, was sure it was yours; but on second thoughts, I felt certain, in spite of great likeness of style, there was a feminine touch in it and sent my letter.

He continued:

> All the same, however, I was not quite satisfied you were not taking us in, especially as your book with Blanche Willis Howard had shown one how womanly a tone you could adopt when it suited you; and I shan't feel absolutely at rest on the subject till I have seen the "beautiful lassie" in person. If she turns out to be W. S. in disguise, I shall owe you a bad one for it: for I felt my letter had just that nameless twinge of emotion one uses towards a woman, and a beginner.

Allen would be glad to meet Sharp's cousin in October, "supposing her to exist," when he hoped the Sharps would bring her to visit him in Hindhead, his village in Surrey. It is interesting to note in the context of this correspondence that Grant Allen wrote and published in 1897 a novel — *The Type-Writer Girl* — under the female pseudonym Olive Pratt Rayner. Like Sharp, he must have thought a work so titled would be taken more seriously if by a woman.

These letters illustrate the problems Sharp encountered from the start maintaining the fiction of a real Fiona Macleod. A year later he was still trying to assure Allen of Fiona's existence. By that time their mutual friend Richard Le Gallienne, who saw from the start the linkage between Sharp's writings and Fiona's, was sure of the deception and said so in print. That so alarmed Sharp he sent Le Gallienne a letter telling him to "shut up." When next they met face to face, he told Le Gallienne the truth after obtaining a firm promise of confidentiality.

In early June Sharp sent from Fiona a copy of *Pharais* and positive quotes from several reviews to John Lane. He hoped to entice Lane into publishing *The Mountain Lovers*, the second Fiona romance. As Fiona, Sharp wrote: the publisher John Lane

> Possibly you may care to make me an offer in advance for "The Mountain Lovers." It will be a book of about the same length as "Pharais," probably a little longer. The note that is dominant is the Return to Joy. The story deals with the love of two young mountaineers, Alan Gilchrist and Sorcha Cameron: but there is an interweaving of dramatic and tragic episodes in the lives of those directly connected with the Mountain Lovers. For the rest, there is, in a more marked degree than in "Pharais," a constant recurrence to the intimate relationship we have, or may have, with Nature. It is here, I know, that I have "something to say": but I will not trouble you with details which in embryo, can be of no interest to anyone until duly and finally set forth.

He sent Lane the opening chapter of the new romance and promised the completed manuscript "by the end of August, or, possibly, a little earlier." He knew Lane was the principal in the firm, but Fiona, unfamiliar with the London publishing scene, was not sure: "If I have been misinformed as to your being the literary representative or chief partner in your firm, I beg you to excuse the informality of my addressing myself to you direct." If Lane was unwilling to accept the book without seeing it, Fiona asked him to return the opening pages so she could find "a publisher on my own terms elsewhere." She would soon be going abroad for two or three months, so she hoped Lane would reply at his very earliest convenience. Though a remote novice, Fiona could demonstrate some of Sharp's backbone in her dealings with Lane. The favorable reception of *Pharais* suggested there was money to be made by the Fiona deception, and Sharp set about acquiring it.

On July 7 Sharp, under his own name, admonished John Lane for not responding to Fiona's early June letter. He was too pressed with his own work "to attend properly to other people's affairs." He had "quite enough trouble" arranging the publication of *Pharais* with Murray. He even had to read the proofs since "Miss [sic] Macleod when not on one of her visits to Edinburgh or Glasgow lives in a very remote spot." He had promised to see *The Mountain Lovers* through the press, but he could not "undertake all the preliminary 'skirmishing' as well." He is critical of both Miss Macleod and Mr. Lane: "What with an exasperatingly vagrant — if dear and lovely — cousin on the one hand, and an exasperatingly dilatory publisher on the other, the fate of a kindly intermediary who happens to be frantically busy is not a pleasant one!" The distinction between Sharp and his cousin is clearly drawn, and Lane is put on notice. Sharp further baited the hook by saying he thought he would arrange with Miss Macleod the publication of her next book, a volume of "fantasies, short stories, and poems called 'A Celtic Wreath'," with Macmillan in London and a Boston firm. The letter had its desired effect. Sharp was able to write again to Lane within a couple of weeks, this time as Fiona, to say she was glad Lane entertained her proposal favorably and set forth the terms she would require if Lane went on to publish the book. Whether or not he met all the terms, Lane published *The Mountain Lovers* in 1895.

At the beginning of August, Sharp went to the west of Scotland to stay with his mother and sisters who were on holiday in Kilcreggan on the Firth of Clyde. In a letter to Elizabeth, he said he was learning legends and customs from "a Celtic Islesman from Iona" who gave him "a copy of an ancient MS. map of Iona with all its fields, divisions, bays, capes, isles, etc." While out with the Islesman in his "two-sailed Wherry," a storm sprang up which he quite enjoyed:

> We flew before the squalls like a wild horse, and it was glorious with the shriek of the wind, the heave and plunge of the boat, and the washing of the water over the gunwales. Twice 'the black wind' came down upon us out of the hills, and we were nearly driven under water. He kept chanting and calling a wild sea-rune, about a water-demon of the isles, till I thought I saw it leaping from wave to wave after us.

In addition to that rune, he learned the rune of "the reading of the spirit" and the rune of the "Knitting of the Knots."

On August 15 he returned to Edinburgh where he wrote a long letter to Herbert Stone regarding the American edition of *Vistas* which Stone and Kimball planned to publish. The firm had initiated a small trade magazine called the *Chap-Book* to advertise its publications. The September 15 number would be devoted to William Sharp and *Vistas*. It would contain a poem by Sharp ("To E. C. Stedman"), an "appreciation" of Sharp's poetry by his friend, the Canadian poet Bliss Carman, and "The Birth of a Soul," a new "dramatic interlude," which would be included in the American edition of *Vistas*. He enclosed a photograph for the *Chap-Book* that had been taken in the spring by Frederick Hollyer. Sharp remained a very handsome man, only slightly greying at the age of thirty-nine. His frequent illnesses, physical and mental, had yet to take their toll.

Fig. 29 Photograph of William Sharp by Frederick Hollyer (1894). Reproduced from *Poems by William Sharp*. Selected and arranged by Mrs. William Sharp (London, William Heinemann, 1912). Wikimedia, https://commons.wikimedia.org/wiki/File:William_Sharp_1894.jpg#/media/File:William_Sharp_1894.jpg, Public Domain.

Sharp also included with his August 15 letter to Stone a dedication of *Vistas* to Henry Alden. It described the contents of the book as "vistas into the inner life of the human soul, psychic episodes," and acknowledged their debt to Maeterlinck, "the Belgian poet-dramatist" who had "introduced a new and vital literary form." During his visit to New York in 1891, Sharp and Alden, editor of *Harper's Magazine*, became friends, and the dedication was "a tribute of affection and admiration" to one he honored and esteemed. From Kilcreggan in early August, Sharp sent Alden two articles for possible publication in *Harper's*. He hoped for the best because money was short: "What with illness & consequent 3 or 4 months' idleness or next to idleness, my wife's long illness, & serious financial distress, we have gone thro,' & are still suffering from, a rather bad time lately." Alden responded positively, and both articles appeared in *Harper's* in 1895: "Rome in Africa" in June and "The Hebrid Isles" in December. The editors Sharp met during his two trips to New York opened a new outlet for his writing and provided a welcome source of income.

Fig. 30 Portrait of Henry Mills Alden (1836–1919), who edited *Harper's Magazine* for fifty years, in 1910. Unknown photographer. Wikimedia, https://commons.wikimedia.org/wiki/File:Henry_Mills_Alden_portrait_in_In_After_Days_(1910).jpg, Public Domain

In mid-August, Elizabeth joined her husband in Scotland, and they spent the next six weeks exploring and collecting materials in the western isles. When they reached Oban, they sailed to the Isle of Mull, crossed to its western shore, and boarded a small ferry to Iona. This was Elizabeth's first visit to the island, and she was deeply moved by its beauty and its history. In the Fiona writings, Sharp turned often to the story of St. Columba who established a religious colony on Iona in the sixth century, built an abbey, and brought Christianity from Ireland to Scotland. He captured the romanticism Iona induces in a September Fiona letter to the Irish poet and novelist, Katharine Tynan-Hinkson.

> I read your letter last night, at sunset, while I was lying on the Cruac-an-Angeal, the hillock on the west where the angel appeared to St Columba.

> [...] It was a very beautiful sight to see the day wane across the ocean, and then to move slowly homeward through the gloaming, and linger awhile by the Street of the Dead near the ruined abbey of Columba. But these Isles are so dear to me that I think everyone must feel alike!

Sharp wanted to establish a close friendship between the two ladies as he hoped Fiona would become the foremost female writer in a Scottish Celtic Renaissance as Mrs. Hinkson had become for the Irish Celtic Renaissance. Iona was an ideal place to achieve that objective as it linked Scottish and Irish history. The impressions Sharp gained during this and subsequent visits provided the material for the Fiona Macleod essay "Iona" that formed part of *The Divine Adventure* in 1900. Fiona would become part of the lore of Iona where her books are available even today for purchase by tourists who descend on the island. After several more weeks exploring the islands south of Oban and hearing more stories, the Sharps returned at the end of September to their new residence in Hampstead.

During the fall, Sharp worked on the stories and sketches Stone and Kimball published in 1895 as *The Gypsy Christ and Other Tales*. To maintain the separate identity of Fiona and that stream of income, he continued to publish under both names. Elizabeth often blamed the strain of dual authorship for his frequent illnesses, physical and mental, but those illnesses plagued him in the 1880s, long before the advent of Fiona. In October and November, he wrote several Sharp articles while also working on Fiona's *The Mountain Lovers*, the Fiona short stories he began in August, and the poems that would appear in Fiona's *From the Hills of Dream* in 1896.

In mid-October, he wrote a conciliatory letter to Theodore Watts (from 1897 Watts-Dunton) hoping to repair a breach in their friendship. Before the break occurred, Sharp sent Watts a birthday letter each year. This letter, resuming that practice, contained a paragraph that demonstrates the amiability frequently attributed to Sharp by his friends.

> In the old days, before your feelings towards me changed somewhat, you were not ill-pleased that (more Scoticè, looking upon the remembrance of a friend's birthday as a scrupulous, almost a religious observance) I used to drop you a line on each 12th Oct. Nor, I hope, will you be ill-pleased now: for the remembrance & the good wish arise from an affectionate regard, and, I need hardly say, high esteem. No doubt I have given you cause of irritation: as, in turn, I was resentful because of things

repeated to me, said of me by you. Right or wrong, I don't think anything is to be gained now by going over the ground of complaint either may have or may imagine against the other. For myself, I bear you nothing but good will: and hope you entertain something of the same feeling towards myself. It is a pity that between friends of material difference in age, differences and divergences are so apt to occur: but I like to believe that in most instances these are not fundamental, but only, as it were, the surface currents.

Born in 1832, Watts was twenty-three years Sharp's senior, and this letter had its intended effect as the two men resumed their friendship, and Sharp regained occasional access to Algernon Swinburne, Watts's housemate. This letter included a poignant passage:

> This has been a sad year, in the loss of friends: J. Addington Symonds, John M. Gray, Mrs. Augusta Webster, Roden Noel, Walter Pater. The death of the last named is a deep loss to everyone who loves what is beautiful and dignified and nobly helpful, in literature.

First Symonds and then Pater befriended the young and handsome William Sharp in the early 1880s and helped pave the way for his acceptance as an editor and writer. All five individuals were writers and friends of Watts and Sharp.

In a late October letter Sharp informed Herbert Stone *The Gypsy Christ* was complete. In mid-November he told Murray Gilchrist he was busy writing articles "for *Harpers*, the *Atlantic Monthly*, *Nineteenth Century*, and three or four other monthlies, and weekly art-articles, etc." Of the titular story of *The Gypsy Christ*, he wrote to Gilchrist:

> The locale of this story is the moorland country where my dear friend & comrade, Murray Gilchrist lives. I wonder what you will think of the tragic atmosphere I seem to have gained from your remote moorlands. There are descriptions and episodes which you will be able to read between the lines.

It is unclear what Gilchrist might read between the lines. It is also unclear what Sharp meant by telling Gilchrist he was "steadily gaining ground. The prolonged mental strain I was under being gone, the chief cause is removed." The removed "chief cause" may have been financial as the articles he was writing and the popularity of Fiona promised a more secure future. It may have been the environment of Phenice Croft which he had left. It may have been that arrangements had been worked out between the two Sharps and the two Rinders to enable Sharp and Edith to maintain their relationship. In early December Sharp went to Scotland — St. Andrews and Edinburgh — for the three weeks preceding Christmas. Having agreed with Elizabeth that Sharp should not be left alone, Edith may have joined him for all or part of his escape from the fogs of London. After Christmas, his doctor advised a rest near the sea, and the Sharps spent a week on the Isle of Wight. Thus ended 1894, a year in which Sharp launched Fiona Macleod upon the world and produced, despite frequent illnesses, an abundance of writings, hers and his own.

Chapter Twelve

January–June 1895

In January 1895 William Sharp wrote to a friend: "London, I do not like, though I feel its magnetic charm, or sorcery. I suffer here. The gloom, the streets, the obtrusion and intrusion of people, all conspire against thought, dream, true living." The city is "a vast reservoir of all the evils of civilised life with a climate which makes me inclined to believe that Dante came here instead of to Hades." Elizabeth recognized the problem, "the noise and confused magnetism of the great City weighed disastrously" on her husband. "The strain of the two kinds of work he was attempting to do, the immediate pressure of the imaginative work [by which she meant the work of Fiona Macleod] became unbearable, 'the call of the sea,' imperative" (*Memoir*, 242). Attempting to alleviate the crisis, the Sharps went to Ventnor on the Isle of Wight on January 6. Before they left, Sharp managed several letters. On January 1, he wrote to the editor of a Scottish paper recommending the publication of an article by Frank Rinder about the Scottish poet Robert Fergusson, who died at the age of twenty-four in 1774. He described Rinder, who at thirty-two was only seven years younger than Sharp, as an "able and promising young writer."

After attending the funeral of Christina Rossetti on January 2nd, Sharp proposed an article about her to Horace Scudder at the *Atlantic Monthly*. It would be similar to his article on Walter Pater which appeared in the December 1894 issue of the magazine. Scudder accepted the suggestion, and Sharp's "Some Reminiscences of Christina Rossetti" appeared in the July 1895 issue. He also proposed an article on "The Celtic Renaissance," a subject that was "becoming recognized as one of profound interest and indeed of paramount significance." He was "a specialist in old and contemporary Scots-Irish Celtic literature," but he would, of course, restrict himself to "the Celtic spirit: not to what is written in Scottish Gaelic or Irish Gaelic." The new "Celtic movement in Ireland & Scotland, & in a less degree in Wales, is, in a word, of vital importance." Fiona would be the movement's dominant literary voice in Scotland, but William Sharp would also play a role. Scudder must not have accepted Sharp's proposal as no such article appeared in the *Atlantic*.

Writing to Catherine Janvier on January 5, he said he resented "too close identification" with the "so-called Celtic renaissance." To survive, his work "must be beautiful in itself." *Pharais*, he wrote, came from the core of his heart; it was the beginning of his true work. While writing it, his pen was "dipped in the ichor" of his life. He could not say more about *Pharais* without telling her about his whole life, but one day he would confide "some of the strange old mysteries of earlier days I have part learned, part divined, and other things of the spirit." He could write out of his heart as Fiona in a way he could not as William Sharp.

> This rapt sense of oneness with nature, this cosmic ecstasy and elation, this wayfaring along the extreme verges of the common world, all this is so wrought up with the romance of life that I could not bring myself to expression by my outer self, insistent and tyrannical as that need is [...] My truest self, the self who is below all other selves, and my most intimate life and joys and sufferings, thoughts, emotions, and dreams, must find expression, yet I cannot save in this hidden way.

In this, his most concise and forthright justification of the pseudonym, there is no mention of supernatural beings or of a separate person, but simply a recognition of two "selves." His most basic self could be expressed only by adopting a feminine pseudonym and projecting a separate identity for his hidden feminine self. That the deeper self was female raised a question that has plagued Sharp's reputation since it was revealed upon his death in 1905 that he was Fiona. Of the book's reception, Sharp told Mrs. Janvier "It had reached people more than he dreamt of as likely" and "created a new movement" in Scotland. In England, it was hailed as a "work of genius" by the likes of George Meredith, Grant Allen, H. D. Traill, and Theodore Watts. It was "ignored in some quarters, abused in others, and unheeded by 'the general reader,'" but Sharp was nonetheless "deeply glad with its reception."

The Sharps met Anna and Patrick Geddes in the fall of 1894, and the couple figured prominently in their lives as 1895 unfolded. There arose between Sharp and Geddes

> a friendship with far-reaching results for "Fiona Macleod" [...] Both were idealists, keen students of life and nature; cosmopolitan in outlook and interest, they were also ardent Celts who believed in the necessity of preserving the finer subtle qualities and the spiritual heritage of their race against the encroaching predominance of materialistic ideas and aims of the day (*Memoir*, 248–249).

The Geddes lived in Dundee, where he was Professor of Botany at University College. They were also active in the intellectual and social life of Edinburgh where, in 1887, Geddes established a summer school of arts, letters, and science and Scotland's first student hostel. The summer school continued every August until 1899 and attracted students and scholars from Great Britain and the Continent. In 1894 he transformed a town mansion known as "Laird of Cockpen," located near the Castle on Edinburgh's High Street, into the Outlook Tower, where he created the

Fig. 31 Sir Patrick Geddes (1854–1932). Photograph by Lafayette, 30 December 1931. © National Portrait Gallery, London. Some rights reserved.

world's first "sociological laboratory." The building became the locus of the Scottish version of the Celtic Revival, and Geddes became the dominant figure in that revival. He fostered the movement as a means of furthering his ambition to restore Edinburgh as a major European center of learning. The Celtic Renaissance article Sharp offered Horace Scudder for the *Atlantic Monthly* was one of a series of lectures Geddes asked Sharp to deliver in August 1895 at the Summer School. The lectures, as we will see, had an unfortunate result, but the invitation initiated a friendship between the two men and opened the way for significant contributions to the Celtic movement by Sharp as an editor and Fiona Macleod as a writer.

From Ventnor on January 10, Sharp asked Anna Geddes if she was surprised when her husband told her "W. S. and Fiona Macleod are one in the same person." Since the Fiona writings were his "Celtic" credentials for taking part in the publishing firm Geddes was organizing, he had confided in Geddes and given him permission to share the secret with his wife. Sharp's purpose in writing to Anna was to emphasize the need for "absolute preservation of the secret." Before she was apprised of Fiona's identity, she received a letter from Fiona in the Fiona handwriting. Now Sharp wrote in his own hand and signed the letter, fittingly, "Fiona Macleod and William Sharp." This is a unique instance of the double signature in a letter and of the Fiona Macleod signature in a letter written in Sharp's hand. Signing both names and asserting W. S. and F. M. were one in the same implied the presence of two personalities. Sharp was trying to find a means of defining and describing his duality. Elizabeth believed her husband's frequent ailments were exacerbated by the strain of appearing to the world as William Sharp while experiencing insights and feelings that found an adequate means of expression only through the female persona.

On January 15 Sharp wrote again to Geddes from Ventnor to say he thought he should go to Edinburgh to discuss details of the publishing firm and "Celtic matters." They would accomplish more in a day than in "months of correspondence." The Sharps were returning to London on January 18 and would be fully occupied through the weekend, but he might be able to get away on January 21 and spend the next two days in Edinburgh. He could ill afford the trip, but it seemed a necessity. Geddes replied he would come to London for the meeting, and Sharp wrote on

January 21 to say he would keep the afternoon and evenings of January 29, 30, and 31 entirely free to talk with Geddes. The Sharp's flat had only one bedroom, but he would arrange with a nearby friend — probably Mona Caird — a place for him to stay.

In his response to Sharp's January 15 letter, Geddes suggested Sharp consider moving to Edinburgh where he could play a leading role in the publishing firm and avoid extensive travel between London and Edinburgh. In his January 21 response Sharp said he found the idea tempting: "I have a profound & chronic distaste for London & London life and a nostalgia for the north." The chief drawback of a move would be financial as a good deal of his income derived from reviewing London art exhibits and works of literature. Editors were less likely to ask for reviews beyond the London postal zone "partly on account of late transmissions & early return of proofs." He doubted there was "publishing, secretarial, tutorial, or other work in Edinburgh that, without more expenditure of time and energy than I now give to my reviewing, would ensure me say £300 & leave me time for my own particular work." In addition to the financial disadvantage of a permanent move to Edinburgh, the Sharps had many acquaintances and some dear friends in London, and the city was a great meeting place, a "bazaar of fortunate & smiling chances." Sharp mentioned his ambitions in the direction of the stage and his wife's love of music, one of her chief joys. He didn't see how he could "throw up Fogtown — at present." Perhaps he might have "rooms in Edinburgh (or the flat in Ramsey Gardens we want to take if possible [...] and come & go a good deal: in fact, if the publishing idea develops, & you entrust me with a responsible part in it, I would need to be in Edinburgh for one week & perhaps two weeks in each month." On the other hand, if his work for the Geddes publishing firm were to develop to the point where he could receive a guaranteed salary of £300 per year, the move might be possible as he would be glad to drop all his "miscellaneous pen-work."

Having addressed his situation and his availability for the new publishing venture, Sharp described at some length how he thought the firm should develop. "The effort," he wrote, "should be to produce at first certain books of as pronounced a character as possible — books of significance so to say: so that the Firm be known at once for a certain distinction." To help the firm get a good start, he suggested "a little

Fortnightly," like Stone and Kimball's *Chap-Book* which sold for only two pence and was "a splendid advt. of their wares." He had given Geddes a copy of the *Chap-Book* that featured his photograph and an article publicizing the American edition of his *Vistas*. He would be glad to undertake the required careful editing and handling. Geddes penciled "Agreed" against this suggestion, which was the genesis of a more elaborate publication, *The Evergreen: A Northern Seasonal*, the first issue of which appeared in the spring of 1895.

Sharp went on to say the firm should engage in "no haphazard publishing at first": "There might be, to start with, a biological book by A. Thomson: a sociological or other work by yourself: 'A New Synthesis of Art' or other work by myself [...] a Celtic romance by Fiona Macleod [...] (for it is on Celtic lines, I think, the most development will take place first)." He estimated the firm would need an initial outlay of about £1,000; authors would be paid on a royalty system. As for his own involvement,

> If you intend me to be the literary "boss" in the firm (tho' perhaps I mistake your intent!) I would give my best thought, care, & experience to making the venture a success in every way, & ultimately a potent factor in the development of Scotland & of Edr [Edinburgh] in particular. Of course, my editorial experiences, & far-reaching literary connections, would stand me in good stead: & in a year or so we could have a varied and potent "staff."

As he continued Sharp's thoughts expanded to include Wales and Ireland, "If I were lity. 'boss,' as I say, one effort would be to centralise in Edinburgh all the Celtic work now being done by Scottish, Irish, and Welsh writers." Capital would be needed to "grease the wheels" and then "patience" and "wise discretion." Here Geddes again wrote, "Agreed." There is always room at the "top of the tree," Sharp asserted, and "We are too enthusiastic, too determined, not to get to that top if it be possible, as I firmly believe it is, and as I know you do." To this statement, Geddes gave his final blessing: "Quite so. Full speed ahead!" Sharp concluded by apologizing for writing "so scrappy and unsatisfactory a note," but said the writing of it moved him out of his "depression & 'doleful dumps.'" This letter provided the basis for their discussion in London as Geddes noted his agreement with many of Sharp's suggestions and moved ahead with them without involving

Sharp. He must have sensed Sharp's inability to stay focused for long on the practical details of management.

In early February 1895, Sharp put the finishing touches on the second Fiona Macleod romance, *The Mountain Lovers*, which John Lane published in the summer. He also wrote Fiona stories for a volume called *The Sin-Eater and Other Tales* which was published in November of 1895 by the Geddes firm in Edinburgh and by Stone and Kimball in Chicago. He was corresponding as Fiona with Herbert Stone about that volume and as William Sharp about *The Gypsy Christ and Other Tales* which Stone and Kimball published, also in 1895. Two weeks of intensive writing and arranging took a heavy toll, physically and mentally. An incident brought home to Elizabeth the seriousness of his condition.

> A telegram had come. I took it to his study. I could get no answer. I knocked, louder, then louder, — at last he opened the door with a curiously dazed look in his face. I explained. He answered, "Ah, I could not hear you for the sound of the waves!" It was the first indication to me, in words, of what troubled him (*Memoir*, 242–243).

It was "the noise and confused magnetism of the great City" and his estrangement from the sea. Since there were no waves to be heard in London, he soon left for the West of Scotland.

After spending a weekend in Edinburgh, he went to Corrie, a village on the western Island of Arran, and described his arrival on February 18 in a February 20 letter to Elizabeth:

> It was a most glorious sail from Ardrossan. The sea was a sheet of blue and purple washed with gold. Arran rose like a dream of beauty. I was the sole passenger in the steamer, for the whole island! What made the drive of six miles more beautiful than ever was the extraordinary, fantastic beauty of the frozen waterfalls and burns caught as it were in the leap. Sometimes these immense icicles hung straight and long, like a Druid's beard: sometimes in wrought sheets of gold, or magic columns and spaces of crystal. Sweet it was to smell the pine and the heather and bracken, and the salt weed upon the shore. The touch of dream was upon everything, from the silent hills to the brooding herons by the shore.

Sharp was the sole passenger on the ferry between the mainland and the port of Brodick on the island. From there he traveled six miles north to the seaside village of Corrie.

After a cup of tea, I wandered up the heights behind. In these vast solitudes, peace and joy came hand in hand to meet me. The extreme loneliness, especially when I was out of sight of the sea at last and could hear no more the calling of the tide, and only the sough of the wind, was like balm. Ah, those eloquent silences: the deep pain-joy of utter isolation: the shadowy glooms and darkness and mystery of night-fall among the mountains.

"In that exquisite solitude," he continued, "I felt a deep exaltation grow. The flowing of the air of the hills laved the parched shores of my heart."

Fig. 32 Winter on the Isle of Arran. By Archie46 — Own work, CC BY-SA 3.0, Wikimedia Common, https://commons.wikimedia.org/w/index.php?curid=30013029

Years later, Sharp retold the story of his 1895 experience in an essay called "Earth, Fire, and Water" which appeared in Fiona Macleod's *The Divine Adventure: Iona; By Sundown Shores* (1900). After repeating several tales about men who were called to the sea by the sound of waves, the narrator continued:

I have myself in lesser degree, known this irresistible longing. I am not fond of towns, but some years ago I had to spend a winter in a great city. It was all-important to me not to leave during January; and in one way I was not ill-pleased, for it was a wild winter. But one night I woke, hearing a rushing sound in the street — the sound of water. I would have thought no more of it, had I not recognized the troubled noise of the tide, and the sucking and lapsing of the flow in weedy hollows. I rose and looked out.

It was moonlight, and there was no water. When, after sleepless hours, I rose in the grey morning I heard the splash of waves. All that day and the next I heard the continual noise of waves. I could not write or read; at last I could not rest. On the afternoon of the third day the waves dashed up against the house. I said what I could to my friends and left by the night train. In the morning we (for a kinswoman was with me) stood on the Greenock Pier waiting for the Hebridean steamer, the Clansman, and before long were landed on an island, almost the nearest we could reach, and one that I loved well. We had to be landed some miles from the place I wanted to go, and it was a long and cold journey. The innumerable little waterfalls hung in icicles among the mosses, ferns, and white birches on the roadside. Before we reached our destination, we saw a wonderful sight. From three great mountains, their flanks flushed with faint rose, their peaks white and solemn, vast columns of white smoke ascended. It was as though volcanic fires had once again broken their long stillness. Then we saw what it was: the north wind (unheard, unfelt, where we stood) blew a hurricane against the other side of the peaks, and, striking up the leagues of hard snow, drove it upward like smoke, till the columns rose gigantic and hung between the silence of the white peaks and the silence of the stars.

That night, with the sea breaking less than a score yards from where I lay, I slept, though for three nights I had not been able to sleep. When I woke, my trouble was gone.

The word painting of this passage is precise and moving. The description of his arrival in the 1895 letter to Elizabeth germinated into a striking and controlled passage of poetic prose. While there are subtle efforts to feminize the narrative voice earlier and later in the essay, Fiona, the supposed author, is absent from this passage.

Elizabeth addressed the issue: "Although the essay is written over the signature of 'Fiona Macleod' and belongs to that particular phase of work, nevertheless it is obviously 'William Sharp' who *tells* the story, for the 'we' who stood on the pier at Greenock is himself in his dual capacity; his 'kinswoman' is his other self." After inventing Fiona, Sharp sometimes portrayed himself as two persons in one body, one male and one female. In the 20 February letter of 1895, after telling Elizabeth he was alone on the ferry to Arran, he wrote,

There is something of a strange excitement in the knowledge that two people are here: so intimate and yet so far-off. For it is with me as though Fiona was asleep in another room. I catch myself listening for her step sometimes, for the sudden opening of a door. It is unawaredly that she

> whispers to me. I am eager to see what she will do — particularly in *The Mountain Lovers*. It seems passing strange to be here with her alone at last.

It was one thing for Sharp to create and name a secondary personality over whom he had control. It was quite another, as here, to turn that personality into a woman over whom he had no control.

When Sharp objectified the Fiona persona as a separate person, she was sometimes a stand-in for a real person. The kinswoman who accompanied him to Arran in mid-winter 1895, stood on the pier with him, and was sleeping in the next room, may have been not the imagined Fiona, but Edith Rinder. Ever kind and generous, we recall Elizabeth writing of Mrs. Rinder:

> Because of her beauty, her strong sense of life and of the joy of life; because of her keen intuitions and mental alertness, her personality stood for him as a symbol of the heroic women of Greek and Celtic days, a symbol that, as he expressed it, unlocked new doors in his mind and put him "in touch with ancestral memories" of his race.

In an 1896 letter to Elizabeth, Sharp wrote "to her I owe my development as 'Fiona Macleod' though, in a sense of course, that began long before I knew her, and indeed while I was still a child," but "without her there would have been no 'Fiona Macleod'" (*Memoir*, 222).

It is impossible to pin down the precise role Edith played in the work Sharp signed Fiona Macleod. Near the end of 1895, writing to his friend Sir George Douglas who knew Fiona was Sharp, he referred to her not as a separate personality, but as a "puzzling literary entity." The previous January, we recall, he told Catherine Janvier, "My truest self, the self who is below all other selves, and my most intimate life and joys and sufferings, thoughts, emotions and dreams, *must* find expression, yet I cannot save in this hidden way." Here Fiona was not a separate person, but one of several "selves" demanding expression. Elizabeth believed Edith Rinder enabled her husband to drop his defenses, release his deepest "self," and exercise most fully his creative imagination. She accepted his claim that he could write most fluently as Fiona when he and Edith were alone together. Some of his letters, especially those to E. C. Stedman, imply he used his need to be away from the city, his need for solitude, as an excuse to be alone with Edith. The build-up of frustration that preceded his escape to the West of Scotland in February 1895 and again in June of that year may have been partly a build-up of sexual tension. The sense of relief and renewal in his February 20 letter to Elizabeth and, after a similar escape, in a June 4 letter to Geddes is palpable.

In early March, Sharp was back in London sending Geddes a detailed proposal for a quarterly which would be a vehicle for stories, articles, poems, and visual art and also a means of advertising the firm's other publications. He had in mind "a thoroughly representative Anglo-Celtic 'quarterly'" that would be "well-supported" in all the big towns of Great Britain and America and draw "Anglo-Celtic writers to look to Edinburgh." He enclosed a draft of what he thought the first number should contain and volunteered to be its editor (with the help of his wife). Drawing on his London connections, he would assemble a strong list of contributors. He envisioned the quarterly, entitled "The Celtic World," as a "valuable record" of the entire Celtic Revival. Rather than naming an editor, it should say only: "Published by Patrick Geddes and Colleagues" or "Edited and Published in Edinburgh." He constructed a Table of Contents for a "Summer Number" that included items by the most notable Irish, English, Welsh, and Scottish Celticists: W. B. Yeats, Ernest Rhys, Patrick Geddes, Katharine Tynan, George Russell (Æ), and, of course, Fiona Macleod. Planning expansively, he proposed a Frontispiece and Celtic Ornament by John Duncan, the principal visual artist of the Scottish revival.

Ignoring Sharp's offer of himself as editor, Geddes took the idea of a quarterly issued as a book and quickly implemented it. After securing an arrangement with T. Fisher Unwin in London to market the book, he produced not a summer issue, as suggested by Sharp, but a spring issue simply called *The Evergreen: A Northern Seasonal*. This would be followed, in accordance with Sharp's suggestion, by Summer, Fall and Winter issues. Geddes asked William Macdonald, an aspiring poet, to assemble and oversee the publication of the first volume. It began with a seven-page "Proem" by Macdonald and J. Arthur Thomson, a biologist, which set forth Geddes's ideas for reforming not only Edinburgh's Old Town, but the industrialized cities of Britain and beyond. It equated the decadence that pervades literature and the arts with the decay of cities and asserted there were signs of a New Birth "against the background of Decadence."

The music of the coming Renascence is heard so far only in "broken snatches," but in these snatches four chords are sounded, which we would fain carry in our hearts — That faith may be had still in the friendliness of fellows; that the love of country is not a lost cause; that the love of women is the way of life; and that in the eternal newness of every Child is an undying promise for the Race.

One hears in that sentence attributed to the aspiring poet William Macdonald the distinctive voice of Patrick Geddes.

The content of the Spring volume was divided into four sections: "Spring in Nature," "Spring in Life," "Spring in the World," and "Spring in the North." Each story, poem, and essay touches on the theme of renewal. The authors are not the luminaries of the larger Celtic renaissance Sharp proposed, but comparatively unknown Scots. It contained two essays by Geddes ("Life and its Science" and "The Scots Renascence"), a Fiona story ("The Anointed Man"), and three Sharp poems, one under his own name and two signed Fiona. Headpieces and Tailpieces of Celtic design appear throughout the volume which

Fig. 33 "Apollo's School Days," John Duncan, in *The Evergreen: A Northern Seasonal, The Book of Spring* (Edinburgh: Patrick Geddes and Colleagues, 1895). Photograph by William F. Halloran of his copy in 2020

was printed on fine paper by Constable in Edinburgh. Several copies were produced with tan leather bindings and a full-page design on the front cover embossed in green. The finest of several full-page drawings is John Duncan's "Apollo's School-Days" which echoes the drawings of the decadent Aubrey Beardsley.

As a sidelight, my wife and I spent the summer of 1962 in Edinburgh where we met Arthur Allhallows Geddes — Patrick Geddes' son and William Sharp's godson — at the National Library of Scotland. He was a Lecturer in Geography at Edinburgh University who always wearing a kilt as he moved about the Old Town. When he learned I was examining the papers of his godfather, he offered to sell me for five pounds his set of the four *Evergreens* bound in leather. When he failed to locate his set, he arranged for me to receive the set, also bound in leather, belonging to Lady Mears, his sister, Patrick Geddes' daughter, and the widow of Sir Frank Mears, (1880–1953). Trained as an architect, Mears became Patrick Geddes' assistant in 1908 and married Norah Geddes in 1915. Scotland's leading planning consultant from the 1930s to the early 1950s, he was knighted in 1946. There followed an invitation to have sherry with Lady Mears at her home in the Morningside district of Edinburgh. She hoped to learn more about William Sharp and his relationship with her father. After a pleasant visit and well-fortified with sherry, we returned to our humble flat in Edinburgh's New Town with Lady Mears' set of *The Evergreen* which may or may not have been replaced by Arthur's missing set.

In a letter to Geddes dated May 15, Sharp said he liked much of what was in the spring volume, but some of it lacked "distinctiveness as well as distinction." It was promising and with "careful piloting" should "come to stay." He read Geddes's two contributions "with particular interest and pleasure, not only with the affection of a friend but with the sangfroid of a critic." The poetry in the volume, including that of Fiona Macleod, did not seem as good as the prose. The editorial control, he wrote, "must be more exigent." And the illustrations, he thought, perilously weak: "With the exception of Duncan's "Apollo's School Days" & some of the head-pieces, there is not a drawing […] which is not crude in draughtsmanship and in design — or in one or two instances frankly meaningless!" John Duncan's "Anima Celtica" was weakly imitative and lacking in any redeeming features. He judged this kind of work as "the mere dross and debris of the 'fin-de Siècle' ebb." It had "the same effect on one's optic nerves as a scraping nail has on one's auditory ditto." He expected much adverse criticism of the volume because of its art; "*The Yellow Book* drawings are at least clever if ultra-fin-de-Siècle, while the majority of these of *The Evergreen* are fin-de-Siècle without being clever." He recognized his criticism may be too severe, but he felt so strongly "that a really valuable & significant future awaits the 'Evergreen' if it preserve & develop its best, in literature & art, & disengage itself from what is amateurish."

The second volume of *The Evergreen* appeared in the fall of 1895, while the third (summer) and the fourth (winter) followed in 1896. Sharp's critique had the effect of improving the quality of the later volumes. In a note called "Envoy" at the close of the fourth volume Geddes and Macdonald announced the end of the first series and declared the need to take some seasons off before producing a second series. Since the publication was without an editor and invited authors were free

Fig. 34 The Outlook Tower, Castlehill, Edinburgh., locus of the Scottish Celtic Revival. Photograph by Kim Traynor (2013), Wikimedia, https://commons.wikimedia.org/wiki/File:Outlook_Tower,_Castlehill,_Edinburgh.JPG#/media/File:Outlook_Tower,_Castlehill,_Edinburgh.JPG, CC BY-SA 3.0

to contribute as they wished, *The Evergreen* reflected Geddes's effort to create an artistic commune in the Outlook Tower and its surrounding buildings, in which writers, visual artists, and scientists would live happily together and stimulate each other's creativity. According to the "Envoy," the artists and scientists now recognized the need to go off on their own and do their own work before coming back together in a new synthesis. *The Evergreen* was not revived.

In early April Sharp wrote a long letter of complaint to Herbert Stone; he had not received proof sheets of *The Gypsy Christ* which had been promised in February, and Fiona Macleod was upset for not having heard from him about the agreement to publish an American edition of *Pharais*. Sharp was beginning to have doubts that Stone and Kimball would be a reliable American publisher of his books. It was an early sign that stresses had developed between the two young publishers. In fact, Melville Stone — Herbert's father and publisher of the *Chicago Daily News* — who supported the publishing venture had begun to wonder if it would develop into a viable business.

In mid-April Sharp went to Paris to cover a salon for the *Glasgow Herald*. He was back in London by the twenty-seventh when he wrote to Geddes apologizing for not having time in Paris to look up Thomas Barclay, a Scottish barrister and asking him to support Geddes's scheme to create a Franco-Scottish College somewhere in France. He promised to contact Barclay when he was back in Paris on May 5, this time with his wife, to review another salon.

Prior to the second Paris trip he wrote Geddes another long letter (April 29) describing an elaborate plan for book publications. He would be in Scotland around May 20 and would like to stay with the Geddes in Dundee for a few days to confer "about the publishing business." The two men must have came to an arrangement during Geddes's late January visit to London, for Sharp to oversee the publication of books, and his April 29 letter contained proposals for discussion. Sharp thought the firm's first book should be an "R. L. S. volume" — that is, a volume either about or by Robert Louis Stevenson — followed by a romance composed by "a well-known Man." Here Geddes wrote in the margin "Mrs. Mona Caird — Agreed 23/5/5." Though not a man, Mona Caird was a well-known advocate for the rights of women and a close friend of the Sharp's. Geddes's marginal note, surely suggested by

Sharp, raises the possibility that Mona Caird, who published in 1894 her ground-breaking novel, *The Daughters of Danaus*, was working on or had completed her next book, *The Pathway of the Gods: A Novel*, which was published in London by Skeffington in 1898. Neither a Stevenson book nor a Mona Caird romance was published by the Geddes firm.

The first two books, Sharp continued, should be followed by Fiona's volume of short stories, *The Sin-Eater and Other Stories*, which would be ready in late fall. Stories of the kind were in demand, Sharp explained, and its sales should be helped by the June appearance of Fiona's second romance, *The Mountain Lovers*. Geddes wrote in the margin of Sharp's letter next to Fiona's *Sin-Eater*, "Press for July," and then, during his meeting with Sharp on May 23, he wrote "Agreed 23/5/5/ for the Autumn." *Lyra Celtica*, an anthology of Celtic poetry, would also be ready for publication in the fall. Sharp suggested the firm publish a series of short books of fiction called "The Evergreen Series" and a "Cosmopolitan Series" containing translations of works by "foreign authors of marked power & distinction in the 'new movement' — a vague phrase that really means little save the onward wave of the human mind." He listed fourteen authors from six countries, including the United States, whose work might be translated. Finally, he thought it best to leave until 1896 the publication of a book called *The Literary Ideal*, which would contain the lectures he planned to deliver in August in Geddes's Summer School. Geddes wisely wrote in the margin "Discuss in August," as he wanted to see the lectures before agreeing to publish them.

Though few of the ideas proposed in this letter materialized, Sharp served briefly as Manager of Patrick Geddes and Colleagues and, when that proved impracticable, as its Literary Adviser. The firm produced, under Sharp's supervision, several beautiful books that rival in design and format those published by established firms in Dublin and London for the Irish contingent of the Celtic Revival. In a series called The Celtic Library, Fiona's *Sin-Eater and Other Tales* appeared in the fall of 1895 and her *Washer of the Ford* in 1896. The series also included in 1896, *The Fiddler of Carne: A North Sea Winter's Tale*, a Welsh romance set in the late eighteenth century by Sharp's friend Ernest Rhys, and, in 1897, *The Shadow of Arvor; Legendary Romances and Folk-Tales of Brittany*, translated and retold by Edith Wingate Rinder. The presence of Wales and Brittany reflected Sharp's determination to have the firm reach beyond Scotland in its portrayal of Gaeldom. A collection of Fiona poems called *From the Hills of Dream, Mountain Songs and Island Runes* was published in 1896. It was dedicated to Geddes' son and Sharp's Godson, Arthur Allhallows Geddes, who was one year old on Halloween in 1896. In 1897, the firm issued Fiona's *Songs and Tales of St. Columba and His Age* and *The Shorter Stories of Fiona Macleod*, a rearrangement and reissue in three inexpensive paper-covered volumes of the stories published in *The Sin-Eater* and *The Washer of the Ford*. While under his direction, the books published by Patrick Geddes and Colleagues were limited to those by Sharp disguised by the pseudonym, his wife, and his friends. It became, nonetheless, the principal voice of the Scottish Celtic Revival due principally to the writings of Fiona Macleod; and with those writings she became, according to an article in the *Irish Independent*, "the most remarkable figure in the Scottish Celtic Renascence." In that context, we need to keep reminding ourselves she was William Sharp.

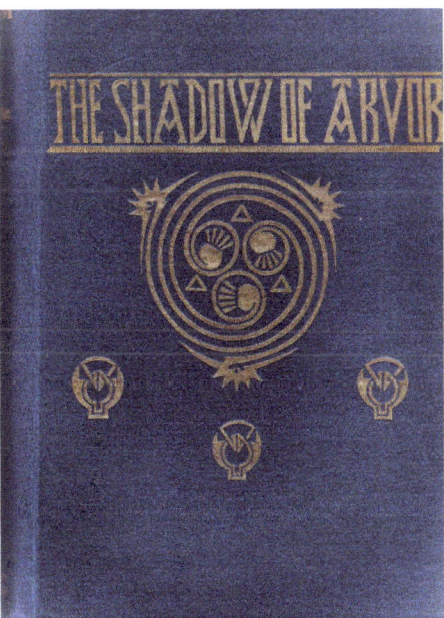

Fig. 35 An example of a Patrick Geddes and Colleague book: *The Shadow of Arvor: Legendary Romances and Folk-Tales of Brittany*, Translated and Retold by Edith Wingate Rinder (Edinburgh: Patrick Geddes & Colleagues, 1897). Printed by W. H. White and Co. Ltd., Edinburgh Riverside Press. Photograph by William F. Halloran (2019).

In his April 29 letter to Geddes, Sharp said *Lyra Celtica*, an anthology of Celtic poetry, would be ready for publication in the fall of 1895. He thought its editor of record should be neither F. M. nor W. S., but Elizabeth Sharp. This was advisable, he thought, "for several reasons (one among them, its inclusion of F. M.'s runes & Celtic lyrics)." Sharp, however, would write a "critical introductory essay (as distinct from an ordinary preface)." When it appeared, the book's editor was Elizabeth A. Sharp, but it was largely the work of her husband who selected the poems, contributed copious notes, and wrote a lengthy introduction. *Lyra Celtica* contains ancient Irish, Scottish, and Cornish poems and early Armorican (Breton) and Cymric (Welch) poems, but most of the volume is devoted to representative poems by "modern and contemporary" poets — Irish, Scottish, Welch, Manx, Cornish, and Breton. Even Canada is represented by Bliss Carman, chosen because he was Sharp's friend, but justified by his Scottish ancestry. The volume's definition of Celtic is very broad; poems by Lord Byron and George Meredith are included. It reflects the suggestion in Sharp's April 29 letter to Geddes that the firm publish a "Cosmopolitan Series." That series did not materialize, but Sharp knew Geddes wanted the Scottish Celtic Revival's inclusiveness to signal its "cosmopolitanism," then fashionable in Europe, and the restoration of Scotland's centrality as a European center of learning and culture. E. A. Sharp was joined as editor by J. Matthay for the second revised and enlarged edition of *Lyra Celtica* which was published by John Grant's Edinburgh firm in 1924 and 1932.

Patrick Geddes and William Sharp shared a propensity to dream grandly and cast a wide net in their interests and concerns. It is no wonder they became good friends. Neither was a well-organized businessman, and the publishing firm soon descended into financial insolvency. Sharp's efforts to sustain his writing and publication under two signatures, his frequent bouts of ill-health and depression, and his inability to remain for long in one place placed a strain on his relationship with the individuals Geddes enlisted to save the firm. He was ever patient with Sharp and concerned for his well-being. Their close friendship produced a great deal in a brief period, but Geddes soon moved beyond the Celtic Revival as his interests expanded into town planning on a grand scale.

As promised in his April 29 letter to Geddes, Sharp left London on May 18, spent two nights in York with his friend George Cotterell,

Fig. 36 Title page of the first edition of *Lyra Celtica, An Anthology of Representative Celtic Poetry*, edited by Elizabeth A. Sharp, with an Introduction and Notes by William Sharp (Edinburgh: Patrick Geddes and Colleagues, 1896), https://archive.org/details/lyracelticaantho00shar/mode/2up

editor of the *Yorkshire Herald*, and went on to the Geddes home in Dundee on May 20. On the 23rd he left for a long weekend of relaxation in the West. During their brief visit Geddes became concerned about Sharp's physical and mental well-being. He wrote to ask Elizabeth's opinion about her husband's health and to propose a stipend from the publishing firm that would enable him to spend less time reviewing and more time on his poetry and fiction. In a late May response, Elizabeth expressed her deep appreciation for Geddes's concern and generosity. She was thankful to have someone else who "sees how he is expending health and strength — and encroaching on his reserve — in work of a kind he ought not to do." She continued:

> Like you, I have a great belief in the future of W. S. and Fiona M., and I am equally persuaded that he must give up the fretting hack-work in order to give his real work its chance. But it is so difficult to make him do so; he grows nervous, and, I regret to say, chiefly on my account. But I feel sure, that now, your kind interest in him, and thought for him will

do more [than] anything else to make him, not only feel, but act on our advice — which coincides. You are indeed a most valuable ally.

It was a relief for her "to see that there is a friend who understands Will and sees his persistent overwork and delicacy." She would discuss Geddes's offers with her husband when he returned to London and put him into "his doctor's hands" to deal with the weakness in his back, which was the result of overwork. She assured Geddes of her interest in all the "schemes" he and her husband were discussing and hoped she might be allowed "to share in a little of the work."

After he returned to London on May 29 and saw the Geddes letter, Sharp wrote again to Geddes on June 3. He expressed his gratitude for his "solicitude about his health and welfare" and called Geddes "a good & loyal comrade as well as a dear friend." He promised to ponder all Geddes's "arguments and advice," but he was sorry Geddes had written "so exigently" about his health, especially about his back, as he had hoped not to worry Elizabeth about that "passing trouble." That said, he launched into a lengthy description of his brief sojourn:

> I had the most glorious weather in the West and had a true sun-bath every day. Friday, Saty, Sunday, & Monday last I spent at one of my favourite remote places on Loch Fyne in Western Argyll. There I lived mentally, spiritually, & physically (excuse the unscientific specifications!) in rainbow-gold. All day from sunrise to midnight I was on the higher mountain slopes, or in the pine-woods (full of continuous solemn music with the north wind), or on the sea. On Sunday forenoon I rowed across (2 miles or so) to the uninhabitable rocky solitudes opposite (South of Ceann More) — went for a long glorious swim of about an hour! — lay naked in the sunlight below a pine on a mossy crag, & dreamed pagan dreams, & fell asleep, & had a wonderful vision of woodland lives unknown of men, and of a beautiful Child God, of which you will hear something from Fiona in due time — & wakened two hours later, still sun-bathed, tanned & burnt & midge-bitten — then another swim — then rowed across the loch again &, after tea etc., away up to the summit of a hill set against a marvellous vision of mountains & peaks & lofty ranges, which I have baptised with a Gaelic name meaning the Hill of the Beauty of the World — then watched the sunglow till 10 p.m. & came down thro' the dewy heather to the pinewoods, where I climbed into the branches of a great red brother & lay awhile listening to the wind, with its old-world wonder-song of the pines, & watching the moon sail upward.

This impressive paragraph of prose, with its long concluding sentence, pulls the reader into sharing the experience. It must have so affected Geddes who shared Sharp's affinity for escaping into the natural world.

> Sharp then proceeded to the effect of the experience:
> I have come away with a sense of the sunflood through & through me: of magic rhythms and hints of secret voices and cadences haunting-sweet: & with the almost passionate health & eagerness of that young Norse god who in sheer extravagance of joy wove the rainbows into a garland for the moment's mountain he made out of falling worlds.

Sharp's physical and mental state certainly improved during the brief interlude, but the main impetus of the letter was to convince Geddes he was well enough to undertake work for the publishing firm, and well enough to prepare the lectures he promised to deliver for Geddes's Summer School in August. All this, Sharp asserted, "means I am well." He thanked God "for life — for a swift pulse & red blood — and fever in the heart and brain," and stated his intention to "be good, & to lecture, & to publish, & behave, & always love Mrs. Geddes & yourself." The letter is yet another example of Sharp's ability to recover quickly from his too frequent bouts of illness and depression. The overt "Paganism" and his promise to behave raise the possibility he was not alone in this restorative interlude. Though he remained well enough through June to do a good deal of work, his recovery, as usual, was only temporary.

Chapter Thirteen
July–December 1896

During the first three weeks of July, Sharp was writing and corresponding with Herbert Stone about American editions of *The Gypsy Christ and Other Tales* by W. S. and *Pharais* and *The Sin-Eater* by F. M. He told Stone his arrangement with Elkin Mathews in London specified Stone and Kimble had the right to publish another collection by Sharp, *Ecce Puella and Other Prose Imaginings*, in America, and the book was issued simultaneously by the two publishers in November. On July 5 he and Elizabeth went to Hindhead in Haslemere, Surrey to spend the weekend with the Grant Allens, "a brief respite," he told Stanley Little. In a letter thanking Mrs. Allen for an enjoyable time, Sharp assured her she need not be concerned about a rumor floating through London involving her husband and a "literary Parisian." Since he was anxious to assure Mrs. Allen it would soon pass, the rumor must have come up during the weekend. Most people, he wrote, knew Allen had been in Paris not with a French woman named Belloc, but with his wife. Sharp's focus on this rumor is notable given the likelihood he was recently in Paris with a woman not his wife — before she was replaced by his wife.

In a postscript, Sharp declared the publisher John Lane "should be careful how he speaks," and advised Allen "not to give himself away." Having received the manuscript of Allen's *The Woman Who Did* and agreed to publish it, Lane let it be known Allen was its author. Allen intended to publish the novel pseudonymously, and Sharp advised him to stick with that intent despite Lane's indiscretion. When the novel appeared several months later, its author was Grant Allen. The book attracted a great deal of attention, positive and negative, and made its author both famous and infamous. Soon after it appeared, Victoria Crosse produced *The Woman Who Didn't*, and Mrs. Lovett Cameron

Fig. 37 "The Croft," Grant Allen's House in Hindhead, Haslemere, Surrey (1906). © The Francis Frith Collection, https://www.francisfrith.com/hindhead/hindhead-grant-allen-s-house-1906_55569

produced *The Man Who Didn't*. The woman in one and the man in the other adhered closely to the norms of Victorian society. Allen's woman believed women should throw off the shackles of male dominance and assert their equal rights, views shared by Sharp. In recommending Allen publish pseudonymously, Sharp knew the book would generate a good deal of outrage. The novel has recently emerged from obscurity as an important contribution to the *fin de siècle* feminist movement known as the "New Woman." The Paris rumor, Sharp's concern about Lane's indiscretion, and the negative response to Allen's novel offer a glimpse of the self-reflective and interconnected London publishing scene in the 1890s.

Allen shared Sharp's interest in authorial deception. He published several books as the work of invented males, and in 1897 he issued *The Type-Writer Girl* as the work of a woman, Olive Pratt Rayner. By that time, he knew Fiona was Sharp, and Sharp's use of a female pseudonym may have encouraged him to follow suit. Two years earlier, however, in 1895, Sharp worried Allen might learn the truth. Writing to Allen on July 15 as Fiona, he made a "small request." If Allen intended to write anything about her *Mountain Lovers*, she hoped he would "not hint playfully at any other authorship having suggested itself." She continued, "And, sure, it will be a pleasure to me if you will be as scrupulous with Mr. Meredith or anyone else, in private, as in public, if chance should ever bring my insignificant self into any chit-chat." Sharp was especially anxious to keep Fiona's true identity from George Meredith as he thought he might lose his friendship if he discovered the deception. Fiona ended her letter by telling Allen she looked forward to meeting him "when she came south in late Autumn."

In early July Sharp began writing the ten lectures totaling, he estimated, 70,000 words promised Patrick Geddes for his August Summer School. On July 13, he went down to the Burford Bridge Hotel in Surrey for a dinner meeting of the Omar Khayyam Club, an organization of literary figures dedicated to the pleasures of good wine and food. Many important writers attended, among them Grant Allen, Thomas Hardy, Theodore Watts-Dunton, George Gissing, and George Meredith who was the guest of honor. Meredith seldom appeared in public, but he was lured to the dinner by his friend Edward Clodd, the club's president, and arrived only for the dessert course. Clodd welcomed him "in a charming and eloquent speech not devoid of pathos," and Meredith, overcoming his famed reticence about speaking in public, responded graciously and wittily. After Sharp attended this dinner as a guest, Edward Clodd recommended him for membership in the Club, and he joined in November (*Memoir*, 246).

In a July 11 letter, Sharp told Richard Le Gallienne, who was living near Allen and Meredith in Surrey, he hoped to see him at the Omar Khayyam dinner to arrange a private meeting. He knows Fiona will be gratified by Le Gallienne's "kind words of praise for *The Mountain Lovers*" in that evening's *Star*, but he must again make "a friendly protest" against Le Gallienne's "inference as to her pseudonymity." He concluded: "Please Don't! — for her sake much more than for that of Yours ever in Friendship, William Sharp." Four days later, on July 15, he wrote again to Le Gallienne. He was sorry Le Gallienne had not attended the Omar Khayyam dinner. It was "a memorable as well as a pleasant one because of George Meredith" who has sent Fiona "a letter of splendid praise & encouragement." He appreciated anything Le Gallienne says about Fiona in print, but "she and her unworthy cousin [Sharp] earnestly hope for no more confusion respecting her actual authorship of 'The Mountain Lovers,' publicly or privately." Le Gallienne had compared the two writing styles and concluded — first privately and then publicly — Fiona was Sharp. Sharp wanted a private talk, probably to tell Le Gallienne a version of the truth and extract a pledge of secrecy, but Le Gallienne could not meet that week, and Sharp could not meet the following week. He was leaving London and would not return until October, by which time Le Gallienne would be in America. The July 15 letter was his only hope of silencing Le Gallienne, and he concluded by returning to Meredith who knows, he wrote, Fiona is "my cousin, but, I hope, will never be 'put about' by hearing any other rumor." Wherever the fires threatened to rise, Sharp tried to extinguish or at least contain them.

Sharp also wrote to Patrick Geddes on July 15: he would be in Scotland the following week, but not in Edinburgh until the end of the month when his wife would join him. He enclosed the titles of his Summer School lectures and informed Geddes he ("or rather Fiona") received a letter from Meredith in which he "slips the laurel into Fiona's dark locks right royally & prophesizes big things of her." When Geddes learned Sharp was coming north in advance of his wife, he proposed a hiking trip. Sharp declined, saying he could "see no one for the week I shall be 'hanging about.'" He would be in Edinburgh only intermittently until the end of July when he would be available to talk with Geddes about *The Evergreen* and other publications of the new firm. He planned to visit Murray Gilchrist on his way to Scotland, but he wrote on the 18th to say he could not leave London until the morning of the 22nd and had to be in Edinburgh that evening. Few of his lectures had been written, and he was beginning to panic. Before leaving London, he found time to write a heartfelt letter to Annie Alden, whose mother, Susan Alden, recently died after a long and debilitating illness. While visiting the Aldens in Metuchen, New Jersey during his visit to America in 1891, he developed a sincere affection for the family. The letter reveals something of his conception of death and the afterlife. Everyone who knew Annie's mother loved her. Certainly, he did. In fact, he had a special spiritual connection with her. He often dreamed of her, and once he had "a kind of vision of her, white and sunlit, walking through a shadowy wood that was all bright where she went." She was one of the few who "go through life as white spirits clothed with the accident of body," and now she has been "born into new life." She has had "still another resurrection — that resurrection in the minds of all who knew her, which keeps new and fresh a vivid and dear memory." She now lives twice, as a spirit in the afterlife and in the memory of all who knew and loved her. In concluding, Sharp hoped Annie would enjoy the copy of Fiona's *The Mountain Lovers* he sent to her father and asked her to preserve the secret of her identity he had shared with the Aldens.

In a late July letter Fiona thanked Grant Allen for his favorable review of *The Mountain Lovers* in the *Westminster Review*. The letter contains a clue as to Sharp's whereabouts during the week of July 22. As he passed through Edinburgh, he had his sister copy the letter into the Fiona hand with a "temporary" return address of 144 North St. | St. Andrews | Fife, (now a shopping area across the street from the University), and Sharp mailed it from there. In the letter, Fiona says she is visiting friends in St. Andrews and that her cousin Will Sharp is "coming to spend the weekend" with her — "or I with him, I should say, as I am to be his guest, at almost the only Celtic place we know of on this too 'dour' shoreland of Fife." From later correspondence, we know Edith Rinder was vacationing in or near St. Andrews until late August, when she left for Brittany to collect folklore. Sharp's insistence on being alone that week and his claim Fiona was visiting him in St. Andrews suggest he was using a rendezvous with Fiona as a cover for one with Edith. As the years went by, Sharp claimed Fiona as his cousin, and sometimes he implied they were romantically involved, though both were married to another. Fiona's movements as portrayed by Sharp in correspondence and conversations often modeled those of Edith. When Edith was in Scotland, Fiona was there; when Edith was abroad, so was Fiona; when Edith was with him, Fiona was with him. This was a convenient way to keep track of Fiona's whereabouts and, if necessary, account for the presence of a female companion. It also signaled his predisposition to conflate the two women, one real and the other imagined.

In an early August note Sharp assured Stanley Little his lectures were going well, but they had "told upon" him heavily, and he was "far from well." According to Elizabeth, while he was delivering the first of ten scheduled lectures on "Life & Art" in the Summer School, he "was seized with a severe heart attack and all his notes fell to the ground. It was with the greatest effort that he was able to bring the lecture to a close: and he realized that he must not attempt to continue the course; the risk was too great" (*Memoir*, 251). The plural in the letter to Little implies more than one lecture was delivered, but apparently that was not the case.

At the end of August, he informed Herbert Stone he had not been at all well, "the strain of lecturing" had been too great. As much as he liked to sketch out the topic of lectures, Sharp was less successful in forming his notes into a coherent narrative. Delivering a lecture provoked great anxiety. The "heart attack" must have been an episode of angina brought on by nervous apprehension. Whatever the case, he repaired across the Firth of Forth to recuperate at the Pettycur Inn in Kinghorn where Edith Rinder could visit from St. Andrews. Elizabeth stayed on in Ramsay Gardens "to keep open house for the entertainment of the students."

Fig. 38 Ramsay Gardens from Princes' Street, Edinburgh. The Outlook Tower is on the High Street behind this impressive group of buildings. Photo by David Monniaux (2005), Wikimedia, https://commons.wikimedia.org/w/index. php?curid=228032#/media/File:Edinburgh_old_town_dsc06355.jpg, CC BY-SA 3.0.

In an August 12 letter with a Ramsey Gardens return address, Sharp informed Herbert Stone "Miss Macleod" was staying with him and Elizabeth for a day or two to hear his lectures, "particularly that on The Celtic Renascence." This was the fifth lecture of the ten he had planned to give, and, if Elizabeth's recollection was correct, he did not get beyond the first. Having Fiona with him at Ramsey Gardens at the halfway point of his planned lectures explains why he was able to add a brief note to a Fiona letter to Stone, also dated August 12. The simultaneity of the two letters was possible because Sharp's sister Mary was close by in Murrayfield to supply the Fiona handwriting. In an August 30 letter to Stone, Sharp reported Edith Rinder had entered the Ramsay Gardens milieu during the previous week. She had been staying in Fifeshire during August, and she was leaving the next day for Brittany "to work up Breton legends and folklore." Sharp was sure Stone would be pleased with her Belgian book, *The Massacre of the Innocents and Other Tales by Belgian Writers*, which his firm published in its Green Tree Library series in November 1895. He offered to write "a short article on the Belgian Renascence" for Stone's *Chap-Book* to publicize the book.

There followed one of Sharp's many stratagems. Edith, he wrote in the August 30 letter to Stone, was "Miss Macleod's most intimate woman-friend" and the "dedicatee of *Pharais*." Since she was William Sharp's "most intimate woman friend" and since it was William Sharp who dedicated *Pharais* to her, he was equating himself with Fiona. Continuing, he said Edith and Fiona had been "staying together recently and (I believe) writing or planning something to do together." It was William Sharp and Edith Rinder who had been staying together recently. After broaching the possibility of joint authorship, Sharp quickly denied it — "that, from what I know of Miss F. M., will never come off, as she is far too essentially F. M. to work in harness with anyone." The passage increases the likelihood Edith was with him on St. Andrews and at the Pettycur Inn, but why, we wonder, did he raise with Stone the possibility of joint authorship only to dismiss it. Since he was corresponding with Stone about the writings of both Fiona and Edith, Stone might succumb to rumors and equate Fiona with Edith or, more likely, with William Sharp. Edith was not Fiona; nor was she collaborating with Fiona. Rather, she was translating and editing continental stories and folktales, including those of Celtic Brittany. By sharing these details of the Sharp | Macleod | Rinder triangle with Stone, Sharp reinforced the separate identity of Fiona. The three were good friends and compatriots in the Celtic cause, but quite independent of each other.

Sharp's careful manipulation of people's locations was not limited to Edinburgh. He and Elizabeth had taken a cottage with his mother and sisters for September in the west of Scotland. In his August 30 letter to Stone, Sharp said he was leaving the next day for Tigh-Na-Bruaich in the Kyles of Bute, in Argyll where he planned to stay at least ten days and where "his cousin, Miss Macleod," would be with him "most of the time." A postscript to Fiona's August 12 letter informed Stone that her address throughout September would be "c/o Mrs. William Sharp [not Mr.] | Woodside | Tigh-Na-Bruaich | Kyles of Bute | Argyll | Scotland." Having brought Fiona to Ramsey Gardens in mid-August, he would have her in the West with him during September. More correspondence with Stone about the publication of *The Sin-Eater* and *Pharais* would be necessary, and sister Mary would be in Tigh-Na-Bruaich to supply the requisite handwriting. Correspondence could move back and forth more rapidly between Chicago and Tigh-Na-Bruaich without having to pass through Edinburgh. This sort of manipulation of Fiona's whereabouts was a fact of Sharp's life until his death in 1905. It was necessary to sustain the fiction of Fiona's separate existence, and he enjoyed orchestrating the complexities.

In mid-September, the Sharps were joined in the Kyles of Bute by Agnes Farquharson Sharp, Elizabeth's mother and William's aunt. On September 18 Sharp told Stone their party was breaking up the next day, but he and Elizabeth would stay on till the end of the month. By September 26, the plans had changed. Sharp wrote Gilchrist to say he was taking his aunt back to London because she was prostrated by a telegram from abroad saying her son had suddenly developed a malignant cancer and was dying so rapidly he had given up hope of coming home. This turn of events disrupted his plan to visit Gilchrist, but he promised to stop for a visit in late October when he would be returning to Edinburgh.

On September 27, William, Elizabeth, and Agnes left the Kyles of Bute for Edinburgh, where Sharp posted a long birthday letter to E. C. Stedman; he should receive from Stone and Kimball "on or about the 8th" — Stedman's birthday — a copy of *The Gypsy Christ*. He wanted to send a book of "prose imaginings," *Ecce Puella*, but Elkin Mathews had delayed publication until late October. Stedman would also soon receive from Stone and Kimball as a special present a copy of the American edition of *The Sin-Eater* by his cousin Fiona Macleod, who "is now admitted," Sharp wrote, "to be the head of the Scots-Celtic movement — as W. B. Yeats is of the Irish-Celtic." The British edition of *The Sin-Eater*, which would be published in Edinburgh, "is novel & beautiful as a piece of book-making." He was responsible for its type, paper, binding, & general format. Apart from *The Evergreen* it was the first publication of Patrick Geddes & Colleagues of which he was "chief literary partner." The books published by the Geddes firm in 1895–1896 are, indeed, beautiful examples of bookmaking. As described in the previous chapter, Sharp also played a critical role in their content since all the initial publications were written by 1) Sharp as Fiona Macleod (*The Sin-Eater*, *The Washer of the Ford*, and *From the Hills of Dream*), 2) his wife (*Lyra Celtica*, with a lengthy introduction by her husband), and 3) his close friends Edith Rinder (*The Shadow of Arvor*) and Ernest Rhys (*The Fiddler of Carne*).

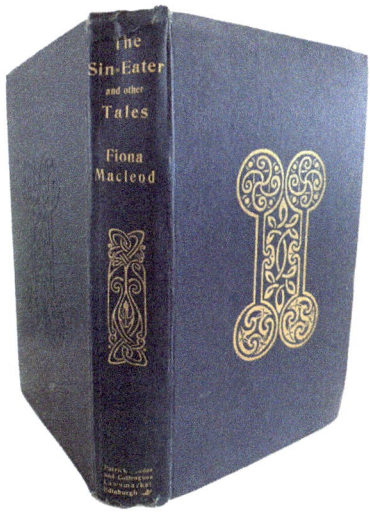

Fig. 39 Fiona Macleod, *The Sin-Eater and Other Tales* (Edinburgh: Patrick Geddes & Colleagues, 1895). Photograph by William F. Halloran (2019).

From Edinburgh on 28 September, Sharp sent Stone an article on the Belgian Renaissance for publication in the *Chap-Book* and told him it would not be necessary to send Mrs. Rinder proofs of her *Massacre of the Innocents and Other Tales by Belgian Writers*, since she was anxious for it to appear. It was published on November 15, 1895 in Stone and Kimball's Green Tree Library series. The book took its title from its first story, "The Massacre of the Innocents," by Maurice Maeterlinck, whose dramas had established his substantial reputation. In her introduction to the volume Edith wrote, "even the most enthusiastic admirers of the author need not be surprised at never having heard of the story" as Maeterlinck himself was amazed that she had unearthed his only published prose tale from an "obscure and long since defunct French periodical where it made its first appearance before anyone had heard a word concerning its author." Edith was in touch with Maeterlinck and the other authors as she assembled and translated their stories for the volume.

Sharp wanted to issue works by W. S. and F. M. at about the same time "in part to sustain what reputation belonged to his older Literary self, and in part to help preserve the younger literary self's incognito" (*Memoir*, 251). To counterbalance the publication of Fiona's *Sin-Eater* by the Geddes firm in October 1895, Sharp produced two books by W. S. One was *The Gypsy Christ and Other Tales*, which Stone and Kimball published in Chicago as the first in their "Carnation Series." The volume's titular story drew upon Sharp's experience as an adolescent with a band of gypsies in Scotland, and on a recent encounter while walking with Murray Gilchrist on the moors of Derbyshire. When the book was published in England by Archibald Constable and Co. in 1897, its second story was given preference in the title: *Madge o' the Pool: The Gypsy Christ and Other Tales*.

Sharp dedicated a second book, *Ecce Puella and Other Prose Imaginings* (published by Elkin Mathews in London on November 1) to his friend George Cotterell, editor of the *Yorkshire Herald*. Not one to pass up dedicatory possibilities, he ascribed each of the book's sketches to a close female friend. The title piece, "Ecce Puella," a revised and condensed rendition of "Fair Women in Painting and Prose," which Sharp wrote for P. G. Hamerton's *Portfolio of Artistic Monographs* in 1894, celebrates the beauty of women. Dedicated "To the Woman of Thirty," it begins with a quotation by H. P. Siwäarmill, an anagram of William Sharp: "*A Dream of Fair Women*: Every man dreams his dream. With some it happens early in the teens. It fades with some, during the twenties. With others it endures, vivid and beautiful under grey hairs, till it glorifies the grave." Sharp's dream of a fair woman became a reality and endured in the person of Edith Rinder who, born in 1865, was a "Woman of Thirty" in 1895, and was the dedicatee.

The second piece in the book, "Fragments from the Lost Journals of Piero di Cosimo," is one of Sharp's attempts to produce a prose version of Robert Browning's "dramatic monologues." Cosimo, an Italian Renaissance painter, records in old age his failure to measure up to the promise of his youth. Sharp dedicated this piece to E. A. S. — Elizabeth Amelia Sharp — who introduced him to the paintings of Cosimo and his more accomplished contemporaries. The next piece — "The Birth, Death, and Resurrection of a Tear" — is dedicated "To A. C." whose identity remains a mystery. She must have been a woman of great beauty, since the narrator elaborately parallels the course of his unrequited love for her with the course of a tear which falls down "the lovely sunbrown cheek no bloom of any 'sun'd September apricock' could outvie." Next, "The Sister of Compassion," is dedicated "To A. M. C." or Alice Mona Caird. The woman of the title is "so wrought by the tragic pain of the weak and helpless" that she laid down her life in order that she might be "a messenger of that tardy redemption which man must make in spirit and deed for the incalculable wrong which he had done to that sacred thing he most values — Life." A well-known spokeswoman for the rights of women, Mona Caird was a vocal participant in the animal rights movement. The first-person narrator, a stand-in for Sharp, "loves and honors" her as Sharp surely did since she supplied shelter and sustenance for the Sharps whenever they were in need.

The next piece, "The Hill-Wind," resembles the impressionistic prose poems Sharp was writing as Fiona Macleod, and he dedicated it to F. M. Personified as a beautiful woman, the Hill-Wind sees the "whiteness of her limbs beneath the tremulous arrowy leaves and the thick clusters of scarlet and vermillion berries" as she descends to become the bride of the Sea-Wind. The image of red berries against the white flesh recalls Sharp's "Swimmer of Nemi" in *Sospiri di Roma*, the volume of poems he published in Italy in 1891. Since he associated that poem with the birth of Fiona Macleod, the dedication to Fiona is fitting, but the overwrought description of the forest through which the winds blow contrasts sharply with the restrained language of the poem.

"Love in a Mist," the final piece in the volume, is dedicated "To a Midsummer Memory." In this poem, "Love" is a young Cupid who spends a good deal of time examining a beautiful forest in search of something to do. He comes upon a handsome man and a beautiful woman, and they provide an opportunity to carry out his designed function; he shoots each with an arrow. He is concerned as they appear to fall in agony, but he soon realizes "they were not dead or even dying, but merely kissing and fondling each other, and this too in the most insensate fashion." Sharp's memory of this encounter, one supposes with the woman of thirty who was his dedicatee in the first essay, enabled him to end a book dedicated to the women in his life with a note of titillation for his female readers. *Ecce Puella* is yet another example of Sharp's preoccupation with women, this example focused on the women in his life.

In a series of letters to Murray Gilchrist in the fall of 1895, Sharp revealed his deeply conflicted state of mind. His unfulfilled promises to visit caused Gilchrist to wonder if a rift had developed. From Argyle on September 26, addressing Gilchrist as "My dear boy," he wrote, "*Of course*, my dear fellow, there is no 'shadow of a shadow of hill or sea,' as they say here, between us. At all times I bear you in affectionate remembrance: and then, we are comrades." He was sorry Gilchrist's year was filled with "mischances and misadventures." His own year had such extremes of "light and shade' that it was no wonder his friends noted the progressive greying of his hair. To further allay Gilchrist's concern, he closed the letter: "to you, my dear friend & comrade, my love, sympathy, & affectionate heed." With the letter, he sent a set of proofs of the "Tragic Landscapes" section of Fiona's *Sin-Eater* and asked Gilchrist, who knew the Fiona secret, what he thought of the three prose poems. He especially wanted to know what Gilchrist thought of the third piece — "Summer Sleep" — which Gilchrist would know was

> an exact transcript of — Phenice Croft at Rudgwick, and that the three men are — you, Garfitt, and myself. I cannot explain aright: you must read into what you read. The most tragic & momentous epoch of my life followed that visit of yours to Phenice Croft, & is, so far, indissolubly linked with that day I met you, and that time.

Published as the work of Fiona Macleod, the "Summer Sleep" section of "Tragic Landscapes" recounts an incident that occurred when Gilchrist and Garfitt were staying with Sharp at Phenice Croft in 1894. As discussed at some length in Chapter Eleven, Sharp wanted Gilchrist to read that section carefully and decipher its hidden meaning.

Shortly after returning to London, Sharp wrote another letter to Gilchrist to say he would spend a day with him between the October 13 and October 19. He was disappointed by Gilchrist's failure, in his note of acknowledgement, to say what he thought of "Tragic Landscapes." He would elicit Gilchrist's thoughts when they met in person. Sharp returned to Edinburgh on October 12 without stopping to see Gilchrist, and, on October 14, he asked Gilchrist by what means he could go from York to his house in Derbyshire when he returned to London at the weekend. Two days later, he told Gilchrist he was ill with a diarrheic weakness and wondered if Gilchrist could meet him on Friday October 18 after 9:00 p.m. at the Station Hotel in York where he would spend that night and where Gilchrist would be his guest. The meeting did not take place.

On November first, Sharp wrote again to Gilchrist thanking him for a letter praising *The Sin-Eater*. Grateful for Gilchrist's favorable opinion, he remained unsatisfied by what he did not say in his "little message." He wanted to know what Gilchrist felt and thought about the entire book which, he wrote, "is full of myself, of my life — more than any (save one other than myself) can ever know." Edith Rinder, as we shall see, was the only one other than himself who knew *The Sin-Eater* was full of his life. That he would make Gilchrist the third to know shows he considered him an intimate friend and trusted him to preserve the secret of Fiona Macleod. He continued with another confession: "I am in the valley of Deep Shadow just now. Great suffering, of a kind that must not be shown, has led me stumbling and blindfold among morasses and quicksands. I see the shining of my star — and so have hope still, and courage. But, while I stumble on, I suffer." He wanted Gilchrist to know he was in the throes of a deep depression.

What, we must wonder, had Sharp embedded in *The Sin-Eater* that he hoped Gilchrist would uncover? The tales in the first section — "The Sin-Eater," "The Ninth Wave," and "The Judgment of God" — each tell the story of a man who commits an infraction of the norms of the Gaelic islands and ends up naked and consumed by the sea. In his depressed state, Sharp must have identified with these poor bedraggled men. In each of the volume's final three stories — "The Daughter of the Sun," "The Birdeen," and "Silk o' the Kine" — Sharp, disguised as Fiona, described a beautiful woman. In the first, she is Ethlenn "with her tall, lithe, slim figure, her dark-brown dusky hair, her gloaming eyes, her delicate features, with, above all, her radiant expression of joyous life." In the second, the Birdeen, or baby girl, grows into a young lady who is

> tall and slim, with a flower-like way wither: the way of the flower in the sunlight, of the wave on the sea, of the tree-top in the wind. Her changing hazel eyes, now grey-green, now dusked with sea-gloom or a violet shadowiness; her wonderful arched eye brows, dark so that they seemed black; the beautiful bonnie face of her, wither mobile mouth and white flawless teeth; the ears that lay against the tangle of her sun-brown shadowed hair, like pink shells on a drift of seaweed; the exquisite poise of head and neck and body.

In the third, Eilidh was the "most beautiful woman of her time." Because of her "soft, white beauty, for all the burning brown of her by the sun and wind, she was also called Silk o' the Kine." She slays the man the King forces her to marry and joins Isla, the man she loves. They shed their clothes and swim out "together against the sun," and they were "never seen again by any of their kin or race." Sharp hoped Gilchrist, reading deeply, would recognize that in each of these stories of female beauty, intense love, and inevitable tragedy, Sharp was telling the story of his troubled relationship with Edith Rinder, which he had described to Gilchrist when they met at Phenice Croft. He concluded the November first letter with a dramatic appeal to Gilchrist: he needed his help, and he needed it "just now."

That plea reached its apotheosis in a late December letter, where he recalled for Gilchrist the "tragic issues" underlying his despair:

> To me, 1896 comes with a gauntleted hand. It will be a hard fight against the squadrons of Destiny (for I hear the trampling of an obscure foe and menacing vague cries) — but perhaps I may — for a time, and that is the utmost each of us can expect — emerge victor. What a bitter strange mystery fate is! You know, dimly and in part, out of what tragic pain and amid what tragic issues I wrote "Summersleep," the third of the "Tragic Landscapes"? Well, every environment is changed, and circumstances are different, and yet the same two human souls are once more whelmed in the same disastrous tides & have once more to struggle blindly against what seems a baffling doom.

The imagery recalls that of the "Silk o' the Kine," but Sharp and Edith could not shed their responsibilities and swim out "together against the sun," never to be seen again. Sharp was "wrought by overwork, anxiety, and the endless flame of life," and he needed to have a long talk with Gilchrist. He told Gilchrist he was in financial trouble due to the indisposition of his wife, who had to spend the three winter months in Italy. He asked again if *The Sin-Eater* "wore" with Gilchrist. He wished Gilchrist would write a long letter, not "one of his usual notelets." He would be thankful if he could leap over "the black gulf of January" and be "safe on the shores of February."

Over-dramatized, but with a ring of truth, the letter is a long cry of desperation and a plea for help. It ends with an "offering" to Gilchrist, a "specially bound proof-revise copy of his last book: *Ecce Puella*:

And Other Prose Imaginings." The volume's extensive ruminations on beautiful women were unlikely to interest Gilchrist, but the intensity of Sharp's adoration might drive home the seriousness of his dilemma. The letter raises Gilchrist to the status of a secular priest whose receipt of an offering might elicit an absolution, a way forward. It is not clear how Sharp thought Gilchrist could help, but he may have assumed the restrictions placed on Gilchrist's relationship with Garfitt resembled those on his relationship with Edith. Gilchrist's experience may have produced insights that would alleviate Sharp's depression. Gilchrist's writings offer another clue to the intense language of Sharp's appeal for help and to his repeated requests for Gilchrist's response to Fiona's "Summer Sleep" in which Sharp saw and feared the "Gates of Hell."

Gilchrist was drawn to speculating about the dark mysteries embedded in the human psyche. Hugh Walpole, in his *The Apple Trees: Four Reminiscences* (Waltham Saint Lawrence, Berkshire: Golden Cockerel Press, 1932), described a visit to Gilchrist (42–51):

> So dark was the house that we lived for most of the day in candle-light. [...] He liked candles and Elizabethan thickness of atmosphere and, if possible, the rain beating on the leaded windows. [...] He liked to sit in the low heavily-beamed room and, as the candles flickered in the old silver candlesticks, and read aloud some of his favorite pieces from his writings.

In their introduction to a selection of Gilchrist's tales — *The Basilisk and Other Tales of Dread* (ix–xvi) — John Pelan and Christopher Roden wrote:

> The themes of madness and doomed love echo through the majority of his stories and in rare instances where his protagonists survive their encounters with the supernatural, it is a close call, and we know that they will carry the psychic scars left by their encounter with the Otherworldly for ever more. Gilchrist's tales are High Tragedy; stories with an air of the morbid and grim, compressed into vignettes of just a few thousand words.

Sharp was especially interested in Gilchrist's response to *The Sin-Eater* because Gilchrist's tales of "doomed love" and "psychic scars" resembled those he was writing as Fiona Macleod. Sharp's attraction to Gilchrist was rooted in his belief that Gilchrist's circumstances, his view of the world, and his state of mind resembled his own.

Pelan and Roden also described the "duality of Gilchrist," as shown by his shift in the late 1890s from "ornately crafted fantasies" to "deftly limned sketches of the Peakland District," from horror stories to local color. "It has been posited" they continue, "that Gilchrist abandoned the realm of the fantastic due to concerns for his own safety following the arrest of Oscar Wilde." They reject that supposition. While they agree that Gilchrist, as "a homosexual living in homophobic times [...] had reason to be concerned," their analysis of the full scope of his writings indicates Gilchrist turned to "charming travel books and mainstream novels" primarily because he recognized a change in the literary market and decided to produce writings that would sell.

In addition to the duality in his writing, Gilchrist, like Sharp, experienced a further, more basic splitting of self. Though he was living with George Garfitt in a homosexual relationship, the nature of the relationship unknown to those outside the relationship. Less flamboyant than Wilde, Gilchrist was not averse to distinctive role-playing. In *Eyam — The "Milton" of Robert Murray Gilchrist*, a small pamphlet of unknown date written by a resident of Eyam and available locally, Clarence Daniel recalled his father saying Gilchrist attended church services wearing "a cassock and girdle, as though it indicated membership of some religious order," while another villager said that Gilchrist was "a huge man, full of tricksy humor, who could rattle off anything on a piano and surprise the stranger with the sweetness of a tenor voice coming from his massive frame." With occasional lapses, Gilchrist projected a distinctive but decidedly masculine image to the world. Sharp also projected that image while secretly wondering if he was more a woman than a man. Gender identity is not openly addressed in Sharp's 1895 letters to Gilchrist, but it is clearly a subtext. The confidential tone and confessional content of the letters suggest they shared while together their concerns about dual identities and gender fluidity. Gilchrist may have been surprised, if not perplexed, by the desperation conveyed in Sharp's 1895 letters, but he must also have recognized similarities in their interests and circumstances: their shared fascination with the supernatural, the psychic traumas lurking below accepted patterns of behavior, and their unconventional relationships, his with Garfitt and Sharp's with Edith. Sharp's pursuit of an intimate relationship with Gilchrist was based, at least partially, on his hope the younger man might provide some solace, a path of escape from depression. Gilchrist's refusal to accommodate Sharp's repeated pleas for a more detailed and intimate response to *The Sin-Eater* reflected, as Sharp feared, his reluctance to deepen and shift the nature of their friendship.

Sharp seems not to have desired or needed a sexual relationship with another man, but he had a compelling need for a male friend to whom he could confide his deepest feelings. That need was rooted in his emotional distance from his father during his childhood, and in his father's early death, which prevented a healing of the breach. In the late 1870s and 1880s, Sharp confided in John Elder, the brother of Elizabeth Sharp's close friend, Adelaide Elder. They met just before Elder immigrated to New Zealand for reasons of health, and the intensity of their relationship, which ended abruptly in Elder's premature death, is preserved in Sharp's letters. Dante Gabriel Rossetti adopted Sharp as an acolyte in the early 1880s, and Sharp became a willing supplicant. Recently discovered letters to Hall Caine show how he became Sharp's confidant after Rossetti died in 1882. In the early 1890s, Sharp developed a close friendship with J. Stanley Little who found Phenice Croft for the Sharps and lived nearby in West Sussex. When he met Gilchrist in 1894, Sharp, sensing their compatibility and the comparability of their circumstances, adopted him first as a confidant and then made him a confessor, a role Gilchrist resisted.

Sharp met his first cousin, Elizabeth Amelia Sharp, a well-educated girl from London, when they were children, and they became engaged when they were twenty. She became his companion and mentor, and she remained such until he died. In mid-life, he met, and came to depend on, the beautiful and brilliant Edith Rinder. The "needs and desires, interests and friends" of the Fiona Macleod side of his "nature," which was "deepening and becoming dominant," needed her presence. It was she who enabled him to summon and objectify his female self. "Without her," he said, "there would have been no 'Fiona Macleod'" (*Memoir*, 222). He came to love her; he needed to be with her; and several unpublished Sharp sonnets in the National Library of Scotland suggest his despair was deepened by the circumstances that prevented them from having a child. A passage in Elizabeth's *Memoir* (292) offers further insight into the state of mind that caused Sharp to reach out in despair to Gilchrist:

> The production of the Fiona Macleod work was accomplished at a heavy cost to the author as that side of his nature deepened and became dominant. The strain upon his energies was excessive: not only from the necessity of giving expression to the two sides of his nature; but because of his desire, that, while under the cloak of secrecy F. M. should develop and grow, the reputation of William Sharp should at the same time be maintained. Moreover, each of the two natures had its own needs and desires, interests, and friends. The needs of each were not always harmonious one with the other but created a complex condition that led to a severe nervous collapse.

Here Elizabeth described her husband's condition in 1898, but the problem surfaced four years earlier when he first faced the effects on his psyche of his creation of a female persona.

To the extent Sharp identified Edith with the woman he experienced in himself, one might say one part of his nature had fallen in love with another — that, like Narcissus, he had fallen in love with himself. In November 1880, when he was twenty-five years old, he unabashedly declared his love to John Elder:

> Don't despise me when I say that in some things I am more a woman than a man — and when my heart is touched strongly I lavish more love upon the one who does so than I have perhaps any right to expect returned; and then I have so few friends that when I do find one I am ever jealous of his or her absence.

This sentence should be read in the broader historical context of Tennyson's relationship with Arthur Henry Hallam, Matthew Arnold's with Arthur Hugh Clough, and many similar relationships between men in nineteenth-century Britain. In this case, however, Sharp was seriously attempting to come to terms with his gender identity: sometimes he identified as a man, and other times as a woman. The norms of his society dictated he identify as one — that of a man — not both.

Despite his mental anguish, Sharp continued writing and negotiating with Stone and Kimball about the publication of his *Gypsy Christ* and Fiona's *Pharais* and *Sin-Eater*. Annoyed by the firm's delays in sending proofs and checks, he was unaware of the managerial and financial problems that soon led to its dissolution. In late December he wrote to Sir George Douglas, a family friend in Scotland who had identified Sharp as the author of the Fiona writings. When confronted, Sharp admitted the truth and asked Douglas to refrain from telling anyone.

He also spoke of Fiona as though she were a separate person. He included several lines about the role of Edith Rinder in the emergence of Fiona Macleod, and then crossed them out as "too personal." Sharp's characterization of Fiona in this letter as a "puzzling literary entity" is both apt and revealing of the limits to his understanding. In his response to Sharp's letter (*Memoir*, 253–234), Douglas obliged by speaking of Miss Macleod as a separate person, but said he detected her "mystical tendency" in the poems Sharp wrote in the early 1880s. He insightfully implied that Fiona had been there all along. In Sharp's letter to Douglas, there is no hint of the troubled state of mind expressed so forcefully in his letters to Gilchrist.

He told Douglas Elizabeth's doctor had ordered her to spend the three winter months in a warm climate, but he shared only with Gilchrist his worries about the strain this order placed on their finances. Far more worrying, however, was his state of mind. "Two human souls," he wrote in his December letter to Gilchrist, "struggle blindly against what seems a baffling doom." He and Edith were bound together in a hopeless love. In the story entitled "Daughter of the Sun" in *The Sin-Eater*, the narrator states: "We have all our dreams of impossible love. Somewhere, sometimes, the impossible happens. Then a man and a woman know that oblivious rapture of love […] the ecstasy of the life of dream paramount over the ordinary human gladness of the life of actuality." For Sharp, the impossible had happened, but the fact that he and Edith could not live together and build a family was tearing him apart. One cannot help but wonder if Elizabeth's decision to spend three months in Italy was motivated, at least in part, by her desire to remove herself from what seemed a hopeless situation and give her husband and Edith time and space to work matters out for themselves.

1895 saw the launching of the Geddes publishing firm in Edinburgh with Sharp responsible for its literary affairs; *The Evergreen*'s appearance from the Geddes firm; the publication in London of Fiona's *The Mountain Lovers* and Sharp's *Ecce Puella*; the publication in Edinburgh of Fiona's *The Sin-Eater*; and the publication in the United States of Sharp's *Vistas* and *The Gypsy Christ* and Fiona's *Pharais* and *The Sin-Eater*. It is not surprising that this level of productivity under two names, his extensive negotiations with publishers, his responsibilities with the Geddes firm, and the frustrations and fears in his personal life had, by the end of the year, taken a heavy toll on Sharp's physical and mental well-being.

Chapter Fourteen
January–June 1896

In December 1895, Elizabeth's doctor was worried about her health and recommended three months in a warm climate. In the first week of January, her husband accompanied her as far as Calais, and she went on to Florence, where she stayed for several weeks with her aunt. From there, she continued to Rome, accompanied by her friend Mona Caird. After returning to London, Sharp wrote several letters on January 6. One informed the publisher Elkin Mathews that Elizabeth was ill and unable to continue her editing of *Musa Catholica*, an anthology of Catholic poetry. Mathews was free "to arrange with Mrs. Meynell, or Mr. Lionel Johnson, or Mrs. Katherine Tynan Hinkson, or any other Catholic poet or writer, to undertake the volume." In letters to W. Scott Tebb, a physician, and Richard Garnett, Keeper of Printed Books at the British Museum, Sharp asked if he could borrow their editions of Matthew Arnold first two books. He wanted to collate their texts for an edition of Arnold's poetry Walter Scott would publish in the Spring. Short of money, Sharp was writing as many reviews as he could and becoming more active in Patrick Geddes and Colleagues. On January 12, that work took him to Edinburgh for four days. From there, he sent Geddes, who was teaching in Dundee, letters from several Belgian writers whose stories Edith Rinder had included in *The Massacre of the Innocents*. They thanked her for copies of the book and praised the quality of her translations. He also enclosed for Geddes a "digest of press opinions" of Fiona's *Sin-Eater*, some twelve from Scottish, Irish, and English papers and all favorable. He wanted to assure Geddes his work as Literary Editor was attracting attention and bode well for the firm.

At a social event in London on January 9, Grant and Nellie Allen invited Sharp to spend a few days with them in Surrey. The next day he wrote a note to Nellie Allen asking if Sunday, January 19 would be convenient. Still trying to assure her husband he was not Fiona, he added: "If I were Fiona Macleod, as Grant seems to 'hanker after believing,' I would call you *Deo-Grein*, for you are of the Sunbeam kind." After a "very fatiguing time in Edinburgh," Sharp returned to London and spent the weekend of January 18 with the Allens. In a thank you note he told Nellie Allen he "had good news from Lill [...] tho' she is still very far from well." The Allens were considering a move to London, where Grant would be better able to defend and enhance his reputation. Sharp recommended strongly against a move to the "fog and gloom" of the city. If the Allens could only sleep a little better and be brave, they would know their luck and "feel inclined to throw the cat across [their] shadow for mere delight." He asked for "a pat on the head for not being obviously down" during his visit, for he "arrived at a moment of great anxiety and profound heart-sinking, & one of the telegrams was not calculated to allay either." He remained worried and depressed about the personal tensions and financial problems he described to Murray Gilchrist in December, but he managed to surface from the "black gulf of January" during his weekend with the Allens.

On January 24 he wrote "a chronicle of woe" to Herbert Stone. In Edinburgh he found Miss Macleod ill and unable to work, which meant *The Washer of the Ford* would not be published by the Geddes and Stone firms until May. When he returned from Edinburgh to London, he found Edith Rinder in bed with a serious infection, also unable to work. She hoped to be up and about soon but could not have the manuscript of *The Shadow of Arvor* ready until mid-March. Sharp had proposed to Stone that he undertake United States publication of Ernest Rhys' *The Fiddler of Carne* and Elizabeth Sharp's *Lyra Celtica*, both in preparation under his direction at the Geddes firm. Everything except the anthology was delayed, including Sharp's romance, *Wives in Exile*, which Stone had accepted. He told Stone he was "far from well." Apart from "the trouble connected with Mrs. Sharp's break-down & going to Italy, & the heavy extra strain thrown on me, & having her work to do for her [...] I have been under a great strain of anxiety & suffering of another kind," about which he could only hint to Stone. Ever anxious to present an optimistic face to publishers, he closed by telling Stone the "strain" was passing. He hoped to complete *Wives in Exile* in February and receive the one-hundred pounds Stone had agreed to pay upon receiving the manuscript. Tapping all sources of money, he sent a statement to John Ross on January 28, which showed the firm owing him seventy-five pounds.

In the January 25 issue of the *Highland News*, John Macleay published the first of a two-part article on Scottish Highland writers. He praised Fiona Macleod's first three books and called on other Highlanders to follow her lead. It is to be hoped, he said, that "Miss Macleod is but the first in a movement which shall bring the Highlands into line with the great band of young Irish writers who are at present attracting so much attention in the literary world." In the next issue of the *Highland News* (February 1), under a section entitled "The Highlands in Literature: A Symposium," Macleay printed letters dated January 28 from William Sharp and Fiona Macleod. The Sharp letter refuted the notion that the Gaelic language was disappearing:

> In Scotland at this moment there are estimated to be 310,000 people who speak both Gaelic and English, and about 48,800 who speak Gaelic only. [...] Doubtless, it will be a further surprise for many to learn there are nearly three-and-a-half million persons who to-day use one or other of the Celtic dialects, and that of these it is estimated 1,156,730 speak no other than their native tongue. Numerically, it is not Wales that comes first, as commonly supposed, but Brittany, of whose population nearly a million and a-quarter speak the Armorican dialect, while 700,000 of these can speak no other language.

He called for the expansion of Gaelic — written and spoken — beyond Ireland, Wales, Brittany, and the western isles of Scotland. He also thought it would be "a good plan to establish in Inverness, with branches in Oban, Glasgow, Edinburgh, and London, a society to be called say, The Gaelic Literary Union."

The Fiona letter proclaimed "a new spirit of intellectual and spiritual life is to go forth; not indeed merely to gleam in fantastic beauty, as bewitching but as insubstantial as a rainbow, but to merge into the larger spirit of intense life which makes everywhere for beauty." For that to happen, Highlanders

> must be true to our old love of two of the noblest of human ideals — Beauty and Simplicity. We must not only love but revere Beauty in Nature, in Art, in Life, in the souls of men and women: and we must not only praise

> Simplicity, we must practice it again. It is better to live on porridge and have the spiritual birthright of our race, than to be bondagers to the palate and the belly, and live less in the spirit and more in the body: and it is better to be wrought by what is Beautiful than by social ambitions and the chronic pathetic effort to live at a tangent.

In the previous issue of *The Highland News*, Macleay assigned Fiona the leadership role in the Scottish contingent of the Celtic Literary Movement. In this letter, Fiona encouraged Macleay in his "timely crusade" and thanked him for his "much too generous words" about her place and work. Sharp proceeded to use the Fiona letter to set forth his expansive goals for the Celtic Revival. Its apocalyptic rhetoric echoes that of several Irish writers, chief among them W. B. Yeats and George Russell (Æ).

In Macleay, Sharp found a champion for his Celtic writings. He sent copies of *The Highland News* to Elizabeth in Italy and told Murray Gilchrist "the chief North of Scotland paper […] is printing two long articles devoted in a most eulogistic way to F. M. and her influence 'already so marked and so vital, so that we accept her as the leader of the Celtic Renaissance in Scotland.'" He "welcomed the opportunity of appearing in print in two guises for he believed that would help shield the true identity of Fiona" (*Memoir*, 258). Before long, Macleay began repeating rumors and engaging in speculation about the identity of Fiona. When forced to write letters of denial, Sharp became decidedly less enthusiastic about Macleay.

After a hectic month of January — trips to France and Edinburgh; physical and mental illness; dealing with the affairs of Patrick Geddes and Colleagues; trying to keep track of the progress of his publications with Stone and Kimball in Chicago; financial worries; and the need to keep writing essays, reviews, and stories as two different people — Sharp went north to the relaxing environment of the Pettycur Inn on the Firth of Forth for the first two weeks of February. Shortly after arriving, he wrote a brief note to tell Nellie Allen he was ill the previous week and sick of London. He canceled his plans to visit Le Gallienne in Surrey where he would also have called on the Allens. Instead, he came to "a remote inn on a little rocky promontory on the Fife coast" where he could hear "the lapping of the tide on the rocks below the windows, and a strange low casual moaning of the sea-wind far out on the water." He would be joined by a friend in a day or so, and he thought Nellie could guess who that friend was. She would guess Fiona Macleod which suggests the guest was Edith Rinder. Several days later, in a letter thanking Macleay for copies of the *Highland News* with his articles on Fiona and the letters from Sharp and Fiona, he assured him "Fiona Macleod is very tangible indeed." She and his sister Mary visited him the day before, and he had to pay for their luncheon. "One doesn't pay for phantoms," he asserted. Macleay had begun to have doubts. Sharp was certain Fiona would not allow her photograph to be published anywhere. She values her privacy, and "anyone who once saw her photograph would recognize her in a moment anywhere, for her beauty is of a very striking kind." In his effort to create Fiona's identity, he again conflated her with Edith Rinder.

Elizabeth had written to suggest he focus on his creative work rather than articles, reviews, and essays. He responded positively to her suggestion, promising to concentrate in February on "finishing *Wives in Exile* and *The Washer of the Ford*." His diary for the first ten days of the month shows he was still balancing the two kinds of work. On February 3, he wrote a lengthy "*Prologue*" to *The Washer of the Ford*; while on February 7, he dictated a 1750-word article for the *Glasgow Herald* on "Modern Romantic Art." On February 9, he wrote Fiona's "The Festival of the Birds;" while on February 10, he produced another article for the *Glasgow Herald* on "The Art of the Goldsmith." He also wrote a long Fiona letter to Herbert Stone about publishing and copyright problems. She would be late in completing *The Washer of the Ford* because she had been ill,

> though not so seriously as Mrs. Sharp, who is now in Italy or my dear friend Edith Rinder, whom you know, and from whom at Christmas I received a copy of "The Massacre of the Innocents," so delightfully got up — or as Mr. Sharp himself, who has had influenza, and is still in the doctor's hands, from that cause and a superadded dangerous chill.

All four — Elizabeth, Edith, Fiona, and Sharp — were ill, and their illnesses, though varying in seriousness, set them behind in their work.

Still sick and depressed when he returned to London in mid-February, Sharp continued working. On February 21 he told Elizabeth he had finished the introduction and notes to Matthew Arnold's *The Strayed Reveller, Empedocles on Etna, and Other Poems*, which was published by Walter Scott's Canterbury Series in the spring. Also on February 21,

Elizabeth's poetry anthology, *Lyra Celtica: An Anthology of Representative Celtic Poetry*, with her husband's lengthy introduction and extensive biographical and critical notes, was issued in Geddes's "Celtic Library" series. He also finished the remaining tales for Fiona's *Washer of the Ford*, which was published in Edinburgh by the Geddes firm on May 12, and by Stone and Kimball in New York on June 10.

In the *Memoir* (263), Elizabeth included a paragraph about *The Washer of the Ford* from an early April letter she received from her husband. It is one of Sharp's most insightful paragraphs about his own work:

> I know you will rejoice to hear that there can be no question that F. M.'s deepest and finest work is in this "*Washer of the Ford*" volume. As for the spiritual lesson that nature has taught me, and that has grown within me otherwise, I have given the finest utterance to it that I can. In a sense my inner life of the spirit is concentrated in the three pieces "The Moon-Child," "The Fisher of Men," and "The Last Supper." Than the last I shall never do anything better. Apart from this intense summer flame that has been burning within me so strangely and deeply of late — I think my most imaginative work will be found in the titular piece "The Washer of the Ford," which still, tho' written and revised some time ago, haunts me! and in that and the pagan and animistic "Annir Choille." We shall read those things in a gondola in Venice?

When one lays down *The Sin Eater* and takes up *The Washer of the Ford*, one moves into a new universe, subjectively and qualitatively. It is the same author writing about similar locales and championing the Celtic cause, but the chief concern is not star-crossed lovers swimming out in the ocean never to be seen again and the impossibility of achieving the perfect amorous relationship while alive. For three years, Sharp had been consumed by the barriers preventing his living a full life with the woman he had found too late, and this burden made its way into his writings. Following the psychological maelstrom that beset him in the fall of 1895, described in his letters to Murray Gilchrist, and after Elizabeth left for Italy in January, Sharp, with the assistance of Edith and Frank Rinder, began to work his way out of the conundrum, come to terms with the facts of his life, and move on to other concerns and other subjects.

The over-arching aim of *The Washer of the Ford* was to illuminate the transition between the Druidic religion that prevailed in the Western Isles and the new religion (Christianity) St. Columba brought to Iona and to show how many of the beliefs and rituals of the old religion were absorbed into the new. The title story is Sharp's rendition of the *bean-nighe*, or the washer at the ford — a woman who sits beside a stream washing blood from the linen and grave clothes of those who are about to die. All the stories are infused with the religion of nature or, as Sharp wrote to Elizabeth, the "spiritual lesson" nature had taught him. "Natural religion" was Sharp's recourse from Darwin's mid-century revelations. In stories like "The Fisher of Men" and "The Last Supper," he treats biblical stories as myths with universal applications and transposes them via dreams or visions into stories set in the Western Isles of Scotland, where they acquire new trappings. In "The Last Supper," for example, Ian Mor of the Hills recounts a dream he had as a young child. Separated from his mother and crying, he was approached by the Prince of Peace, who took him to a hut where a table was set for thirteen men. The Prince told the child he dies daily, and "ever ere I die the Twelve break bread with me." Asked by the child his name, the Prince replied "Iosa mac Dhe," Jesus son of God. The child then saw twelve men sitting at the table with "eyes of love upon Iosa." Each had three shuttles with which they wove phantoms that arose and left the room to enter the lives of men and women. The child liked most to look at the two men sitting on either side of Iosa. One was the Weaver of Joy and the other the Weaver of Love. The remaining men were Weavers of Death, Sleep, Youth, Passion, Laughter, Tears, Prayer, Rainbows, Hope, and, finally, Glory (who turned out to be Judas, and who the Prince named the Weaver of Fear). When Glory left the room, his shadow "entered into the minds and into the hearts of men and betrayed Iosa who was the Prince of Peace." After the child was led by Iosa from the room, he looks back and sees only the Weaver of Hope and the Weaver of Joy "singing amid a mist of rainbows and weaving a radiant glory that was dazzling as the sun." Finally, Ian Mor of the Hills recalls waking against his mother's heart, with her tears falling on him and her lips moving in prayer. It is a compelling story told with precision, restraint, and compassion.

As Fiona, Sharp dedicated the book to Catherine Ann Janvier. A lengthy "Prologue" addressed "To Kathia," begins:

> To you in your faraway home in Provence, I send these tales out of the remote North you love so well, and so well understand. The same blood

is in our veins, a deep current somewhere beneath the tide that sustains us. [...] You will find much that is familiar to you; for there is a reality, beneath the mere accident of novelty, which may be recognised in a moment as native to the secret life, that lives behind the brain and the wise nerves with their dim ancestral knowledge.

If this sounds like William Sharp writing about a woman fourteen years his senior with whom he has bonded, it is. In what follows, he says things to and about Kathia that would have been awkward had he not attributed them to a woman. In an article titled "Fiona Macleod and Her Creator William Sharp" published in the *North American Review* in 1907, Catherine Janvier recalled receiving a letter from Sharp in April 1896 saying he had dedicated *The Washer of the Ford* to her and commenting "if a book can have a soul that book has one." A copy of the book did not arrive in Provence until mid-May, but on the first of May she received "an especially printed and bound copy of the Prologue, and a letter stating it had been materially improved and strengthened and largely added to." Later, Sharp gave her his original draft of the Prologue. Comparing the draft with the printed version, she noted "the precise choice of word, the careful ordering of phrase and placing of paragraph," and was moved to write "Never was there a more careful writer than Fiona MacLeod, while of her creator this cannot always be said." Catherine Janvier valued the "Prologue" and her friendship with Sharp.

Elizabeth included two of the letters Sharp received about *The Washer of the Ford* (*Memoir*, 264–265). One dated June 22, 1896 is from Catherine's husband, Thomas Janvier, who agreed with his wife about the quality of the writing:

I am sensitive to word arrangement, and some of your work has made me rather disposed to swear at you for carelessness. [...] But these stories are as nearly perfect in finish, I think, as literary endeavor can make them. [...] Of all in the book, my strongest affection is for "The Last Supper." It seems to me to be the most purely beautiful, and the profoundest thing you have done. [...] I feel some strong new current must have come into your life; or that the normal current has been in some way obstructed or diverted. [...] The Pagan element is entirely subordinated to and controlled by the inner passions of the soul. In a word, you have lifted your work from the flesh-level to the soul-level.

Janvier also thought the stories in *The Washer of the Ford* were quite clearly written by a man. It was not only that the masculine Sharp, though nominally a woman, addressed his wife in the Prologue, but a great part of the book was "essentially masculine."

> If *The Washer of the Ford* were the first of Fiona's books, I am confident the sex of the author would not have passed unchallenged. [...] The "Seanachas," and "The Annir Choille," and the opening of "The Washer": not impossible for a woman to write, but unlikely. [...] The fighting stories seem to me to be pure man — though I suppose there are Highland women (like Scott's "Highland Widow") capable of their stern savagery. But on these alone, Fiona's sex scarcely could have been accepted unchallenged.

Sharp sometimes said he was more a woman than a man, while Janvier claimed Fiona, in *The Washer of the Ford*, was more a man than a woman. One's head spins at the reversal, but Janvier, like Sharp and many of his close friends, was reaching toward an understanding of human sexuality that became widely accepted in western culture only a century later.

In one story in the volume, "The Annir Choille," Janvier continued, Fiona showed her "double sex" more completely than in any other. The story has "a man's sense of decency and woman's sense of delicacy — and the love of both man and woman is in it to a very extraordinary degree." He concluded by moving beyond the masculine/feminine dichotomy:

> What seems to me plainest, in all the stories together, is not the trifle that they are by a man or by a woman but that they have come out of your spiritual soul. [...] With their freshness they have a curious primordial flavor — that comes, I suppose, from the deep roots and full essences of life which are their substance of soul. Being basic, elementary, they are independent of time, or even race.

Men have feminine traits, and women have masculine traits, and basic human traits are shared by men and women. Though he maintained the distinction between the two sexes, he had come to believe it was not unusual for an author to be both a man and a woman who loved both men and women.

The second letter Elizabeth included is from Frank Rinder:

> My dear Will, From my heart I thank you for the gift of this book. It adds to the sum of the precious, heaven-sent things in life. It will kindle the fire of hope, of aspiration and of high resolve in a thousand hearts. As one of those into whose life you have brought a more poignant craving for what is beautiful in word and action, I thank you for writing it. Your friend, Frank.

The letter is remarkable for the praise it conveys and its expression of gratitude for what Sharp has brought to his life. It also suggests an understanding had been reached between Sharp and the Rinders about the future of their relationship.

If during Elizabeth's absence in the first four months of 1896 Sharp overcame the anxiety and depression that arose from the frustrations of his relationship with Edith Rinder, another problem still plagued him. He was short of money. A letter to Geddes early in March reveals the pressure of his work, and the precariousness of his finances. He had come to rely heavily on an American woman, Lillian Rea, in his work for the Geddes firm. She was based in Edinburgh, but Sharp needed her in London. He was trying to finish Fiona's *Washer of the Ford* and her *Green Fire* for Archibald Constable, and his own *Wives in Exile* for Stone and Kimball. He was also managing the distribution of Elizabeth's *Lyra Celtica*, doing her reviewing work for the *Glasgow Herald*, and corresponding with Stone and Kimball regarding the publication of his books in America. Sharp's doctor ordered him to obtain the help of, or "give up at once" his connection to, Patrick Geddes and Colleagues, and do nothing besides his "own imperative work."

> I am under extreme pressure of work of my own — which has been so terribly interfered with by *Lyra Celtica*, E's work, & my own ill health & absence — and in order to meet E's heavy expenses abroad & my own here I must put my best foot forward. In order to do this work, I must have help for the correspondence etc. involved with printer, binder, & the question of distribution, reviews, etc. etc. of L/C, Rhys, etc. — besides, Evergreen correspondence, etc. In a word, it is not only W. S.-F. M. who wants an opportunity to get well & to do his own work, but the Manager of P.G. & Co. who wants a clerk or at least an office-boy!

"If I could have Lilian Rea's services clear for about three weeks (or at most a month)," I would be able "to put all straight, for myself and others, at the least possible expenditure of my rather too severely drawn upon reserve."

There was another reason he needed Lillian Rea in London. He had been given "medical injunctions not to be alone," and Geddes, Sharp wrote, didn't realize how "down" he had been: "I don't care to speak about it. I want to forget it. I want to be well. I want to work." Sharp did not want to slip back into depression, and he informed Geddes he did not feel well if left alone — "particularly in the evenings." There was no one at present who could suitably come to him, except Lillian Rea. Elizabeth was in Italy and Edith Rinder was ill. When alone it was "not only the terrible (& to me novel) depression I then experience, but the paralysis that comes upon my writing energy." The operative word is "depression." It was this condition he described to Murray Gilchrist at the close of 1895. It was this condition he could only hint at in the "chronicle of woe" he sent to Herbert Stone in January. And it was this condition that caused his wife and Edith Rinder to agree that one or the other or a suitable substitute must always be with him. To be sure, he could not work — and sustain necessary income — when alone, but a greater worry was the possibility of his depression leading to suicide.

It becomes ever clearer that Sharp was manic-depressive, a condition augmented and partly caused by the precarious condition of his heart and other physical ailments. In this early March letter to Geddes, he summarized his situation as follows:

> If I find myself unable to do my F. M. work — & it is imperative that for the next six weeks F. M.'s work should prevail — I must sever my connection with the firm. At all hazards, F. M. must not be "killed." *But this is sure*: she cannot live under present conditions. Leaving aside then the Doctor's & E's urgent requests as to my not being alone (partly because of my heart, & partly because of a passing mental strain of suffering and weariness) it comes to this: (1) I have help (& mind you an "outsider" is absolutely worthless to me just now, & probably at any time) & stay here, and do both F. M. & W. S. & P. G. & Co. — each in proportion and harmony: or else [(2)] I definitely sever my connection — at any rate pro: tem: — before all correspondence: & go away somewhere where F. M.'s funeral wd. not be so imminent, & W. S.'s nervous health could not be so drained. My plans all hang upon (1) how much I can get done before the end of March, (2) and at what mental cost. God need not send poets to hell: London is nearer, & worse to endure.

Geddes responded positively to this appeal and sent Lillian Rea to London. Not a frugal person himself, he also responded as far as he could to Sharp's need for money. At the same time, after receiving this letter and considering Sharp's collapse at the Celtic summer session the previous August, Geddes began to realize that, just as working for the firm was not good for Sharp, Sharp was not good for the firm.

By early April, Sharp's need for money reached crisis level. In another letter to Geddes, he said Stone and Kimball had not sent the money promised for his books, and what he was writing currently would bear no fruit until summer. It was essential that he receive one-hundred pounds from Geddes before the end of the month. He was due that much for managerial fees and book contracts. Also, he had one-hundred pounds invested in Geddes's Town and Gown Association. Failing money for his work, he would retrieve his investment. With one or the other, he would be able to borrow the rest to cover his expenses in London and those of a trip to Italy he planned for May. It was not only that he wanted to meet his wife and accompany her home, but he had to go abroad because he had come to the end of his tether: it was "no longer a case of an *advisable* complete rest & change — but of that being imperative." Shocked at his "startling loss in vitality," his doctor ordered him not to travel far at a time. Consequently, it would be at least a week or ten days after he left Paris before he met up with Elizabeth. "I am told to go by the Riviera & stay somewhere 3 or 4 days on the way, at least — This for the head." He would spend the next three weeks making "the cauldron boil," but that would produce money only after he and Elizabeth return.

Sharp was also trying to understand the lack of communication from Stone and Kimball. On May 4, he vented his frustration in a letter to Herbert Stone:

> If, when I wrote to you expostulatingly exactly a month ago today, I was then more than merely surprised and annoyed at the extraordinary delay in hearing from you concerning the matters about which you were to write to me, and in many weeks past-promised receipt of my MS. of "The Gypsy Christ" & Proofs — you may perhaps imagine how I regard the matter now: — now that you have had time to receive and answer that letter sent to you on April 4th.

He was "utterly at a loss to understand this most unbusinesslike and apparently grossly discourteous conduct." He understood Miss Macleod was being treated similarly. For the extraordinary discourtesy, he demanded "an immediate and absolutely explicit explanation." Unless Fiona heard from him before the end of May, she would take legal action in accord with her contract.

With Geddes's aid, he managed to put enough money together to leave for Italy in early May. After stopping briefly in Paris and then in

Provence to visit the Janviers, he went on to the Riviera, which turned out to be a profit center. In a May 6 note to Murray Gilchrist, he reported that he had made forty pounds on the gaming tables the previous night, almost half as much as he sought from Geddes. From the Riviera, he went on to Venice, where he joined Elizabeth on May 16. After a few days, they went north to the Italian lakes. On May 28, a card from Bellagio on Lake Como informed Gilchrist they would be in England on June fourth. Elizabeth would go directly to London, but he, having to break up his journey, would spend a few days — as it turned out a week — in Dover. After a week in the remote seaside hotel at St Margaret's Bay near Dover, he spent another week in London with Elizabeth. In mid-June he escaped to Edinburgh and stayed until the end of the month across the Forth at the Pettycur Inn.

During his absence, there had been no communications from Herbert Stone. As Fiona, Sharp wrote a letter to Stone dated June 9 in which he said he understood *The Washer of the Ford* had been published in the United States and requested his agreed upon twelve copies and advance of "£25 due on publication." Fiona was "strongly disinclined to publish further" with his firm unless she met with "more prompt courtesy and more satisfactory business relations." The next day — June 10 — Sharp wrote a letter to Hannibal Ingalls Kimball to say he received Kimball's letter dated May 22 which had followed him around Europe. In the letter Kimble said he had bought out Stone's interest in the firm and moved it to New York. He intended to go ahead with the publication of Sharp's *Wives in Exile* as soon as possible. Sharp replied he was willing to make allowances for the disruption, but he expected to receive 1) the £100 Stone promised on receipt of the manuscript of *Wives in Exile* and 2) proofs of the book to offer Archibald Constable for a possible British edition. Within a few months Kimball ran out of money and closed the business without publishing *Wives in Exile* or sending Sharp the promised money. Stone and Kimball was an excellent vehicle for introducing Fiona Macleod to the American public. With its dissolution, Sharp was left without an American publisher and a vital source of income.

In early June, Sharp received a letter from W. B. Yeats which must have buoyed his spirits, at least temporarily. In his lengthy introduction to Elizabeth's *Lyra Celtica*, Sharp singled out W. B. Yeats as "pre-eminently representative of the Celtic genius of today," and praised his poetry:

> He has grace of touch and distinction of form beyond any of the younger poets of Great Britain, and there is throughout his work a haunting sense of beauty. He is equally happy whether he deals with antique or with contemporary themes, and in almost every poem he has written there is that exquisite remoteness, that dream-like music, and that transporting charm which Matthew Arnold held to be one of the primary tests of poetry, and in particular, of Celtic poetry.

High praise indeed to assert that Yeats's poems met the high test of Matthew Arnold, whose poetry Sharp had edited for Walter Scott's Canterbury Poets Series. He went on to quote and praise passages of several Yeats's poems. In the early June letter, Yeats told Sharp he had read *Lyra Celtica* "with greatest delight." No book for a long time had given him so much pleasure. It was certain "to be very influential & to help forward a matter" that meant a good deal to him: "the mutual understanding & sympathy of the Scotch, Welsh, & Irish Celts." Yeats lavishly praised a Fiona Macleod poem in the anthology: "In the Scottish part Fiona Macleod's 'prayer of women' filled me with a new wonder it is more like an ancient than any other modern poem & should be immortal." These words (as transcribed in *Collected Letters II*) must have given Sharp enormous pleasure and encouraged him to continue putting Fiona forward as the leader of the Scottish contingent of the Celtic Revival. Yeats concluded by accepting Sharp's invitation for dinner as he had some "Celtic matters" to talk over with him, and that meeting may have occurred the following week. When Yeats first met Sharp in the late 1880s, he was not impressed, but *Lyra Celtica* changed his mind. Sharp was a comrade in the Celtic cause. Thus began a close relationship that developed quickly and lasted for several years.

In mid-June, while her husband was at the Pettycur Inn, Elizabeth wrote a poignant letter to thank Geddes for his friendly welcome home, to tell him she felt stronger and better than she had for years after spending the winter in Italy, and to express her deep concern about the state of her husband's health. When she met him in Venice, he "was so weak and feeble I was very alarmed. He had long fainting fits which at first I thought were heart attacks." Geddes had offered the Sharps his seaside cottage, but Elizabeth could not go north right away because of her work for the *Glasgow Herald*. And Will had to be near the Edinburgh office of Patrick Geddes and Colleagues. She asked Geddes not to allow her husband, when he saw him, "to discuss business matters for any length of time at one sitting. He needs all his time and strength to get well."

> Each spring, she told Geddes, her husband got worse, and she could see that "if he works at the present speed & with the present complications, he will not see many more springs. The dual work of F. M. and W. S. is a great drain on his strength, at the present moment too great a drain; & his state at present is unsatisfactory."

Ignoring Elizabeth's concern, Sharp continued his work with the Geddes firm. On June 22 and June 30, the day before he left the Pettycur Inn, he wrote long letters to Geddes about the firm's publications and his work as Literary Director. The positive notices of the Fiona Macleod publications and the praise from Yeats were surely factors in his burst of energy during the last two weeks of June.

Chapter Fifteen

July–December 1896

Less than three weeks after Sharp returned to London from Edinburgh in early July, he and Elizabeth left for a long summer holiday in the north. Before leaving, Sharp asked his friend Murray Gilchrist to join them for a few days on the Northumberland coast. In mid-letter, he changed course and asked if it would be convenient for him and Elizabeth to spend a few days with Gilchrist and his mother at Cartledge, her home in Derbyshire. Neither visit materialized. They spent the night of July 20 at the Station Hotel in York and went on to Bambrough, a coastal village in Northumberland. After a week of "sea bathing," as Elizabeth described it, they crossed to "the little Holy Isle of the Eastern Shores, Lindisfarne, Iona's sister." During the years he was writing as Fiona Macleod, Elizabeth noted, her husband "was usually in a highly wrought condition of restlessness, so that he could not long remain contentedly anywhere" (*Memoir*, 266). After two weeks on Lindisfarne, they went to Edinburgh, and, after a few days, left for Dunoon, a seaside resort town on the Firth of Clyde west of Glasgow, to be near Sharp's mother and sisters who were there on holiday.

In Bambrough, in late July, Sharp wrote a long letter to John Macleay of the *Highland News* in which he tried to dispel rumors he was Fiona.

> I confess I share to some degree in Miss Macleod's annoyance in this persistent disbelief in her personality to which you allude — as, indeed, to some extent in her resentment against the impertinence of those persons who try to intrude upon her privacy or seek to ascertain what for good reasons of her own she does not wish made public. [...] Did you not see the explicit statement I caused to be inserted in the "Glasgow Evening News," & elsewhere (because of one of these perverse misstatements) to the effect that "Miss Fiona Macleod is not Mr. William Sharp; Miss

Fiona Macleod is not Mrs. William Sharp; and that Miss Fiona Macleod is — Miss Fiona Macleod." Surely that ought to have settled the matter: for it is scarcely likely, I imagine, that I should put forth so explicit a statement were it not literally true. I trust, therefore, that you will do your best at any time to counteract all other misstatements.

Near the close of this letter, Sharp said he hoped to go north to Inverness in early October and, if so, he "might perhaps say something on, say, 'The Celtic Spirit.'" Macleay took that possibility seriously and informed Sharp he was working with others to find a venue for Sharp's lecture, which would be welcomed by many in Inverness. In Edinburgh, on his way to Dunoon, Sharp quashed that possibility in another letter to Macleay: his doctor had forbidden him from lecturing "on any condition whatever, this year at any rate." He thanked Macleay and others who would have given him a friendly welcome, but he would have to defer a lecture till the spring of 1897, or even the autumn, when Inverness would host the Mod, a large annual gathering of Celtic enthusiasts which moved and still moves from city to city in Scotland.

When Sharp arrived in Dunoon on August 15, he saw the August 14 issue of the *Highland News*, which contained a lead article by John Macleay titled "Mystery! Mystery! All in a Celtic Haze." Hoping to attract attention and increase readership and disregarding Sharp's assertions, Macleay described an article in the *Glasgow Evening News* that asserted Fiona Macleod was William Sharp. This unexpected development produced a flurry of letters from Sharp to Macleay during the next week — nearly one per day — in which he indignantly denied he was Fiona and tried, with expressions of camaraderie and implied threats of legal action, to dissuade Macleay from pursuing the issue further. Intended as an interlude of rest and relaxation, the visit with his family in Dunoon turned stressful as Macleay seemed intent on discovering and broadcasting the truth. Sharp summoned all his verbal skills in a hasty effort to preserve the fiction and thus prevent both embarrassment and erosion of income. He had received a letter from Fiona which expressed "deep resentment" against the writers of the *Glasgow Evening News*. She was especially insulted by the cruel & inexcusable phrase: "I hear again & again that she is a greater fraud than Macpherson of Ossianic fame." She would "ignore all unwarrantable interference, conjecture, & paragraphic impertinence." Macleay's initial praise of the Fiona writings and support for the cause of Scottish Celticism was a welcome stimulus for the sale of the Fiona books in Scotland. Now Macleay's pursuit of Fiona's identity, unless handled properly, threatened a public debacle. By the end of the week, Sharp had derailed Macleay's probes and decided the conflict had the beneficial effect of focusing attention on the Fiona publications.

On Saturday, August 22, the Sharps took his mother to Edinburgh, stayed for only two days, and left again on Monday with Sharp's sister Mary for Tigh-Na-Bruaich, west of Glasgow on the Kyles of Bute. From there, in early September, William and Elizabeth paid a brief visit to Inverness, where they met Macleay, and went on to see the Falls of Lora. In mid-September, Elizabeth returned to London and her art reviewing for the *Glasgow Herald*. William and his sister took the ferry across Loch Fyne to Tarbert where Edith and Frank Rinder were vacationing. Elizabeth reproduced (*Memoir*, 166–167) a section of a letter Sharp wrote to her from Tigh-Na-Bruaich, and sections of two letters he wrote from Tarbert, one on September 23 and one on September 26. His writing was going well, but he was not well enough to carry out his plan to go off by himself in the Hebrides.

Sharp found it easier to write as Fiona Macleod when Edith was nearby, and a burst of creativity in Tarbert produced many pseudonymous stories, poems, and letters. On September 23 he told Elizabeth he had written "the long-awaited 'Rune of the Passion of Women' the companion piece in a sense to the 'Chant of Women' in *Pharais*." On September 26 he said he had finished what had stirred him "so unspeakably, namely the third and concluding 'Rune of the Sorrow of Women.'" That rune, he said, had tired him "in the preliminary excitement and in the strange semi-conscious fever of composition." All three runes appeared in *From the Hills of Dream*, the volume of Fiona poems Patrick Geddes and Colleagues published in the fall of 1896, where he said he did not use the word "Rune" in "its ancient or exact significance, but rather as a suitable analogue for 'Chant.'" Occasionally, he continued, they have "something of the significance of the old Ru'n, meaning a mystery, or the more or less occult expression of mystery." All three runes express the travails of women suffering at the hands of men. Recalling Sharp's early poem called "Motherhood," they focus particularly on the burden of bearing children and then being cast aside for younger women. The runes deserve attention for the varied nuances of Sharp's critique of the repression of women. Equally interesting is his description of the composition process in his letter to Elizabeth:

> In a vague way not only you, Mona, Edith and others swam into my brain, but I have never so absolutely felt the woman-soul within me: it was as though in some subtle way the soul of Woman breathed into my brain — and I feel vaguely as if I had given partial expression at least to the inarticulate voice of a myriad women who suffer in one or other of the triple ways of sorrow.

The image of breath entering the brain aside, Sharp admitted his need to become a woman in order to write as Fiona. He projected himself into the minds of the three women he knew well (Elizabeth, Mona, and Edith), identified the qualities he shared with them, and coalesced those qualities into a fourth woman he introduced to the world as Fiona who was, herself, an advocate of women's rights. This is one of Sharp's several efforts to explain the emergence of Fiona Macleod.

A letter he wrote to W. B. Yeats from Tarbert in late September continued his lengthy and complicated relationship with the Irish poet. In an August 25 letter to Sharp from Tillyra Castle, Edward Martin's home in western Ireland, Yeats described a recent vision:

> I invoked one night the spirits of the moon & and saw between sleep & waking a beautiful woman firing an arrow among the stars. That night she appeared to [Arthur] Symons who is staying here, & so impressed him that he wrote a poem to her, the only one he ever wrote to a dream, calling her the fountain of all song or some such phrase. She was the symbolic Diana (*Collected Letters II*, 47–49).

Yeats described his archer vision in a letter to Fiona the previous day, but that letter has not surfaced. At Tarbert in late September Sharp composed Fiona's response, which began with an apology for "unforeseen circumstances" that prevented her from writing sooner. She claimed to have begun a letter describing her archer vision in a letter to Yeats before she received his of August 24:

> Alas, a long penciled note (partly apropos of your vision of the woman shooting arrows, and of the strange coincidence of something of the same kind on my own part) has long since been devoured by a too voracious or too trustful gull — for a sudden gust of wind blew the quarto-sheet from

off the deck of the small yacht wherein I and my dear friend and confrère of whom you know were sailing, off Skye.

Sharp's goal was to convince Yeats of Fiona's visionary compacity, and he made further use of the archer vision by tacking it to the end of a Fiona story he finished earlier called "The Last Fantasy of James Achanna."

Fig. 40 William Butler Yeats (1865–1939). Photograph by Alice Boughton (1903), Wikimedia, https://commons.wikimedia.org/wiki/File:Yeats_Boughton.jpg#/media/File:Yeats_Boughton.jpg, Public Domain.

The story begins in the authorial voice of Fiona, who says she will tell a story she heard from a fisherman named Coll McColl. In the story, a woman who is married falls in love with another man but finally chooses to remain with her husband. It would kill him to choose otherwise, and, not surprisingly, the body of the spurned lover is found several days later. Sharp attached two archer visions to this depressing story and changed its name to "The Archer." On the night the dead body was found, Coll McColl saw "a tall shadowy woman" draw "a great bow" and shoot an arrow through the air, which pierced the heart of a fawn. He believed "the fawn was the poor suffering heart of Love" (or the spurned lover) and the "Archer was the great Shadowy Archer that hunts among the stars." The next night, Coll saw a woman "shooting arrow after arrow against the stars."

Arthur Symons, who was staying with Yeats at Tillyra Castle, was editor of the *Savoy*. Encouraged by Yeats, he had asked Fiona to submit a story for publication. In his September 23 letter to Elizabeth, Sharp said he had "done the *Savoy* story 'The Archer' (about 4,500 words)," and shortly thereafter he sent it to the *Savoy*. He assumed correctly Symons would mention Fiona's archer story to Yeats when they returned to London in early October. As Sharp expected, Yeats decided Fiona could not have heard about his archer vision before she wrote "The Archer," and that buttressed his belief in Fiona's visionary powers.

In the last paragraph of Fiona's late September letter to Yeats, Sharp burnished her visionary powers by recounting yet another vision:

> I had a strange vision the other day, wherein I saw the figure of a gigantic woman sleeping on the green hills of Ireland. As I watched, the sun waned, and the dark came, and the stars began to fall. They fell one by one, and each fell into the woman — and lo, of a sudden, all was wan running water, and the drowned stars and the transmuted woman passed from my seeing. This was a waking dream, an open vision.

After claiming not to know what the vision means, Sharp, as Fiona, suggests a meaning:

> I realise that something of tremendous moment is being matured just now. We are on the verge of vitally important developments. And all the heart, all the brain, of the Celtic races shall be stirred. There is a shadow of mighty changes. Myself I believe that new spirits have been embodied among us. And some of the old have come back. We shall perish, you and I and all who fight under the "Lifting of the Sunbeam" — but we shall pioneer a wonderful marvelous new life for humanity.

Having provided evidence of Fiona's visionary powers, Sharp proceeded to place her firmly in line with Yeats's aspirations by having her forecast "a new life for humanity" arising from the spiritualist heart of the Celtic revival.

Sharp incorporated another stratagem in the late September Fiona letter. She was sailing off Skye with her "dear friend and confrère of whom you know." That good friend, William Sharp, was with her during "much sailing about and faring in remote places," and he has participated in the "work we are doing and putting together the volume of verse." The volume of verse was *From the Hills of Dream: Mountain Songs and Island Runes* which was published in November 1896. When Sharp composed the Fiona letter, he and his sister Mary were in Tarbert. Uniquely, two manuscripts of this letter survive: Sharp's draft is in the National Library of Scotland, and Mary's copy is among the Sharp letters in Yale's Beinecke Library. In the draft, Sharp first wrote "our" when referring to the volume of poetry, but he crossed this out and replaced it with "my [Fiona's] own book of verse." Mary copied "my own book of verse," but there is a caret after "my" in the copy and "(our)" is written above the line in Sharp's hand and then lightly crossed through. Since Mary was with him in Tarbert, he saw Mary's copy before it was posted and added the "our." The main purpose of the letter was to convince Yeats he had found in Fiona a fitting companion in the Celtic cause, but it also introduced Sharp as an enabler of the Fiona writings and raised the possibility of some collaboration. In substituting "our" for "my" and then crossing it out, Sharp wanted Yeats to recognize he was responsible for more than the "putting together" of the book of poems. Later, as we shall see, he told Yeats Fiona was a separate personality speaking through him. In reviewing *From the Hills of Dream* in the *Bookman* of December 1896, however, and in his January 1897 reply to Fiona's September letter, Yeats treated Fiona as a woman entirely separate from Sharp and entirely responsible for the poems in *From the Hills of Dream*. Events in January 1897, as we shall see, indicate Sharp succeeded in convincing Yeats he and Fiona were bound inextricably together.

Sharp left Tarbert on October 2 spent the night at the Caledonian Station Hotel in Glasgow and continued to Edinburgh and London. Before leaving Tarbert, he wrote an exuberant birthday letter to E. C. Stedman which announced his intention to come to New York in early November. The trip was necessary if he hoped to recover the money Stone and Kimball promised for works the firm had published and promised to publish. He asked Murray Gilchrist to accompany him to America, both for the sake of Gilchrist's health, and for "friendship's sake." Gilchrist declined the unexpected invitation, and Sharp wrote from London on October 18 to say he wanted to see Gilchrist when he returned in December. After three weeks in London, Sharp went to Southampton on October 22 and boarded the "Augusta Victoria" of the Hamburg American line which left for New York the next day. He arrived in New York on Saturday, October 31 and found "the streets thronged with over two million people" in the weekend before the fiercely contested Presidential election in which William McKinley, the Republican candidate, defeated the Democrat William Jennings Bryan. Since no business could be done until the following Wednesday, he crossed the Hudson River to spend a few days with Henry Mills Alden. On Sunday, he described the pre-election scene to his wife:

> New York itself is at fever heat. I have never seen such a sight as yesterday. The whole enormous city was a mass of flags and innumerable Republican and Democratic insignia. The whole business quarter made a gigantic parade that took 7 hours in its passage — and the businessmen alone amounted to over 100,000. Everyone — as indeed not only America but Great Britain and all Europe — is now looking eagerly for the final word on Tuesday night (*Memoir*, 174–175).

Following McKinley's victory, business resumed, and Sharp returned to the city where E. C. Stedman's son Arthur arranged for him to stay at the Century Club as a temporary member.

Before leaving London, Sharp threatened lawsuits against Stone and Kimball and armed himself with power of attorney from Fiona so he could act on her behalf as well as his own. One can but wonder who drew up a document that authorized one aspect of Sharp's personality to act for the other. During his week in the city, however, Kimball succeeded in charming Sharp into submission. He described Herbert Stone's loss of interest in the firm, the withdrawal of financial support by Stone's father, Kimball's acquisition of the firm's stock of bound volumes, sheets, and plates, and his move of the enterprise to New York, where he was determined to make a success of it. The firm remained in perilous condition, but Kimball managed a small check for Sharp to take back to Fiona. On Friday November 13 Sharp thanked Kimball for his hospitality and expressed his hope that Kimball would soon visit London where his kindnesses would be repaid. His faith in Kimball had been rekindled to the extent that, ever optimistic, he proposed a book for him to publish the following year. When Sharp boarded the Fürst Bismarck on Saturday November 14 for his return to London, he was satisfied with the results of his American trip.

During his absence, Archibald Constable and Co. in London, and Harpers and Brothers in New York published Fiona Macleod's *Green*

Fire: A Romance. The first half of the novel takes place in Celtic Brittany, and the second on a remote island near Skye in the Hebrides. The two parts are held together by the love of Alan de Kerival for his beautiful cousin Ynys de Kerival. When Ynys' father kills Alan's father in a duel, the two realize they cannot remain together in Brittany, and they escape to a Hebridean island where they both have family roots and where the second half of the romance, "The Herdsman," takes place. Years later, Sharp rewrote the Hebridean section and published it separately in Fiona Macleod's *The Dominion of Dreams*. Before he died in 1905, he asked Elizabeth to promise she would never reissue *Green Fire* in its entirety. In fulfilling that promise, she said Sharp thought only the second "Herdsman" section was produced by the Fiona impetus, while the first — "The Birds of Angus Ogue" — was the work of William Sharp.

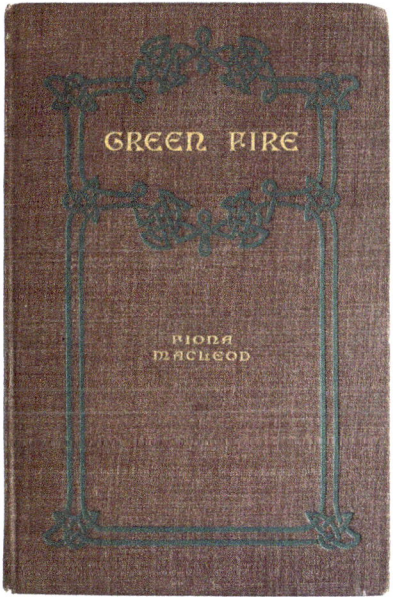

Fig. 41 The first American edition of Fiona MacLeod's *Green Fire. A Romance* (New York: Harper & Brothers, 1896). Photograph by William F. Halloran (2019).

While it is true that the first half of the romance sounds more like Sharp and the second, set in the Hebrides and focusing on a deeply held folk belief of the native Gaels, sounds more like Fiona, a closer look at the two sections reveals a deeper reason for suppressing the Brittany section of the romance. While studying in Paris, Alan dreamed of Ynys with "ever deepening joy and wonder." She was his "real life; he lived in her, for her, because of her." She was "his strength, his inspiration." When Alan returned to Brittany, Ynys saw him as "the fairest and comeliest of men," and when Alan turned

> the longing of his eyes upon Ynys he wondered if anywhere upon the green earth moved aught so sweet and winsome, if anywhere in the green world was another woman so beautiful in body, mind, and spirit as Ynys — Ynys the Dark, as the peasants call her, though Ynys of the dusky hair and hazel-green eyes would have been truer of her whom Alan de Kerival loved. […] there was but one woman in the world, but one Dream, and her name was Ynys.

Alan was a poet, and Ynys "was the living poem who inspired all that was best in life, all that was fervent in his brain." Beyond that, recalling Sharp's fascination with women, it was Ynys who gave Alan his "sense of womanhood, […] In her, he recognized the symbol as well as the individual." She was "his magic; the light of their love was upon everything: everywhere he found synonyms and analogues of Ynys. Deeply as he loved beauty, he had learned to love it far more keenly and understandingly, because of her." Recalling Sharp's early poem "Motherhood," Alan, through his love for her, "had come to understand the supreme hope of our human life in the mystery of motherhood." Ynys "was at once a child of nature, a beautiful pagan, a daughter of the sun; was at once this and a soul alive with the spiritual life. […] Indeed, the mysticism which was part of the spiritual inheritance came with her northern strain that was one of the deep bonds which united them."

In Alan, Ynys "had found all that her heart craved," but she had found that "nearly too late." While Alan was in Paris, Ynys was "formally betrothed" to Andrik, a friend of her childhood, and in Brittany a betrothal was "almost as binding as marriage." Ynys asserted that "betrothal or no betrothal" she belonged only to Alan: "How could she help the accident by which she had cared for Andrik before she loved Alan." She still cared for Andrik, but what she felt for him paled in comparison to her love of Alan. She was the flame that lit his torch. Even if forced to marry Andrik, she would still love only Alan. "Affection, the deepest affection, is one thing; the love of man and woman" as they knew it was "a thing apart."

The only way Alan and Ynys could escape the betrothal and build a life together was to board a ship and sail to the Hebrides, where their love prevailed, despite further complications arising from the case of mistaken identity that became the story of the Herdsman. Those complications caused Alan to slip in and out of depression, "a melancholy from which not even the love of Ynys would arouse him." To ward off that depression, he dwelt upon the "depth and passion" of his love for Ynys,

> upon the mystery and wonder of that coming life which was theirs and yet was not of them, itself already no more than an unrisen wave or an unbloomed flower, but yet as inevitable as they, but dowered with the light which is beyond where the mortal shadows end. Strange, this passion of love for what is not; strange this deep longing of the woman — the longing of the womb, the longing of the heart, the longing of the brain, the longing of the soul — for perpetuation of the life she shares in common with one whom she loves; strange this longing of the man, a longing deep-based in his nature as the love of life or the fear of death, for the gaining from the woman he loves this personal hostage against oblivion. For indeed something of this so commonplace, and yet so divine and mysterious tide of birth, which is forever at the flow upon this green world, is due to an instinctive fear of cessation. The perpetuation of life is the unconscious protest of humanity against the destiny of mortality.

When this abundance of overwrought prose is disentangled, we identify the belief often expressed by Sharp — that the love between a man and a woman reaches its zenith only in the production of children as "hostages against oblivion." When the complexities of the Herdsman section were cleared away, Alan and Ynys boarded a ship and returned to Brittany, where Alan assumed his rightful position as Lord of the Manor, and the two lovers would produce a child. Unlike the lovers in earlier Fiona Macleod productions, Alan and Ynys find a way to consummate their love and live happily ever after.

The love story of Alan and Ynys is the central theme of both sections of *Green Fire*. Again, and most directly, Sharp, disguised as Fiona, was attempting to reconcile his passionate love for Edith Rinder with his affectionate love for his wife. In a letter to John Macleay dated late July 1896, Sharp said the book was written "a year or so ago," which would be the late summer and fall of 1895, a period in which he was in agony over the conundrum. The title page carries the following lines below the author's name: "While still I may, I write for you | The love I lived, the dream I knew." The book is dedicated "To Esclarmoundo" followed by the Latin phrase from Ovid, "Nec since te nec tecum vivere possum," which translates: "Neither without nor with you is it possible to live." The book was written for and about Edith Rinder.

Esclarmonde of Foix was a prominent figure associated with Catharism in thirteenth-century southern France. She figured prominently as a heroine in several medieval epic poems, including one titled "Esclarmonde" by Bertran de Born. Esclarmonde was also the heroine of an opera by that name composed by Jules Massenet and first performed in Paris in 1889. Sharp's more immediate source for the name was a Provençal poem, *La Glorie d'Esclarmonde*, edited in both Italian and French by Marius Andre, and published by J. Roumanille in Avignon in 1893. Characteristic of the Provençal tradition, a beautiful woman inspired the poem. Sharp dedicated his novel, which recounts his own

Fig. 42 Poster advertising the premiere of *Esclarmonde*, libretto by Alfred Blau and Louis de Gramodt, music by Jules Massenet's, Paris, May 1889. August François-Marie Gorguet, *Esclarmonde* (1889), chromolithograph. Wikimedia, https://commons.wikimedia.org/wiki/File:Esclarmonde.jpg#/media/File:Esclarmonde.jpg,Public Domain.

love of a beautiful woman, to Edith Rinder — the object of his love disguised as the heroine of a Provençal love poem and further protected by his female pseudonym.

How can we be sure? There is another equally revealing Esclarmoundo. While Sharp was in America, Fiona Macleod's *From the Hills of Dream: Threnodies, Songs and Other Poems* was published. Sharp dedicated the book to Arthur Allhallows Geddes, the newborn son of Patrick and Ann Geddes who would become Sharp's godson. Arthur was born in 1895 on Halloween, the day Sharp arrived in New York and the anniversary of William and Elizabeth Sharp's marriage. The last section of the volume — a series of "prose rhythms" called "The Silence of Amor" (the silence of love) — is dedicated "To Esclarmoundo." Cast in the usual heightened Fiona prose, the dedication exposes the intensity of Sharp's love for Edith and his manic state of mind:

> There is one word never spoken in these estrays of passion and longing. But you, White Flower of these fugitive blossoms, know it: for the rustle of the wings of Amor awakens you at dawn, and in the last quietudes of the dark your heart is his dear haven of dreams.
>
> For, truly, that wandering voice, that twilight-whisper, that breath so dewy-sweet, that flame-wing'd lute player whom none sees but for a moment, in a rainbow-shimmer of joy, or a sudden lightening-flare of passion, this exquisite mystery we call Amor comes, to some rapt visionaries at least, not with a song upon the lips that all may hear, or with blithe viol of a public music, but as one wrought by ecstasy, dumbly eloquent with desire, ineffable, silent.
>
> For Amor is ofttimes a dreamer, and when he dreams it is through lovely analogies. He speaks not, he whispers not, who in the flight of the wild swan against the frosty stars, or the interlaceries of black branches against the moonlight, or the abrupt song of a bird in the green-gloom of the forest, hears the voice that is all Music for him, sees the face of his unattainable Desire. These things [the poems that follow in this section] are his silences, wherein his heart and his passion commune. And being his [Amor's], they are mine: to lay before you, Dear; as a worshipper, wrought to incommunicable pain, lays white flowers before the altar, which is his Sanctuary and the Ivory Gate of his Joy.

The author of this dedication identifies with Amor or Cupid, the male personification of love. Since he cannot express his love openly, the poems that follow are silences, but in them his heart and passion "commune." He lays them before the object of his desire just as a worshipper, hoping for salvation, lays flowers before an altar. He is "dumbly eloquent with desire" and "wrought by ecstasy," but also wrought to "incommunicable pain" by the need to be silent about the love and passion he shares with his beloved.

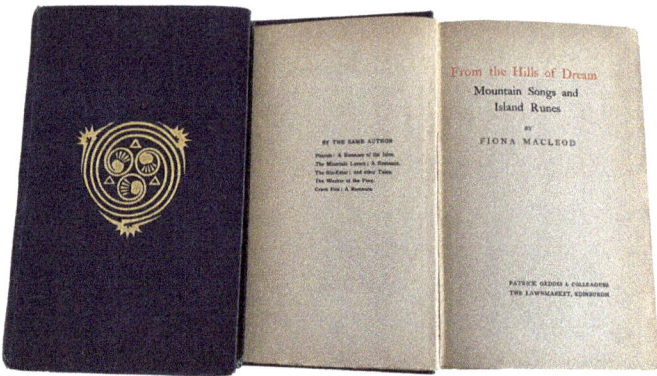

Fig. 43 Cover and title page of the first edition of Fiona Macleod's *From the Hills of Dream* (Edinburgh: Patrick Geddes & Colleagues, 1896). Photograph by William F. Halloran (2019).

All that is clear enough, but the author of the dedication and the "silences" that follow was nominally was Fiona, a woman. Was anyone paying close attention to what she was saying? Surely Elizabeth Sharp, a bright and well-educated woman fluent in French, knew what her husband was saying under the cover of Fiona. Edith and Frank Rinder surely knew. By the fall of 1896, when *Green Fire* and *From the Hills of Dream* were published, the two couples had reached an understanding that Sharp and Edith would continue their relationship discretely, but neither would leave the spouse they also loved. Sharp must have intended Fiona's readers to assume she was inventing a male persona, an interesting reversal to be sure. More likely, her readers simply ignored the matter. Sharp was able to disguise the identity of Fiona Macleod for a decade because a part of the reading public needed her. He recognized the need and set about fulfilling it. Descent into the Celtic past was an escape from the negative effects of rapid industrialization and the scientific discoveries challenging the tenets of Christianity. More to the point, Fiona's sentimentalizing of love and passion appealed mightily to many women and some men, one of whom claimed to have fallen in love with her.

In an October 18 letter, Sharp told Murray Gilchrist *Green Fire* was just published and called it "a strange book — some will say a mad book." Gilchrist knew its true authorship and would read it as a disguised account of Sharp's love of a beautiful woman. When the flame of his passion had cooled in 1899, Sharp repressed the book's account of the love affair. He dropped the first half of "Green Fire" and erased from the second, which he called "The Herdsman," any mention of the love affair. There is no Ynys, and there is no dedication to Esclarmoundo. At the start Alan Carmichael leaves Brittany and lands on a small island near Skye. He has "wed and lost" the unnamed daughter of the man who killed his father. His only companion is his "servant and old friend Ian M'Ian." Sharp also eliminated "The Silence of Amor" section from editions of *From the Hills of Dream* published after 1900. In 1902, Thomas Mosher of Portland Maine printed *The Silence of Amor | Prose Rhythms by Fiona Macleod* in a beautifully designed book on Van Gelder paper limited to 400 copies. Sharp wrote as Fiona a "Foreword" asserting his preference for calling the contents of the volume "prose rhythms" rather than "prose poems" and described the form as he conceived it. He also dropped the dedication to Esclarmoundo without replacing it but retained the dedicatory statement, slightly revised, which he prefaced with the following quotation from Fiona Macleod's *The Distant Country*: "Love is more great than we conceive, and Death is the keeper of unknown redemptions." In this edition the passion of the first is less intense. It is still Sharp disguised as Fiona laying the prose rhythms before his "Dear." In 1896 he laid them "as a worshiper, wrought to incommunicable pain, lays white flowers before the alter, which is his Sanctuary and the Ivory Gate of his Joy." In the 1902 iteration he does so calmly "as a wind, that has lifted the blossoms of a secret orchard, stoops, and lays milk-white drift and honeyed odors at the open window of one who within sleeps and dreams."

Despite the perceived success of Sharp's New York trip and the publication of two Fiona Macleod books in his absence, matters soon took a turn for the worse. He fell ill again, this time with influenza, and needed money to recuperate in a warmer climate. Herbert Stone, acting for the firm, had promised Sharp £300 for a yachting romance called *Wives in Exile* (£100 on the submission of the manuscript and £200 upon publication). Kimball claimed ignorance of this commitment, and he could not afford to honor it. The book was submitted for copyright under the Stone and Kimball imprint in September 1896, but not issued. When they met in New York, Kimball agreed to relinquish all rights to the book, whereupon Sharp arranged for a young Boston publishing firm, Lamson, Wolffe & Company, to buy the loose sheets and plates, and they published it in January 1897 with a new title page. The Boston firm gave Sharp a promissory note due in January for £150, which he carried home only to discover it was not negotiable in Britain. He had hoped to borrow against it but was forced to send it to Stedman and ask him to advance the money until the note could be redeemed in January. While in New York, Sharp also met Melville Stone, Herbert's father, in an effort to recover the remaining £150 due for *Wives in Exile*. The elder Stone agreed his son was morally, if not legally, obliged to pay Sharp some of the missing £150. He suggested E. C. Stedman arbitrate the matter, and Sharp accepted his suggestion. In his December 5 letter to Stedman, Sharp presented the history of the affair in a manner designed to convince Stedman, as arbiter, to award him the compensation he thought due from the Stone family.

After recovering from influenza, Sharp began to exhibit in early December "disquieting symptoms of nervous collapse" which were brought on, Elizabeth said, by "the prolonged strain of the heavy dual work added to by an eager experimentation with certain psychic phenomena with which he had long been familiar but wished further to investigate, efforts in which at times he and Mr. W. B. Yeats collaborated" (*Memoir*, 282). Sharp had engaged in various attempts to communicate with the spirit world, augmented by drugs, while living at Phenice Croft in 1891–1892. That was one reason Elizabeth disliked the place and insisted they give it up and return to the city. After returning from America, he resumed those investigations. Suffering both physically and mentally in late November and early December, he needed a respite from damp and depressing London.

Stedman's efforts to recover money from the Stone family had not produced results, but he loaned Sharp — against Lamson's promissory note — enough money to leave England. In a letter of December 16, Sharp thanked him profusely for his generosity and said he was leaving the next day for the South of France. He stopped for a few days in Tarascon and then went on to St. Remy where the Janviers were living.

From there he wrote to Elizabeth: St. Remy, with its "hill-air and beauty," was a most welcome change from Tarascon. He realized he "must give up everything to getting back" his "old buoyancy and nervous strength. [...] Prolonged rest and open air were paramount needs." Catherine Janvier recalled Sharp's visit in a 1907 *North American Review* article:

> In December of 1896 — preceded by the announcement that he was old and gray-haired — William Sharp superb as a young Viking, burst in on us in quiet Saint-Remy. After the excitement of the first joyous meeting was over, it was plain to see that this magnificent presence gave false promise. He was exhausted by the long strain of double work and had been ordered away from the smoke and fog of London to the sunshine of the Riviera, there to seek the rest he nowhere had found. While with us strange moods possessed him; and, perhaps, because of these strange things happened. At times it was as though he struggled against an evil influence; was forcing back a dark tide ever threatening to overwhelm his soul. Warring presences were about him, he thought; and he believed that these must be conquered, even at the risk of life. The culminating struggle came, and through one winter night my husband watched over him as he battled against unseen but not unfelt influence. The fight was won, the dark tide stemmed, but at great cost of vitality, his victory leaving him faint and exhausted. "Nevermore," he told us, "would he tamper with certain forces, for such tampering might mean destruction."

Having passed through the dark night, according to Mrs. Janvier, Sharp recovered from his severe psychic episode and enjoyed the Christmas celebrations in the village. After Christmas he left for the warmer Riviera where, according to Mrs. Janvier, "he wandered restlessly from place to place" before returning to the Janviers in St. Remy shortly after the start of 1897. As it turned out, the New Year brought another entanglement that, despite his "Nevermore," involved his return to spiritualist experiments.

Chapter Sixteen

1897

On New Year's Day, Sharp wrote to the Janviers from Saint-Maxime to say he felt lonely and "craved help and companionship in a way foreign to his self-sufficing nature." After sending the Janviers several telegrams, he reappeared in St. Remy, saying "he wished to be looked after and to be made much of." In her *North American Review* article, Catherine Janvier recalled,

> During this second stay with us, he was utterly unlike the mystery-surrounded, dual-natured dreamer of his previous visit: he was William Sharp, and William Sharp in his blithest mood. Though Fiona might smile, it is impossible to imagine her as bursting into a hearty laugh; while her creator could be the gayest of companions, full of fun and frolic, displaying at times a Pucklike impishness worthy of a twelve-year-old boy. He left our town in this joyous trim, waving his blue beret from the carriage window until the train was out of sight.

Initially Sharp planned to spend the entire month of January in southern France, but the warm weather and the hospitality of the Janviers worked their magic. In late December, Yeats wrote a lengthy letter to Fiona Macleod which Mary received in Edinburgh and forwarded to St. Remy where it awaited Sharp's return. It described his intent to incorporate occult materials in his writings and hinted at plans to create a Celtic Mystical Order. He was working on a play, the Shadowy Waters, which was "more magical and mystical" than anything he had written. Mr. Sharp had heard some of it "in its first very monotonous form." He hoped Sharp would come to Paris before mid-January on his way back to England, for he had "much to talk over with him." This invitation contributed to Sharp's "joyous trim" as he boarded a train to Paris on January 4 or 5.

The references to Sharp in Yeats' letter indicate he considered Fiona a separate person closely associated with Sharp. Since they met in 1887, the two men moved in some of the same London circles, and they may have experimented together in drug-induced (hashish and mescal) spiritualist experiments. They were not close friends, but Yeats interest in Sharp quickened with the advent of Fiona Macleod. Ten years younger than Sharp, he was attracting notice for the quality of his poetry and for his efforts to promote Celticism in Ireland and beyond. Having invented Fiona and positioned himself as her friend or relative, Sharp hoped to be drawn more closely into the Celtic Revival that was centered in Ireland. A conversation with Yeats in Paris might offer the entrée he sought.

When he arrived in Paris, Sharp discovered Yeats was offering a closer relationship than anticipated. The ruse he perpetrated the previous August involving the Archer vision assured Yeats of Fiona's visionary powers. Now he wanted to know if Sharp had similar powers. Years later, he recalled Sharp visiting him in his hotel in the Boulevard Raspail:

> When he stood up to go, he said, "What is that?" pointing to a geometrical form painted upon a little piece of cardboard that lay upon my windowsill. And then before I could answer, he looked out of the window, saying, "There is a funeral passing." I said, "That is curious, as the Death symbol is painted on the card." I did not look, but I am sure there was no funeral. A few days later he came back and said, "I have been very ill; you must never allow me to see that symbol again" (*Autobiographies*, 339–340).

Although Sharp may have known the geometrical form was a death symbol, Yeats assumed he did not and that reassured him of Sharp's powers of clairvoyance. In his *Autobiographies* Yeats recounted an astonishing demonstration of Sharp's effort to prove his psychic abilities. He told Yeats a phantom woman visited his hotel suite. Appearing and disappearing, she finally escaped down a flight of stairs into the street. Sharp followed her around many corners constantly seeing and losing her, until he came to the Seine. She stood at an opening in the wall looking down into the river, and then she vanished. Yeats recalled Sharp's words:

> I cannot tell why, but I went to the opening in the wall and stood there, just as she had stood, taking just the same attitude. Then I thought I was

in Scotland, and that I heard a sheep-bell. After that I must have lost consciousness, for I knew nothing till I found myself lying on my back, dripping wet, and people standing all around. I had thrown myself into the Seine.

Yeats continued:

I did not believe him, and not because I thought the story impossible, for I knew he had a susceptibility beyond any one I had ever known to symbolic or telepathic influence, but because he never told anything that was true; the facts of life disturbed him and were forgotten.

When Yeats recounted this incident, he had succumbed to the general opinion that Sharp was a hopeless prevaricator, an oddity who pretended for years to be a woman. His opinion of Sharp was quite different when he heard the story in 1897.

Having proved his visionary powers, Sharp was elated to receive Yeats's invitation to join him and Maud Gonne in evoking visions to obtain the talismans and rituals of a Celtic Mystical Order that would "unite the radical truths of Christianity to those of a more ancient world" and gradually transform first Ireland and then the world. The Order's design, as planned by Yeats, resembled that of the Order of the Golden Dawn. He was an active and Sharp a less active member of that Order's London branch. Yeats' Order would be centered not in London, but in the abandoned Castle of the Rock in Loch Key in western Ireland. Young men and women would be invited to the castle to learn the order's rites and then go out into the world to spread the word and recruit others. Members would also use the castle for "occasional retirement from the world."

To begin this difficult project, Yeats needed "mystical rites — a ritual system of evocation and meditation — to reunite the perceptions of the spirit of the divine, with natural beauty." He was deeply in love with Maud Gonne and thought she exceeded him in "seership." She shared his ideas, and he hoped to "entirely win her" for himself as they engaged in the evocations together.

I could therefore use her clairvoyance to produce forms that would arise from both minds, though mainly seen by one, and escape therefore from what is merely personal. There would be, as it were, a spiritual birth from the soul of a man and a woman. I knew the incomprehensible life could select from our memories and, I believed, from the memory of the

> race itself; could realize of ourselves, beyond personal predilection, all it required of symbol and of myth. I believed we were about to attain a revelation.

Sharp was to engage in evoking visions only in the company of and in partnership with Fiona Macleod. Since Sharp and Fiona had clairvoyant powers and were in love, Yeats thought their relationship paralleled his with Maud Gonne. The two couples would augment each other's visionary capacities in the secret and laborious work of finding the symbols and rituals of the Order. [The quotations in this and the preceding paragraphs are from the first draft of Yeats's autobiography in *Memoirs*, 123–125.]

During the ten days he spent in Paris with Yeats and his friends — Maud Gonne, and Moina and Macgregor Mathers who were busy setting up a Paris branch of the Order of the Golden Dawn — Sharp was in a heightened state of mind. The invitation to join the inner sanctum of a revolutionary movement whose ultimate purpose was to prepare the world for the apocalypse produced a state of euphoria. There was one missing part; he had to enlist Fiona Macleod in the undertaking. He left Paris on or about January 15, stopped briefly in London, and went on to Edinburgh where he crossed the Forth to the Pettycur Inn. He told Stedman in a January 25 letter he was "staying with a friend, F. M." at a "remote place among the hills." He had led Stedman to believe he was having an affair with Fiona, but it was Edith Rinder who was with him at the Pettycur Inn. It was she he had to convince to play the role of Fiona in the spiritualist work. It was she who must play Maud Gonne to his W. B. Yeats. Edith must have been astonished by and skeptical of Sharp's proposal, but he succeeded in convincing her to play at least a passive role. By 1897, their original passionate commitment had begun to fade. The search for talismans and rituals gave their relationship a new and serious purpose. Sharp continued to write as Fiona for the rest of his life, but his experience in Paris in January 1897 was a critical turning point. The occult and its psychic experiments influenced the prose he wrote as Fiona during the last three years of the century and published in *The Dominion of Dreams* (1899) and *The Divine Adventure* (1900). He turned to philosophic, symbolic, and ritualistic stories and essays, and wrote fewer about the people who lived amid tragedies and in close touch with spirits and with ancient myths in Gaelic Scotland. Though Edith may not have been enthusiastic about the psychic investigations, she was a significant enabler of Sharp's participation in the Celtic Mystical project and the concurrent shift of emphasis in his Fiona writings.

In a January 25 letter, Sharp thanked for a check which was about half what he was due from E. R. Lamson for *Wives in Exile*. He deposited it right away, to the relief of his "wife and his bank manager," since his "worldly fortune" had sunk to "about £3." After signing the typed letter, Sharp added a handwritten note:

> The time on the Riviera did me a lot of good and still more this unexpected and wild flight straight from France to the Scottish hills. And now I am going back to settle down to hard work till the end of July — and at the same time manage to give both my wife and myself a good time — and be a good boy — and always endorse my cheques — and love you and Mrs. Stedman and Miss McKinney — and "Generally" be your loving and grateful W. S.

This handwritten note was intended to inform Stedman he had spent the last couple of weeks in "a remote place among the Scottish hills" with the woman he loved. He did not want to share that information with Lillian Rea who typed the letter. .

Financial problems continued to plague Sharp through the winter and spring, aggravating his physical and mental illnesses. He wrote as Fiona to ask the Geddes firm's accountant for an advance of twenty-five pounds against the royalties of a three-volume edition of her short stories that would be published in March. If twenty-five pounds was too much, she hoped for at least ten. Another Fiona letter went to Hannibal Kimball in New York asking if he would like to undertake the American publication of the three-volume edition or, if not, a single volume edition of her stories. In mid-February, he asked Murray Gilchrist whether he would like to contribute a serial romance to *My Social World*, a periodical Frank Rinder, his "intimate friend," was editing. He also offered Gilchrist a glimpse of his current state of mind:

> Alas, my dear boy, I can tell you neither that I am well nor happy. I am content, at present, to tell you that I am not actively unhappy, and that I am, I hope, slowly gaining ground physically. I have not done a stroke of original work for weeks past but am eagerly hoping to be able to begin again soon.

In a late February letter, he invited Richard Le Gallienne to be his guest at an Omar Khayyam Banquet at Frascati's, an elegant and expensive restaurant on Oxford Street. Shortage of money seemed not to limit his expenditures. Another Fiona letter went to Kimball, who was considering a trip to England and hoped to meet Fiona. She informed him it would be "unpractical" for her to see him because she was "going to Italy immediately, and when I return in the late spring or early summer it will be direct to Glasgow or rather Greenock, to sail thence to my relatives in the Hebrides."

Fig. 44 Fiona Macleod stories reissued in paperbacks by Patrick Geddes and Colleagues in 1896. Photograph by William F. Halloran (2019).

Though Sharp told Stedman he was going to work hard until July, give his wife a good time, and be a "good boy," he wrote again in early March to thank him for a twenty-pound advance from Lamson and added a personal note:

> Pour moi, my brief spell of reform (three weeks and three days) convinced me that systematic reform would never suit me in mind or body. I have very happily relapsed into my Pagan ship, and the Sunbeam flies again at the Peak. My mate in this delectable craft smiled at my attempt, and now laughs joyously that I am myself once again.

He asked Stedman to destroy a postscript that identified his mate: "Two days ago I was by the sea, with F. M. In mind and body, I am ten years younger, with that joy and delight." The improvement in his mental and physical state did not last long. A March 10 letter informed Catherine Janvier he "had an unpleasant mental and physical set-back the last three days." He hoped he was "steadily gaining ground," but he had not been able to regain the "health and spirits" he was in during his visit to St. Remy, though even then he was "far more worn in mind and body" than she had guessed.

In mid March, Sharp thanked his friend, the popular novelist Coulson Kernahan for generously promising "to do what he could for the Reissue of Miss Macleod's shorter tales." He would be "personally indebted" for any helpful word Kernahan might say "for the reasons I hinted to you." We can only wonder what Sharp had hinted. If it was not Sharp's authorship of the Fiona tales, it must have been his close relationship with her. Sharp was sorry to hear the painter Harvey Moore had been ill, but it was kind of Kernahan to go sit with him. He asked Kernahan to thank his wife for her kind letter thanking him for a copy of *Vistas*. Elizabeth was "hors-de-combat" as she had been in bed for several days and was likely to be there for several more days "with an attack of rheumatism. Next and surprisingly, Sharp casually mentioned a "conflagration." The other night, just after Murray Gilchrist left him, his study caught fire, and it was with difficulty that the conflagration was extinguished. Fortunately, he continued, no harm was done to his books or pictures, and the insurance would cover the rest. A house fire, no doubt caused by a misplaced cigarette, and Elizabeth sick in bed unable to work must have been upsetting, but Sharp was only "distracted," and he continued asking friends to help boost the sale of the Fiona stories. That Murray Gilchrist made it to London and visited him must have warmed his heart. He was not producing much writing, but he was quick to escape into Yeats-inspired millennialism.

Energized by the beginning of Spring, he proclaimed to Catherine Janvier on March 22:

> It is the season of sap, of the young life, of green fire. Heart-pulses are throbbing to the full: brains are effervescing under the strong ferment of the wine of life: the spiral flames of the spirit and the red flower of the flesh are fanned and consumed and re-created and fanned anew every hour of every day… . This is going to be a strange year in many ways: a year of spiritual flames moving to and fro, of wild vicissitudes for many souls and for the forces that move through the minds of men. The West will redden in a new light — the "west" of the forlorn peoples who

Fig. 45 Coulson Kernahan (1853–1943). Photography by Elliot and Fry (1903). Public Domain. Wikipedia, https://commons.wikimedia.org/wiki/File: Coulson_Kernahan_by_Elliott_%26_Fry.jpg

congregate among our isles in Ireland — "the West" of the dispeopled mind. The common Soul is open — one can see certain shadows and lights as though in a mirror.

Printing this passage in the *Memoir* (284), Elizabeth noted "The letter ends abruptly." Its rhetoric implies a manic state of mind, and the "red new light in the West" ties it to his participation in the work of Yeats' Order. We recall Elizabeth writing: "During the most active years of the Fiona Macleod writings, the author was usually in a highly wrought condition of mental and emotional tension," and, later: "The prolonged strain of the heavy dual work added to by eager experimentation with certain psychic phenomena with which he had long been familiar but wished further to investigate, efforts in which at times he and Mr. W. B. Yeats collaborated — began to tell heavily on him and to produce very disquieting symptoms of nervous collapse" (*Memoir* 266, 282). Periodic escapes with Edith enabled him to engage in psychic experiments in search of Yeats' rituals, but they evoked manic episodes that often collapsed into depressions.

The Irish writer Katharine Tynan Hinkson, after favorably noticing Fiona's *From the Hills of Dream* in the *Speaker*, wrote to ask for more information about her personal life for an article she proposed to write for the *English Illustrated Magazine*. Sharp composed in late March a long Fiona reply designed to project her as the preeminent female contributor to the Celtic revival in Scotland just as Hinkson was the preeminent female Celtic revivalist in Ireland. He responded first to Hinkson's mention of the questions about Fiona's identity.

> Oh yes, dear Mrs. Hinkson, I am now well aware of much of the mystery that has grown up about my unfortunate self. I have even heard that Fleet Street journalist rumor to which you allude — with the addition that the said unhappy scribe was bald and old and addicted to drink. Heaven knows who and what I am according to some wiseacres! A recent cutting said I was Irish, a Mr. Chas. O'Connor, whom I know not. A friend of a friend told that friend that I was Miss Nora Hopper and Mr. Yeats in union — at which I felt flattered but amused. For some time, a year or so ago, there was a rumor that "Fiona Macleod" was my good friend and relative, William Sharp. Then, when this was disproved, I was said to be Mrs. Sharp. Latterly I became the daughter of the late Dr. Norman Macleod [a distinguished minister of the Scottish Church]. The latest is that I am Miss Maud Gonne — which the paragraphist "knows as a fact." Do you know her? She is Irish, and lives in Paris, and is, I hear, very beautiful — so I prefer to be Miss Gonne rather than the Fleet Street journalist!

Writing as Fiona to another woman, Sharp projected his most feminine voice and employed irony to counter the "wiseacres." He also stressed Fiona's need for privacy: "I do most urgently wish not to have my privacy made public, partly because I am so "built" and partly for other reasons. Next, he revealed just a bit:

> But this much I will confide to you, and gladly: I am *not* an unmarried girl, as commonly supposed, but am married. The name I write under is my maiden name. Perhaps I have suffered, as well as known much joy, in my brief mature life: but what then — all women whose heart is in their brain must inevitably suffer. And so, you will, I know, at once excuse me and forgive my inability to give you any material particulars. This past week I have had no fewer than four editorial applications for my photograph for reproduction — but now, as ever, I have had to decline. Two friends in London have my photograph, and perhaps you may see it someday: but now I do not even let friends have a photograph, since one allowed someone to take a sketch of it for an American paper. I can't

well explain why I am so exigent. I must leave you to divine from what I have told you.

And a bit more: "I don't object to its being known that I come of an old Catholic family, that I am a Macleod, that I was born in the southern Hebrides, and that my heart still lies where the cradle rocked. If, perchance, I should be in London this autumn or early winter — on my way to the Riviera (for I am not strong) — I hope to be able to make your acquaintance in person." Several friends had drawn Fiona's attention to Mrs. Hinkson, among them Mr. William Sharp who "is a great admirer of your writings, both in prose and verse." Carefully structured, the letter is one of Sharp's most revealing and extensive efforts to construct the personality of his invention.

The possibility of a London meeting suggests Sharp thought he could convince Edith to impersonate Fiona. Two days later he broached the idea in a Fiona letter to George Meredith: "There is a chance I may be south this Spring or early Summer. If so, I look with keen pleasure to the often-anticipated visit to you." Sharp succeeded in convincing Edith to play the role in a visit to Meredith at Box Hill on June 10, 1897. Meredith described her in a letter to Alice Meynell dated June 13 as "a handsome woman, who would not give me her eyes for awhile." In a letter to Maud Gonne dated January 14, 1907, Yeats recalled Meredith saying, "she was the most beautiful woman he ever saw." It is not surprising Edith, a woman of great beauty, appeared shy and almost voiceless. Neither is it surprising this was the only time she agreed to meet one of Sharp's friends as Fiona. The ruse was successful because Meredith lived in relative isolation in Surrey, far removed from London literary society where he might have come upon Edith.

In late March, Sharp sent his latest "phiz" to Louise Chandler Moulton for her birthday, told her he was leaving England for three weeks or so, and he hoped to find her in London when he returned. He sent the same message to Stanley Little. If he planned to go abroad, he changed plans and opted for a hotel in St. Margaret's Bay, near Dover. Without the pressures of life in London and, for part of the time at least, with Edith Rinder, he hoped to regenerate his writing as Fiona and renew efforts to find talismans and rituals for Yeats. In the *Memoir*, Elizabeth recalled: "Towards the end of April I went to Paris to write upon the two 'Salons,' and my husband, still very unwell, went to St. Margaret's Bay" (*Memoir*,

Fig. 46 An etching of William Sharp, dated about 1897, by William Strang (1859–1921). Printed by David Strang (1887–1967), the artist's son. Photograph by William F. Halloran of his copy (2019).

285). Since the "Old Salon" opened on April 14 and the "New Salon" on April 20, Elizabeth must have been in Paris for the "Press Preview" of the "Old Salon" on April 13.

On Sunday April 18, Sharp wrote to Elizabeth from St. Margaret's Bay. He was "on the shore by the sea and in the sunshine," and he felt very near to her in spirit, as he always did when he was "reading, hearing, seeing any beautiful thing." Filled with "a passion of dream and work," he felt he would soon be able to write again. "More and more absolutely," he wrote, W. S. and F. M. were "becoming two persons — often married in mind and one nature, but often absolutely distinct." Omitting passages of the letter, Elizabeth added a final sentence: "Friendship, deepening into serene and beautiful flame, is one of the most ennobling and lovely influences the world has." She wanted to imply the sentence referred to her, but Sharp was using the flame metaphor to describe his relationship with Edith. Here it increases the likelihood she was with him in St. Margaret's Bay. How neatly it coalesces with the splitting of selves since she was often the embodiment of the second person. The letter is signed "Wilfion," a name Elizabeth described in the *Memoir*:

> In surveying the dual life as a whole I have seen how, from the early partially realized twin-ship, "W. S." was the first to go adventuring and find himself, while his twin, "F. M.," remained passive, or a separate self. When "she" awoke to active consciousness "she" became the deeper, the more impelling, the more essential factor. By reason of this severance, and of the acute conflict that at times resulted therefrom, the flaming of the dual life became so fierce that "Wilfion" — as I named the inner and third Self that lay behind that dual expression — realized the imperativeness of gaining control over his two separated selves and of bringing them into some kind of conscious harmony (*Memoir*, 423).

Having postulated yet a third self trying to gain control over her husband's two separated selves, Elizabeth described one characteristic of the unifying self. "The psychic quality of seership," she thought, "linked the dual nature together" for both as F. M. and W. S., Sharp "dreamed dreams" and "saw visions." She said little about her husband's psychic experiments because she was worried about their effects, but a few friends, she wrote, knew him only as a "psychic and mystic." From time to time, "he interested himself in definite psychic experimentation, occasionally in collaboration with Mr. W. B. Yeats; experimentation that sometimes resulted in such serious physical disturbance that he desisted from it in later years" (*Memoir*, 424). That brings us back to William and Edith in St. Margaret's Bay and the likelihood — recalling Yeats's opinion that visions come more readily when a man and woman who love each other evoke such visions together — they were engaged in the work Yeats set for them.

Before Sharp left for St. Margaret's Bay, he dictated a Fiona letter which Mary copied and dated April 9, to Benjamin Burgess Moore, an undergraduate at Yale University who had written an article about her in the *Yale Literary Magazine*. She thanked him for his "profoundly sympathetic" and "most welcome appreciation" of her work. She had seen nothing in any American paper or magazine which "can be compared with it — either in knowledge of the writings, sympathetic understanding, and general insight — and this, I may add, not merely because you honor me with such cordial praise." As in the letter to Katharine Hinkson, Sharp, writing as Fiona, fleshed out her approach to human life:

> I believe in one intensity of emotion above all others, namely the intensity of this brief flame of life in the heart and the brain, an intensity no one

can have who does not account the hours of every day as the vanishing pawns in that tragic game of chess for ever being played between Time and Eternity. [...] I live truly only when I am in the remote Isles or among the mountains of Argyll — a solace and inspiration which come to me much attenuated through the human medium. [...] though young in years, I have a capacity for sorrow and regret which has come to me through my Celtic ancestry out of a remote lost world.

Despite her sorrow, Fiona was not a melancholy person: "I am young, and life has given me some of her rarest gifts, and I am grateful." Having lived, she will be ready when her hour comes. She is "ever aware of the menace of the perpetual fugitive shadow of Destiny." While lying among the dunes on Iona, she had a dream that summed up her approach to life. She "heard a voice saying in Gaelic that the three Dominions or Powers were 'The Living God, the Dying World, and the mysterious Race of Man,' and that behind each gleamed the shadowy eyes of Destiny." Fiona's confidences indicate Sharp thought Moore might shore up Fiona's reputation in the United States. To further that aim, he sent him a copy of Fiona's *Washer of the Ford*, a copy of *From the Hills of Dream*, and a sympathetic review of the latter. Later, when Moore decided to seek out Fiona in Scotland in the hope of a Celtic romance, Sharp had cause to regret Fiona's openness in this letter.

Fig. 47 Cartledge Hall, Holmesfield, Derbyshire. Home of R. Murray Gilchrist and family. Photograph by Dave Hobson (2014). Courtesy of Vale of Belvoir Ramblers, https://vbramblers.blogspot.com/2014_04_01_archive.html

In early May, Sharp was back in London, and Elizabeth, in poor health, had gone to St. Remy in the south of France where the Janviers lived in the winter months. On May 3 she wrote to thank Murray Gilchrist for his photograph which she had requested to become better acquainted with "Will's firm friend." She was gathering strength, resting, and enjoying herself in a lovely sunny spot where she had been taken to the heart of a "wonderful literary movement" — the Provençal poets, led by Frederick Mistral, who she hoped to meet soon. Sharp went north to spend the night with Murray Gilchrist on Saturday, May 8, and returned to London the next afternoon. In a letter of thanks, he reminded Gilchrist to include his photograph when he wrote to Mrs. Wingate Rinder, whose address was 11 Woronsow Road, in St John's Wood, a fashionable area of northwest London. Despite his worries about finances, Sharp, restless as ever, decided to visit his wife in St. Remy on her birthday. He left London on Friday, May 14, arrived in Tarascon on Saturday, made his way to St. Remy, and surprised Elizabeth the next morning, Sunday May 16. After resting that day and celebrating her birthday on Monday May 17, he left that evening, and was back in London late Wednesday.

Elizabeth described the occasion: Early in the morning, the waiter brought my coffee and "told me gravely that a large packet had arrived for me, during the night, with orders that it should not be delivered to me till the morning. Should it be brought upstairs? The next moment the door was pushed open and in came the radiant smiling unexpected apparition of my Poet!" (*Memoir*, 286). The "interlude" seemed "strange and dreamlike," he wrote to Elizabeth, on Friday the 21st, the "hurried journey, the long afternoon and night journey from Paris, the long afternoon and night to Tarascon — the drive at dawn and sunrise through beautiful Provence — the meeting you — the seeing our dear friends there again. And then that restful Sunday, that lovely birthday!" After returning to London, he left again to spend the weekend with his mother and sister in Edinburgh. When he returned the following Monday, May 24, he told Little he could not go down to Sussex to visit him until Elizabeth returned from St. Remy on June 14 or 15. He was busy all week and planned to leave again on the weekend. He went on to say:

> What with the autumn in Scotland, the early winter in America, Jany in the Riviera, Provence, Scotland, & France three times, I've not been much

here since last summer! I'm as nearly bankrupt as I've ever been in my life — but I've lived up to the hilt, and it's Spring, and Summer's still to come, and heads or tails it's still good to be alive, and may the Dispenser of Laughter & Tears smile benignly on both of us, cher ami!

In that spirit he left at the end of May to spend the first week of June with Murray Gilchrist and his family at Cartledge Hall in Derbyshire. Following his stay in St. Margaret's Bay, his trip to St. Remy, his visits to Gilchrist, and the advent of Spring, his spirits were high, but the constant movement — reflecting his efforts to stave off loneliness and depression — prevented him from writing much as W. S. or F. M.

For most of June, Sharp was in London. As the summer progressed, he worked on several Fiona tales which would appear in 1899 in *The Dominion of Dreams*. He also wrote, as Fiona, *The Laughter of Peterkin* — a collection of Celtic stories for children, which Archibald Constable and Co. published in November. In mid-August, he and Elizabeth spent two weeks in Southwold, Sussex with the Janviers, who were visiting England. They returned to London for two days on August 28 and then left for Parkstone in Dorset, where they stayed until September 12, Sharp's forty-second birthday.

While in Dorset, Sharp constructed a birthday letter from Fiona to Will which is in Sharp's hand. It reflects the splitting defined by Elizabeth and his belief Fiona was becoming a separate personality distinct from that of W. S. It provides a glimpse of how Sharp viewed his life in the fall of 1897:

> Now, dear Billy, forgive me if I say that I am very much disappointed with you this past year. You have not been well, it is true: but you have also been idle to a painful degree, and your lack of method makes me seriously anxious. I will not dwell upon your minor and to me irritating faults: you know well to what I allude, and I think too you are often greedy, for it is not necessary always to have both marmalade and butter at breakfast. That is a small thing, but it is significant: I can only hope that you will control your appetites better in 1897–8.
>
> But do for heaven's sake put your shoulder to the wheel and get soon in good working trim at something worth doing. You ever put pleasure first and think so much of youth that you don't like billiards merely because the balls are bald. This is sad, Billy.
>
> I shall keep all the rest till we meet. What an uncomfortable half hour you will have!

Still, you're a dear, and I like you with all your faults. Be a good boy and I'll love you.

Your loving twin, | Fiona

It is Sharp's view of himself, but it also that of a sister or mother figure, who expresses her displeasure with Sharp's putting pleasure first and failing to control his appetites.

On September 14, Sharp sent the typed manuscript of Mona Caird's "The Pathway of the Gods," to William Meredith, George Meredith's son, who was an editor of the Edinburgh publishing firm, Archibald Constable and Co. The firm was about to publish Fiona Macleod's *Laughter of Peterkin*, and Sharp recommended they publish Caird's manuscript. He was back in London when he wrote to Edward Martyn on September 22. Yeats had encouraged Martyn, a well-off member of the Irish landed gentry, to invite Sharp and others to his home, Tillyra Castle in County Galway, to discuss the kind of plays Yeats wanted for his projected Irish Theater. With the dates for the theater discussion set for early October, Sharp told Martyn he was leaving the next day (Thursday, September 23) for Dublin, where he would see George Russell (Æ) on Friday and, on Saturday morning, go on to the Royal Hotel in Greenore, a port village on the coast north of Dublin. Here, he could be contacted on Sunday and Monday morning (September 26 and 27). His plans after that, he told Martyn, would be "guided by weather and other circumstances." He implied he would be travelling in Ireland until Saturday October 2, when he would take the train to Ardrahan in Galway. Letters that follow show he made his way on September 27 back across the Irish Channel to the Isle of Arran off the west coast of Scotland, where he stayed four nights, before returning to Ireland and boarding the train to visit Martyn.

Sharp's annual birthday letter to E. C. Stedman, dated September 28 from The Corrie, Isle of Arran, began: "I send you a line from this beautiful island (more beautiful than ever to me because of a beautiful friend and comrade who is here too)." He went on to name that comrade as F. M. The brief Arran interlude seems to have been preplanned to enable him to be alone for a few days with Edith Rinder, who was spending September, as usual, on the mainland near Tarbert just north of Arran. After leaving Arran, he told Stedman, he would be going "to the West of Ireland (Connemara) to stay at an old castle with a strange and delightful host — with a fellow guest, my friend W. B. Yeats." In a September 29 letter from Arran, he asked John Macleay to see that the *Highland News* "for this and the next two weeks" be sent to him at Tillyra Castle.

After arriving at Tillyra, he wrote a long letter to Elizabeth on October 4 which described his arrival two days earlier and Martyn's plans to take him to see the Cliffs of Moher and other West Country sights before Yeats arrived on Thursday. He was delighted to have finally made it into the heart of the Irish literary revival, a distinguished group that included, besides Martyn and Yeats, Lady Gregory (whose Coole Park was nearby), Douglas Hyde, and Martin Morris, a neighbor who would become, in 1901, Baron Morris of Killanin. As the days went by, he was less than well-received by the group. Lady Gregory memorably described him (*Diaries*, 153–154) as

> an absurd object, in velvet coat, curled hair, wonderful ties — a good natured creature — a sort of professional patron of poets — but making himself ridiculous by stories to the men of his love affairs & entanglements, & seeing visions (instigated by Yeats) — one apparition clasped him to an elm tree from which he had to be released.

I have described Sharp's strange and amusing visit to Tillyra for what Lady Gregory called a "Celtic party" at some length in a section called "The Soul of the Tree and the Hermaphrodite" in *Yeats Annual, No. 14*, 184–199. Lady Gregory recalled having suspected Sharp was Fiona Macleod. That may have been only hindsight, but Yeats knew Sharp was the key to Fiona Macleod, and he wanted Fiona, not Sharp, to contribute plays for the theater. Throughout the visit Sharp played a double role, and portraits taken in a Dublin studio on his way to or from Tillyra confirm Lady Gregory's description. With two large blond curls on his forehead and the velvet coat, he seems to have decided his appearance at Tillyra should offer at least a hint of his feminine self.

Writing to the Grant Allens from London on November 5, Sharp reported he had returned a few days earlier from the west of Ireland, where he had a delightful time. Having left Tillyra in mid-October, he spent some time in Dublin and Scotland. But he was not long in London. "Owing to the excitable condition of his brain," according to Elizabeth (*Memoir*, 290), "London proved impossible, and "he took rooms in

Fig. 48 This photograph of William Sharp was taken in Dublin in late September 1897, and sent to Henry Mills Alden, editor of *Harper's Magazine* and Sharp's friend, at Christmas, 1897. Courtesy of the University of Delaware Library (The Henry Mills Alden Papers), Public Domain.

Hastings." That decision recalls his residence in Phenice Croft in 1893, when he was alone and experimenting with drugs to evoke visions. One reason for the "excitable condition of his brain" which Elizabeth did not mention was the need for a place where he could be alone — and at times with Edith Rinder — to conduct psychic experiments for Yeats. The fragment of a letter he sent Elizabeth from Hastings which she included in the *Memoir* reflects the state of his mind as 1897 ended:

> I am so glad to be here, in this sunlight by the sea. Light and motion — what a joy these are. The eyes become devitalized in the pall of London gloom…. There is a glorious amplitude of light. The mind bathes in these illimitable vistas. Wind and Wave and Sun: how regenerative these elder brothers are. Solomon says there is no delight like wisdom, and that wisdom is the heritage of age: but there is a divine unwisdom which is the heritage of youth — and I would rather be young for a year than wise for a cycle. There are some who live without the pulse of youth in the mind: on the day, in the hour, I no longer feel that quick pulse, I

will go out like a blown flame. To be young; to keep young: that is the story and despair of life.

Sharp fixated on "flame" as the image of youth and desire he desperately wanted to preserve. The desire to "keep young" is central to the story of Sharp's life. The increased difficulty of sustaining his youth was one cause of the despair he suffered in 1897 and, periodically, for the rest of his life.

On December 4 he was back in London briefly to attend a meeting of The Irish Literary Society, where Yeats read an important lecture on "The Celtic Movement." Without Yeats's approval, the Society officials had asked Sharp to chair the meeting. Influenced no doubt by Sharp's behavior at Tillyra Castle, but also because it was an Irish society, Yeats asked him to withdraw. He refused, whereupon Lady Gregory, ever ready to come to Yeats' aid, intervened and charmed Sharp into acceding to Yeats's request. She arranged what she called "a little festa" after the lecture at the Metropole restaurant for a group that included the Sharps, Yeats, Yeats's father and sisters, and Arthur Symons. She said: "It went off very pleasantly." The rest of December seems to have passed uneventfully, though at the end of the month, Elizabeth, who Lady Gregory came to know and like, contacted the flu, whereupon her husband took her to his flat in Hastings to recuperate. 1897 was a full year for the Sharps, with many highs and many lows.

Chapter Seventeen

1898

Early in the new year Sharp suffered a "an acute depression" which Elizabeth attributed to the strain of maintaining a double identity. "Each of the two natures," she continued, "had its own needs and desires, interests, and friends. The needs of each were not always harmonious one with the other but created a complex condition that led to a severe nervous collapse (*Memoir*, 292). This collapse, as we have seen, was not Sharp's first. Others predated his invention of Fiona Macleod, and they became more serious when his feminine "nature" was given a separate identity. Ernest Rhys was not alone among Sharp's friends to comment on his ability to recover quickly from periods of illness. His ability to emerge from a deep depression into state of euphoria that foreshadowed another lapse into depression signals from this distance a bipolar disorder or, more simply, manic depression. In January 1898, according to Elizabeth, his depression required a "change of environment." He left London "for the southern coast and moved from place to place — Bournemouth, Brighton, and St. Margaret's Bay near Dover." He was "much alone, except for the occasional visit of an intimate friend."

In a January or February letter to Catherine Janvier, from which Elizabeth quoted a passage, Sharp described his condition:

> I am skirting the wood of shadows. I am filled with vague fears — and yet a clear triumphant laughter goes through it, whether of life or death no one knows. I am also in a duel with forces other than those of human wills — and I need all my courage and strength. At the moment I have recovered my physic control over certain media. It cannot last more than a few days at most a few weeks at a time: but in that I am myself.

In addition to alleviating depression, but unnamed by Elizabeth, there was another purpose in Sharp's moving from place to place along England's southern coast. He was trying to create conditions that induced dreams and visions he could share with Yeats. That effort, often aided by drugs, rather than alleviating depression contributed to the mood swings he described to Catherine Janvier. When his spiritualist activities at Phenice Croft in 1894 produced similar results, Elizabeth insisted they give up the house and return to the city. In December 1896 she attributed his illness to "experimentation with certain psychic phenomena [...] efforts in which at times he and Mr. W. B. Yeats collaborated" (*Memoir*, 282). Sharp and Yeats may have engaged together in psychic experiments earlier, but their collaboration began in earnest in January 1897and reached a crescendo in early 1898. As described in the previous chapter, Yeats convinced Sharp, referencing his own relationship with Maud Gonne, that visions came more easily when jointly evoked by a man and a woman who were in love. He urged Sharp to partner with Fiona who he thought the better "seer" just as he thought Maud Gonne's psychic capacities exceeded his own. Edith Rinder, who was playing the part of Fiona in the search for rituals, was the "intimate friend" who occasionally visited Sharp on the south coast. Whether or not Edith shared his faith in the supernatural, her presence for the spiritualist activities reflected her concern for Sharp's health and productivity. Given Elizabeth's worry about her husband's spiritualist activities, it is interesting to note that a diary, now in the British Library, which Elizabeth kept for some years after her husband died in 1905, records in considerable detail her contacts through a medium with the spirit of her dead husband.

In mid-February, shortly after arriving at the St. Margaret's Bay Hotel near Dover, Sharp wrote Elizabeth a letter which expressed the sense of peace and happiness that came to him that afternoon after leaving the station, walking through the village, and finding himself "alone, alone 'in the open.'" It was not "merely healing to me but an imperative necessity of my life." He was weary of "the endless recurrence of the ordinary in the lives of most people." To his own "wild heart [...] life must come otherwise or not at all." He wished he was "a youth once more" so he could "lie down at night smelling the earth and rise at dawn, smelling the new air out of the East, and know enough of men and cities to avoid both, and to consider little any gods ancient or modern, knowing well that there is only 'The Red God' to think of, he who lives and laughs in the red blood." He described the tension between the need to produce articles and reviews that generated income and his desire to live freely in nature, "a wild instinct to go to my own."

In a letter about this time to "a friend," who may well have been Edith, he was even more specific about his desire to shed his human qualities and become a creature of nature:

> I wish I could live all my hours out of doors: I envy no one in the world so much as the red deer, the eagle, the sea-mew. I am sure no kings have so royal a life as the plovers and curlews have. All these have freedom, rejoice continually on the wind's wing, exalt alike in sun and shade: to them day is day, and night is night, and there is nothing else (*Memoir*, p. 298).

Elizabeth read this letter as providing "an insight into the primitive elemental soul that so often swayed him and his work." Taken together, the two letters — to Elizabeth and to a friend — express Sharp's passing desire to escape the bonds of rational life, to live an "elemental life" in the natural world, to recover the freedom he experienced as a youth in the Hebrides.

Before leaving St. Margaret's Bay, he explained his illness to Murray Gilchrist and said his two weeks there had been restorative:

> I know you will have been sorry to hear that I have been ill — and had to leave work, and home. The immediate cause was a severe and sudden attack of influenza which went to membranes of the head and brain, and all but resulted in brain fever. This evil was averted — but it and the possible collapse of your friend Will were at one time, and for some days, an imminent probability. I have now been a fortnight in this quiet sea-haven and am practically myself again.

At the letter's close, he added: "I have suffered much, but am now again fronting life gravely and with laughing eyes." In a March 1 letter, after returning to London, he told Stedman "he had been seriously ill, had just returned from two-months convalescence, and was well again partly due to what he called "alleviations" or "to be more exact, it should be in the singular! You can guess the name, & perhaps remember something of a rare beauty, of life-lifting eyes." He must have shown Stedman a photograph of Edith Rinder during his trip to New York in November

1896. Later in the letter he was more specific about his illness and Edith's role in his recovery:

> Although I have had so bad a time with a dangerous collapse (culminating in severe meningitis) I am now feeling better than I have done for at least two years past — and am quite determined not only to work hard but to get as much of the sunshine & joy & romance and dear delight of life as may be! And what's more, I've had it! And what's more, I have laid in a treasure of it quite recently! And what's more — by my Queen's full consent and approval — I've been a very bad boy with a very dear & delightful "friend," now alas returned to her home in Brussels — & generally I've been "spoilt" & made much of, & have enjoyed it, and am thinking of reforming 20 years hence, but meanwhile cling to my Sunshine Creed — to live sunnily, to think blithely, to act on the square even in my "sinning," & to try to give sunshine to others. After all, it's not such a bad creed — indeed, it's a very good one, and it has my dear poet E. C. S. as Prophet!

In the *Memoir*, Elizabeth said she welcomed Edith's cooperation in the efforts to maintain her husband's health, but this paragraph is the only known instance of Sharp's stating explicitly that Elizabeth (his Queen) consented in and approved of his relationship with Edith. Stedman would have known Edith Wingate Rinder's translations of the stories of Belgian writers, *The Massacre of the Innocents*, which Stone and Kimball published in 1895. Sharp may have given him a copy and suggested she was the woman he loved. Edith visited Belgium in the summer of 1895 and interacted with the writers she translated. In 1899, she published in the *Dome* her translation of Maeterlinck's "Massacre of the Innocents" (January, 49–60), a review of Maeterlinck's *Wisdom and Destiny* (January, 93), and "A Child of the Marshland" (December, 49–60). She may have visited Brussels again in 1898, or Sharp, for reasons unknown, simply invented the idea to remove her from London.

Toward the end of the letter, in a burst of enthusiasm reflecting his restored health and enhanced devotion to the creed of which Stedman was the prophet, Sharp revealed his plan to meet Edith again in France in mid-April:

> If all goes well, you can think of me (and my friend) in a lovely green retreat, on the Marne, near Paris, during the last fortnight of April. If you were there too, I would drink to you in white wine, and she would give you a kiss — which, with the glory in her beautiful eyes, would make

you "wild with the waste of all unnumbered Springs." You will be with us in Spirit, dear poet of youth & romance — and *I* will kiss her for you, & likewise drink the sweet wine of France!!

Following this passage several lines are blacked out and undecipherable. They precede the following lines which are also crossed through but can be read: "[…] hope, and I trust that her sunny smile and youthful heart often rejoice you. You will be a dear youth till the end, E. C. S., — & may the Gods reward you!" Stedman's life must also have been enriched by a young woman as he tried to live the creed of which, at least in Sharp's mind, he was the Prophet. Sharp concluded by saying his letter had better be entrusted to "the oblivious flame." The letter was not so entrusted, but Stedman or someone expunged the name of the young woman who brought joy to his life.

In his St. Margaret's Bay letter to Gilchrist, Sharp said Fiona, "before she got ill," had nearly finished a group of stories that might appear in the spring under the title *There is But One Love*, a volume Elizabeth identified as Fiona's *The Dominion of Dreams*, which was not published until the spring of 1899. Four of those stories appeared first in periodicals in 1898: "Children of the Dark Star" (*Dome*, May); "Enya of the Dark Eyes" (*Literature*, September); "The Wells of Peace" (*Good Words*, September); and "The White Heron" (*Harper's*, December). Two more failed to make their way into *The Dominion of Dreams*: "The Four Winds of Desire" (*Good Words*, 245) and "The Wayfarer" (*Cosmopolis*, June). Despite his illnesses during the first several months of 1898, Sharp produced by mid-year a considerable volume of writing.

Yet another spiritualist entered Sharp's life in late March when he wrote the first of several Fiona letters to Dr. John A. Goodchild, whom he met through their mutual friend Grant Allen. As Fiona, he thanked Goodchild for a copy of a book of his poems and for a proof copy of his *Light of the West*, which would be published in April by Allen's nephew, Grant Richards. Goodchild was a highly regarded medical doctor who cared for his British patients in England and in Italy where many spent the darker months. He was also a serious student of the early civilizations of Ireland, England, and Scotland and had a special affection for the Celts, especially the early converts to Christianity. More significantly, important messages were delivered to him during sleep and reveries. He bought from a tailor in Italy a beautiful glass bowl he thought might be the Holy Grail, the cup Jesus used at the last supper. After keeping it on display in his library for several years, a master spirit directed him to bury it in a stream near Glastonbury in the West of England, the reputed domain of King Arthur and his grail-seeking knights. The purpose of the burial is not clear, but it had some interesting results. Given Sharp's involvement with Yeats's Celtic Mystical Order, it is not surprising he was drawn to Goodchild who, in turn, was drawn to the Celtic stories of Fiona Macleod.

Since Elizabeth included in the *Memoir* (294–296) part of a letter from her husband dated March 29, he must have been away again. Her inclusion of this letter in the *Memoir* addresses concerns about her acceptance of her husband's relationship with Edith. It is a carefully crafted argument not for free love, but for loving more than one person at a time. Elizabeth introduced the letter by saying it expressed views she and her husband held in common, thus echoing Sharp's opening assertion in the letter:

> Yes, in essentials, we are all at one. We have both learned and unlearned so much, and we have come to see that we are wrought mysteriously by forces beyond ourselves, but in so seeing we know that there is a great and deep love that conquers even disillusion and disappointment.

Having assured Elizabeth of his continuing love, he portrays his love for Edith as a powerful force impossible to control:

> Not all the wishing, not all the dreaming, not all the will and hope and prayer we summon can alter that within us which is stronger than ourselves. This is a hard lesson to learn for all of us, and most for a woman. We are brought up within such an atmosphere of conventional untruth to life that most people never even perceive the hopeless futility in the arbitrary ideals which are imposed upon us — and the result for the deeper natures, endless tragic miscarriage of love, peace, and hope. But, fortunately, those of us who to our own suffering *do* see only too clearly, can still strike out a nobler ideal — one that does not shrink from the deepest responsibilities and yet can so widen and deepen the heart and spirit with love that what else would be irremediable pain can be transmuted into hope, into peace, and even into joy.

More simply, loving more than one person can cause deep pain, but it can become a source of hope, peace, and even joy for those who know it can "widen and deepen the heart and spirit."

It strains credulity to believe Sharp's relationship with Edith Rinder brought "hope, peace, and even joy" to Elizabeth, but her inclusion of the letter is a clear sign she shared its basic tenets. For most people, Sharp continued in the letter, "the supreme disintegrate" of happiness is "the Tyranny of Love — the love which is forever demanding *as its due* that which is wholly independent of bonds, which is as the wind which bloweth where it listeth or where it is impelled, by the Spirit." Men and women are taught "hopeless lies." They start life

> with ideals which seem fair but are radically consumptive: ideals that are not only bound to perish, but that could not survive. […] That ought not be — but it must be as long as young men and women are fed mentally and spiritually upon the foolish and cowardly lies of a false and corrupt conventionalism.

Mona Caird, Elizabeth's best friend and Edith's cousin by marriage, was arguing forcefully against the conventional constraints of marriage. Elizabeth asserted several times in the *Memoir* that she and her husband shared Mona's views. Her main goal was to free women from the legal and conventional constraints of marriage and recognize them as equal partners with their husbands. In this letter Sharp goes much further to argue that men and women ought to be freed from the convention that marriage required them to love and have intimate relations with only their marital partner.

The letter casts an important light on Sharp's psychological make-up. "False and corrupt conventionalism," he wrote, subjects "many fine natures, men and women," to "lifelong suffering." Some never learn their unhappiness is the result of impossible ideals, while others "learn first strength to endure the transmutations and then power to weld these to far nobler and finer uses and ends." Both suffer, and Sharp places himself among the second class of sufferers. Everyone, he says, tends to nurse grief. "The brooding spirit craves for the sunlight, but it will not leave the shadows. Often, *Sorrow* is our best ally." Sharp's frequent bouts of depression which he described to intimate friends were rooted in the impossible ideals installed in his youth. The letter to Elizabeth ends as follows:

> I dreamed that a beautiful spirit was standing beside me. He said, "My Brother, I have come to give you the supreme gift that will heal you and save you." I answered eagerly: "Give it me — what is it?" And the fair

> radiant spirit smiled with beautiful solemn eyes and blew a breath into the tangled garden of my heart — and when I looked there, I saw the tall white Flower of Sorrow growing in the Sunlight.

Whether or not the dream occurred, Sharp's rendition is revealing. When he was twenty-one, his father, with whom he had a strained relationship, died. From that point onward, he had an overpowering need for an intimate relationship with a man or a woman with whom he could share his deepest thoughts and feelings. Elizabeth, Edith, and Catherine Janvier fulfilled the female need, and a succession of men — Hall Caine, J. Stanley Little, R. Murray Gilchrist, E. C. Stedman, and starting in 1900 Alexander Nelson Hood, the Duke of Bronte — fulfilled his need for a male confidant, a brother who would blow a breath into the tangled garden of his heart and allow his sorrow to grow into a beautiful white flower in the bright sunlight. These individuals and others fulfilled a deep psychological imperative that reasserted itself throughout his troubled life. Among his surviving letters, those to Murray Gilchrist express that need most vividly. The white Flower of Sorrow neatly symbolized the beauty as well as the temporality of periods of relief from dark depression.

Sharp's trip to France was delayed. On April 22, he told Gilchrist he was leaving for Paris "next Friday," April 29. The purpose of the trip was to introduce Fiona to Yeats and those who were helping him with the Celtic Mystical Order: Maud Gonne, Macgregor Mathers, and his wife Moina. The six would engage in psychic experiments, and Yeats would discuss with Fiona the plays he wanted her to write for the Celtic Theatre he was planning for Dublin. Yeats described the gathering in an April 25 letter to Lady Gregory:

> I have been here in Paris for a couple of days. [...] I am buried in Celtic mythology and shall be for a couple of weeks or so. Miss Gonne has been ill with bronchitis. [...] She comes here to-morrow to see visions. Fiona Macleod (this is private as she is curiously secret about her movements) talks of coming here too, so we will have a great Celtic gathering (*Collected Letters II*, 214–215).

In a postscript, he told Lady Gregory he was staying with Macgregor Mathers, "a Celtic enthusiast who spends most of his day in highland costume to the wonder of the neighbors."

Sharp left for Paris on April 29, but he made it only as far as Dover where he again checked into the St. Margaret's Bay Hotel. He wrote to Yeats the next day: "A sudden and serious collapse in health will prevent Miss M. from coming to Paris" and will "probably end in her having to go to some remote Baths for 2 months." He added, "As for myself, partly for this and partly because being myself (as you will understand) seriously indisposed in the same way, I am unable to go to Paris either." This sentence indicates Sharp, by this time, had told Yeats confidentially that Fiona was a second personality and there was another woman he loved who facilitated the emergence and shared many of her qualities. She was working with him psychically on the Celtic Mystical Order. This was the Fiona Yeats expected in Paris. However improbable that construction may be, Yeats accepted it. He was in love with Maud Gonne who loosened his creative powers just as the real Fiona released Sharp's. He was also deeply committed to the possibility of communicating with spirits. Since neither Maud Gonne nor the Mathers knew anything about the woman within, the woman he was taking to Paris would be Fiona Macleod.

Fig. 49 Maud Gonne McBride (1866–1953). Wikimedia https://commons.wikimedia.org/wiki/File:Maude_Gonne_McBride_nd.jpg#/media/File:Maude_Gonne_McBride_nd.jpg, Public Domain.

In agreeing to take Fiona to Paris, Sharp must have thought he and Edith, as Fiona, would engage briefly with Yeats and company and then go to "the lovely green retreat on the Marne, near Paris," he described to Stedman on March first. He expected Edith to play the role of Fiona in Paris as she had done for an hour or two with George Meredith the previous June. Though sympathetic to the Celtic Revival, she was neither a Scot nor immersed in the myths and legends of the Hebrides. She must have considered the Paris plan as one of Sharp's romantic fantasies that would evaporate. When she realized he was about to implement the plan, she demurred, and Sharp was forced to invent Fiona's illness. Ensuing events bordered on the fantastic.

After learning Sharp and Fiona were not coming to Paris, Yeats sent Sharp a letter dated May 3:

> My dear Sharpe [sic]: please send the enclosed to Miss Macleod. I have been compelled to seal it up, because it concerns the affairs of an astral form which appeared to me & to my fiends last night. I will probably be able to tell you about it later. Please send it at once. Also please tell me what is the tartan of your family & what kind of person was Miss Macleod's father. What did he look like? What was his tartan? Were you conscious of being in any unusual state on either May 1 or May 2nd? You will understand these questions later but I may not speak more clearly now except to say that I have had an astral experience of the most intense kind & that your answers are necessary before certain things which I was asked to do can be done.

Such was the atmosphere Yeats and his friends had created in Paris. Yeats, of course, had minimal interest in tartans, so it was Mathers who asked him to do "certain things." Years later, Yeats recalled (*Memoir*, 105) that Mathers "had seen a vision of 'a man standing in an archway' wearing a kilt with the Macleod and another tartan." Yeats himself had begun "to shiver," and the shivering was associated in his mind with William Sharp and Fiona Macleod. In a second "self-induced clairvoyant experience Mathers had seen Sharp in need" and proclaimed, "It is madness, but it is like the madness of a god" (*Collected Letters II*, 219–220). A professional Scot, the tartan wearing Mathers, with help from his wife Moina, he was setting up a Paris Lodge of the Order of the Golden Dawn. He must have had some doubts about the Sharp/Fiona duo. Their tartans, if any, might prove them legitimate Scots. He was more interested in asserting his Scottish credentials and getting on with the Golden Dawn than in Yeats' Celtic Order.

In his May 5 reply to Yeats' May 3 letter, Sharp said Fiona was with him at St. Margaret's Bay.

> She was on her way to Paris, but as I told you she was suddenly taken too unwell. She was sleeping when your letter came, but I left the enclosure for her at her bedside — & if she wakes before the post goes, she will doubtless give you a message through me, unless she feels up to writing herself. If well enough, she leaves here on Saturday morning — but to go north again.

In response to Yeats' questions, Sharp said he experienced on May 1 "a singular depression, and a curious sense if unreality for a time," as though he was really elsewhere, but on May 2 he suffered in a way he could not explain, "owing to what seemed ... an unaccountable preoccupation of Miss M." Responding again to Yeats: Fiona's "father was tall, fine looking, with a rather singular concentrated expression. The Macleod tartan is dark (dark green and dark blue almost black)." Fiona, he continued, "sees a startling likeness between me & her father, though I am taller & bigger & fairer than he was. There are, however, many similarities in nature, etc., and also in the accident of baptismal name." One need not look far for the origin of that detail; Edith Wingate Rinder's father, then deceased, was William Wingate (1828–1884) of Ludford, Leicestershire. Sharp didn't understand why Yeats was asking about the tartan though he must have suspected the questions about Fiona's father came from Mathers. He was nervous about Mathers's interest in Fiona's family, and he saw no need to share the spotlight by introducing a second male into the mix.

In his sealed note to Fiona dated May 3, Yeats said he was suddenly visited the previous night "by the intellectual body of some one who was passing through an intense emotional crisis." He was inclined to believe Fiona was his visitor, and he asked if she, either last night or the previous night (the "intellectual body sometimes appears a little after the emotional crisis that causes its appearance") was passing through some state of tragic feeling. He does not ask in an "idle spirit," but because his help and the help "of the far more powerful occultist [Maud Gonne], with whom he was working, was undoubtedly asked last night by some one."

Just before Sharp posted his letter to Yeats, Fiona awoke, read Yeats' letter, and asked Sharp to reply for her:

> I *have* been going through an intense emotional crisis. One less poignant period was on the evening or night of the 1st, but far more so, and more poignantly on the 2nd. But this, being private, I cannot speak further. I was on both occasions (though differently & for different reasons) undergoing tragic feeling, I am at present at a perilous physical & spiritual crisis. I can say no more. The one who shares my life & self is here. It is as crucial for him. I will talk over your letter to us — for to us it I, though you send it to me. Are you sure it was not Will whom you felt or saw?

Having again neatly shifted the focus to himself, Sharp revealed nothing substantive, but echoed Yeats' vague "tragic feelings" and "emotional crisis." Perhaps because he thought he had been less responsive than expected, he added the following:

> Note *this* time today: About 3 p.m. today Thursday she went through (& I too) a wave of intense tragic emotion — and last night, between 10 and 12 or later, we nearly lost each other in a very strange way. Something I did by the will was too potent, & for a time severed some unconscious links (we were apart at the time: I thought she was sleeping) —& we both suffered in consequence. But I think the extreme crisis pf tragic psychic emotion is over. God grant it.

Since Yeats knew Sharp was producing the Fiona writings, his sealed letter to Fiona must have been intended for the woman who inspired the Fiona writings and was helping Sharp with the rites for his Order. That woman, we know, was Edith Rinder who must have been the Fiona who was with Sharp in St. Margaret's Bay. Convinced of that woman's psychic powers, Yeats added to his Fiona note the following postscript: "I had hoped to see you in Paris, having heard from Mr. Sharpe that you might be here. The opening ceremonial of the celtic mysteries, of which he will have told you, is now ready."

In a May 7 response to Sharp's May 5 letter, Yeats detailed Sharp/Fiona's appearances in Paris (*Collected Letters II*, 222–223). Fiona's father had appeared in a Macleod tartan to Mathers in a dream on Sunday [May 1]. On Monday [May 2], Yeats "fell into a strange kind of shivering & convulsive trembling" whereupon he felt the astral presence of first Fiona and then Sharp. Moina Mathers then saw a face

Fig. 50 Moina Mathers (1865–1928), the wife of Macgregor Mathers and sister of Henri Bergson, was an artist, occultist, and founder of the Alpha et Omega Lodge of the Golden Dawn. Left: Moina Mathers from her performance in the Rites of Isis in the Paris Lodge of the Golden Dawn (1899), Wikimedia, https://commons.wikimedia.org/wiki/File:Picture_of_Moina_Mathers_from_her_performance_in_the_Rites_of_Isis_in_Paris.jpg, Public Domain. Right: Moina Mathers (c. 1887). Public Domain. Wikimedia, https://commons.wikimedia.org/wiki/File:Moina_Mathers.jpg

which she drew, and it seemed to Yeats to be the face of William Sharp's daemon which George Russell (Æ) had seen in the spring of 1897. Next, Moina saw someone who must have been Fiona and then a man with a tartan who, Yeats wrote, "was probably the astral of some dead person." After all these sightings, Yeats, Moina, and Macgregor retired "into a room used for magical purposes" and there made themselves "magical principals rather than persons." Fiona appeared, Yeats continued, and told them "certain things about her spiritual & mental state & asked for Occult help, of which I prefer to talk rather than to write." Fiona, he affirmed, "is suffering physically," as Sharp had told him, "but the cause of this suffering is not physical & can be remedied." It would be best if Sharp and Fiona "could come to Paris for a couple days on (say) Monday [May 9]." Otherwise, Yeats might see Sharp in London at the end of the next week.

Yeats was left shaken for a time by this intense experience. He had spoken in a dream to Sharp's daemon during the night. If Sharp can come to Paris, his friends in "the order of the Rosy Cross," really the Order of the Golden Dawn, and specifically the Mathers, will give any help they can. These friends "have a boundless admiration for the books of Fiona Macleod." As if all this were not enough to set Sharp's teeth on edge and feed his manic fantasies, Yeats added a postscript, which reads as follows:

> I think you should do no magical work with Miss Macleod until we meet. I mean that you should not attempt to use the will magically. The danger of doing so just now is considerable. You are both the channels of very powerful beings & some mistake has been made. I tried to send a magical message, as I have said, last night. It was something which you were to say to Miss Macleod. I can but remember that it was a message of peace. I did not try to appear or make you aware of my presence. I was in a dream for a [...] time too, far off from my surroundings, & believe that our daemons met in someplace of which my bodily self has no memory & that the message which I spoke with my bodily lips was carried thither.

Yeats was an active member of the London Lodge of the Order of the Golden Dawn where his motto was *Daemon est Deus*. His encounter with Sharp's daemon was rooted in the secret rituals of the order, and Sharp, though a less active member of the London Lodge, knew many of its rituals.

Many years later, Yeats wrote of the St. Margaret's Bay exchange of letters:

> I was fool enough to write to Sharp and [received] an unbelievable letter from a seaside hotel about the beautiful Fiona and himself. He had been very ill, terrible mental suffering and suddenly my soul had come to heal him, and he had found Fiona to tell her he was healed — I think that I had come as a great white bird. I learnt, however, from Mrs. Sharp years afterward that at the time he was certainly alone but mad. He had gone away to struggle on with madness (*Memoirs*, 105).

Sharp may have written another letter to Yeats or mentioned the "great white bird" in conversation, but if not and he was referring to Sharp's May 5 letter, his recollection was inaccurate. Not only is there no bird, but the assertion — attributed correctly or falsely to Elizabeth — that Sharp was surely alone and struggling with madness was not true. If Sharp's descriptions of Fiona's actions were, as I believe, beyond Sharp's ability to create out of thin air, Edith must have been with him in St. Margaret's Bay. Moreover, many of the letters he wrote to others during the two weeks were perfectly sane and rational. He was experiencing depression, a condition worsened by the psychic experiments, but he was not insane. The description in his May 5 letter to Yeats of his depression and "tragic emotion" and Fiona's "perilous physical & spiritual crisis" had some basis in fact, but the letter's purpose was to sustain Yeats's confidence in his psychic abilities. It is always difficult to distinguish between genuine Sharp's experiences and his fabrications. They are often combined, and the mix varies. That said, this letter displays both Sharp's canniness and the intensity of his desire to participate in Yeats's spiritual quest

Yeats's three May letters from Paris — one to Fiona and two to Sharp — also exhibit his attraction to Fiona and the ease of his relationship with Sharp in 1898. He was joined with both in a secret project known to only a few of his close friends. His later disparaging remarks arose, I believe, from an effort to obscure the extent of his psychic activities in the 1890s. Sharp was trying his best to follow Yeats's directions and contribute to his project. In the first draft of his "Autobiography," Yeats wrote of Sharp,

> I feel I never properly used or valued this man, through whom the fluidic world seemed to flow, disturbing all; I allowed the sense of comedy, taken by contagion from others, to hide from me my own knowledge. To look at his big body, his high colour, his handsome head with the great crop of bristly hair, no one could have divined the ceaseless presence of that fluidic life (*Memoirs*, 128–129).

On the other hand, we recall Yeats's remark many years later that Sharp "never told one anything that was true." Taken together, the two comments show Yeats continued for years to unravel the mysteries and grasp the truth about Sharp/Fiona. His failure reflects the complexity of Sharp's personality and exemplifies the difficulty his friends faced understanding him while he lived and many have faced since he died.

The letters Sharp wrote to Yeats contrast starkly with perfectly sane business letters he wrote from St Margaret's Bay to his publisher Grant Richards, John Macleay, and Benjamin Burgess Moore. It is no wonder Sharp's state of mind was fragile, that he was often depressed and on the edge of mental collapse. His life was defined by dichotomies and contradictions as he tried to comply with Yeats's spiritualist expectations, write poems and stories as though by two different writers, get them published to produce income, and deal with the tensions that inevitably arose from his love for two remarkable women, both of whom loved him and worried about his mental and physical health. Yeats's warning that Sharp not engage with Miss Macleod in any "magical work" until they could meet provided Sharp some respite for serious writing during his second week at the St. Margaret's Bay Hotel.

After returning to London on May 13, Sharp described his condition to Gilchrist: "After months of sickness, at one time at the gates of death, I am whirled back from the Iron Gates and am in the maelstrom again — fighting with mind and soul and body for that inevitable losing game which we call victory." After mentioning what he was writing, he asked Gilchrist to write to him soon, "by return best of all. You can help me — as I, I hope, can help *you*." Despite his return with renewed health to the "maelstrom," his condition remained fragile; he needed Gilchrist's help, if only through a letter. "It is only the fullest and richest lives," he wrote, "that know what the *heart* of loneliness is." He placed Gilchrist and himself among those who live full and rich lives. Sharing confidences about their deepest feelings and desires would, he thought, alleviate their loneliness. He concluded by calling Gilchrist his "comrade" and assuring him he had his love. More openly here, but throughout his correspondence with Gilchrist, there is the suggestion that Sharp had shared with Gilchrist, whose desires were directed entirely toward men and who lived with a male lover, his need for an intimate relationship with another man and the duality of his sexual orientation.

After St. Margaret's Bay, Sharp stayed in London only long enough to celebrate Elizabeth's birthday on May 17. On the 18th he left for what Elizabeth called "a delightful little wander in Holland" with Thomas Janvier, "a jovial, breezy companion." She thought a walking trip with a sound and sensible friend would be restorative, and she was right. Sharp described in a May 20 letter to Elizabeth from the south Zuyder Zee the "marvelous sky effects" and the island of Marken where "the women are grotesque, the men grotesquer, and the children grotesquest" and where the babies are "gorgeous-garbed, blue-eyed, yellow haired, imperturbable." They alone, Sharp wrote, were worth coming to see.

Only a few Sharp/Macleod letters survive from the second half of 1898. Elizabeth glossed over this six-month period by describing her husbands need to express his deepest thoughts and feelings in the writings of Fiona while also continuing to write and publish as William

Sharp to maintain their income and preserve the fiction of Fiona's separate existence.

> There was a great difference in the method of production of the two kinds of work. The F. M. writing was the result of an inner impulsion, he wrote because he had to give expression to himself whether the impulse grew out of pain or out of pleasure. But W. S., divorced as much as could be from his twin self, wrote not because he cared to, because the necessities of life demanded it (*Memoir*, 301).

In this context, Elizabeth mentioned two William Sharp novels: *Wives in Exile, A Comedy in Romance* which he wrote in 1895 for Stone and Kimble and *Silence Farm* which he was writing in 1898.

When Grant Richards started his publishing firm in 1897, Sharp saw an opening and convinced Richards to publish a British edition of *Wives in Exile*, which was written in 1896 for Stone and Kimble and finally published in 1897 by Lamson, Wolffe and Co. in Boston. He made some revisions in the spring of 1898, and the book appeared in the summer. It is a light romance in which the men go off sailing, leaving their wives behind to make do. In 1899 Richards published *Silence Farm*, a "tragic tale of the Lowlands, founded on a true incident." According to Elizabeth, her husband had to keep "a considerable amount of himself in check" in order to avoid "obvious kinship to the work of F. M." since he knew "many of the critics were on the watch." Therefore, she continued, "he strained the realistic treatment beyond what he otherwise would have done." Still, "the book was the one he liked best of all the W. S. efforts, and he considered that it contained some of his most satisfactory work." Neither *Wives in Exile* nor *Silence Farm* attracted a sizable readership or critical acclaim. Their failure caused Sharp to turn to travel writing, art history, and criticism for publications signed William Sharp. Despite his efforts to maintain a distinction between publications signed F. M. and those signed W. S. the difference began to fade.

On or about June 20, Yeats sent Fiona a letter which has not surfaced. In it he praised two Fiona stories and asked for a further explanation of the relationships between William Sharp, the female responsible for the Fiona writings, and the real woman who inspired them. Portions of Fiona's reply dated June 28 have been crossed out or erased, but it is possible to read some lines through the markings and infer some of the erased words. In a postscript Fiona asked Yeats to destroy the letter.

When Sharp had not received word that Yeats had done so, he wrote again as Fiona on July 6 to tell Yeats he was anxious about the letter. In a July 4 letter to Sharp, Yeats said he had heard from Fiona and "done as she wished about the letter" (*Collected Letters II*, 250). Fortunately, he had not done as she wished, and the letter survives. In it Sharp evoked a metaphor to describe his relationship with Edith Rinder and her role in his creative process. Since he was writing as Fiona to explain how he created and sustained her, the letter portrays Fiona describing her own origin.

The relevant section reads as follows:

> I have been told that long ago one of the subtlest and strangest minds of his time — a man of Celtic ancestry on one side and of Norse on the other — was so profoundly influenced by the kindred nature and spirit of a woman whom he loved, a Celt of the Celts, that, having in a sense accidentally discovered the mystery of absolute mental and spiritual union of two impassioned and kindred natures the flame of [?vision] that had been his in a far back day was in him, so that besides a strange and far [?reaching] ancestral memory, he remembered anew and acutely every last clue and significance of his boyhood and early life, spent mostly among the shepherds and fishers of the Hebrides and Gaelic Highlands. His was the genius, the ancestral memory, the creative power — she was the flame — she, too, being also a visionary, and with unusual and all but lost old wisdom of the Gael. Without her, he would have been lost to the Beauty which was his impassioned quest: with her, as a flame to his slumbering flame, he became what he was. The outer life of each was singular, beyond that of any man or woman I have heard of: how much stranger that of their spiritual union. A profound and resolute silence lay upon the man, save when he knew the flame of the woman "through whom he saw Beauty," and his soul quickened. She gave him all she could, and without her he could not be what he was, and he needed her vision to help his own, and her dream, and her thought, and her life, till hers and his ceased to be hers and his and merged into one, and became ...... a spirit of shaping power born of them both.

Sharp enabled Fiona to recall a tale from the ancient past about a man who was half Celt and half Norse and had one of the subtlest and strangest minds of his time. Sharp was half Celt and through his mother half Norse, and he certainly had one of the strangest, if not the subtlest, minds of his time. To understand how his relationship with Edith Rinder enabled him to write as Fiona, Yeats had to untangle the metaphor of a torch, a match, and a flame. My best effort of entanglement makes Edith the match that brought flame to the otherwise dark and silent torch. They became one in the resultant fire, which was the fire of passion, the fire of creativity. The torch (Sharp) was the vehicle that carried that fire while the match survived within the fire and sustained it. How Yeats interpreted this metaphor of creativity we cannot know, but it came to dominate Sharp's imagination. After describing it, Fiona asked Yeats: "How does that strike you as a subject for a tale, a book? It would be a strange one. Does it seem to you impossible? It does not seem so to me." Indeed, it did not, for Sharp as Fiona incorporated the match, the torch, and the flame into "The Distant Country," a story he began writing in the summer of 1898 and included in Fiona's *The Dominion of Dreams* which Archibald Constable and Co. published in May 1899. The story will be discussed in some detail in the next chapter.

Sharp was in London for most of July 1898 writing and dealing with the publication details of *Wives in Exile*. In mid-July, he received a letter from Yeats addressed to Fiona informing him that a certain legal obstacle to the establishment of a Celtic Theater in Dublin had been resolved and asking which plays Fiona would have for production by the fall. In her reply, Fiona said that three plays ("Fand and Cuchulain," "The King of Ys," and "Dahut the Red') would be ready for consideration. And there might be a fourth, "The Hour of Beauty." The first three were never finished, but "The Hour of Beauty," was retitled "The Immortal Hour" and published in the *Fortnightly Review* in 1900. The play was not performed in Dublin, but it became the libretto for Rutland Boughton's opera, which was an enormous success on the London stage in the 1920s and is still performed. Though Sharp was working on plays during the summer of 1898, he managed to complete only two ("The Immortal Hour" and "The House of Usna"). His plan to write a series of short dramas under the general title *The Theatre of the Soul* came to naught, but "The House of Usna" was also published in the *Fortnightly Review* in 1900. On April 29, 1900, it was performed at the Globe Theatre in London under the auspices of the Stage Society of which Sharp was President. Only a few in the audience knew he was the play's author.

On July 19 the Sharps went to Holmesfield in Derbyshire to visit Murray Gilchrist at Cartledge Hall, where he lived with his mother, his two sisters, and his companion George Garfitt. They returned to London on July 26, and Sharp left for the West of Scotland on July 31. A letter carrying that date from Fiona to Benjamin Burgess Moore, the American fan she had enlisted in approaching publishers, informed him that "it is not quite true that Mr. Yeats and I are collaborating on a drama: but we are each writing a drama, which we hope to see brought out in the new Celtic Theatre in Dublin next year." She concluded by telling him that as soon as she finished her new book (*The Dominion of Dreams*) she would "get on with two short plays, 'The Hour of Beauty' and 'The King of Ys and Dahut the Red.'" Yeats's efforts to encourage Sharp/Fiona to write plays for his projected theatre in Dublin soon came to an abrupt end when Irish Nationalists forced him to change its name to the "Irish Theatre" and exclude all but Irish authors.

In a July 4 letter to Sharp from Coole Park, Yeats said Edward Martyn was too upset by his mother's death (on May 12) to invite anyone to Tillyra Castle, his home in County Galway. If he changed his mind, Yeats would speak to him about inviting Sharp who spent three weeks at Tillyra in October 1897. Encouraged by Yeats, Martyn sent Sharp an invitation, but the formality of Sharp's early August reply suggests it was less welcoming than that of the previous year. Having gone by himself to the West of Scotland at the end of July, Sharp stayed in and around Kilcreggan, near where Edith Rinder was vacationing, for most of August. He returned to London on the 24th and went on to Holland to gather material for an article on Rembrandt which *Cosmopolis* commissioned and published in its November issue. He was back in London by September 17, the date of a Fiona letter to Benjamin Moore which mentioned "prolonged absence" as reason for his delay in writing.

Sharp's annual birthday letter to E. C. Stedman on September 28 mentioned "illness — followed by heavy work & latterly a big exigent writing commission in Holland for *Cosmopolis*" (the Rembrandt article) as excuses for the relative brevity of the letter. Still, he managed to inform Stedman that he "had a very wonderful & happy time this summer with the dear friend of whom you know, & whose writings you admire so much — & I look to another week at least about mid-October." The dear friend was Edith Rinder, who Stedman thought was Fiona Macleod. She and Sharp were frequently together during the three weeks he spent in the West of Scotland. He concluded the Stedman letter by highlighting his recent successes: "In another letter I must tell you of my many literary doings — more ambitious now. (In a magazine way, see *Fortnightly* for August, etc. etc. Also, *Cosmopolis* in Nov. — am now writing for *all* the big mags here and U.S.A.)." The August *Fortnightly* contained his tribute to Edward Burne Jones, the Pre-Raphaelite painter who recently died.

It is difficult to chronicle Sharp's activities in the fall of 1898 because very few letters survive. He may have had another holiday with Edith Rinder in October, as he told Stedman he was planning, and he was continuing the mystical efforts to obtain talismans and rituals for Yeats. In that connection, it is interesting to note that Sharp proposed Grant Richards ask Edith Rinder to translate Jules Bossière's *Fumeurs d'Opium*, a collection of stories first published in 1896 examining the effects of opium on mind and body.

Near the end of December, just before Christmas, he wrote to Catherine Ann Janvier with enthusiasm and optimism from the Pettycur Inn across the Forth from Edinburgh. His time there had been "memorable,'" and he had written three stories for *The Dominion of Dreams* that he thought some of his best work.

> What a glorious day it has been. The most beautiful I have ever seen at Pettycur I think. Cloudless blue sky, clear exquisite air tho' cold, with a marvelous golden light in the afternoon. Arthur's Seat, the Crags, and the Castle and the 14 ranges of the Pentlands all clear-cut as steel, and the city itself visible in fluent golden light.

Then he was moved to reflect on what he had accomplished and to welcome "a new birth," without specifying whether it would occur in this world or the next:

> And now I listen to the gathering of the tidal waters under the stars. There is an infinite solemnity — a hush, something sacred and wonderful. A benediction lies upon the world. Far off I hear the roaming wind. Thoughts and memories crowd in on me. Here I have lived and suffered — here I have touched the heights — here I have done my best. And now, here, I am going through a new birth. "Sic itur ad astral!" [Thus, onward to the stars]

It is fitting that the first and last surviving letters of 1898 were addressed to Catherine Ann Janvier, the American artist and writer who was fourteen years older than Sharp, and with whom he shared some of his deepest thoughts and dreams.

Chapter Eighteen
January–June 1899

In a lengthy article entitled "A Group of Celtic Writers" in the January issue of the *Fortnightly Review* William Sharp, disguised as Fiona, offered his views of the Celtic Revival. He thought there was too much looseness of phrase among journalists who wrote about "the Celtic spirit, the Celtic movement, and that mysterious entity Celticism." To clarify the issue, he offered a definition:

> What is called "the Celtic Renascence" is simply a fresh development of creative energy colored by nationality and molded by inherited forces, a development diverted from the common way by accident of race and temperament. The Celtic writer is the writer the temper of whose mind is more ancient, more primitive, and in a sense more natural than that of his compatriot in whom the Teutonic strain prevails.

After detailing more differences between Celtic and Teutonic writers, he settled on a simple definition:

> All that the new generation of Celtic or Anglo-Celtic (for the most part Anglo-Celtic) writers hold in conscious aim, is to interpret anew "the beauty at the heart of things," not along the lines of English tradition but along that of racial instinct, colored and informed by individual temperament.

The writers he singled out as fitting the definition were Anglo-Irish: W. B. Yeats, George Russell (Æ), Nora Hopper, and Katharine Tynan Hinkson. Designed to solidify Fiona Macleod's position in the Celtic Renascence and curry favor among the Irish, the article was favorably noted in the Irish press.

It also elicited an unexpected response. The sections reproduced above are enough to show its prose was unlike Fiona Macleod's and resembled that of the articles William Sharp was writing for London periodicals. It precipitated an unsigned article entitled "Who is Fiona Macleod: A Study in Two Styles" in the January 28 issue of the *London Daily Chronicle* which set passages of prose side by side, and challenged Sharp to deny his authorship: "Will Mr. Sharp deny that he is identical with Miss Macleod? That Miss Macleod is Mr. Sharp. I for one have not a lingering doubt, and I congratulate the latter on the success, the real magic and strength of the work issued under the assumed name." This article was notable for its detailed comparisons and its praise of the pseudonymous writings. Sharp was worried about its effect, but since it was hard to refute he decided to ignore it. Several months later, at the insistence of his publishers, he placed a brief denial by Fiona in the *Literary World* (*Memoir*, 305).

Concern about a possible unmasking contributed to the various maladies Sharp suffered during the winter months of 1899, but he managed to finish two books: Macleod's *The Dominion of Dreams* was published by Archibald Constable and Co. on May 27, and Sharp's *Silence Farm* was published by Grant Richards on June 13. The former was a collection of stories and ruminations Sharp considered the deepest and most significant of the Fiona writings. The latter, as described in the previous chapter, was a realistic novel about a young farmer falling in love with his father's ward and incurring his father's wrath. On January 18, he told Richards he thought it was "the strongest and best piece of work I have done in fiction." Richards agreed to publish it, and, when it appeared, Sharp promoted it among his friends and fellow writers hoping to elicit favorable reviews that would boost sales. Unfortunately, trying to read *Silence Farm* one becomes emersed in a verbal swamp, and it disappeared quickly into the silence of its title. Sharp was a skillful and energetic editor and critic, but he fell short when venturing into short fiction, and the novel eluded him. On the other hand, adopting the persona of an elusive lady who roamed the western isles of Scotland released his creative and formative powers. The fiction is uneven and too often over-written, but as Fiona he could mold stories from start to finish, stories that enabled readers to suspend disbelief and identify with characters. Sharp thought his ability to adopt the Fiona Macleod persona and tell the stories depended on maintaining the fiction of her existence as a real person.

Richards' decision to publish *Silence Farm* may have been based in friendship rather than the work's quality. In May 1897, he married Elisina Palamidessi de Castelvecchio (1878–1959), the great-great-granddaughter of Napoleon's brother Louis. In the spring of 1898, they were planning a delayed honeymoon on the French Riviera. Sharp suggested Richards contact Thomas Janvier who had a home in Provence and was currently living in London. Should Janvier fail to respond, Sharp offered his assistance. He knew the area well, Mistral and Felix Gras were friends, and he was engaged in "a critical study of modern Provençal literature." Years later, in *Author Hunting by an Old Literary Sportsman*, Richards credited William Sharp and Thomas Janvier with drawing up the itinerary for his honeymoon.

In a late January letter to Richards, Sharp mentioned the success of Mrs. Wingate Rinder's translation of C. Le Goffic's *Le Crucifié de Keraliès*, recently published as *The Dark Way of Love* by Archibald Constable and suggested he commission Mrs. Rinder to translate Jules Boissiere's *Fumeurs d'Opium*. Richards must have expressed interest, since Edith sent him Sharp's copy of *Fumeurs d'Opium* and a sample of her translation. Either it failed to reach Richards, or he mislaid it which caused Sharp to tell him in a late April letter he hoped it might still be traced, as copies were not easy to come by. Mrs. Rinder was naturally put out about it as her translating had to be stopped, and it was not resumed.

In late March, the Sharps spent a long Easter weekend (March 30–April 4) in Hazelmere, Surrey with the Grant Allens, Grant Richards' uncle and aunt. Accepting the invitation in a March 25 letter, Sharp said his insomnia required a separate bed; he would stay at a nearby inn if a room having two beds was not available at the Allen's. To mitigate his request for separate beds, he informed the Allens Elizabeth was about to return from a month-long absence in Scotland and commented: "How fortunate that I am an austere Anchorite — eh?" In a follow-up letter to Nellie Allen, who must have assured him of the separate sleeping arrangement, Sharp hoped the "fine air" would provide "a surcease from too much nervous headache and from indifferent sleep."

On March 25, Fiona thanked Frederick Ernest Green, a prolific writer on agricultural policy, for his letter praising her *Washer of the Ford*, and Green published the letter in his "Book of the Week" column in the January 21, 1909 issue of the *New Age*. The book that occasioned

Fig. 51 The elaborate cover design of *The Dark Way of Love*, Edith Wingate Rinder's translation of C. Le Goffic's *Le Crucifié de Keraliès*, published by Archibald Constable in 1898. Photograph by William F. Halloran of his copy.

Green's column was Fiona's *Songs and Poems, Old and New*, published posthumously in 1909 by Eliot Stock. In his column, Green recalled sitting next to Richard Whiteing at a dinner in 1899 following the publication of his *No.5 St. John Street*, a popular novel that went through sixteen editions, made Whiteing famous, and became Grant Richards' first commercial success. Green asked Whiteing if he knew William Sharp and said it had been rumored that Sharp "was either Fiona Macleod or else a near relation to that personality." Whiteing replied, "Yes, I do. Now, he is my ideal of a Man — magnificent physically as well as intellectually." Green commented, "How I should have liked to see these two Titans among men of letters standing together or walking arm-in-arm down Fleet Street." Sharp would have been surprised and pleased to be called a "Titan among men of letters."

Green also recalled having talked with W. B. Yeats, the honored guest and speaker at another dinner which took place on March 1, 1899:

> From telling me how he could cast a spell upon an Irish peasant and make him see a ghost, we got on to talk of crystal-gazing and from thence to Fiona

Macleod, whose writings were to me the most beautiful efflorescence of the Celtic Renaissance. I remember asking him point-blank if he knew who Fiona Macleod was. He answered in the affirmative. He spoke about a pilgrimage, too, that she had made to George Meredith, and how in her was wedded beauty and intellect. This inspired me to speak of my wife, who had died a few years anterior to this, and I promised to send him a little book of her poems.

Green then printed what he termed a "strange reply" from Mr. Yeats:

My dear Mr. Green, — I thank you very much for your wife's little book. What a beautiful face she must have had. Her photograph is a little like Miss Fiona Macleod's, curiously enough. I have been so busy about "The Irish Literary Theatre" that [I] have put off writing to you from day to day. Again thanking you, I remain, yours sincerely, W. B. Yeats.

After receiving this letter, Green wrote Fiona the letter which produced her reply of March 25. Yeats's letter to Green is of interest for its direct evidence Sharp had shown Yeats a picture of Edith Rinder and identified it as a portrait of the woman who inspired Fiona. Green commented: "Whether or not Mr. Yeats ever knew the truth and felt obliged to sustain the fiction invented by the author himself I cannot say." Yeats did know a version of the truth. He knew Sharp was the vehicle of the Fiona stories and poems, and he accepted Sharp's contention Fiona was a secondary personality inhabiting his body inspired by a beautiful woman with whom he was in love. He had seen a picture of Edith Rinder, the woman who enabled the emergence of Fiona, the woman Sharp sometimes identified as Fiona.

In a mid-April letter Sharp thanked Yeats for a copy of *The Wind among the Reeds*, his "long-awaited" book of new poems: "It is beautifully got up — and you know what intimate appeal and constant charm its contents have for me. Some of your loveliest work is here. And the notes (which I must read again and again) have, in their kind, a like charm." He ended: "Either I or Miss M. — or both, separately — will review your beautiful book in one or two places. Miss M. has written to the Express — 'Literature' is already secured." Fiona's review appeared in the *Dublin Daily Express* on April 22, 1899 under the title "Mr. Yeats' New Book":

It is not often, I imagine, that titles are as apt as that which Mr. Yeats has chosen for this little book. These fewer than two-score poems, most of them within the boundary of a page, are small and slight as reeds; and the wind which moves them, which whispers or sings from them a delicate music, is as invisible, as mysterious, as elemental as that "strong creature, without flesh, without bone, that neither sees nor is seen," of which long ago Taliesin sang.

Having defined the spirit of the poems, Fiona turned to praise:

> Mr. Yeats is assuredly of that small band of poets and dreamers who write from no other impulse than because they see and dream in a reality so vivid that it is called imagination. With him the imagination is in truth the second-sight of the inward life. Thus it is that he lives with symbols, as an unimaginative nature might live with barren facts.

A note of caution creeps in: "When the reader, unfamiliar with 'the signature of symbol,' shall read these and kindred lines, will he not feel that this new priest of the Sun should translate to a more human key his too transcendental vision?"

That question leads to a discussion of the notes which comprise half of the book: "If all notes afforded reading such as one may read here! Mr. Yeats turns round mentally and shows us the other side, where the roots grow and the fibers fill with sap, and how they grow to that blossom we have already seen, and what the sap is." They are full of learning and "have something of the charm of the poems to which they stand interpreter," but

> one cannot ignore the incongruity which lies in the wedded union of brief lyrical poems with many explicatory pages. It is not their presence, then, that one objects to, but their need. Poetry is an art which is, or should be, as rigorously aloof from the extraneously explicative, as the art of painting is, or as sculpture is, or music. When Mr. Yeats gives us work on a larger scale, with a greater sweep, he will, I trust, remember that every purely esoteric symbol is an idle haze — and haze, as we know, is apt to develop into a blank mist.

From questioning the need for the notes, learned though they might be, and asserting that poetry should stand by itself without explication, Fiona reverted to high praise:

> what a lovely gift of music and spiritual intensity and beauty Mr. Yeats delivers in this book, ...No lovelier, more convincingly poetic verse has been given to us of late than these light, yet strenuous, airs of a wind that is forever mysterious, though we hold it more familiar when it blows

across the mind of some poet such as Mr. Yeats whom we know, and to whom we look.

A revised and expanded version of this review appeared as "The Later Work of Mr. W. B. Yeats," in the October 1902 issue of the *North American Review* (473–485). There, Fiona called the volume the "beginning of a new music" and included, "This little book has the remoteness, the melancholy of all poetry inspired by spiritual passion." Concerns about the obscure symbolism and the copious notes were retained, but the praise was more excessive: Yeats was "one of a small company" of "pioneers in that intimate return to nature from which we may and do expect so profound and beautiful a revelation."

Couched as they are amid words of praise that would warm the heart of any young poet, the review's critical comments contributed to the breach that occurred between Yeats and Sharp/Macleod over the next few years. Coolness had begun to surface during Sharp's visit to the West of Ireland in the fall of 1897. Yeats's Irish friends were not hesitant in sharing their reservations about Sharp's strange behavior and lack of enthusiasm for Irish nationalism. Fiona was not alone among reviewers in questioning the arcane symbolism and lengthy notes in *The Wind among the Reeds*. Yeats anticipated the criticism when he described the volume to Henry Davray (*Collected Letters II*, 306): the notes, he said, had given him "a good deal of trouble & will probably make most of the critics spend half of every review complaining that I have written very long notes about very short poems" (see also R. F. Foster, *W. B. Yeats, A Life, I*, 214–218).

Davray reviewed the book favorably in the July 1899 issue of *Mercure de France* (267–268). Interestingly, he addressed both Yeats's book and Fiona Macleod's *The Dominion of Dreams* as the work of the two major exemplars of the Celtic movement in Britain. Though Yeats knew his symbols and notes would invite criticism and though he eliminated the notes in later printings of the poems, he did not expect any critical remarks from Sharp/Macleod, his secret confederates in the Celtic Mystical Order and a major voice in the Celtic Revival. Sharp, of all people, should have appreciated the symbols, some derived from the Golden Dawn and the Celtic Order, as well as the attempt to enlighten the world about Celtic myth and lore. It was not long until Yeats's reciprocated with a critique of Fiona's *The Dominion of Dreams*.

In mid-April, having finished *Silence Farm* and with *The Dominion of Dreams* in galleys, Sharp was set to go to Paris to review the Salons and then on to the country for a period of rest and relaxation. Difficult negotiations with Grant Richards about *Silence Farm* delayed his departure. On April 16, he was leaving the following week. On April 26, he would leave on the 28th; on the 28th he could not leave until April 30 or May 1. The problem was Sharp's need for an advance from Richards to fund his trip. On April 25 he told Richards he was willing to accept fifty pounds instead of a hundred pounds upon delivery of the manuscript. Two days later he returned the manuscript to Richards (who had shipped it back to him) and agreed to accept twenty-five pounds if he could have the money now. He needed it "owing to an unforeseen emergency." Richards had the upper hand, since the sale of Sharp's previous novel, *Wives in Exile*, was disappointing, but it is sad to witness Sharp, who wanted so much to be in his own right a successful writer of fiction, pleading with the young publisher for money.

Once in France, Sharp spent about two weeks reviewing the salons in Paris. While there, he met Moina and Macgregor Mathers and read aloud several stories from his proof copy of *The Dominion of Dreams*. The Mathers were impressed. In a letter to Yeats dated May 29, Moina Mathers wrote: "We have been much delighted to meet William Sharp, who was over here. It is impossible to say how much we liked him — We felt greatly in sympathy — He is a very remarkable being I think — in every respect, & so strangely psychic." After signing the letter "Yours fraternally ever | Vestigia," her name in the Golden Dawn, she added a footnote: "Have just received 'The Dominion of Dreams' — & am much looking forward to it" (*Collected Letters II*, 51). An enthusiastic reader of Fiona, Moina became an enthusiastic admirer of Sharp, though she did not know he was Fiona.

On May 14, Sharp left Paris to spend a week in the countryside. During that week, we learn from later letters, he became ill enough to need two physicians, but he was able to return to London on May 22, where he found an author's copy of *Silence Farm*. The next day, he told Grant Richards he was pleased by the appearance of the book: "the binding, the print, the paper, are just what I would choose." He was sorry Richards had postponed publication until June 13, and gave him a list of people who should, along with the weeklies and monthlies, receive complimentary copies so they could write reviews or otherwise spread word about the book.

The year's work began to bear fruit when *The Dominion of Dreams* was officially published on May 27. Sharp sent one of his author's copies to Frank Rinder. He wanted him to have one of the first copies because the book "is at once the deepest and most intimate that F. M. has written." The letter should be read with the knowledge that Sharp's relationship with Rinder's wife was the disguised subject of many of the book's stories. Sharp told Rinder, "Too much of the book is born out of the incurable heartache, 'the nostalgia for impossible things.'" He hoped "the issues of life have been woven to beauty, for its own sake, and in divers ways to reach and help or enrich other lives." That, he said, is "a clue to the whole book," and it was at once his solace, his hope, and his ideal. "If ever a book," he continued, "came out of the depths of a life it is this." He then turned to the future of the Fiona writing: "F. M.'s influence is now steadily deepening and, thank God, along the lines I have hoped and dreamed. ... In the writings to come I hope a deeper and richer and truer note of inward joy and spiritual hope will be the living influence." More explicitly, he intended future Fiona writings to turn from love affairs and their inevitable tragic endings to stories of joy and hope. Concluding the letter, he quoted the final sentence of "The Distant Country," one of the book's stories: "Love is more great than we conceive, and Death is the keeper of unknown redemptions."

Sharp began writing "The Distant Country" in the summer of 1898, not long after he invented, in his June 28 letter to Yeats, the metaphor of the match, the flame, and the torch to describe his relationship with Edith. He concluded that letter, we recall, by saying: "How does that strike you as a subject for a tale, a book? It would be a strange one. Does it seem to you impossible? It does not seem so to me." "The Distant Country" is the tale that did not seem impossible.

Writing as Fiona in the first person, Sharp announced the story would be about love: "There is a poet's tale that I love well and have often recalled: and of how in the hour of death love may be so great that it transcends the height of hills and the waste of deserts and the salt reaches of the sea." One night Fiona dreamed of Red Ithel and Pale Bronwen in the far east and the next night of Aillinn and Sweet-spoken Baile in the Gaelic west. Both couples loved intensely, but sadly their love was consummated only in death. From those four star-crossed lovers, Fiona moved on to a pair of lovers she "loved well" who "had their day in this West of rains and rainbows, of tears and hopes" and have now passed on to the "Distant Country." The body of the tale is an effort by Sharp, speaking as Fiona, to describe and understand his relationship with Edith Rinder. Before launching the story, Sharp announced its theme by introducing the metaphor of the flame.

> Love is at once so great and so frail that there is perhaps no thought which can at the same time so appall and uplift us. And there is in love at times for some an unfathomed mystery. That which can lead to the stars can lead to the abyss. There is a limit set to mortal joy as well as to mortal suffering, and the flame may overlap itself in one as in the other. The most dread mystery of a love that is overwhelming is its death through its own flame.

Fiona then proceeded to the story of the couple she knew. The woman, who was a "flame" to the man's "mind as well as to his life," fears their all-consuming love, as it becomes more powerful, will burn itself out. At first the man rejects that fear and describes his love as "more enduring than the hills." The woman senses the end approaching when the man becomes "strangely disquieted": "'Too many dreams,' he said once, with double meaning, smiling as he looked at her, but with an unexpressed trouble in his eyes." Soon her love for him becomes "too great a flame" and implodes. She has not ceased to love him. She will continue to give him her entire being, but it has become "an image that has no life." Love came close, the man decides, and looked at them in its "immortal guise," a tameless and fierce thing "more intense than fire," which consumes what death only silences.

Here Sharp ventured into the spiritualist experiments he was conducting with Edith. The "immortal had become mortal." The man had not foreseen the result when "by a spiritual force, he accomplished that too intimate, that too close union in which none may endure." Fiona believed in the "mystery," but could not explain it. She knew of it "only through those two who broke (or of whom one broke) some occult but imperious spiritual law." The two lovers "lived long after this great change. Their love never faltered. Each, as before, came close to the other, as day and night ceaselessly meet in dawns and twilights. But that came to her no more which had gone. " And for him, "he grew slowly to understand a love more great than his. His had not known the innermost flame, that is pure fire." Fiona turned next to the depressions that often clouded the man's life: as they sometimes clouded the life of William Sharp: "Strange and terrible thoughts came to him at times. The waste places of the imagination were peopled. Often, as he has told me, through sleepless nights a solemn marching as of a vast throng rose and fell, a dreadful pulse.'"

Fiona did not know "what, in the end, clouded or unclouded" the man's spirit. But she, "who knew them, who loved them," has her "assured faith: the more, not the less, now that they have gone to that distant country of Splendour and Terror." Then the climactic sentence: "Love is more great than we conceive, and Death is the keeper of unknown redemptions." That sentence became fixed in Sharp's mind and in the minds of many readers of Fiona Macleod; it is inscribed on his gravestone under a Celtic cross in a remote protestant cemetery in Sicily.

For all its contradictions and excesses of language, this story was Sharp's effort to explain how his love for Edith Rinder and hers for him quickened his imagination and enabled him to write as Fiona Macleod. Augmented by their efforts to contact and join the realm of spirits, their love became too passionate, too intense. Whereupon they broke, or, more precisely, he broke "some occult but imperious spiritual law" that produced his intense mental conflicts. Either the flame of his love was so intense it burned itself out or, he speculates, he had not reached the "innermost flame," the flame of pure fire which can burn forever. Either way, the love became unsustainable. It could be fulfilled only in some "distant country of Splendour or Terror," wherever their spirits may live when they die.

The story's ending — the fire that fueled their love burned itself out — explains Sharp's sending the book to Frank Rinder and highlighting this story. The sentence he quotes from the story, moreover, is a plea for forgiveness. Deep love is beyond our ability to understand and control. Redemption from the pain it causes may come only after death. That conclusion must also explain Elizabeth's decision to include in the *Memoir* portions of her husband's letter to Rinder. If the operation of love is a mystery beyond human comprehension, the actions it precipitates are beyond human control and unreconcilable on this side of the shade that separates life and death. Sharp intended the story and this letter as signals to Rinder that the intensity of his relationship with his wife had begun to fade. Elizabeth surely grasped her husband's intent and included the letter in the *Memoir* for her readers to unravel.

The importance of the story is reaffirmed in two letters to Yeats. In the first in late May Sharp said of *The Dominion of Dreams*, "Few can guess how personal much of it is. You almost alone will read 'The Distant Country,' for example, with 'other eyes.'" Yeats would recognize the two principal characters are based on Sharp and the woman he loved, and he would understand the occult underpinnings and their effect. In the second, dated September 16, Sharp, writing this time as Fiona, had more to say about the story and its central metaphor which will be discussed in the next chapter.

On May 29 Sharp also wrote letters about *The Dominion of Dreams* to Æ (George Russell) and Coulson Kernahan, and he drafted Fiona letters to Benjamin Burgess Moore in the United States and to Edith Lyttelton in London. The latter presents a telling instance of Sharp's efforts to ingratiate himself with the London establishment. Edith Sophy Balfour Lyttelton, later Dame Edith Lyttelton, was a writer and an enthusiastic reader of Fiona Macleod. She was also a prominent hostess and the wife of Alfred Lyttelton (1857–1913), a Member of Parliament and, for a time, Secretary of State. In responding as Fiona in early May to a fan letter from Mrs. Lyttelton, Sharp wrote:

> I would like to know a little more of you, though more than likely we may never meet. Will you tell me? (Are you Miss or Mrs.?) But just as you like, of course. I ask, partly because of yourself as revealed in your letter: partly because of a keen personal association unwittingly awakened. But it does not matter. I am content that you are a friend, that you bear a name dear to me, and that you have been generous enough to write whole heartedly to a stranger.

Edith Lyttleton's name was dear to Sharp/Macleod, of course, because she shared her given name with Edith Rinder. Fiona continued,

> You live in London and know Mr. Yeats. Do you know his, and my friend and kinsman, Mr. William Sharp? As doubtless you have seen in the papers — for the controversy about myself seems as recurrent as the sea-serpent — he is often supposed to be me, or I to be him, or both of us to be each other, with many other speculative variations! I would like you to meet.

Fig. 52 Dame Edith Sophy Lyttelton (née Balfour) after a picture by Romney; by Lafayette, photogravure by Walker & Boutall, 1897; published 1899. © National Portrait Gallery, London. Some rights reserved.

Sharp did meet Edith Lyttleton at a social gathering shortly after he returned from France in mid-May. She told him, in what must have been a brief conversation, she had been ill. Sharp passed this news to Fiona and used it as an excuse to have Fiona tell Edith how sorry she was to hear of her illness, adding "You will, of course, know at once how I have heard of your illness." She continued,

> After your second letter I wanted you to meet Mr. William Sharp, and he would have called a month or more ago but that he had to go to France. I am glad you have met for as I think I told you, he is my most intimate friend, as well as my kinsman. If you like him, you would like me: if you do not like him, you would not like me. There! It is a woman's argument — but perhaps none the less convincing.

Farcical as those sentences sound, Sharp was not simply having fun with Mrs. Lyttleton. He was angling for another meeting, this time just the two of them. "So, you live in an old house in Westminster and have 'a swift and individual mind,' and are 'keenly sensitive to impressions,' and 'seem tuned to that finer inward suffering which goes with every nature open to mystery and to beauty.' That is what Sharp told Fiona, and she knew that. She mentally reproached Sharp for not being more explicit where upon he said frankly "It is not only that I have no time, but that I am unable to say more. If ever I meet her alone, I will see and know what, in a first visit, in the circumstances and with others present, was of necessity fugitive or uncertain." Sharp was using Fiona to prepare the way for his calling on Edith in the hope of finding her alone and prepared for an in-depth discussion of their dreams and desires. He was especially attracted to women he thought might become confidants, and this one had the added advantage of being highly placed in society.

It did not take long for Edith to invite Sharp and for him to accept. The next Fiona letter, dated June 18, is a reply to a recent letter from Edith Lyttleton:

> I am very glad that you can feel to me as to a friend. I hope you will write when so ever you will. I shall always be glad to hear from you. Indeed, I feel that we *are* friends. There are things — but above all there is *something* — in your letter which comes home to me intimately.
>
> As some slight sign of this I sent you the "Kingdom of Silence," and also asked Mr. Sharp to send you from me (I thought he had an extra copy of mine, but he hadn't!) a copy of my most personal or intimate book, "From the Hills of Dream."
>
> Do you not "write" yourself? Your letters (with their eager note, and distinctive touch) make me think you do. If so, I wish you would let me see something.
>
> I am glad you have seen my friend again. I think you and he will become friends. It is my hope. He says you are "the Hon. Mrs. Lyttelton," and wife of one of whose family I know something.
>
> And I am sure I would like you now as much as he does.

Sharp's use of Fiona to begin a friendship with a woman of importance mirrored the relationship he developed — via Yeats — with Lady Gregory, and both friendships were limited in duration. .

In late May, Sharp assured Yeats he had read and carefully considered the draft of a Celtic Mystical Order Rite. He thought it needed "something more definite in visionary insight and significance." It needed "spiritual recasting." He was waiting for inspiration, a "resurrection," that would enable him to recast the Rite. He would let Yeats know when the rebirth occurred if it was of "any worth." His "stream of inward thought" was "moving that way." He had been ill and was now better, but his doctor had ordered "hill and sea air" native to him. He and Elizabeth would forego their plans to visit Scandinavia and go instead to Ireland at the end of July, to the East coast, as it would be too expensive to go to the West. He hoped Yeats will like *The Dominion of Dreams*, which will appeal to few but hopefully "sink deep." The play Fiona Macleod would soon finish for Yeats's Celtic Theatre would no longer be called "The Tarist," but "The King of Ireland's Son." Sharp asked if Yeats will be at Gort (with Lady Gregory) or Tillyra (with Edward Martyn) in August? If so, Sharp said, he envied him as his heart was always in the West. Having to stay in hotels would make the West too expensive for their Ireland visit. Yeats surely got the unspoken point that an invitation from Lady Gregory to stay at Coole Park or from Martyn to stay at Tillyra would make the West affordable. In a postscript, Sharp sent his "most cordial remembrances & regards to Lady Gregory"

Through most of June, Sharp remained in London, trying to promote sales of his two books through friends and reviewers. On or around June 5, he wrote again to Yeats. He was still too weak to undertake the psychic effort to comment in detail on the draft copy of the Rite. It needed more work, and he would get to it as soon as he could muster the energy. Again, he asked Yeats what he thought of *The Dominion of Dreams* and wondered if he would be reviewing it. He remained curious on this point through June. Having heard nothing in response, he was surprised when Yeats's review appeared in the July *Bookman*.

After asking Yeats to do something for *Silence Farm* in his early June letter, he said he and Elizabeth would be leaving their South Hampstead flat (30 Greencroft Gardens) for good around July 20. If Yeats would be in town before then, he hoped to see him. He told Yeats for the second time he and Elizabeth would spend some time on the east coast of Ireland, north of Dublin. Then he explicitly stated his hope that Edward Martyn or Lady Gregory would invite them to the West. The lines containing that hope are crossed through with a single wavy line, but the text is clearly visible. If the line was Sharp's, he must have wanted Yeats to think he had thought better about conveying his hope for an invitation while leaving the hint highly visible. Uncharacteristically, Sharp ended by telling Yeats he was suffering one of his periodic bouts of depression: "I doubt if I'll ever live in London again. It is not likely. I do not know that I am overwhelmingly anxious to live anywhere. I think you know enough of me to know how profoundly I feel the strain of life — the strain of double life. Still, there is much to be done yet. But for that..." The mention of his double life reminds us again Sharp told Yeats in 1897 the Fiona writings flowed through him, she was a separate alternative personality triggered and inspired by a real woman with whom he enjoyed an intimate relationship.

Yeats also sent a draft copy of the rite to Fiona asking her to comment. Rather than asking Sharp's second self to respond, the letter must been intended for the woman who inspired Sharp to write as Fiona, the woman he knew only as Fiona who was helping Sharp with the Celtic Rites. In a June 14 letter Sharp as Fiona asked Yeats to be patient about the Rite for a bit longer. Sharp would be coming to see her in Scotland at the end of the following week (around June 24), and "it is important he and I should talk over, rather than correspond about this."

In late May, Sharp told Æ (George Russell) he would receive a copy of *The Dominion of Dreams* "from Miss Macleod & myself (per the publishers)." When they met in Dublin the previous fall, Sharp claimed authorship of the Fiona writings and said, as he told Yeats, she was a separate personality inhabiting his body. Russell knew Sharp was talking about one aspect of his self when he said the book "comes from deeper depths of life, both of suffering & spiritual exaltation, than any other of F. M.'s books." Preserving the fiction of Fiona's separate existence, Æ sent her a letter, which has not surfaced, that mixed praise with criticism. Writing as Fiona, Sharp responded on June 17 to Æ's "friendly and sincere letter," echoing Æ's heightened prose:

> I am like one in an apparently clear wood which is yet a mysterious maze out of which I cannot escape, or even reach the frontiers so as to discern where I am and what vistas are beyond me: nay, even the stars themselves become confused often in the darkness of the branches, and the sun's way seems equally to lead west or east, or north or south, so that I fare often bewildered even at full noon.
>
> Perhaps your letter — perhaps your will and thought — can help me. I hope so. I can say neither "yea" nor "nay" to the central part of your letter. But that spiritually I have been furnishing the palaces of the mind with empty shadows is, I fear, true. Well, I *hope* — and *believe*.

The letter ended with a request for a copy of the review Æ was writing for the *Dublin Daily Express*. When Æ sent the review to Fiona later in the summer, he excused his delay by saying he had said all he wished to say directly to her in the earlier letter. He told her "The review is sincere if critical. But I can judge by no other than an absolute standard." He concluded with a sad admission: "if you hope and believe you are on the path: Faith and hope are companions only met on the straight road and having them you have help I could not give you having lost them awhile."

Sharp went to Edinburgh on or around June 24. On the 27th he mailed a card to Grant Richards from Sterling on his way to Glasgow and the West. He wanted to assure him he would answer his letter when he returned to Edinburgh in "about a week." In the June 14 Fiona letter to Yeats, she said Sharp planned to meet her in Edinburgh and go with her to the western isles. It was his habit to talk about the time he spent with Edith Rinder as time spent with Fiona, who he claimed variously was both his cousin and his beloved. He was constructing and taking part in a drama with multiplying complexities that only he understood, and it was becoming difficult to manage. He began to tell people different and contradictory details about Fiona — who she was and how they were related — and it became harder to keep his stories straight. Sequencing Fiona's movements with those of Edith enabled him to attain some consistency. It is likely Sharp and Edith were together in the country southwest of Glasgow, in or near the Kyles of Bute, in late June, a respite that may well have lasted longer than a week and one that provided an escape from his financial problems and the nagging doubts of friends and fellow writers about the authenticity of Fiona.

Chapter Nineteen

July–December 1899

Sharp asked Yeats several times in May and June to review Fiona's *Dominion of Dreams*. Yeats praise would boost the book's sales. On July 3, while he was in the west of Scotland, Sharp began a letter to Yeats about the Celtic Order and the plays he was writing as Fiona. Before he finished, the post brought a letter from a London friend telling him Yeats had reviewed the book negatively in the July *Bookman*. Distraught, he began another letter to Yeats in which he quoted extensively the letter from his friend who had a conversation with several "literary men" who spoke favorably about Sharp's *Silence Farm*. But then,

> the talk drifted to your friend (she is your friend, is she not?) Miss Macleod's new book, and what a notable thing it is for a book of that kind to go into a second edition within three weeks of publication. So, there is a split in the Celtic Camp! I admit it amuses me. I never have believed, never can believe, in the ability of these folk to sink minor matters for a common end. I'm speaking of course of W. B. Yeats's article on Miss M. in *The Bookman*. Mr. _____ laughed & said that it was the worst snub Miss M. had received. Have you seen it? Yeats says she has enough faults to ruin any ordinary writer, and that there's not a story in her book which should not have many words struck out. As he doesn't say a word of praise or welcome about it, but only something about her surely unquestioned mythopoeic faculty — it's obvious he either doesn't find much in the book, or wants to take her down a peg or two.

Sharp had not seen the July issue of the *Bookman*, but he expected it to arrive the next day. "Meanwhile," he continued the second Yeats letter, "I can hardly credit what my friend writes."

> I hope it is not true. It will greatly distress & dishearten Miss Macleod, who had hoped so much for a cordial & generous word from you about

her maturest & most carefully wrought book: but I hope it is not true for the sake of the plays also, for if once deeply discouraged Miss M. may not touch them again for months. And still more, & far more importantly than for any individual concern, I hope it is not so — for the always bitterly opposed idea of unselfish & united action among "our scattered few" will be grievously handicapped by any suggestion that you have "gone for" or even "snubbed" Miss Macleod.

When a copy of the *Bookman* arrived the next day, Sharp found in Yeats's review two paragraphs of praise and only one expressing reservations about Fiona's overly florid style. He decided not to send Yeats the second letter, and it has surfaced in a batch of Sharp letters to John Macleay recently acquired by the National Library of Scotland. How it came into Macleay's hands is unknown, but Elizabeth may have mistakenly included among letters she returned to Macleay after using them in the *Memoir*. Instead of sending that letter, Sharp wrote to Yeats as Fiona and asked him "to indicate the passages he took most exception to." According to Elizabeth, Yeats sent "a carefully annotated copy of the book," and "a number of the revisions that differentiate the version in the *Collected Edition* from the original issue are the outcome of this criticism" (*Memoir*, 309).

The person most likely to have stirred up trouble between two leading figures of the Celtic Renaissance was Sharp's publisher, Grant Richards. He knew where Sharp was staying in Scotland, and he knew Sharp would be sensitive to any criticism of Fiona's *Dominion of Dreams*, particularly anything negative by Yeats. The letter writer's conversation with the "literary men" took place at the Savile Club in London. According to the Club's records, Richards became a member on March 24, 1899. That the men spoke positively about Sharp's *Silence Farm* is not surprising since Grant Richards published it. Nor is it surprising the men were amused by Yeats's criticism of *The Dominion of Dreams* and viewed it as a "split in the Celtic camp." Some in London's literary establishment, Richards among them, viewed Fiona Macleod and other Celtic Revivalists with a mixture of humor and contempt.

On July 20, the Sharps, back in London, stored their furniture and vacated their South Hampstead flat. They stayed briefly with Elizabeth's mother in Bayswater and then returned to their "dear West Highlands, to Loch Goil, to Corrie in Arran, and to Iona" (*Memoir*, 311). In August they crossed to Belfast and, after a few days in the city, went north to

Ballycastle on the Antrim coast. On August 26, they moved south to Newcastle in County Down, stayed there three weeks, and spent ten days in Dublin before returning on September 26 to London.

Benjamin Burgess Moore, the Yale undergraduate who fell in love with Fiona, announced he was coming to England and hoped to meet her. In a July 12 letter, Fiona assured him he was one of the few for whom she would break her invariable rule, but she needed complete and prolonged rest and was about to leave Edinburgh for a two- or three-month yachting trip in the far north. She suggested Moore meet instead with her "most intimate friend, Mr. William Sharp," who "asked me to say he hoped you would call next Monday afternoon (17th) about 3 or 3.30." Moore accepted that suggestion, and Fiona, in an August 11 letter, said she was glad Moore liked Sharp. Surprisingly, she continued, "If you had not, you would not like me! Truly: for we are not only close kindred but at one in all things." Mr. Sharp had taken a liking to his "American friend" and hoped he would call again in October on his way back to America from the continent. He was leaving his South Hampstead address at the end of July and would be living from October first in Chorleywood, just northwest of London and reachable by train. Moore could call on him either there or at his club, the Grosvenor in New Bond Street. He was currently in Ireland, "on the north Antrim coast called Ballycastle (the neighborhood whence Deirdre and the Sons of Usna sailed for Scotland when fleeing from Concobar)." Fiona had just received a letter from Sharp in which he described his "titanic swim among rough breakers on a wild coast near the Giant's Causeway, so, after all, his hated London life does not seem to have sapped his vigor!" Later she will go to Ireland to meet him. She already knew "the wild Antrim coast — and the lonely, remote, Gaelic-speaking isle of Ragherry (Rathlin) where the grandson of the great Nial the Victorious went down with all his fleet." Why Sharp wanted to portray himself to Moore as strong and vigorous is not clear, but the mentions of Gaelic mythology were designed to sustain his interested in Fiona.

Having now met Moore and decided he was a sensible young man who might become a useful promoter of Fiona in America, Sharp had Fiona share some details about her work. She planned several revisions of *The Dominion of Dreams*. They were too late for the third edition, but she hoped there would be a fourth so she could insert the changes despite the publisher's opposition. She mentioned an "exceedingly good" review the book received the previous week in the *Publisher's Circular*, and a complimentary notice of the book in, of all papers, *Punch*. Then surprisingly, given the favorable reviews and Sharp's claims that it was the best Fiona had done, he wrote as Fiona: "I am very dissatisfied with it — and would gladly rearrange and rewrite it all from beginning to end." During the fall, Fiona hoped to finish a volume of spiritual tales that would be named either "the Reddening of the West" or, after its chief essay, "The Divine Adventure." Unless she could finish one of its crucial pieces, an essay on Iona, she would delay its publication until the spring of 1900. She also hoped to finish before Christmas a volume of three plays: "The King of Ireland's Sons," "The Immortal Hour," and "Queen Ganore." That volume did not materialize, but the first play, retitled "The House of Usna," was performed in April 1900 and published in July 1900 in the *National and English Review*. The second play, "The Immortal Hour," was published in the *Fortnightly Review* in November 1900. More will be said about them in the next chapter. After sounding more like Sharp than the modest lady of the Isles, Sharp revived her coyness in concluding: "Now after all this personal detail see that you write to me from France, or I will not forgive you, nor ever write to you again. | So, conditionally, your friend, Fiona Macleod."

Sharp wrote several other remarkable letters in Ireland. In late August, he told his new friend, Edith Lyttelton, that Fiona sailed to Iceland but did not stay long before being blown south to the Inner Hebrides by "a continuous polar wind which almost made sails as swift as steam." He spent some time with her before coming to Ireland, and she might join him there "for a week or so in Connemara, and again in Antrim." After reading Sharp's *Silence Farm*, Edith Lyttelton had written to ask about his other writings. Among other books Sharp mentioned *Sospiri di Roma*, the lyrics he wrote and published in Italy in 1891. He promised to give or lend Mrs. Lyttleton a copy of the rare, limited edition and described some of the circumstances of its composition. He might tell her more in person than he cared to write. Was that only another effort to land a meeting with Mrs. Lyttelton, or did he intend to tell her about a beautiful young woman who inspired the poems. Had he done so he would not have identified the woman as Edith Rinder, but simply as Fiona Macleod. He sometimes claimed the mysterious and elusive

Fiona was his cousin, and sometimes he went further, implying they were lovers. Edith was often conflated in his mind with Fiona, and the fictional Fiona story was intricately interwoven with the facts of his life.

On September 12, his forty-fourth birthday, Sharp, in a reflective mood, wrote a letter to Adelaide Elder, Elizabeth's girlhood friend, in which he recalled that on his twenty-second birthday in 1877 she had given him "a beautifully bound book by a poet with a strange name and by me quite unknown — Dante Gabriel Rossetti." Had he not received that gift, the whole course of his life would have been different. He mentioned the book to Sir Noel Paton, a Scottish painter, a family friend, and a friend of Rossetti who dissuaded him from "going abroad on a career of adventure." Later, in 1881, Paton provided the introduction he presented to Rossetti when he knocked on his door in Cheyne Walk and was invited in for the first of many visits. That event, Sharp wrote, "completely redirected the whole course of my life." He knew Adelaide understood how "in the complex spiritual interrelation of life," the "single impulse of a friend" can have "so profound a significance." As Sharp approached his fiftieth birthday, they became occasions for reflecting on his past and mustering resolve to get on with unfinished projects.

A Fiona letter to Yeats dated September 16 thanked him for returning a copy of *The Dominion of Dreams* with suggested revisions. According to Fiona the book had "already been in great part revised by my friend" [Sharp himself] who had "in one notable instance followed [Yeats's] suggestion." She did not bother to say why Sharp was revising her book. In an October 20 letter to John Macleay, Sharp, as Fiona, said *The Dominion of Dreams* was now in its fifth edition, but she had still been unable to make any revisions. She hoped to be able to make revisions in the seventh edition, and it seemed probable that would occur by or shortly after the first of the year. As it turned out, the revisions had to wait until 1910 when Elizabeth, in accord with her husband's instructions, reprinted *The Dominion of Dreams* in Volume III of the Uniform Edition of *The Works of "Fiona Macleod"* (London: William Heinemann).

From revisions, Sharp as Fiona turned in the September 16 letter to "The Distant Country," one of the stories in *The Dominion of Dreams*:

> Of one thing only I am convinced, as is my friend (an opinion shared with the rare few whose judgment really means much), that there is

> nothing in *Dominion of Dreams* or elsewhere in these writings under my name to stand beside "The Distant Country." Nothing else has made so deep and vital an impression both on men and women — and possibly it may be true what a very subtle and powerful mind has written about it, that it is the deepest and most searching utterance on the mystery of passion which has appeared in our time. It is indeed the core of *all* these writings — and will outlast them all.

Nowhere else was Sharp so direct in asserting the autobiographical underpinnings of the Fiona writings and the importance therein of love and sexual passion. He continued writing as Fiona:

> Of course, I am speaking for myself only. As for my friend, his heart is in the ancient world and his mind for ever questing in the domain of the spirit. I think he cares little for anything but through the remembering imagination to recall and interpret, and through the formative and penetrative imagination to discover certain mysteries of psychological and spiritual life. (Apropos, I wish you very much to read, when it appears in the *Fortnightly Review* — probably either in October or in November — the spiritual "essay" called "The Divine Adventure" — an imaginative effort to reach the same vital problems of spiritual life along the separate, yet inevitably interrelated, lines of the Body, the Will (Mind or Intellect), and the Soul.) ["The Divine Adventure" appeared in the November 1 and December 11 issues of the *Fortnightly Review*.]

The Dominion of Dreams, Fiona implied, embodied the feminine approach to life and love, while *The Divine Adventure* embodied that of her friend, the masculine William Sharp. *The Divine Adventure*, the articles in the fall of 1899 and the book in the summer of 1900, was, nevertheless, published as the work of Fiona Macleod Such were the contradictions that surfaced in Sharp's management of the dual authorship and double identity.

From the two modes of writing, Sharp as Fiona turned to yet another effort to define the role of Edith Rinder in the Fiona Macleod writings. Yeats had asked Fiona which of her tales she liked best, and she responded, "Temperamentally, those which appeal to me most are those with the play of mysterious psychic force in them." She singled out, "The Distant Country" as displaying the "mysterious psychic force" and "the core of all" the Fiona writings. As indicated in the previous chapter, the story was Sharp's attempt to fictionalize and thus come to terms with his relationship with Edith Rinder. He hoped Yeats would read the story as a coded effort to describe how his love for Edith quickened his imagination and enabled him to write as Fiona.

Yeats knew Sharp was the author of the Fiona stories and poems, but he continued to ask if Fiona was a real person who inspired Sharp to write as Fiona, a secondary personality of Sharp's, or a spiritual being inhabiting Sharp's body and using him as an amanuensis. After drawing Yeats's attention to "The Distant Country" Sharp, as Fiona, turned to the story's fire metaphor which he had introduced to Yeats in a June 1898 letter. Here, more than a year later, he expanded and transformed it into an elaborate allegory involving the match, the torch, and the spiritual wind, a new element which fans the flame.

> Again, I must tell you that all the formative and expressional as well as nearly all the visionary power is my friend's. In a sense only his is the passive part; but it is the allegory of the match, the wind, and the torch. Everything is in the torch in readiness, and, as you know, there is nothing in itself in the match. But there is the mysterious latency of fire between them: in that latent fire of love — the little touch of silent igneous potency at the end of the match. Well, the match comes to the torch, or the torch to the match — and, in what these symbolize, one adds spiritual affinity as a factor — and all at once flame is born. The torch says all is due to the match. The match knows that the flame is not hers, but lies in that mystery of thitherto awakened love, suddenly brought into being by contact. But beyond both is the wind, the spiritual air. Out of the unseen world it fans the flame. In that mysterious air, both the match and the torch hear strange voices. But the match is now part of the torch, lost in him, lost in that flame. Her small still voice speaks in the mind and spirit of the torch, sometimes guiding, sometimes inspiring, out of the deep mysterious intimacies of love and passion. That which is born of both, the flame, is subject to neither — but is the property of the torch. The air which came at the union of both is sometimes called Memory, sometimes Art, sometimes Genius, sometimes Imagination, sometimes Life, sometimes the Spirit. It is all.

The match is Fiona, the presumed author of the letter, and the torch is Sharp. Most people admire the flame and wonder only at the torch. A few "look for the match beyond the torch, and, finding her [Edith Rinder], are apt to attribute to her that which is not hers, save as a spiritual dynamic agent." Occasionally the "match may also have *in petto* the qualities of the torch — particularly memory and vision: and so can stimulate and amplify the imaginative life of the torch. But the torch

[Sharp] is at once the passive, the formative, the mnemonic and the artistically and imaginatively creative force." More explicitly: "he and he alone is the flame, his alone both the visionary, the formative, and the expressional." Sharp, as both the torch and the flame it produces, was the sole author of the Fiona writings and Fiona, or more precisely the real woman behind her, was his muse. The wind — or spiritual force — was introduced to appeal to Yeats who believed spirits intervened and energized the creative process. Once its complexities are unraveled, the letter assigns William Sharp full credit for the writings of Fiona Macleod. It is no wonder he asked Yeats to destroy it. ["Read — copy what you will, as apart from me — and destroy this."]

In "The Distant Country," Sharp implied the love that defined his relationship with Edith had changed shape. In this letter he was more explicit: Edith's role as Sharp's muse, as his inspiration for the Fiona Macleod writings, was diminishing. "Of late," he wrote, "the 'match' is more than ever simply a hidden flame in the mind of the 'torch.' When I add that the match never saw or heard a line of "Honey of the Wild Bees" (which you admire so much) till after written, you will understand better." In that story, Sharp introduced what he called "ancient Celtic lore" to equate Love and Death. Rinn, known as "Honey of the Wild Bees," fell in love with Aevgrain, the beautiful daughter of Deirdre and Naois. Having seduced her and caused her to love and follow him, he announced he was the Lord of the Shadow whose name in this world is Death. As in "The Distant Country," passionate love can be perfectly and permanently consummated only in the afterlife, the realm of spirits. In drawing Yeats's attention to this story, Sharp wanted him to know the woman behind Fiona was becoming less important in producing the writings published as her work. It was Sharp who introduced the spirit from the shadow world to portray the impossibility of perfect love in this world. It was Sharp who foresaw the inevitable ending of his relationship with the woman behind Fiona and the gradual reintegration of his personality.

Fiona, Sharp posits, was speaking only for herself in expressing her preferences for stories in *The Dominion of Dreams*, not for her friend Sharp:

> [His] heart is in the ancient world and his mind forever questing in the domain of the spirit. I think he cares little for anything but through

> the *remembering* imagination to recall and interpret, and through the formative and penetrative imagination to discover certain mysteries of psychological and spiritual life. (Apropos, I wish you very much to read, when it appears in the *Fortnightly Review* — probably either in October or in November — the spiritual 'essay' called "The Divine Adventure" — an imaginative effort to reach the same vital problems of spiritual life along the separate, yet inevitably interrelated, lines of the Body, the Will (Mind or Intellect), and the Soul.)

The forthcoming "Divine Adventure" would be published as the work of Fiona Macleod, but it would be an expression of William Sharp's attempt to discover through "the *remembering*, formative and penetrative imagination certain mysteries of psychological and spiritual life." Sharp had tried hard to maintain in his fiction and poetry the gender difference between the voice of Fiona and his own, but the difference had become less essential. Moving forward, the Fiona writings would project a voice that combined feminine and masculine sensibilities, a voice closer to that Sharp adopted in his reviews and essays on literature and art.

For financial and health reasons, the Sharps decided "to make the experiment of wintering at Chorleywood," a small town immediately northwest of London, now part of greater London. Ever in need of money, they hoped to economize by living outside London and avoid having to go abroad to escape the city's smoke and smog in the winter. On the first of October 1899, they occupied the first floor of a new building named Wharncliffe with floor-to-ceiling windows overlooking Chorleywood's High Commons. A baker named Frederick Baldwin owned the building, and his bakery occupied the ground floor. A member of the Hertfordshire Genealogical Society, recognizing William Sharp's occupancy of the building at the turn of the 20th century, has posted a contemporary photograph on the Society's website and seeks older photographs so the building can be restored. On October 8, Sharp told Richard Garnett they had settled in Chorleywood, a "bracing & delightful place, near Milton's Chalfont St. Giles and Arnold's beloved Chess" where he hoped Garnett would "feel inclined to come for a breath of vivid air." Concluding an October 19 letter to Watts-Dunton, he remarked: "How lovely autumn is at this moment. The trees here are divinely lovely."

Fig. 53 Recent photograph of Wharncliffe, Chorleywood, London, http://www.hertfordshire-genealogy.co.uk/images/!/c/chorleywood/chorleywood-wharncliffe-google.jpg

On October 25, Grant Allen suffered a painful death from liver cancer. His family arranged for his body to be cremated on October 27 following a brief ceremony in the Brookwood Crematorium in Woking. Sharp was deeply moved by the death of his friend who shared many of his "advanced" views about the nature of love and the restraints of marriage. His effort to attend the service in Woking was stymied by poor communications and missed connections. Having failed to reach Woking, he returned to Chorleywood and wrote a sympathy letter to Allen's son. Only in that morning's paper had he learned of Allen's death and the service set for three o'clock that afternoon: "I at once changed my clothes, caught the one available train, & drove straight across — but, in the hurried departure, I had unfortunately read 'Charing Cross' for 'Waterloo' — & so I missed the train after all, to my profound regret everyway." He also explained his absence and conveyed his sympathy to Grant Richards, his publisher and Allen's nephew. In a letter to Murray Gilchrist that day, he said he was acutely saddened by the death of his good friend, Grant Allen: "I loved the man — and admired the brilliant writer and catholic critic and eager student. He was of a most winsome nature. The world seems shrunken a bit more. As yet, I cannot realise I am not to see him again. Our hearts ache for his wife — an ideal loveable woman — a dear friend of us both." He also told Gilchrist he had undertaken, for financial reasons, a huge study of art in the nineteenth century that, with his other writing, occupied all his time. Still, he remained pleased with Chorleywood and the beauty of the fall season: "We like this most beautiful and bracing neighborhood greatly […] It has been the loveliest October I remember for years. The equinoxial bloom is on every tree. But today, after long drought, the weather has broken, and a heavy rain has begun."

In early November Sharp invited Gilchrist to come to London for a few days at the end of the month to be his guest at a dinner of the Omar Khayyam Club: "You know that the Omar Khayyam Club is the 'Blue Ribbon' so to speak of Literary Associations, and that its occasional meetings are more sought after than any other. As I think you know I am one of the 49 members — and I much want you to be my guest at the forthcoming meeting on Friday Dec. 1." It would be a special occasion. The President of the club had honored Sharp by asking him to write and recite a poem at the dinner. The invitation meant a great deal as it confirmed his presence among London's literary elite. Though Elizabeth seconded the invitation to Gilchrist, he did not appear.

An undertow soon diminished the pleasure of life in Chorleywood. As November darkened into December, Sharp had to take the unusual step of asking Watts-Dunton for a loan:

> What with long and disastrous illness at the beginning of the year — having to help others dear to me — and, finally, losses involved through the misdeed of another, I find myself on my beam-ends. By next Spring I hope to have things righted so far, if health holds out — but my pinch is just now, with less than £5 in the world to call my own at this moment!

Much of their income derived from journalistic art criticism, and all such work had been cut back by two-thirds due to the Boer War. When he finished the history of fine arts in the nineteenth century, it would repay the time and effort he was devoting to it, but nothing until then. He asked Watts-Dunton if he could lend him fifty pounds. If that was too much, he might be able to manage with twenty-five pounds, which had the buying power of 2,766 contemporary pounds and 3,350 dollars. He would be able to repay that much by February or even sooner. How ironic that Sharp who was about to be honored by his peers at the Omar

Khayyam Club dinner had only five pounds to his name. A man of means and considerable compassion, Watts-Dunton came through with twenty-five pounds.

"The Divine Adventure" appeared in the November and December issues of the *Fortnightly Review*. On December 30, Sharp told Gilchrist, who knew Fiona was Sharp, "It was written *de profundis*, partly because of a compelling spirit, partly to help others passionately eager to obtain some light on this most complex and intimate spiritual destiny." On that day, he also wrote to Frank Rinder, his "dear friend and literary comrade" to wish him "health and prosperity in 1900." He wanted him to read the opening pages of the Fiona Macleod essay called "Iona" which would soon appear in a book with "The Divine Adventure": "I have never written anything [...] so spiritually autobiographical. Strange as it may seem it is almost all literal reproduction of actuality with only some dates and names altered." Having asserted his authorship of the essay, he said to Rinder, "But enough of that troublesome F. M.!" This assertion — he is, and he is not Fiona Macleod — is a fitting conclusion to a year in which he made some progress in clarifying, for himself if not for others, the complex relationship of William Sharp, Edith Rinder, and Fiona Macleod.

Chapter Twenty
1900

In early January Sharp sent Nellie Allen a letter with a copy of the poem he delivered at the December meeting of the Omar Khayyam Club. The poem alluded to her husband, and in his preliminary remarks he called Grant Allen "a fine writer and true-hearted man" whose death was a loss to his many friends and to the club. Both Sharps looked forward to seeing Nellie again as soon as she vacated The Croft in Hindhead and settled in London. On January 8, he wrote a long letter to Edith Lyttelton who remained under the spell of Fiona. He was sorry to hear she had been ill through much of the fall. He had also been ill and was determined not "to spend another midwinter in this damp & sunless climate." He asked if she had written anything lately and declared Fiona, having sampled her earlier work, felt assured she "could, and probably some day soon would, write a notable book." Fiona's new book, *The Divine Adventure*, would be published in March by Chapman & Hall. Its title was also the title of its long titular essay which had appeared in the recent November and December issues of Chapman & Hall's *Fortnightly Review*. The book will be "personal" and "autobiographical," unlike anything Fiona has produced. As for William Sharp, he was "at work every available hour on a commissioned 'History of the Fine Arts in the Nineteenth Century' — a kind of synthesis, or coup d'oeil perhaps, of the dominating features and interrelated developments of modern art." He concluded by asking Mrs. Lyttelton to join him the following Monday for tea and a chat at his club or, if she preferred, he could come to her.

During the warm and sunny fall Sharp enjoyed life in Chorleywood, but as winter set in he began to tire of country life and dislike the travel in and out of London in foul weather. In an early February letter, he told Theodore Watts-Dunton he would ask the Walter Scott publishing to make the requested "rectifications" in Watts-Dunton's sonnets in the next edition of *The Sonnets of the Nineteenth Century*. Given his current money problems it is not surprising that he went on to say about that book:

> It's a little hard that for this book I got £10 — & that all I ever had from it since was £5 for preparing a special reprint! It has gone into innumerable editions — & in all forms has sold to an unprecedented extent for a book of the kind, here & in America etc. At even a royalty of 1d a copy I'd had over £400 — so imagine what Scott's profit must be!

The book had sold about 100,000 copies and another edition would be out in the Spring.

He turned next to his ill health since the turn of the year:

> I know you will be sorry to hear that since Christmas I have had a bad time of it. First, I got influenza again, with pneumonic complication — then an inflammatory condition of the veins was set up — & thro' that & an accident on the railway I started a bad varicose vein, badly strained, & constantly threatening a clot (phlebitis) — laming me as though I had the gout! — & keeping me to the house for weeks. Then a very painful & prostrating meningeal neuralgia set in — partly from overstrain of work & financial straits etc. Still, all might have gone well, had not I gone one day (under great stress of agony) to a dentist to be sure there was nothing the matter with my teeth. He was a faddist, & incompetent — & having found all absolutely sound said he wd. take out five sound teeth then & there (& without gas!) as that would cure me! I was weak enough to be persuaded of urgency — but after the second sound tooth had been literally torn out (for my teeth are very sound & strong) I fainted & he could do no more. It now turns out he was wholly wrong as to this — & I have lost two sound molars & have my neuralgia still, only worse! The nervous shock proved so bad for me that my wife, & the doctor, became seriously perturbed. The upshot was that a few days ago I was ordered away for a month to recruit by the sea — & would have gone 2 days ago but for a sudden painful attack of lumbago.

From a twenty-first-century perspective, one can only wonder how people endured such a litany of pain.

The lengthy description of his illnesses was "partly a preamble" to explain his inability to repay the £25 Watts-Dunton loaned him in November. He had hoped to do so in February, but his inability to work

Chapter Twenty: 1900

meant no income. He planned to go into London the next day to see if from his bank or other sources he could raise enough money to go away for a month as recommended by his doctor. Elizabeth was down with bronchitis, and she also needed to "recruit by the sea." His trip to London must have been successful since he and Elizabeth escaped for a month to Broadstair, a coastal resort town on what was then an island and is now a peninsula at the most easterly point of Kent. He concluded the letter by saying he hoped to see Watts-Dunton and be "recuperative & buoyant" when he returned. Shortly after returning in early March, he went to Edinburgh to visit his mother and sister for two days on "family business." On March 15, he wrote to William Blackwood proposing an article for *Blackwood's Magazine* on recent French Art or an article on Breton poets. He planned to visit Paris for the Salon which would open on April 2 and then go on to Brittany where he hoped to meet and interact with poets. Since Blackwood was not in his Edinburgh office when Sharp called, he would not have the pleasure of meeting him since he was returning to London the next morning. The proposed articles did not make it into *Blackwood's Magazine*.

As it turned out, he fell ill again, and instead of leaving Edinburgh as planned on March 16, he stayed an additional ten days. Back in Chorleywood on the 26th, he wrote a note to Stanley Little: "Just returned — but E. still very seedy and at her mother's. I go there now but shall be back tomorrow and hope to write then or Wedny." When he wrote two days later, he began by saying he was months behind with urgent work due to illnesses, his and Elizabeth's. After recounting the progress of their maladies, he turned to the work he had managed to accomplish. Between January 1 and 21, he wrote 50,000 words for what would become *The Progress of Art in the Nineteenth Century*. Then he came down with the flu and was unable to continue. He still had 70,000 words to write, but he could not get to it until mid-April. Elizabeth agreed to write an additional 15,000 words about music, and they hoped to have it all done before the end of May. Commissioned by The Linscott Publishing Company in Toronto and Philadelphia, it became Volume Twenty-Two in their gigantic Nineteenth Century Series. It was published separately in 1902 by W. and R. Chamber, Ltd., in London and Edinburgh.

Little asked Sharp about this work because he had agreed to write another volume for the Linscott series and wondered how much he should charge. Sharp said he "had special terms, without which it wd. have been wholly impossible to take up the book: and not only special terms, but special conditions of payment." Unfortunately, he could not share those terms with Little because he was under a pledge of honor, a given promise, not to do so. He also asked Little not to mention his name or what he had told him about dealing with the Linscott firm. Unless specified in a contract, Little was unlikely to get an advance from Linscott so he should just send in his manuscript and hope for royalties. He was leaving in a few days to review the Salon in Paris and then to spend some time in Brittany.

When he returned to London in mid-April, he began making arrangements for a performance of a Fiona Macleod play. While visiting Grant Allen in 1897, he met Frederick Whelen, one of Allen's nephews, who wanted to find a vehicle for producing contemporary art plays. Sharp expressed interest since he was writing a highly symbolic Fiona Macleod play destined, he thought, for the Celtic Theater Yeats was planning in Dublin. Encouraged by Sharp and some prominent actors and businessmen, Whelen, in July 1899, invited several hundred people to attend an organizing meeting for what became the Stage Society. Seventy-five invitees showed up at his house in London's Red Lion Square. Despite the crowd, Whelen managed to form a seven-member Managing Committee that included Sharp. It was agreed the Society would sponsor several performances of new plays every year. They would take place on Sunday evenings when theaters would otherwise be dark because of the prohibition of public performances on the Sabbath. To circumvent the law, the performances would be called meetings of the Society and only members of the society and invited guests would be able to attend.

The performances began in the fall of 1899, and Whelen, with Sharp's encouragement, scheduled a production of Fiona Macleod's "The House of Usna" for the fifth meeting of the Society in the Globe Theatre on April 29, 1900. Sharp sent a Fiona letter to Whelen dated April 16 which contained her permission for the performance and delegated all final revisions and performance details to her "friend and relative Mr. William Sharp." Her only request had to do with "reserved accommodations." She asked for two contiguous boxes, one for the Sharps and herself if she was able to "come from Scotland for the occasion." The second should be offered to George Meredith in case he was able to attend or, if not, to other friends. She requested eight reserved stall seats which she designated for W. L. Courtney, Editor of the *Fortnightly*; James Knowles Esq., Editor of the *Nineteenth Century*; W. B. Yeats. Esq.; Mr. and Mrs. Ernest Rhys; The Hon. Alfred & Mrs. A. Lyttelton; and Mr. Percy Bunting who edited the *Contemporary Review*. The tickets were to be given directly to Sharp who would either send them to Fiona or forward them as she directed. The absence of Edith and Frank Rinder from the list of people for whom tickets were to be reserved is curious. I expect it was due to the possibility that Meredith might attend. We recall Sharp had introduced Edith as Fiona Macleod to Meredith who described her as one of the most beautiful women he ever met. It would be more than embarrassing if he saw Edith at the performance and identified her as Fiona, the author of the play. Since Meredith, in the end, was unable to attend, the Rinders may have been among the friends who occupied the second reserved box.

"The House of Usna" was one of three Fiona plays Sharp was writing with Yeats' encouragement. On April 29, it shared the bill with two Maeterlinck plays: "The Interior" and "The Death of Tintagiles." Y. M. Capel composed music for the Sharp play, and it was directed by Granville Barker. According to Elizabeth, one critic said the play had beauty and atmosphere, "two very rare things on the stage, but I did not feel that it quite made a drama, or convince, as a drama should, by the continuous action of inner or outer forces. It was, rather, passion turning upon itself, and with no language but a cry." Other reviews were more positive. Elizabeth said Sharp "took the greatest interest in the rehearsals, and in the performance. He thoroughly enjoyed the double play as he chatted about Fiona during the intervals unconcerned about the risks of their detecting the real authorship." The play was printed in the *National Review* in July 1900 and then in book form by Thomas Mosher in Maine in 1903 (*Memoir*, 317–318).

By July 1900, the Stage Society was floundering for lack of resources. Sharp and Whelen developed a plan to rescue it which Sharp described in a letter to the actor/manager Frederick Charles Charrington, a fellow member of the Managing Committee. The plan prevailed, Sharp became the Society's Chairman, and Whelen its Secretarial Manager. The Society went on for forty years and produced more than two hundred plays that would not have succeeded initially in the West End.

For some time, Sharp had used the London address of Lillian Rea rather than that of his sister in Edinburgh as the return address for the Fiona letters. Receiving the letters in London, where he spent most of his time while in Britain, enabled him to draft answers more quickly and send them to Edinburgh for Mary to copy and mail. In a June 1 letter to Grant Richards, Fiona identified Miss Rea as her "late agent and typist" and said she was away recovering from illness. Fiona was having all her correspondence "sent through a literary friend, whose address heads this letter." This address (11 Woronzow Road, London) was the home of Edith Rinder who was often conflated in Sharp's mind with Fiona and who began providing secretarial assistance for Sharp.

In June 1899, Grant Richards, at Sharp's suggestion, asked Fiona to assemble and edit a poetry anthology which would be called "The Hour of Beauty." A year later, a Fiona letter informed Richards she could not promise to have the book done before the New Year. She had been "much of an invalid" since the previous November and unable to do much work. On 20 October 1900, Fiona wrote again to Richards, with the Lillian Rea return address restored, to say she was resting in London for two days before leaving England for Tangiers. She had been seriously ill, and "a southern air" and "absolute rest are imperatively prescribed." She had to "relinquish [...] all hopes" of finishing *The Hour of Beauty* by Christmas. She wanted to give Richards the option of withdrawing from their agreement or letting it stand indefinitely until her health recovered so she could "take up properly that which can be done only absolutely *con amore*, and with scrupulous judgment and care." She wondered, instead, if Richards would like to publish a little volume of her poetry in the spring:

> It would be called either *For a Little Clan* or else *The Immortal Hour* — the latter being the title of the greater part of the little book, a poetic old-world drama, perhaps to be defined as "a symbolist drama" (though I dislike such designations) which is to appear in the *Fortnightly Review* either in November or December (or in both). The remainder of the book would consist of the few selected poems (all I care to preserve) from a volume of verse published some four or five years ago, *From the Hills of Dream*, with some new and uncollected poems.

A Fiona letter to Richards dated October 31 indicates he decided to defer the anthology until she was able to finish it. He liked her suggestion of a small book of poems which would include "The Immortal Hour." In her response, Fiona expressed her hope that she would be able to select the poems and send copy for the book "from Marseille or Malta or Algiers (I do not know where yet) by the end of November." To avoid Richards asking to meet Fiona, her October 20 letter informed him she would be in London only two days on her way South. Her October 31 letter is postmarked from Paris on November 13 which means Sharp held it to avoid a London postmark and mailed it from Paris on his way south.

In the summer and fall of 1899, Sharp implied to several friends he was experiencing a blurring or a reintegration of the two aspects of his personality and suggested his future writings would reflect a merger of the Fiona voice and the William Sharp voice with the former more prominent in his fiction and poetry and the latter more prominent in his nonfiction. In his 8 January 1900 letter to Edith Lyttelton, he said Fiona Macleod's *The Divine Adventure* would be "unlike anything she has done; it would be personal and autobiographical, especially in the essay called 'Iona,'" parts of which would appear in February and March in the *Fortnightly*. The periodical's publisher, Chapman & Hall, would also publish the book containing "Iona" and other essays. When it appeared in May 1900, it carried a longer title derived from its content, *The Divine Adventure: Iona: By Sundown Shores: Studies in Spiritual History*, and it went through several editions during the year. In a Fiona letter to John Macleay in early October 1899 Sharp wrote:

> There is a sudden departure from fiction ancient or modern in something of mine that is coming out in the November and December issues of "The Fortnightly Review." I hope you will read "The Divine Adventure," as it is called — though this spiritual essay is more "remote" i.e., unconventional, and in a sense more "mystical," than anything I have done. But it is out of my inward life. It is an essential part of a forthcoming book of spiritual and critical essays or studies in the spiritual history of the Gael, to be called "The Reddening of the West."

The essay improbably personifies the Body, the Will and the Soul and sets them on a journey to discover the meaning of life: "We had never been at one, though we had shared the same home, and had enjoyed so much in common; but to each, at the same time, had come the great desire of truth, than which there is none greater save that of beauty." Confusion sets in from the start as the narrator of the journey sees his

Body, his Soul, and his Will independently travelling through a Scottish landscape each talking with people they meet along the way. Just who, we wonder, is the observer-narrator? What part is left after the departure of Body, Soul and Will? Perhaps the intellect, but that piece of the puzzle seems to merge with the Will or the Mind as the journey proceeds. It is a decided relief to find the narrator learned at the end:

> There is no absolute Truth, no absolute Beauty, even for the Soul. It may be that in the Divine Forges we shall be so moulded as to have perfect vision. Meanwhile only that Truth is deepest, that beauty highest which is seen, not by the Soul only, or by the Mind, or by the Body, but all three as one. Let each be perfect in kind and perfect in unity. This is the signal meaning of the mystery.

If that is the conclusion, was the thirty-four-page journey worth the author's effort and the reader's patience? It must have been, since the book went through several editions. Its success shines a bright light on the efforts of many in 1900 to come to terms with the previous century's scientific discoveries. With its masculine narrator and the masculine nature of his dissected parts, the essay comes out of the "inward life" of William Sharp. The voice of Fiona Macleod, the nominal author, is nowhere to be heard.

The longest essay in the volume is "Iona" in which the narrative voice of Fiona alternates with that of Sharp in chronicling stories and legends associated with the island. As mentioned in the previous chapter, Sharp, in December 1899, wrote Frank Rinder a letter in which he said he would like him to read

> the opening pages of "Iona," for they contain a very deep and potent spiritual faith and hope, that has been with me ever since, as there told, as child of seven, old Seumas Macleod (who taught me so much — was indeed the *father* of Fiona) took me on his knees one sundown on the island of Eigg and made me pray to "Her." I have never written anything so spiritually autobiographical. Strange as it may seem it is almost all literal reproduction of actuality with only some dates and names altered.

In Iona's opening pages, Sharp as Fiona said she will speak "as befalls her pen" of the multiple meanings of Iona, and she will recount legends and remembrances of her own and others. She will describe "hidden meanings and beauty and strangeness surviving in dreams and imaginations, rather than facts and figures that others could adduce more deftly and with more will." After a hundred and sixty-one Iona pages in the first edition of *The Divine Adventure*, Sharp/Fiona summarized the history of the island:

> To this small, black-brown tarn, pilgrims of every generation, for hundreds of years, have come. Solitary, these; not only because the pilgrim to the Fount of Eternal Youth must fare hither alone, and at dawn, so as to touch the healing water the moment the first sunray quickens it — but solitary, also, because those who go in quest of this Fountain of Youth are the dreamers and the Children of Dreams, and those are not many, and few come now to this lonely place. Yet, an Isle of Dreams Iona is, indeed. Here the last sun-worshippers bowed before the Rising of God; here Columba and his hymning priests labored and brooded; and here Oran or his kin dreamed beneath the monkish cowl that pagan dream of his. Here, too, the eyes of Fionn and Oisìn, and of many another of the heroic men and women of the Fiànna, may have lingered; here the Pict and the Celt bowed beneath the yoke of the Norse pirate, who, too, left his dreams, or rather his strangely beautiful soul-rainbows, as a heritage to the stricken; here for century after century, the Gael has lived, suffered, joyed, dreamed his impossible, beautiful dream; as here now, he still lives, still suffers patiently, still dreams, and through all and over all broods upon the incalculable mysteries.

Fig. 54 Benedictine Abbey on Iona, Inner Hebrides, constructed in 1203 AD on the site of the Celtic Church which St. Columbo built after he settled on Iona in 563 AD and began to establish Christianity in Scotland. Photograph by Paul T. (Gunther Tschuch) (2019), Wikimedia, https://commons.wikimedia.org/wiki/File:Iona_07.jpg, CC BY-SA 4.0.

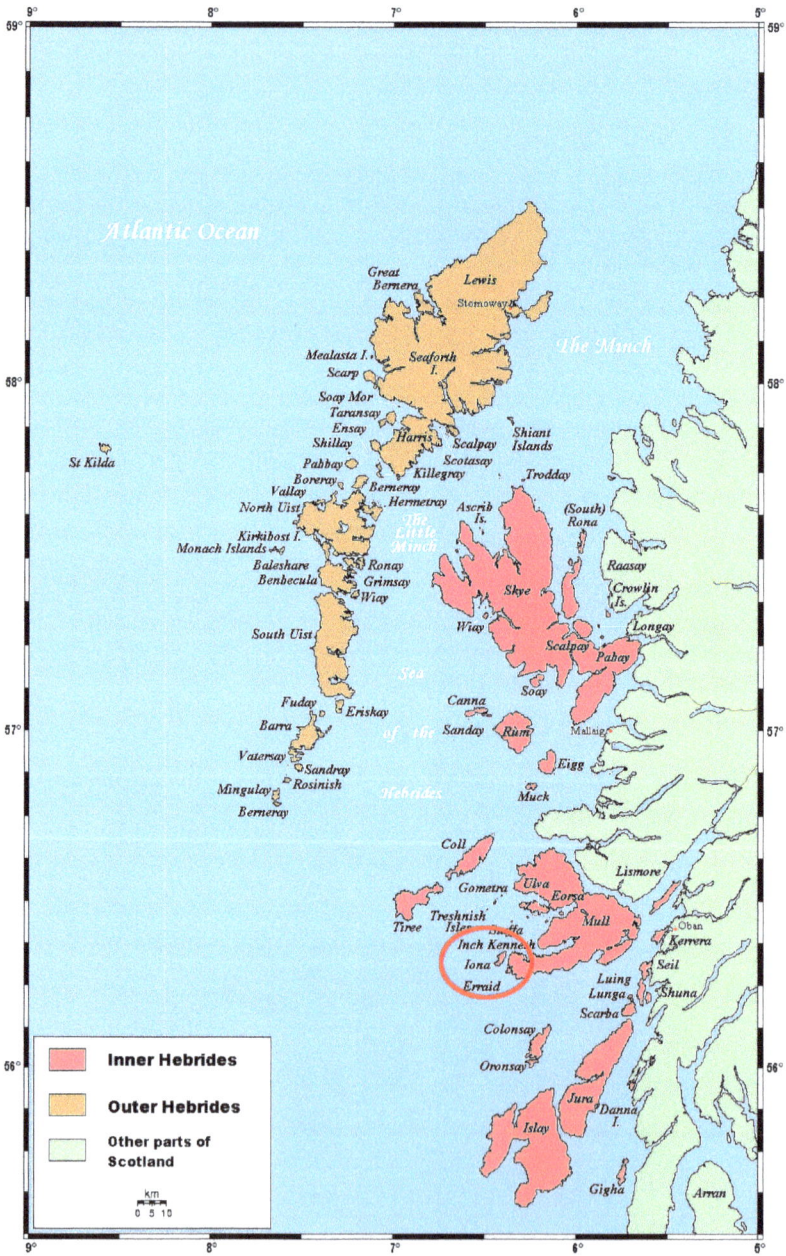

Fig. 55 Map of the Isle of Mull in Scotland's Inner Hebrides. Iona is the tiny island located off Mull's eastern-most tip. Wikimedia, https://commons.wikimedia.org/wiki/File:Ordnance_Survey_1-250000_-_NM.jpg, OGL v.3. Contains OS data © Crown copyright and database right (2021).

The quotation illustrates the power of the essay which is among the most lasting and influential pieces of Sharp's writings. When it was published Iona hosted only a few visitors in fine weather. Many, motivated by this essay, began to take the steamer from Oban to Mull and make their way across that large island to Iona. Nowadays, Iona is flooded with visitors during the summer months, and many purchase a book containing this essay in the island's shops.

The section of *The Divine Adventure* called "By Sundown Shores" contains five short essays and "Celtic," a longer piece which also appeared in the May issue of the *Contemporary Review*. The latter essay exemplifies what Sharp called the merger of his masculine and feminine voices. One hears in it the voice of Fiona, but that of Sharp, the practical literary and cultural critic, predominates. It is as though two separate persons were speaking. Early on we hear Fiona saying the Celtic Movement was not "as so often confusedly stated an arbitrary effort to reconstruct the past," but an "effort to discover the past." As "one imputed to this movement," she sought "in nature and in life, and in the swimming thought of timeless imagination, for the kind of beauty that the old Celtic poets discovered and uttered." Those poets had no monopoly on artistic beauty. No beauty of art excels "that bequeathed to us by Greece," but artists must seek and express their ideals through their own tradition. Fiona placed herself firmly in the Celtic camp, the camp of her heritage: "There is one beauty that has to me the light of home upon it; there is one beauty from which, above all others now, I hope for a new revelation; there is a love, there is a passion, there is a romance, which to me calls more suddenly and searchingly than any other ancient love or ancient passion or ancient romance."

After placing Fiona with her heightened rhetoric firmly among the Celts, Sharp reverted to the plainer language of the literary critic. Still writing as Fiona, he began to sound like the critic William Sharp. Although not a great believer in "movements" or "renascences," he understood the "Celtic Movement" as "the natural outcome, the natural expression of a freshly inspired spiritual and artistic energy." Its source was "a mythology and a literature, and a vast and wonderful legendary folklore […] in great part hidden behind veils of an all but forgotten tongue and of a system of life and customs, ideals and thought that no longer obtains." Then, veering toward dangerous territory, he said he was unable to see the Celtic movement as having "sustenance in elements of revolt." If a movement is to have any force, "it will not destroy itself in forlorn hopes, but will fall into line, and so achieve where alone the desired success can be achieved." He took his examples from the realm of art, but "revolt" and "falling into line" opened the door to politics.

The term Celtic writer, he continued, "must denote an Irish or Scottish Gael, a Cymric or Breton Celt, who writes in the language of his race." Those who write in English, however, are English writers "who in person happen to be an Irish Gael, or Highland, or Welsh." He was willing to be designated

> Celtic only if the word signifies an English writer who by birth, inheritance, and temperament has an outlook not distinctively English, with some memories and traditions and ideals not shared in by one's countrymen of the South, with a racial instinct that informs what one writes, and, for the rest, a common heritage.

The paragraph that stands out among the others in the essay turns overtly from literature to the issue of national identity:

> Above all else, it is time that a prevalent pseudo-nationalism should be dissuaded. I am proud to be a Highlander, but I would not side with those who would "set the heather on fire." If I were Irish, I would be proud, but I would not lower my pride by marrying it to a ceaseless ill will, an irreconcilable hate, for there can be a nobler pride in unvanquished acquiescence than in revolt. I would be proud if I were Welsh, but I would not refuse to learn English, or to mix with English as equals. And proud as I might be to be Highland or Scottish or Irish or Welsh or English, I would be more proud to be British — for, there at last, we have a bond to unite us all, and to give us space for every ideal, whether communal or individual, whether national or spiritual.

Choosing his words carefully, Sharp gathered all people with Celtic roots or inclinations in the British Isles, including Ireland, under the British umbrella.

He knew Æ (George William Russell) and Yeats were intent on establishing Ireland as an independent country free of English rule. His argument for unity was an attempt to discourage them from advocating separation. Though he knew it would not sit well with them or with other Irish writers advocating independence, but he hoped to soften their attitudes and dissuade them from overt revolutionary activities.

He also wanted to maintain, both as Macleod and Sharp, his own position in a Celtic Literary Movement that transcended nationalisms. He underestimated the depth of Æ's feelings, the fire underlying his rhetoric, and the strength of the Irish independence movement.

Such is the background of a June 15 Fiona letter to George Russell who had written to put her on notice he intended to write a review of *The Divine Adventure* that took issue with her "Celtic" essay. In her response, Fiona expressed her regret; she was sorry Æ rejected her effort to "save our Gaelic remnant from extinction." She hoped he would give up "the transitory while inevitable logic of human sorrow and revolt" and adopt "the immortal and inevitable logic of the Spirit." She failed to dissuade Æ.

His review appeared in the July 21 issue of Standish O'Grady's *All Ireland Review*. There were many things in the book everyone could enjoy. In the title essay, "The Divine Adventure," and in "Iona" there was "a graver and more restrained use of that rhetorical eloquence which Miss Macleod perhaps finds it too easy to employ." If at times there was "only vagueness where a mystic meaning was intended," there was also "genuine imagination and frequent beauty of thought and style." That said, he turned to "Celtic" and its "anti-nationalistic" stance. Casting reasoned argument aside, he accused Fiona of "arrogance and shallowness of judgment" and remarked disparagingly, "it is perhaps like a woman to advise a cheap peace between race and race." She was unable, he said, to distinguish "English emotion from Celtic emotion, or from Hindu emotion." She was "devoid of the faculty of analysis or the power of seeing distinctions, not even subtle distinctions, but glaring ones." He imagined a good Briton reading this essay and feeling quite satisfied that "there were to be no more wild Irish; that he was not to be troubled further with revolt or plain speaking; the truth would be modified to suit his capacity for receiving it." He would beam in satisfaction as the Celtic "crown of strange jewels" is placed on his brow. There followed some high-handed advice that drew a clear and foreboding line between the Irish and Scottish revivalists: "It is to be hoped in the future if Miss Macleod wishes to write semi-political essays she will speak only for the Scottish Celt. We are a strange people over here, and we dislike being preached to by foreigners." When we read this review with the knowledge Sharp had told Æ he was Fiona, pledging him to secrecy, we recognize, as did Sharp, that "perhaps like a woman" was a double-barreled shot at the male William and his creation, the female Fiona.

Standish O'Grady attempted to ameliorate Æ's venom by printing immediately following his review a different assessment of *The Divine Adventure* signed by J. S.: "From the beginning of her remarkable career till now Miss Fiona Macleod has done nothing so beautiful and lofty as this wonderful book." The praise became increasingly elaborate. "Iona," J. S. wrote, was "so full of spiritual light, not raying out aimlessly into the void but clothing reality and life with beauty, that it is no exaggeration to describe them [the rays] as adding a new sacredness to the Mecca of the Gael [Iona]." Turning to "Celtic," the reviewer met Æ headlong:

> Miss Macleod showed "that her keen insight does not fail her in a region of thought far removed from that into which she has hitherto taken her readers. A Celt of the Celt, and possessed as no other writer of our time is possessed with a sense of the faculty and mission of the Celt, she shows here not only deep intuition but the power [quoting Matthew Arnold] "to see life steadily and see it whole," of which the Celt, in this country at least, must acquire some greater measure before his flame can burn with any but a destructive power.

The real argument, he concluded, was not between the Scots and the Irish, but among the Irish.

In the next issue of the *All Ireland Review* (July 28) O'Grady printed in the letters section the following sentence: "We overhold an interesting communication from the celebrated Fiona Macleod in reference to strictures recently made in A. I. R. on her latest book 'The Divine Adventure.'" In that communication — dated July 22 and printed in the next edition of the weekly (August 4) — Sharp as Fiona thanked the unidentified J. S. for his praise and responded to Æ's charges. She denied her inability to see distinctions, stated she was not anti-nationalistic, and reaffirmed her belief that "Genius does not lie with any one race," but it is "a calling of the Spirit to one soul here, another there; neither tribe nor clan has the divine mystery as its own." Allowing that some of her fellow Gaels may be "in some things […] astray," she insisted that "others, and the English in particular, are not invariably and inevitably in the wrong, and stupid and malevolent." Justice and love, not hatred and resentment, must accompany nationalism. Taking up Æ's gender challenge, Fiona asserted that even a woman knows "there is a peace which is death." She did not advocate "a cheap peace between race and race," but an ideal for "our broken and scattered race that may not only uplift and ennoble but may bring about a great and wonderful regeneration." Here Sharp referred obliquely to the regenerative goals of Yeats' Celtic Mystical Order which he and Æ shared. Fiona's attempt to clarify her position only caused Æ to harden his. In a letter O'Grady published which constituted the entire front page of the August 18 *All Ireland Review*, he accused Fiona of labeling nationalism as "race hatred," reasserted his adherence to Irish nationalism, and confessed he had no love for England. He called Fiona a Briton and an English writer who, unlike some other Scottish Celts, lacked the aspiration to nationality common among Irish Gaels.

The public exchange of correspondence concluded with a letter from T. W. Rolleston on the front page of the August 25 *All Ireland Review*. After noting Æ's letters contained "so much that is good and true," Rolleston addressed what he considered the major errors of his ideas about nationalism. Taking issue with Æ's emphasis on British oppression, he suggested the Irish had not been so much oppressed as indifferent to the claims of their heritage and that any changes in attitude must be enforced by the Irish people themselves. He also criticized Æ for linking the Celtic spiritual movement with the Irish political movement, adding that "Ireland might have her local legislature and yet be thoroughly denationalized and vulgarized." Or "she might attain nationalism in social life, literature, and art and yet be content with her present voice in the Imperial Parliament." After criticizing the bitterness and hatred underlying much of the political movement, he said Æ and Fiona Macleod were pressing each other to extreme views; their positions were complementary, not contradictory. Finally, he commended Fiona's Celticism, insisted she was a "helper not a hinderer," and condemned Æ's bias against her as a Scottish Celt. Despite the efforts of O'Grady, J. S., and Rolleston to keep Fiona on board and maintain a unified movement, Æ's attack, fueled by the growing spirit of Irish nationalism, caused a rift between the Irish and the Scots that became increasingly difficult to bridge.

In late August Sharp wrote a letter to Yeats in which he expressed his feelings about Æ's attack: "As for Æ, I think I had better not say what

I think: but of one thing I am very sorry, his inevitable loss of prestige among those of his own circle who like myself have thought so highly of him and his work. None can now accept him as a thinker, or as a fair and loyal opponent, however else one may regard him." The letter re-enforced what Sharp had told Yeats about Fiona — that she was an independent individual with a will of her own, mysteriously speaking through him, and that there was a flesh and blood woman whom Sharp loved and depended on to evoke this persona. He wished Fiona would not take notice of critics. He wished he had seen her letter to the *All Ireland Review* before she sent it. And he wished Æ would be "content to be the poet and seer, and not turn aside to these unworthinesses."

Perhaps motivated by encouragement from Yeats and by Rolleston's suggestion that they were pushing each other to extremes, Sharp drafted a Fiona letter to Æ in mid-September saying she wanted to go with him on the "quest," not apart from him. This letter evoked a conciliatory response in which Russell said he had no personal feelings against her: "You are to me so far only a beautiful myth." He never fights, he said, "except when I feel the spiritual life of Ireland is threatened and when I fight why of course I do it with all the energy I can put into it." He often fights with his friends, he said, and remains good friends with his opponents. He hoped to remain friends with Fiona because she belonged to "the clan," the group of Irish or Scottish people "who's ideal is mainly a spiritual one." The clan included O'Grady, Yeats, Hyde, Lady Gregory, and others whom Fiona/Sharp did not know. Finally, he enclosed a spray of heather as a peace offering. The letter was written with the awareness that its recipient would not be "a beautiful myth," but William Sharp. Indeed, Æ had written to Yeats on July 13, a week before his first review appeared in print, that he was "a little sorry" he had been "so savage," but he hoped it would "do Fiona/Sharp some good." We can only wonder if his review would have been so savage had he thought Fiona a real woman.

Sharp responded as Fiona on October 20. Briefly in London on her way to southern France, she accepted Æ's offer of continuing friendship: "Your spray from the sacred hill brought me not only a message from your inward self, but more than you could know perhaps. Some fallen link has been caught up through it — and, too, a truer understanding has come to me in one or two points where we have been at issue." She hoped Æ would read and like "The Immortal Hour" in a forthcoming *Fortnightly Review* and a forthcoming essay in the *Nineteenth Century* on "The Gael and his Heritage" which dealt with "the treasure-trove of the spiritual hymns and ancient lore in the Hebrides." The breach with Æ was papered over, but there followed a decided cooling of enthusiasm for the writings of Fiona Macleod among the independence-minded Irish.

In addition to managing this public controversy, Sharp continued his association with the evolving Stage Society during the summer and fall. He made only two brief trips to Scotland in late summer and continued work on the long essay that was published in 1902 as *The Progress of Art in the Nineteenth Century*. His article titled "Some Dramas of Gabrielle d'Annunzio," appeared in the September *Fortnightly Review*, and the October issue of the *Art Journal* carried his article about the work of Monro S. Orr, a well-known contemporary Scottish painter, etcher, and illustrator. In November, Fiona Macleod's "The Immortal Hour" appeared in the *Fortnightly Review* and her "The Gael and His Heritage" in the *Nineteenth Century*. The latter was a lengthy and adulatory tribute to Alexander Carmichael's recently published *Carmina Gadelica*.

In early November, Sharp began a letter at his club (the Grosvenor) to Murray Gilchrist with the incident that occasioned it:

> A little ago, on sitting down in my club to answer some urgent notes (and whence I now write) my heart leapt with pleasure, and an undeserving stranger received Part I of a beaming welcome — for the waiter announced that "Mr. Gilchrist would like to see you, Sir." Alas, it was no dear Peaklander, but only a confounded interviewer about the Stage Society!

He went on to say he and Elizabeth planned to leave England on November 12 and go first to Provence and then, after Christmas, to Italy, "perhaps first to Shelley's Spezia or to Pegli of the Orange Groves near Genoa: and there we await you, or at furthest a little later, say in Florence. We shall be away till the end of March." He had just returned from Dorset where he saw Thomas Hardy who was well and at work, "the two happiest boons of fortune for all our kinship." He wished Gilchrist would come to London for the Stage Society production that weekend, Sunday November 11, of a play by Hardy, another by Robert Louis Stevenson, and William Ernest Henley's "Macaire." Sharp said he had resigned as Chairman of the Stage Society but was re-elected, so he was extra busy before leaving for France. As usual in his letters to Gilchrist, Sharp told him how he was feeling; "all unpleasantness and incertitude: much to do and little pleasure in the doing: a restlessness too great to be salved short of departure, and the longed for mental and nervous rest far away."

Ill-health continued to plague both Sharps in the late summer and early fall. Mrs. Sharp described their condition:

> Partly owing to the insistence of circumstance, partly from choice, we began that autumn a series of wanderings that brought us back to London and to Scotland for a few weeks only each summer. The climate of England proved too severe. ... Despite his appearance of great vitality, his extraordinary power of recuperation after every illness — which in measure was due to his buoyant nature, to his deliberate turning of his mind away from suffering or from failure and "looking sunwise," to his endeavor to get the best out of whatever conditions he had to meet — we realized that a home in England was no longer a possibility, that it would be wise to make various experiments abroad rather than attempt to settle anywhere permanently. Indeed, we were both glad to have no plans, but to wander again how and where inclination and possibilities dictated (*Memoir*, 323–324).

The Sharps left London on November 12, passed through Paris, and went on to stay near the Janviers in Saint Remy where they socialized with local writers and artists. Sharp finished an essay on "The Impressionists" which appeared under his name in the April 1901 *New Library Review*. He also began an essay on famous Provençal poets called "Modern Troubadours" which appeared in the *Quarterly Review* of October 1901. Stage Society business followed him. On November 19, he hand-printed a letter to the Editor of the *Topical Times* stating his absolute opposition to the official censorship of plays.

On November 30, he wrote a long letter to John Macleay, of the *Highland News*, in which he expressed his regret that he was unable to visit Andrew Carmichael and his family during his brief visit to Scotland in the fall. He praised Carmichael's *Carmina Gadelica* which, he affirmed, "ought to become as precious to the Scottish Gael as the Greek Anthology to all who love the Hellenic ideal, but with a more poignant, a more personal appeal." After eagerly perusing it from "cover to cover" he had given his early copy to Miss Macleod who praised it highly in

"The Gael and His Heritage," an article published in that month's issue of *Nineteenth Century*. Fiona had become dissatisfied with the historical novel she was writing, and ill health, "involving much absolute rest, and latterly change of climate," had interfered with her writing. She wanted to go to Italy, but her doctors recommended Egypt or Algeria, as "drier & sunnier, & to vary this frequently with the sea she loves so well & which suits her splendidly." Sharp saw her a week or two ago in Marseilles on her way south, He does not know where to address her now. She may be in Mustapha, near Algiers. He hopes she will be able to pay a flying visit to Sicily in February, where the Sharps will be, as she will then be yachting in the Mediterranean with friends. Although he does not know her current address, Sharp said he would be writing to her in a few days and would forward Macleay's note. It was an elaborate effort to impress upon Macleay, who had his suspicions, the separate identity of Fiona Macleod. On Christmas Day, the Sharps left Provence for Palermo in Sicily where they spent New Year's Day. A week later, they crossed the island to the east coast and Taormina where events affecting the remainder of Sharp's life would unfold.

Chapter Twenty-One

1901

When they reached Taormina, the Sharps checked into the Hotel Naumachia which was famous for its spectacular views of the bay of Naxos and Mount Etna. In a January 25 letter to Catherine Janvier, Sharp described the joy he felt in the warmth and beauty of Taormina:

> Today it was too warm to work contentedly indoors even upon our little terrace with its superb views over Etna and the Ionian Sea — so at 9 a.m. Elizabeth and I, with a young painter-friend, came up here to a divine spot on the slopes of the steep and grand-shouldered Hill of Venus, bringing with us our writing and sketching materials and also fruit and wine and light luncheon. It is now about 3 p.m. and we have lain here for hours in the glorious warmth and cloudless sunglow — undisturbed by any sounds save the soft sighing of the sea far below, the fluting of a young goatherd with his black flock on a steep across a near ravine, and the occasional passing of a muleteer or of a mountaineer with his wine-panier'd donkeys. A vast sweep of sea is before us and beneath. To the left, under the almond boughs, are the broad straits which divide Sicily from Calabria — in front, the limitless reach of the Greek sea — to the right, below, the craggy heights and Monte Acropolis of Taormina — and, beyond, the vast slope of snow-clad Etna.

In addition to the warm weather and beauty of Taormina, Sharp took special pleasure in the area's association with Greek literature, especially the pastoral poet Theocritus who was born in Sicily *c.* 300 B. C.

> I have just been reading (for the hundredth time) in Theocritus. How doubly lovely he is, read on the spot. That young shepherd fluting away to his goats at this moment might be Daphnis himself. Three books are never far from here: Theocritus, the Greek Anthology, and the Homeric Hymns. I loved them before: now they are in my blood.

While picnicking on Monte Venere above Taormina, Sharp continued his letter to Mrs. Janvier:

> Legend has it that near this very spot Pythagoras used to come and dream. How strange to think that one can thus come in touch with two of the greatest men of antiquity [...] Perhaps it was here that Pythagoras learned the secret of that music (for here both the sea-wind and the hill-wind can be heard in magic meeting) by which one day — as told in Iamblichus — he cured a young man of Taormina (Tauromenion) who had become mad as a wild beast, with love. Pythagoras, it is said, played an antique air upon his flute, and the madness went from the youth.

In the Sicilian sun, the illness and depression that beset both Sharps in the rain and cold of London disappeared as if by magic.

Fig. 56 Taormina on the east Coast of Sicily with Mt. Etna in the distance. Photograph by Miguel Torres (2011), Wikimedia, https://commons.wikimedia.org/w/index.php?curid=17133090#/media/File:Taormina_and_Mt_Etna.jpg, CC BY-SA 3.0.

When word reached Taormina of Queen Victoria's death on January 22, Albert Henry Stopford (1860–1939), a British antiques and art dealer with connections to the royal family, arranged a memorial service in the English Chapel of Saint Caterina. After the service, the Sharps met Alexander Nelson Hood who accompanied his father — the Viscount Bridport in England and the Duke of Bronte in Italy — to the service from his estate on the western slope of Mount Etna. In 1799, King Ferdinand IV of Southern Italy and Sicily gave the estate to Lord Nelson in appreciation for his interception of the French fleet which saved his kingdom from Napoleon. Along with the estate, Ferdinand made Nelson the Duke of Bronte, the name of the area's largest town. Nelson was proud of the title, but he did not survive to visit his Duchy which passed, along with the title, through the marriage of his niece to the Hood family which was headed by a succession of Baron Bridports and, as of 1874, the Viscount Bridport who attended the memorial service in Taormina. The service had a special meaning for Bridport who served for forty years as Queen Victoria's Lord in Waiting.

His younger son, the Honorable Alexander Nelson Hood, was attached to the household of the Duchess of York who later became Queen Mary, but he lived at least six months each year on the Bronte estate where he renovated the residence and introduced farming methods that improved the condition of the people who depended on the estate for their livelihood. Since he had given the Duchy new life and restored it to profitability, Hood inherited both the estate and the Italian title when his father died in 1904. Over the years, he entertained many British artists and aristocrats at the estate's residence, the Castello Maniace. He also constructed a large villa in Taormina where he spent part of the time mingling with artists and enjoying the social life of the English community. Since he never married and had no direct heirs, the title and the estate reverted to his British relatives following his death in 1937. Over the years, they sold most of the estate's land to local farmers, and in 1981 they sold the Castle and 15 hectares of surrounding land to the regional government which presented it to the town of Bronte. The town, in turn, opened the house as a museum in 1982 and renamed it the Castello Nelson. Over the last forty years, the estate's buildings and grounds have been gradually repaired and improved, and the main house, now open to the public, displays a wealth of fine furniture and Nelson memorabilia donated by the Hood family. Many of Lord Nelson's possessions have found a permanent home in the museum which has become one of the main tourist attractions of the Provence of Catania in eastern Sicily.

Following the memorial service in Taormina, Alex Hood invited the Sharps to visit Castello Maniace. Several days later they left Taormina for what Elizabeth described as their first trip "to that strange, beautiful Duchy on Etna, that was to mean so much to us" (*Memoir*, 331). This

 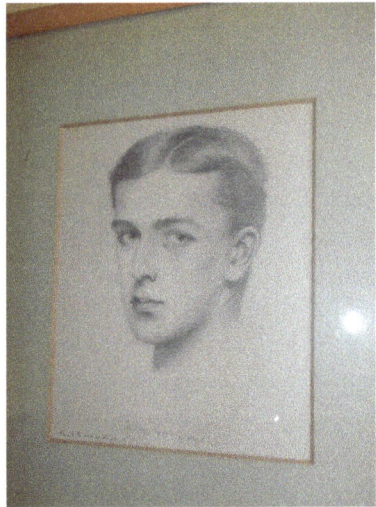

Fig. 57 Bust and portrait of the 5th Duke of Bronté, Alexander Nelson Hood (1854–1937), on display in the Castello Nelson (formally the Castello Maniace). Photographs by Warwick Gould (2014), reproduced with permission.

was the first of five winters in which the Sharps spent time with Hood at Maniace. Sharp died and was buried there in December 1905. His grave in the estate's English cemetery was marked with an imposing Celtic cross commissioned by Hood, which still towers over its lesser neighbors.

Fig. 58 The Greek Theater in Syracuse, Sicily. Built about 470 B. C., it is the largest surviving theater of the ancient world. Photograph by Michele Ponzio (2006), Wikimedia, https://commons.wikimedia.org/wiki/File:Teatro_greco_di_Siracusa_-_aerea.jpg, CC BY-SA 2.0.

After several days with Hood, the Sharps traveled south to Syracuse where, on February 7, William wrote again to Catherine Janvier who shared his interest in Greek history and literature. For Sharp it was the

> Syracuse of Theocritus you love so well — the Syracuse where Pindar heard some of his noblest odes sung, where Plato discoursed with his disciples of New Hellas, where (long before) the Argonauts had passed after hearing the Sirens singing by this fatal shore, and near where Ulysses derided Polyphemus — and where Aeschylus lived so long and died.

They were fortunate to be there for a "special choral performance" in "the beautiful hillside Greek Theatre in honor of the visit of Prince Tommaso, the Duke of Genoa, the late King's brother, and Admiral of the Fleet."

> Imagine our delight! And <u>what</u> a day it has been — the ancient Aeschylean theater crammed once more on all tiers with thousands of Syracusans so that not a spare seat was left — while three hundred young voices sang a version of one of the choral sections of "The Supplicants" of Aeschylus — with it il Principe on a scarlet dais where once the tyrant Dionysius sat! Over head the deep blue sky, and beyond, the deep blue Ionian Sea. It was all too wonderful.

From Syracuse the Sharps returned to Taormina where they were pleased to be accepted among the British elite who wintered there. With their health restored and with some misgivings, they left Sicily on the first of March to spend a month in Florence where they rented rooms and were introduced to the English community by Elizabeth's aunt who lived there. They also spent some time at the Villa Il Palmerino in the hills below Fiesole, as guests of Sharp's friend Eugene Lee-Hamilton, his new American wife, and his half-sister Violet Paget, the well-known English feminist who published under the pseudonym, Vernon Lee.

Coincidentally, on the day the Sharps left Sicily, March 1, Mary Beatrice Sharp, who provided the Fiona Macleod handwriting, gave birth to a baby boy in London. Her oldest sister, Agnes, was with her in a nursing home in Hammersmith, when she gave birth. Mary named her baby Douglas and gave him up for adoption. He was raised by a family in the Midlands, and it was only when he decided as a young man to immigrate to Canada and needed his birth certificate that he learned the identity of his birth mother whereupon he changed his surname to

Fig. 59 A recent photograph of the beautifully restored Villa Il Palmerino in Settignano, north-east of Florence, where Eugene Lee-Hamilton and Vernon Lee lived for many years. Photograph by Sailko (2016), Wikimedia, https://commons.wikimedia.org/wiki/File:Il_palmerino,_esterno_04.jpg, CC BY 3.0.

Sharpe, adding a final "e" that may have come from a mistake on the certificate. In 2004, Douglas Sharpe's son, Derek Michael Sharpe, shared with me this information and his supporting documents. He was living in Canada, and he hoped to learn more about his grandmother who played a critical role in the production of the Fiona correspondence. William and Elizabeth must have been concerned about the progress of Mary's pregnancy and relieved to learn she delivered a healthy baby and survived the birth in good health. Sharp's early poem, "Motherhood," was only the first of many Sharp and Fiona writings about the agonies and dangers of childbirth. Sharp's advanced feminism and focus on the travails of womanhood had its origins in the eight children (six girls and two boys) born to his mother in the twelve years following his birth in 1855. Mary's pregnancy and the birth of her baby were reminders of the complications awaiting the Sharps at home (see Chapter 11 for a photograph of Mary Sharp).

An October 20 letter to Grant Richards may have been the last Fiona letter Mary copied before she gave birth on March first. The next surviving Fiona letter in Mary's script — to David Munro, the Assistant Editor of the *North American Review* — is dated March 15, 1901, two weeks after her baby was born. It was mailed from London, and Fiona explained she had been delayed there by her health on her way to Scotland from Italy. The next surviving Fiona letter — to Mrs. Gertrude Page — is only a draft by Sharp for Mary to copy. The date March 16 is crossed out and "18th Mar" in the Fiona hand is substituted on Sharp's draft. Since Fiona claims in the letter to be writing from Florence, Sharp must have sent the draft to London for Mary to copy and return to him in Florence where he mailed it. The letters to Munro and Page placed Fiona simultaneously in London and Florence, but Munro in New York and Mrs. Page in Bedfordshire would not be comparing dates and locations.

These two letters indicate Mary was sufficiently recovered in mid-March to copy and send the Fiona letters. Meantime, Sharp was making plans to conduct the Fiona correspondence from London after Mary returned to Edinburgh. In the letter to Mrs. Page, Fiona said her "most convenient letter address" was "c/o Mrs. Rinder | 11 Woronzow Road | St. John's Wood N.W." Sometime between October and March, Lillian Rea left the country, and Edith Rinder stepped in as the London transfer agent for the Fiona correspondence. The next Fiona letter, dated June 1, is entirely typed, and its font differs from that of the letters Mary occasionally typed in Edinburgh; even its signature is typed. Edith Rinder, whose return address it contains, must have typed it from Sharp's draft. Meanwhile, Mary transcribed in the Fiona script a card to the American publisher Thomas Mosher dated June 10 and mailed it from Edinburgh. In a lengthy typed letter to Mosher dated July 8 (which included a note and signature in the Fiona script and carried Edith's return address), Fiona referred to Mrs. Rinder as her "friend and literary-correspondence agent." It is somehow fitting that Edith Rinder, who was so intimately involved in Sharp's production of the Fiona writings, became for at least a time the London manager of the Fiona correspondence.

On February 1, while visiting Alex Hood, Sharp wrote to ask Theodore Watts-Dunton to persuade his housemate, Algernon Swinburne, to consent to his editing a selection of his poems for publication by Baron Tauchnitz, whose firm in Leipzig was publishing inexpensive paperback editions of English authors. In a March 19 letter to Watts-Dunton, Sharp said Baron Tauchnitz accepted his terms for the Swinburne volume (£30) and added this message: "Pray give my best regards to Mr. Watts-Dunton as well as to Mr. Swinburne, and tell them that I am proud now to be able to put the name of the greatest living English poet on our list of publications. Sharp received Swinburne's permission, conveyed through Watts-Dunton, but he was concerned that he lacked Swinburne's written consent. He asked Watts-Dunton: "Do you think you could in any case prevail upon Mr. Swinburne to write the briefest line — <u>or to sign one written to you, saying simply 'I consent to the preparation of a Tauchnitz vol. of selections from my poetical writings.'</u>" Whether or not Sharp received that line, Tauchnitz published *Selected Poems by A. C. Swinburne*, selected and arranged and with an introduction by William Sharp, in October 1901. Sharp was under the impression he had complete freedom to select and arrange the poems, but when the volume appeared he received a letter from Swinburne (*Memoir*, 336–337) with several complaints about selection and arrangement.

On or around July 9, the Sharps left London and settled for a month at the Spa House in Cowley within walking distance of R. Murray Gilchrist near the village of Holmesfield. While they were in rural Derbyshire, Edith Rinder gave birth on July 26 to Esther Mona Rinder. The child's middle name recognized the crucial role Mona Caird played in the lives of her parents. As Frank Rinder's cousin and soon to be Esther's godmother, Mona continued to provide material and emotional support for Edith and Frank long after she facilitated their move to London in the late 1880s and their marriage in 1890. Occasionally in his decade-long relationship with Edith Rinder, Sharp lamented, in private notes and in the Fiona Macleod stories, their inability to have a child. Occasionally, he cast Fiona, the product of their collaboration, as their child. Given the interdependence of the relationship between the Sharps and the Rinders and the fact that neither marriage had produced a child, it is not surprising the Rinder's baby girl meant a great deal to both couples.

Since Sharp often referred to Edith as Fiona's very close friend, it was not surprising that Fiona's retelling of the story of *Deirdrê and the Sons of Usna*, published by Mosher in 1903, was dedicated "To Esther Mona." Writing as Fiona, Sharp left a beautiful, loving message for the child which reads in part

Fig. 60 Baron Christian Karl Bernard Tauchnitz (1841–1921). Portrait by Vilma Lwoff-Parlaghy (1901). Wikimedia, https://commons.wikimedia.org/wiki/File:Tauchnitz_Christian_Karl_001.jpg#/media/File:Tauchnitz_Christian_Karl_001.jpg, Public Domain

I shall have bent above the fading warmth, and have risen at last, cold, and gone away, when that little wandering heart of yours shall have become a woman's heart; and so I do not know whether, if I were to look in it, I should see beyond the shaken reeds of the mind the depth-held star of the old passion of beauty, the old longing, the old enchantment. But I hope so. Are you not the child of her, that friend to whom I inscribed my first book; of whom, in its prefatory words, I wrote "we have loved the same things and in the same way [...] take, then, out of my heart, this book of vision and dream." [...] So, little one, come in time to love these things of beauty. Lay your child's heart, that is made of morning joy and evening longing, to that Mother-heart; and when you gather years, as now you gather the little white clan of the grass, it shall be well with you. And you, too, when your time is come, and you in turn pass on the mystery of life to another who will look up from your breast with eyes of still wonder and slowly shaping thought, forget not to tell that other to lay its child's heart of morning joy and evening longing against a more ancient and dream-filled heart than that of any woman, that mother-heart of which I speak to you, the Heart of Beauty (x–xii).

It is one woman speaking to another, but more profoundly it is a man who loved the child's mother expressing his hope the child will come to love the same things they loved, including the Gaelic myth of the beautiful Deirdrê he recounted for the child in "this book of dream and vision." Had Sharp lived longer, he would have been pleased as the hope expressed in Fiona's dedication was realized. Esther Mona (Rinder) Harvey was a woman of many accomplishments as a linguist, artist, wife, and mother. He would have been equally pleased by the accomplishments of the family she left behind when she died in 1993 at the age of ninety-one.

During his visit to New York in the fall of 1896, Sharp spent a few days with Henry Mills Alden, the Editor of *Harper's Magazine*, at his home across the Hudson in Metuchen, New Jersey. One night after dinner he told Alden, who was twenty years his senior and had recently lost his wife, about his relationship with Edith Rinder. In a letter to Alden dated October 22, 1901, Sharp expressed his hope that "all goes well with you in your new life" — Alden had recently remarried — and continued: "I wish too I could tell you of a strange, of a fantastically strange, and to me deeply moving development of that old romance of boyhood which I confided to you one evening before the fire at Metuchen." At a time when the relationship between Sharp and Edith had begun to cool — as he explained directly to Yeats and indirectly in the Fiona writings — Edith gave birth to a daughter. That must have been the "deeply moving development' he wished he could describe to Alden. The Fiona dedication to Esther Mona and Sharp's guarded statement in this letter appear to be his only surviving references to Esther; and her only remembrance of William Sharp was the oranges he sent to the Rinder family from Sicily when she was a child of three and four.

After spending most of July and early August in Derbyshire, the Sharps went to Kilcreggan in Argyll and remained there until mid-October. During the summer, Sharp as Fiona corresponded frequently with the publisher Thomas Mosher in Portland, Maine. Over the course of a lengthy career, Mosher oversaw the design and publication of hundreds of books, mostly reprints of works by British authors. Sharp's enthusiastic praise of Mosher's books in many Fiona letters was genuine and well-deserved. Unsurprisingly, there was also a financial motive. Since the demise of Stone and Kimball five years earlier, Sharp had no outlet for the Fiona books in the United States. Sensing Mosher's publishing firm might fill that void, he moved full steam ahead.

The December 1900 issue of Mosher's *Bibelot, A Reprint of Poetry and Prose for Book Lovers* featured "Lyrics *From the Hills of Dream*," a selection from the book of Fiona poems published in Edinburgh in 1896 by Patrick Geddes and Colleagues. The response to Fiona's poems in the *Bibelot* suggested she might be a reliable source of income for Mosher. When he visited Edinburgh in the spring of 1901, he sought and received permission from Geddes to publish more of the poems. In May 1901 he wrote directly to Fiona proposing an American edition whereupon Sharp accepted the proposal and began to remove some of the poems in the Geddes edition of 1896 and add new ones. *From the Hills of Dream: Threnodies, Songs, and Other Poems* was published in September 1901, in Mosher's *Old World* Series. Mosher published nine more Fiona Macleod books during the four remaining years of Sharp's life — a total of ten — and six more after he died. It was principally through the Mosher publications that Fiona Macleod gained a modest but devoted American readership in the early twentieth century.

A source of concern for Sharp during the summer and fall of 1901 was his involvement with W. B. Yeats in planning the Celtic Mystical Order. As described in Chapter Sixteen, Yeats, in 1897, became convinced Sharp and the woman he called Fiona Macleod were accomplished visionaries, and he invited them to join him and a few close friends in the effort to produce the Order's rituals. Yeats borrowed his model for the Celtic Order from the Order of the Golden Dawn. He was active in the London branch of the Order, while Sharp, though a member, was less so. Sharp had begun to experiment with spiritualism at least as early as 1892. After joining forces with Yeats in 1897, his efforts to contact spirits, sometimes aided by drugs, became more frequent and intense.

With a late May letter from London, Yeats sent Sharp a draft he had "done in a very perfunctory way" of the first, Neophyte, ritual for his Celtic Mystical Order (*Collected Letters IV*, 967–968). He asked Sharp "to try to get a vision of the coming of the seven races," the races that invaded Ireland in ancient times, and to send the rite back with notes "as soon as possible." He also asked Sharp to "try to get Miss Macleod to try her hand at any point that may seem weak." His goal was to "start" the Order with this first Rite when he returned to London from Ireland in the fall, "and then go on Rite by Rite till the whole fabric is finished." A few days later, having received no word from Sharp, Yeats wrote directly to Fiona from Rosses Point near Sligo where he was staying with George Pollexfen, his uncle and a fellow member of the Golden Dawn. By this time Yeats knew Sharp was writing the works attributed to Fiona, but Sharp had convinced him she was a second personality inspired by a real woman he loved who possessed great psychic abilities. He had that woman in mind in his letter to Sharp and the subsequent letter to Fiona. He assumed Sharp had sent her the draft initiation ritual. He thought the structure was right, but it needed to be better written. Could she help with the writing? He went on to describe what he thought the material to be mastered should be in the remaining six Rites. He had worked out the symbolism, the proposed content, and the purpose of all seven Rites, but "the great problem is structure, just as the great problem in a play is structure." Since Fiona's clairvoyant powers were greater than his own and Sharp's, he hoped she would comment on his draft.

Sharp constructed a brief Fiona reply to Yeats which is now lost, but the substantive reply is in a Fiona letter dated July 26, coincidentally the very day of Esther Mona Rinder's birth. Fiona wondered if Yeats would object to a complete reconstruction of the Rite since it seemed to present "insuperable difficulty." "In other words," she continued, "has your Rite <u>finality</u> to you?" She then warned Yeats to be very careful in November: "It is always a month of suffering and mischance for some of us and especially about the 21st (the seven days before or after)." Her friend — Sharp — was feeling especially vulnerable. He had recently had "five very singular visions, each unsought and abrupt." They were followed by a sixth which, she thought, was a warning from the realm of spirits: "Put the four cups of light about you in the seven and seven dark days of the month of the curlew (… i.e., November)." Sharp's vulnerability is understandable. He had other matters on his mind and was trying to cover his inattention to Yeats' Celtic project with language borrowed from the Golden Dawn.

Yeats, on the other hand, was deadly serious. He responded in a brief note to Sharp on August 4 (*Collected Letters IV*, 980). He could not delay much longer the implementation of the first Rite. Once it is finalized and accepted, Sharp will find he is "much less attacked." The ceremonies will be his

> protection — that is indeed part of their purpose. A Rite woven into other Rites is a ceaseless invocation of strong protectors. Make a circle of light about the room before you begin & if you think well — this I got once studying Maud Gonne — set the 4 hosts of the Feann to guard the cardinal points.

For the time being, Yeats concluded, Sharp should simply do whatever he could about the Rite and protect himself from evil forces.

With his August 4 letter to Sharp, Yeats enclosed a much longer letter to Fiona. He dismissed her proposal to recast the first Rite and suggested she start working on the second Rite, which would be "The Mystery of the Cauldron" (*Collected Letters IV*, 974–978). He had been "instructed to work on the six initiations in order," but a plan for the second Rite, the "initiates of the cauldron," had floated before him. The officers, or those conducting the initiation, would speak "as the prow, stern, rudder etc. of a symbolic ship, which is taking the candidate on his way." The initiation would then change to

> a purifying ceremony (the candidate standing symbolically in the stone vessel one sees in New Grange). I got the ship from a ship in "The Book of the Dead" & from a certain Irish peasant ceremony, said to have been obscene by the priests who put it down.

Since Fiona, according to Yeats, was "beyond comparison a greater clairvoyant," he would gladly have her complete reworking of the first Rite, "The Mystery of the Obligation," but that would take time. He wanted to move quickly so he could "initiate certain people who I have in my mind into the Mystery of the Obligation this autumn."

Yeats concluded his letter to Fiona by stating his goal in creating the Celtic Mystical Order and the need for fast action: "I believe that there is a great contest going to come on here in a few years between the Church and the mystics. There have been some premonitory mutterings already. It is absolutely necessary to begin our organization at once." He was creating a spiritualist movement that would rival and eventually replace Christianity, including of course the Catholic Church, which exercised great power over the minds and bodies of the Irish. Though Sharp was certainly interested in contacting the spirit world and maintaining his friendship with Yeats, the obsolescence of Christianity did not figure prominently among his goals.

In the face of Yeats' sense of urgency, Sharp continued to procrastinate. He was losing interest in Yeats' Celtic Mystical Order and shifting his spiritualist interests toward those of his new friend, Doctor John Goodchild, whose geographical locus for spiritualist renewal was not the West of Ireland, but the West of England — specifically Glastonbury and the surrounding area. On October 31, Sharp, as Fiona, told Yeats she wished she could write on magical matters, but regretted it was not possible yet.

> I have never known such continuity of hostile will, of which I am persuaded: and though, owing to the visionary power of our common friend [Sharp], much has been seen and overcome, and much seen and avoided, there is still something to avoid, something to overcome; and something to see. But very soon now, possibly in this very month of November where the dark powers prevail (and if so, a double victory indeed!) that which has been impossible may become possible. Even yet, however, there is much to work against: and not only here: for you, too, move often into the Red and Black, or so at least it seem.

All she could do now was send Yeats a copy of the new edition of her poetry published by Thomas Mosher in Maine. She described in some detail how this edition differed from that published by the Geddes firm in 1896. In addition to the new array of poems, one section of the volume entitled "Foam of the Past" contained a lengthy dedication to Yeats. That dedication will appear, she told him, at the very front of a projected new English edition of her poems, a project that failed to see the light of day until 1907 when William Heinemann published a posthumous edition of *From the Hills of Dream*. She wanted Yeats' advice among three titles she was considering for that English edition. Having brushed quickly past the Celtic order, Sharp sought Yeats' approval of the new poems in the new edition. It must have been clear to Yeats that Sharp's interest in his Order had waned.

On November 23, Sharp sent Yeats a Fiona note accompanying the November issue of Thomas Mosher's *Bibelot* which featured a reprint of her "Celtic" essay, the essay Æ had attacked in his review of *The Divine Adventure* in the July 21, 1900 issue of the *All Ireland Review*. She had expanded its title to "Celtic: A Study in Spiritual History" and written a prologue intended to address some of Æ's concerns which she would like Yeats to read. She hoped he had found "something to care for" in Mosher's *From the Hills of Dream*, and in its dedication of one section to him.

The reminder caused Yeats to respond quickly with apologies for having waited so long to thank her for the book (*Collected Letters IV*, 982–984). He took time to write frankly and perceptively. He liked her prose better than her poetry, but "here and always you are a wonderful maker of myths. They seem your natural mode of expression. They are to you what mere words are to others." He encouraged her to strive for simplicity of language so "the myths stand out clearly, as something objective, as something well born & independent." When she used elaborate words, she invented "with less conviction, with less precision, with less delicacy." He continued:

> I have an advantage over you in having a very fierce nation to write for. I have to make everything very hard & clear, as it were. ... You have in the proper sense far more imagination than I have & that makes your work correspondingly more difficult. It is fairly easy for me who do so much of my work by the critical, rather than the imaginative faculty to be precise & simple, but it is hard for you in whose mind images form themselves without ceasing & are gone as quickly perhaps.

When Fiona spoke in an obviously personal voice, Yeats wrote, she was "not that Fiona who has invented a new thing, a new literary method. You are that Fiona when the great myths speak through you." Yeats made no mention of the volume's dedicatory note to him or to the new prologue to the controversial "Celtic" essay in Mosher's November *Bibelot*. Rather, he concluded by returning to his principal interest. He asked Fiona to send him any notes she had on the Celtic Rite because "there are places where I need the qualities of a different mind from mine."

This carefully crafted letter blends perceptive criticism with generous praise. Yeats shared Æ's displeasure with the heightened rhetoric and imprecision of some of the writings of Fiona Macleod. Yet he believed many of Fiona's works were valuable, indeed that Sharp as Fiona had "invented a new thing, a new literary method." In some of her prose, "myth" was her "language," and the myth spoke directly through her. Although Æ had warned Yeats directly and then through Lady Gregory in August 1900 that Sharp/Fiona should not be trusted with the secrets of the Celtic Mystical Order (*Collected Letters II*, 552 and *Collected Letters IV*, 978), Yeats ignored the warning. Even though Sharp was using some of the symbols and constructs of the incipient Order in Fiona's poems and plays, Yeats continued to seek his assistance because he believed Fiona, or the woman who enabled Fiona, had clairvoyant powers more insightful than his own.

In early 1901, Sharp's proposal for an article on the poetry and prose of Theodore Watts-Dunton was accepted by the weekly magazine *Literature* whose editor wanted "an account and sympathetic appreciation." Sharp submitted the article in June and wrote to Watts-Dunton in early July: "I hope that what I have written will be just such a pronouncement as you would like. Fortunately, *Literature* now carries great weight with its large circulation." In fact, *Literature* was in dire straits, having descended into confusion in February 1900 following the unexpected death of its powerful editor, Henry Duff Traill. It soon combined with the *Academy* and survived for a time as the *Academy and Literature*. Sharp's article never appeared, and Sharp told Watts-Dunton in February 1902 that he had heard nothing from the journal: "neither returned MS [manuscript], nor payment, nor even acknowledgment of my letter." In the meantime, Sharp's friend George L. Halkett, Editor of the *Pall Mall Magazine*, accepted his proposal for an article on Watts-Dunton and his housemate at the Pines, Algernon Swinburne. He finished this article, sent it to Watts-Dunton for review, and put it in final form for Halkett. Entitled "A Literary friendship: Mr. Swinburne and Mr. Watts-Dunton at the Pines," it appeared in the December 1901 number of the *Pall Mall*.

After returning from Argyll to London in mid-October, the Sharps made plans to spend December in Florence and then go south for another extended stay in Sicily. From January to mid-February, they would be in Taormina followed by a fortnight or so with Alexander Nelson Hood at his Castle Maniace. Through Hood, Sharp had met the popular American novelist Marion Crawford who lived with his wife in Italy, near Sorrento. Sharp wrote to say they would be happy to visit the Crawford's in Sorrento on their way to Sicily. Subsequently, the Sharps' December plans were canceled due to illness, their own and, more seriously, that of Elizabeth's mother who required Elizabeth's presence at her bedside at 72 Inverness Terrace in Bayswater.

Chapter Twenty-One: 1901 331

Fig. 61 Theodore Watts-Dunton (1832–1914). Portrait by H. B. Norris (1902). Public Domain. Wikimedia, https://commons.wikimedia.org/wiki/File:Theodore.watts-dunton.jpeg

While still in London in mid-December, Sharp drafted a letter for Mary to copy and send to Thomas Mosher. In response to his request for a photograph of Fiona, Sharp had sent him a picture of Edith Rinder. Mosher asked Fiona to allow him to publish it for her fans in America. Like others who had seen the picture, he was struck by the woman's beauty. The Fiona letter to Mosher of December 15 is an artful response to a reasonable request from someone whose favor she wanted to maintain. Asking him not to think her ungracious, she continued, "I am sure you know me well enough to be sure that neither a foolish 'fad,' nor still less any ungraciousness towards a request so natural and from one whose friendship I value, is responsible for my asking you not to press the point of my photograph." Were she to accept his request, she would be under "continual subsequent nervous apprehension, in itself very bad for work and well-being." In fact, her recent illness was due to the "serious nervous drain" that affected her after she sent the picture to Mosher on loan. She hated to refuse him just as she had hated to refuse a similar request from George Meredith. She promised Mosher he would surely have a photo when she died, or even earlier were she to decide later that the distance between Scotland and Portland was far enough to avoid "peril." Sharp did not tell Mosher the nature of the feared peril, that the woman in the photograph might be recognized as Edith Rinder. Fiona Macleod, Sharp's greatest invention, required frequent fabrication and occasioned near constant anxiety.

While Elizabeth was confined to London with her mother, Sharp went to Hastings in mid-December to "convalesce." On the 19th, he spent a day with Henry James in Rye and described the visit in a letter to Mrs. Philpot:

> I had a most delightful day at Rye with Henry James who now lives there for many months in the year. I went over early, lunched, and then we went all over that wonderfully picturesque old Cinque Port. A lovely walk in a frost-bound still country, and then back by the sombre old Land Gate, over the misty marshes down below, and the flame red Cypress Tower against a plum coloured sunset, to Henry James' quaint and picturesque old house to tea. It was in every way a memorable and delightful day, and not least the great pleasure of intercourse with that vivid brilliant and alive mind.

Mrs. Philpot was the author of *The Sacred Tree in Religion and Myth* and other popular books and pamphlets about spiritualist associations with trees. Little is known about Sharp's relationship with her though he may have met her through Dr. John Goodchild since the three shared the conviction that spirits inhabited the natural world and communicated frequently with those attuned to their messages. She was among the company of women with whom Sharp developed special relationships. In a December 26 letter to another of those women, Louise Chandler Moulton, he said he would leave for Sicily in a week going first to Bordighera on the Italian Riviera, then to Genoa where he hoped to meet Elizabeth, and then to Sicily for January and February. Despite the illnesses and the financial problems, 1901 was redeemed by days like those with Henry James and by the discovery of Thomas Mosher in Maine and Alexander Nelson Hood in Sicily.

Chapter Twenty-Two

1902

In early January, Sharp left for Bordighera where his friend Dr. John Goodchild was caring for his English patients. Elizabeth had planned to join him shortly in Genoa, but instead remained in London caring for her ailing mother. After a few days Sharp went south to Rome where, as he told Ernest Rhys in an early January letter, he had a brief but severe recurrence of the fever he suffered in December. Once recovered, he went on to Sicily where he planned to spend two months in and near his "beloved 'Greek' Taormina." In late January he boarded a narrow-gauge rail car, the Circumetnea, which took him up to the town of Maletto, high on the northwestern slopes of Mount Etna, where he was met and taken by donkey-cart to Alexander Nelson Hood's "wonderful old Castle-Fortress-Monastery-Mansion — the Castle Maniace," as described to Rhys. Elizabeth joined him there in early February, and they remained as guests of Hood for what Elizabeth called "a month of sunshine and flowers" (*Memoir*, 339). On February 10, Sharp told Watts-Dunton he was "convalescent" from his "gastric attack" and "happy to be in this beautiful & 'romantic' place with my dear friend Alex Nelson Hood (in Sicily, the Duke of Bronte)." Spring had come, he continued, "Everywhere is a mass of purple iris, narcissus, Asphodel, & thousands of sweet-smelling violets."

A fellow British guest, the composer Maude Valérie White, suggested Sharp compose a poem to commemorate their time together; she would set it to music and dedicate it to their host. The result was Sharp's "Buon Riposo" or "Good Rest" which became a song that put the guests to sleep when Hood's bagpipers finished marching up and down the main hall playing Christmas airs.

Buon riposo
When, like a sleeping child
Or a bird in the nest,
The day is gathered
To the earth's breast ...
Hush! ... 'tis the dream-wind
Breathing peace,
Breathing rest
Out of the gardens of Sleep in the West.
O come to me ... wandering
Wind of the West!
Gray Doves of slumber
Come hither to nest. ...
Ah, sweet now the fragrance
Below the dim trees
Of the White Rose of Rest
That blooms in the gardens of Sleep in the West.

Fig. 62 Maude Valérie White. Photograph by Herbert Rose Barraud, published by Eglington & Co. Carbon print, published 1889. © National Portrait Gallery, London. Some rights reserved.

Before the Sharps left Maniace on March 7, Sharp wrote a letter to Dr. Goodchild in which he said he was glad to leave, though with regrets. He went on to describe a defining trait of his personality:

> My wife says I am never satisfied, and that Paradise itself would be intolerable for me if I could not get out of it when I wanted. And there is some truth in what she says, though it is a partial truth only. I think external change as essential to some natures as passivity is to others; but this may simply mean that the inward life in one person may best be hypnotized by a "still image," that of another may best be hypnotized by a wavering image or series of wavering images. It is not change of scene one needs so much as change in these wavering images (*Memoir*, 340–341).

Continuing, he said he "should now, in many ways, be content to spend the most of [his] life in some quiet place in the country, with a garden, a line of poplars and tall elms, and a great sweep of sky." This image of the English countryside appealed to Sharp after a month in the barren landscape of Hood's estate, but, as Elizabeth knew, he would not be content to spend much time in such a place.

On March 7, the Sharps returned to Taormina where they spent another month in the warmth and beauty of the town perched high above the Bay of Naxos. Taormina's landscape differs from that of the slopes of Mount Etna though the volcano is visible as a backdrop in the distance. During their first trip to Sicily in 1901, Elizabeth thought her husband's opinions were tarnished by the island's troubled past.

> When I suggested how much the fascination of the beautiful island had seized hold of me, he would say: "No, I cannot feel it for the ground is sodden and every leaf drips with blood." To his great relief, on his return there he found, as he said, that he had got beyond the surface of things, had pierced down to the great essentials of the ancient land, and had become one of her devoted lovers (*Memoir*, 343).

A March 1902 letter to Catherine Janvier conveyed his new-found love of the land. Sometime, he wrote, he would like to come to Taormina without anything to do so he could simply dream and

> relive many of the scenes of this inexhaustible region of romance: to see in vision the coming and going of that innumerable company — from Ulysses and his wanderers, from Pythagoras and St. Peter, from that Pancrazio who had seen Christ in the flesh, from Aeschylus, and

Dionysius and Hiero and Celon [three Sicilian rulers in the fourth and fifth centuries B. C.], from Pindar and Simonides and Theocritus, to Richard Coeur-de-Lion and Garibaldi and Lord Nelson — what a strange company (*Memoir*, 342).

The beauty of Taormina impelled Sharp to some of his most effective word-painting in an April 3 letter to Mrs. J. H. Philpot:

> From my room here in the Castello-a-Mare — this long-terraced hotel is built on the extreme edge of a precipitous height outside the Messina Gate of Taormina — I look down first on a maze of vividly green almond trees sloping swiftly down to the deep blue sea, and over them the snowy vastness of Etna, phantom-white against the intense blue, with its hitherside 11,000 feet of gulfs of violet morning shadow. [...] My French windows open on the terrace, it is lovely to go out early in the morning to watch sunrise (gold to rose-flame) coming over Calabria, and the purple-blue emerald straits of Messina and down by the wildly picturesque shores of these island coasts and across the Ionian sea, and lying like a bloom on the incredible vastness of Etna and its rise from distant Syracuse and Mt. Hybla to its cone far beyond the morning clouds when clouds there are — or to go out at sunrise and see a miracle of beauty being woven anew — or at night when there is no moon, but only flashing of the starry torches, the serpentine glitter of lights, the soft cry of the aziola, and the drowsy rhythmic cadence of the sea in the caves and crags far below. Just now the hum of bees is almost as loud as the drowsy sighing of the sea: among the almonds a boy is singing a long drowsy Greek-like chant, and on the mass of wild rock near the cypresses a goatherd is playing intermittently on a reed pipe. A few yards to the right is a long crescent-shaped terrace garden filled with roses, great shrub-like clumps of white and yellow marguerite, myrtle, lilies, narcissus, sweet-scented blossom-covered geranium, oranges hanging in yellow flame, pale gold lemons. Below the branches a "Purple Emperor" and a snow- white "May Queen" are hovering in butterfly wooing. On an oleander above a wilderness of pink and scarlet geraniums two blue tits are singing and building, building, and singing.

While in Taormina, Sharp wrote "Italian Poets Today," a lengthy survey which appeared in the July issue of the *Quarterly Review*. He also read Greek history and Italian literature and worked on a Greek drama, never completed, titled "The Kôrê of Enna." Shortly after returning to England in the spring, he succumbed to what he called malarial fever, followed by a bout of pneumonia. He was able to spend a week or two in Brittany in late May, and then, in mid-June, he suffered a serious financial blow.

Fig. 63 Photograph of the Hotel Castello-a-Mare taken in 1937. William and Elizabeth Sharp stayed here in April 1902, and he described the view from the terrace outside his window in an April 3 letter to Mrs. J. H. Philpot. Photograph of postcard taken by William F. Halloran (2021). Original photographer unknown.

Fig. 64 Taormina as seen from the Saracen castle overlooking the town. The Hotel Castello-a-Mare is at the far left. The Greek theater is in the background. Photograph by Solomonn Levi, Wikimedia, https://en.wikipedia.org/wiki/File:Taormina_as_seen_from_the_castle_overlooking_the_town..jpg, CC BY-SA 4.0.

Elizabeth attributed their financial difficulties to her husband's ill health and consequent inability to generate income. He no longer had the "energy and buoyancy" to counter "the stress of circumstances," and his need to leave England for a warmer climate in winter forced Elizabeth to give up her art criticism for the *Glasgow Herald* and its attendant income. Sharp frequently ran short of money, and it was not unusual for him to ask friends for loans and editors for advances. This time there was an added problem.

In a July 21 letter to Alden, he described the "very serious disaster" as "the complete & final loss, without any warning, of all I had to depend upon, except what I can make by the pen." The loss came when he was still very

> "down" from a prolonged & health-shaking malarial fever. [...] The loss, though it might seem small to others, is a very material one to me, and above all I miss it as a surety, the one thing I could look to. [...] The trouble was complicated by coincident loss to others dear to me (thro' the mismanagement and defalcations of an agent in Australia) — & what with a pneumonic attack after return to England, & worry, etc., I have had anything but a satisfactory time of it! [...] However, I am now feeling much better in health, & if only health keeps hope to emerge from my present pressing embarrassments, & though I cannot replace the sure income lost forever still I hope I can make enough to get along on. [...] I hope very much, therefore, that one or two of the proposals made to you may appear to you "commissionable."

A relative in Australia had set up a trust from which Sharp had been receiving a modest income. In mid-June he learned the trust had suddenly disappeared due to mismanagement by an agent. His description of the loss in this letter to Alden indicates its seriousness, as does a Fiona letter dated July 19 to Mosher: "Through an unforeseen financial disaster affecting one who had money in trust for me I find myself not only in a most difficult position for the present but strained to get away abroad when the late autumn damps begin, as I am strongly advised to do." Alden would be able to help by accepting his articles for *Harper's*, and Mosher by publishing the Fiona books.

When Alexander Hood returned to England from Sicily in the summer and learned of Sharp's financial problem, he started a petition to have him placed on the Civil Pension List. He began by enlisting the support of Alfred Austin, the Poet Laureate, whom Sharp thanked in a July 12 letter for his concern and his "prompt and generous action." He hoped Austin's influence with James Arthur Balfour, First Lord of the Treasury, would be successful, and he sent names of friends in case others were needed to endorse the petition: George Meredith, A.

C. Swinburne, Thomas Hardy, Theodore Watts-Dunton, Dr. Richard Garnett, Austin Dobson, W. G. Prothero, Editor of the *Quarterly Review*, and the Duke of Sutherland. He went on to describe his need in a compelling manner:

> To show you how urgent things are with me, let me add therefore that I have only a few pounds left, enough with care to carry us on till the middle or end of August (& this because of an advance cheque for a long article of mine on contemporary Italian poetry in the forthcoming "Quarterly Review" July–Sept) — and that at the present moment I see no way, without borrowing (which I am most loth even to consider, apart from being already £50 in debt to my Bank) to meet the living-expenses of the autumn-months, or the winter (& alas, it is even more imperative than before, the doctor says, that I should get abroad before the fogs and damps begin — by the 1st of November, he says, if at all possible). By the turn of the year, of course, I hope that what I am now variously busy upon will begin to bring in money — if health holds, tho' worry and anxiety are heavy handicaps.

That Sharp felt he had to convey these personal details to a man he knew only slightly indicates the seriousness of his plight. Recognizing the petition for a Civil List Petition might fail, he also asked Austin to use his position on the Board of the Royal Literary Fund to obtain a one-time grant.

On July 11, Balfour, to whom Austin had appealed, succeeded his uncle, Lord Salisbury, as Prime Minister. Though Balfour surely had other matters on his mind during July, he managed to send word to Alexander Hood that "the writings of William Sharp, considered alone, would not constitute a sufficient claim." Hood then asked Sharp "to allow him to acquaint the Prime Minister with the authorship of the Fiona Macleod writings, and of the many sacrifices their production had entailed." According to Elizabeth, her husband consented providing Mr. Balfour were told "confidentially" and orally (*Memoir*, 345–349). Hood learned in mid-August the confidential message was insufficient. "A statement of entire claims to consideration" would have to be "laid upon the table of the House of Commons for the inspection of members." Informing Sharp of this requirement, Hood first declined to offer an opinion and then proceeded to do just that: "If you will sacrifice your unwillingness to appear before the world in all the esteem and admiration which are your due, then (I may say this) perhaps you will obtain freedom — or some freedom — from anxiety and worry that will permit you to continue your work unhampered and with a quiet mind."

Sharp refused to disclose Fiona Macleod's identity to members of Parliament since word would soon leak from there to the British press. His letter to Hood of August 21 (*Memoir*, 346–349) is Sharp's clearest and most affecting statement of how he came to view the Fiona Macleod phenomenon:

> Rightly or wrongly, I am conscious of something to be done — to be done by one side of me, by one half of me, by the true inward self as I believe — (apart from the overwhelming felt mystery of a dual self, and a reminiscent life, and a woman's life and nature within, concurring with and often dominating the other) — and rightly or wrongly I believe that this, and the style so strangely born of this inward life, depend upon my aloofness and spiritual isolation as F. M. To betray publicly the private life and constrained ideal of that inward self for a reward's sake would be a poor collapse.

The genesis of Fiona Macleod was "no literary adventure, but a deep spiritual impulse and compelling circumstances of a nature upon which I must be silent." Even to his good friend Hood, Sharp only alluded to the crucial role Edith Rinder played in the genesis of Fiona. Reflecting his grounding in myth and legend and his association with W. B. Yeats and Dr. John Goodchild in spiritualist activities, Sharp offered another explanation of the Fiona presence in his letter to Hood:

> In a word, and quite simply, I believe that a spirit has breathed to me, or entered me, or that my soul remembers or has awakened (the phraseology matters little) — and, that being so, that my concern is not to think of myself or my "name" or "reward," but to do (with what renunciation, financial and other, may be necessary) my truest and best.

Fiona Macleod, the female who had emerged and gained by his agency a wide readership in Britain and America, was both a second personality and a spirit speaking through him from another realm.

Sharp saw no reason to choose between the two explanations of Fiona; he experienced both as true. He had explored both the psychological and the spiritualist approaches to the mysteries of the human mind — indeed of human life — that vied for adherents in a post-Darwinian world which had rejected the comforting beliefs of established religions. The scientific, or materialist, approach recognized the presence of dual or even multiple personalities, some of which, according to his friend Havelock Ellis, might be male and others female. The spiritualist approach manifested itself in many movements and organizations, among them the Order of the Golden Dawn (Sharp was a member of the London branch), Madame Blavatsky's Theosophical Society, Yeats' Celtic Mystical Order, and Dr John Goodchild's Avalonians who fixated on the Holy Grail and sites in and around Glastonbury. Powerfully attracted to spiritualism, Sharp had engaged in elaborate rituals of evocation.

Sharp's letter to Hood of August 21 shows the psychological and spiritualist explanations of Fiona Macleod living together in his mind. He attributed his decision not to reveal the truth to his need for "aloofness and spiritual isolation as F.M." He believed he would no longer be able to write as Fiona if her identity was revealed, and he feared the truth would subject him to endless derision and mockery in the popular press and literary journals. That, in turn, would diminish editors' interest in publishing the pseudonymous writings. The impact on the Sharp's finances would be devastating. Small wonder he was free to assure Hood that Elizabeth, who was on a visit to Fife, would wholeheartedly endorse his decision.

Unable to inform Parliament Sharp was Fiona, but responsive to the appeals of Hood and Austin, Balfour, now Prime Minister, arranged for a one-time government grant. Sharp heard the news directly from Balfour's secretary and later from Austin. In his letter of appreciation to Austin, Sharp asked him to withdraw his request to the Royal Literary Fund since the grant from the government freed him from "present embarrassments and immediate exigencies." The grant, along with some payments and advances for his writings, enabled the Sharps to leave Britain for warmer weather at the end of October.

After learning about the lost trust in mid-June, the Sharps decided to go to the west of Scotland and live as frugally as possible. Writing on June 23 from St. Abbs, a fishing village in Berwickshire in northeast England, Sharp told John MacLeay he planned to leave for Edinburgh two days later. Elizabeth would join him at the end of July, and they would spend August and September in the Highlands before going to Sicily at the beginning of November. Macleay had asked for biographical material he could use in a projected article, but Sharp was reluctant, and frankly too exhausted, to say much about himself in a letter. Near the end of June, Elizabeth joined her husband in Edinburgh, and they went on to Glasgow, southwest to the Isle of Arran, north to Oban, and rented a room in the remote ferryman's cottage at the northern point of "'the Green Isle' of Lismore in the sea-mouth of Loch Linnhe within sight of the hills of Morven"(*Memoir*, 344). In his July 21 letter to Alfred Austin, which carries the return address "Point House | Island of Lismore | (by Oban)," Sharp said he had come to the "quiet farmhouse (already known often) so as to live with the utmost possible saving of expense."

Fig. 65 North Lismore from Port Appin on the mainland with the hills of Kingairloch beyond. Photograph by Alan Partridge (2004), Wikimedia, https://commons.wikimedia.org/wiki/File:Lismore_Island.jpg, CC BY-SA 2.0.

Despite their worries about finances, Elizabeth remembered her month on Lismore as happy, disease-free, and productive (*Memoir*, 344–345): "We spent much of our time on the water in a little rowing boat. A favourite haunt was a little Isle of Seals, in the loch, where we one day found [and freed] a baby seagull, fat and fully fledged, but a prisoner by reason of a long piece of grass that had tightly wound round and atrophied one of its feet." The ferryman sometimes served as their oarsman and guide: "One day when we were out on the loch at sundown, and an exquisite rosy flush lay over hill and water, he stopped rowing and leant over his oars, silent for a time, and at last murmured in his slow Highland English ''Tis-the-smile-of-God-upon-the-waters.'"

In the isolated ferryman's cottage, "a good place for work," Sharp wrote as Fiona: "'The Four Winds of Eirinn' (long); 'The Magic Kingdoms' (longer and profounder), one of the best things F. M. has ever written; 'Sea-Magic' (a narrative and strange Sea-Lore); 'The Lynn of Dreams' (a spiritual study); and 'Seumas' (a memory)." He revised for American publication an 1899 a Fiona review of Yeats' *Wind Among the Reeds* which appeared in the October 1902 issue of *The North American Review* as "The Later Works of W. B. Yeats." He arranged a selection of Fiona stories for a Tauchnitz book to be called *Wind and Wave*, and he prepared *The Silence of Amor* for publication by Thomas Mosher in Maine. This small book contained the prose poems, or as Sharp preferred to call them, "prose-rhythms," from "The Silence of Amor" section of the 1896 edition of *From the Hills of Dream*. As William Sharp he wrote the introduction to his friend Eugene Lee-Hamilton's *Dramatic Sonnets, Poems and Ballads: Selections from and Poems of Eugene Lee-Hamilton* which the Walter Scott firm published in 1903. Earlier in 1902, he wrote an essay called "Sir Walter Scott's Land," which his friend Henry Alden published in the June 1902 issue of *Harper's Magazine*. While on Lismore, he wrote "Robert Louis Stevenson's Country" which Alden published in the September issue of *Harper's*. These were the first of several articles he wrote on the home locations of famous writers. George Halkett, a boyhood friend and editor of the *Pall Mall Magazine*, published eight more of the articles in 1903. In 1904, the Pall Mall Press published a handsome volume called *Literary Geography* which contained twelve such articles and which Sharp dedicated to Halkett, the volume's "godfather." Both Editors — Alden and Halkett — were motivated in part by their desire to help their friend through a financial crisis. Under the pressure of such a crisis and despite what Elizabeth called his "increasing delicacy," Sharp managed to write an amazing amount during the summer and fall of 1902.

While Sharp was on Lismore, he made his way across the water to Oban to meet John Macleay who had come down from Inverness to interview him. In his June 23 letter, Sharp wrote in response to Macleay's request for information about his life and work, "If we should meet in Scotland ... why, I daresay my tongue would be less reticent than my pen, whose shocking apathy at the sight of ink is growing into a disease." His lips were less reticent in Oban since Macleay produced an article on Sharp called a "A Literary Wanderer: The Career of William Sharp" which appeared in the April 1903 edition of a periodical called *The Young Man*. The article's title was derived from Sharp's June 23 letter to Macleay in which he referred to himself as a "homeless wanderer" who might some day, when settled some place, "take up the reminiscent pen." The Macleay article quotes Sharp's reminiscences about his boyhood and early career, but Macleay, whose primary interest was Scottish and Gaelic writings, says little about his writings. He describes Sharp as a well-read, rapid writer who moves from place to place frequently, and he admires the range of Sharp's interests. He implies that Sharp takes on too many writing assignments, thus limiting his proficiency in one genre. In the interview, Sharp tried to focus Macleay's attention on his youth and early career. Macleay had speculated frequently about the identity of Fiona in *The Highland News*, and he continued to suspect she was Sharp despite his repeated denials. The meeting with Macleay provided Sharp another opportunity to allay Macleay's suspicions. If Macleay hoped for a confession, he was disappointed, and the resultant article is devoid of Fiona.

The Sharps left Lismore in mid-August. Elizabeth returned to London, but Sharp rented a room from a Mrs. Rhind at 53 Castle Street in Edinburgh where he stayed for a month. In early September, he spent a long weekend with a friend in Linlathen, north of Dundee, and he became ill again when he returned to Edinburgh. According to an October 31 letter to Grant Richards, he had hardly recovered from the Edinburgh illness when, on his return to London, he was seized with "a dangerous & painful illness through catching a bad internal chill in a fog" on the morning of his arrival. It did not take long for London to make Sharp ill, but the illness provided a convenient excuse for avoiding a meeting with Grant Richards regarding a dispute over a debt he could not afford to repay. That aside, the income from his writings and the government grant made it possible for both Sharps to escape to Sicily.

The couple left London in mid-October, and Sharp wrote to Catherine Janvier from Taormina on October 30: "We reached Messina all right, and Giardini, the Station for Taormina, in fair time; then the lovely winding drive up to unique and beautiful and wildly picturesque Taormina and to the lovely winter villa and grounds of Santa Caterina where a warm welcome met us from Miss Mabel Hill, with whom we are to stay till the New Year" (*Memoir*, 349). Santa Caterina, formerly a convent and now a hotel, was renovated as a winter home for Sir Edward Stock Hill (1834–1902), an English politician who was made a Knight Commander of the Order of the Bath by Queen Victoria in 1892. Hill contributed substantially to the well-being of the English community in Taormina. Following his death, his daughter, Mabel Hill, carried on her father's tradition of philanthropy and focused on improving the condition of Taormina's native residents. She established, for example, a school where women learned the art of embroidery and earned money of their own. Taormina became famous for its intricate embroidery which is still prominently displayed in the shops along the town's main street. Taormina revived Sharp's spirits and again moved him to word-painting in a letter to Catherine Janvier:

> I have for study a pleasant room on the garden terrace, at the Moorish end of the old convent-villa with opposite the always open door windows or great arch trellised with a lovely "Japanese" vine, looking down through a sea of roses and lemon and orange to the deep blue Ionian Sea. The divine beauty, glow, warmth, fragrance, and classic loveliness of this place would delight you. [...] Beneath my Moorish arch I look down through clustering yellow roses and orange and lemon to green-blue water, and thence across the wild-dove's breast of the Ionian Sea.

On November 7, the Sharps and Mable Hill took the narrow-gauge railroad up and around the slopes of Etna to stay with Alexander Nelson Hood at the Castello Maniace. Writing the next day to Catherine Janvier, Sharp described the journey:

> We three came here yesterday (Elizabeth, Miss Hill and I) and enjoyed the marvelous mountain-climbing journey from the sea-level of Giarre (near Catania) up to beautiful Linguaglossa, and Castiglione 2000 ft. high and so on to Randazzo and Maletto (3000 ft.) where we got out and drove thro' the wild lava-lands of this savage and brigand haunted region to Castello di Maniace where il Signor Ducino Alessandro gave us cordial and affectionate welcome.

The ladies stayed a week, and Sharp remained for a second week before returning to Taormina with Hood who went on to Venice.

During November, Sharp worked on a story about Flora Macdonald entitled "The King's Ring" which appeared as the work of Fiona Macleod in the *Pall Mall Magazine* in May and June 1904. Flora MacDonald (1722–1790) was a member of the MacDonalds of Sleat, who helped Charles

Fig. 66 The Ferrovia Circumetnea is a narrow-gauge railway which encircles Mount Etna. From its terminal in Catania the line loops around Mount Etna and eventually reaches the other terminal at the seaside town of Riposto. Its rolling stock has been updated several times, but the route is the same as when the Sharps boarded the train to travel back and forth between Taormina and the Castello Maniace in the early twentieth century. Photograph by Arbalete (2011), Wikimedia, https://commons.wikimedia.org/wiki/File:Mappa_ferr_Circumetnea.png, CC BY-SA 3.0.

Fig. 67 The Randazzo station of the Ferrovia Circumetnea where the Sharps entered and left the train on their trips to the Castello Maniace. Photograph by LuckyLisp (2005), Wikimedia, https://commons.wikimedia.org/wiki/File:Circumetnea_stazione_di_randazzo.jpg, CC BY-SA 3.0.

Edward Stuart evade government troops after the Battle of Culloden in April 1746. Her family supported the government during the 1745 Rising, and Flora later claimed to have assisted Charles out of sympathy for his situation. After her release from the Tower of London in 1747, she married and moved to North Carolina. Sharp's story focused on her life there, and her support of Britain during the American Revolution. As soon as he finished some "pot-boiling" essays, he told Catherine Janvier in an October 30 letter, he planned to put together for publication in Britain "two F. M. volumes, one a vol. of Gaelic essays and Spiritual studies to be called *For The Beauty of an Idea* and the other a volume of Verse to be called probably 'The Immortal Hour and Poems' or else 'The Enchanted Valley'". When the volume of essays and spiritual studies was published in 1904 by Chapman & Hall in London, it had expanded significantly. "For the Beauty of an Idea" became the second half of a 400-page book called *The Winged Destiny: Studies in the Spiritual History of the Gael*. The volume of Fiona Macleod poems did not materialize until two years after Sharp died when Elizabeth organized it as her husband had directed: *From the Hills of Dream: Threnodies, Songs and Later Poems* (London: William Heinemann, 1907).

Sharp's November 19 letter of thanks to Hood exemplifies the renewal he experienced in the warmth and beauty of Sicily: "what a happy time I had at Maniace, and how pleasantly I remember all our walks and talks and times together, and how the true affection of a deepened friendship is only the more and more enhanced and confirmed." Hood was in Venice to collect information for a romance he was writing called *Adria: A Tale of Venice* which dealt with the city's occupation by Austria after that country received it in a trade with Napoleon. When Hood's book was published in 1904 it contained the following dedication:

TO
WILLIAM SHARP
IN TOKEN OF FRIENDSHIP AND GRATEFUL REMEMBRANCE
OF PLEASANT COMPANIONSHIP, THIS "SAGA OF
A BELEAGUERED CITY" — THIS TALE OF
THAT VENICE OF WHICH WE BOTH
HAVE SO GREAT A LOVE

In Hood, Sharp found late in life another man with whom he forged an intimate friendship, as he had earlier with Hall Caine, J. Stanley Little, and R. Murray Gilchrist. That Hood tried so hard to obtain a government pension for Sharp and continued to entertain him for weeks at a time in his Bronte Castle suggests the affection expressed in this dedication was genuine. In late August, Sharp concluded a letter to Hood by saying "I am more than ever glad and proud of a friendship so deeply sympathetic and intuitively understanding. | Ever affectionately yours, dear Friend, | Will." The bond formed between the two men endured until December 1905 when Sharp died in Hood's Castle Maniace.

Fig. 68 Sir Alexander Nelson Hood, Fifth Duke of Bronté (1854–1937). "The Princess's Private Secretary," Caricature by Spy (Leslie Ward), published in *Vanity Fair* in 1905. Wikimedia, https://en.wikipedia.org/wiki/Alexander_Hood,_5th_Duke_of_Bronté#/media/File:Alexander_Nelson_Hood,_Vanity_Fair,_1905-10-26.jpg, Public Domain.

Chapter Twenty-Three

1903

Sharp began a diary at that start of the New Year and, as was his habit, abandoned it a few days later. On New Year's Day, the Sharps had dinner with the novelist Robert Hichens at the Hotel Timeo just down the hill from the Greek Theater in Taormina. Hichens (1864–1950) was a frequent visitor to Taormina and a friend of Alexander Nelson Hood. He was also an established writer, having published ten novels between 1886 and 1904. One of those, *The Green Carnation*, was published pseudonymously in 1894 and withdrawn from publication in 1895. By defining, satirizing, and barely disguising the relationship between his friends, Oscar Wilde and Lord Alfred Douglas, the novel contributed to Wilde's public humiliation and imprisonment. Despite its abrupt disappearance it was widely circulated, and many knew Hichens was its author. Following the Wilde debacle, Hichens, himself a recognized and unapologetic homosexual, spent most of his time away from England — in Switzerland, Egypt, Northern Africa, and Taormina where he found a group of men who shared his temperament and inclinations. Sharp formed a bond with Hichens, as he had with Murray Gilchrist and Alex Hood, but their short-lived friendship ended abruptly with Sharp's death in 1905.

On January 3, the Sharps lunched with Hichens at the Timeo, and, after walking around the theater, called on Maude Valérie White, a member of Taormina's British community admired for her musical settings of poems and ballads. Also, on the third, according to Sharp's diary, he finished the Fiona Macleod story about Flora Macdonald and sent it off to Edinburgh for Mary to type. The Fiona letter sending the story to George Halkett for inclusion in the *Pall Mall Magazine* is dated May 9, 1903. The delay suggests Sharp tried unsuccessfully to have

Fig. 69 Robert Smythe Hichens (1864–1950). Photograph by unknown photographer (1912), in Frederic Taber Cooper, *Some English Story Tellers* (New York: Henry Holt & Co, 1912). Wikimedia, https://commons.wikimedia.org/wiki/File:Robert_Hichens_001.jpg#/media/File:Robert_Hichens_001.jpg, Public Domain.

the story accepted elsewhere before sending it to the *Pall Mall*. Halkett accepted the story, and it appeared a year later in the May/June 1904 issue of the magazine. On January 4, Sharp began an account of the rugged land and the hardy people who occupied the vast Nelson estate which he called "Through Nelson's Duchy." He finished it four days later, and it appeared as the work of William Sharp with photographs selected by Alexander Nelson Hood in the *Pall Mall Magazine* in October 1903.

The Sharps continued to enjoy the beautiful weather and active social life of Taormina while Sharp worked sporadically on his writing and correspondence. In late January, he set off by himself on a trip to Greece to gather material for a book he planned to call Greek Backgrounds. After crossing from Messina in Sicily to Reggio di Calabria, at the western point of the toe of Italy's boot, Sharp took a train to Crotona on the east side of the toe. There he boarded a ferry which took him to the port city of Taranto on the west side of the boot's heel. A train called the Agamemnon took him from Taranto to Brindisi, a port city on the east of the heel, where he boarded a ship bound for Greece. Appropriately named the Poseidon, the ship crossed the Aegean, and as it approached the coast of Turkish Albania the shaft of its main screw broke. In a January 23 letter to his wife written aboard the stranded ship, he described the beauty of the mountainous shoreline and the joy he felt in being on his own amidst scenery that reminded him of his native Highlands. He was rescued by another steamer that took him to Kerkyra on Corfu where he boarded yet another ship which sailed for Athens. Upon arriving he was delighted by the ancient sites familiar from years of reading. "It is a marvelous home-coming feeling I have here," he wrote to Elizabeth on January 29, "and I know a strange stirring, a kind of spiritual rebirth." On February first, he wrote again:

> Yesterday, a wonderful day at Eleusis. Towards sundown drove through the lovely hill-valley of Daphne, with its beautifully situated isolated ruin of the Temple of Aphrodite, a little to the north of the Sacred Way of the Dionysiac and other Processions from Aonai (Athenai) to the Great Fane of Eleusis. I have never anywhere seen such a marvelous splendour of living light as the sundown light, especially at the Temple of Aphrodite and later as we approached Athens and saw it lying between Lycabettos and the Acropolis, with Hymottos to the left and the sea to the far right and snowy Pentelicos behind. The most radiant wonder of light I have ever seen.

Not since 1892 when he reveled in the beauty of the Roman countryside and its ruins had Sharp experienced such joy in exploring the landscape and its monuments.

Sharp returned to Taormina in early February where he found a letter Robert Hichens wrote after returning from Taormina to England. He urged Sharp to winter with him in Africa the following year. They would stay in a first-rate hotel in Biskra, Algeria, and they would be very happy. Hichens continued:

> We must often go out on donkey-back into the dunes and spend our day there far out in the desert. I know no physical pleasure, — apart from all the accompanying mental pleasure, — to be compared with that which comes from the sun and air of the Sahara and the enormous spaces. This year I was more enchanted than ever before. Even exquisite Taormina is humdrum in comparison. Do try to come then as November is a magnificent month (*Memoir*, 365).

Fig. 70 View over the excavation site towards Eleusis, the site of the Eleusinian Mysteries, or the Mysteries of Demeter and Kore, which became popular in the Greek-speaking world as early as 600 BC and attracted initiates during the Roman Empire before declining in the fourth century AD. Photograph by Carole Raddato (2005), Wikimedia, https://commons.wikimedia.org/wiki/File:General_view_of_sanctuary_of_Demeter_and_Kore_and_the_Telesterion_(Initiation_Hall),_center_for_the_Eleusinian_Mysteries,_Eleusis_(8191841684).jpg, CC BY-SA 2.0.

Sharp must have shared with Hichens his newly formed fascination with Greece and his intention to spend the next winter there since Hichens closed his letter by writing, "I can't help being rather sorry that you won't go to Sicily again for a long while. I always feel as if we all had a sort of home there." After reproducing this letter in her *Memoir*, Elizabeth added that Hichens wrote to her: "I still think Taormina the most exquisite place in Europe. On a fine morning it is ineffably lovely." In the fall of 1905, according to Elizabeth, it was planned that "after the New Year Mr. Hood, Mr. Hichens, my husband, and I should go together to Biskra. But as the autumn waned, we realized the unwisdom of any such plans" (*Memoir*, 365–366, 413).

In a February 18 letter to Catherine Janvier, Sharp complained: "with this foreign life in a place like this, with so many people I know, it is almost impossible to get anything like adequate time for essential work — and still less for the imaginative leisure I need [for] dreaming out my work — to say nothing of reading, etc." He described the strains of his double life:

> As you know, too, I have continually to put into each day the life of two persons — each with his or her own interests, preoccupations, work, thoughts, and correspondence. I have really, in a word, quite apart from my own temperament, to live at exactly double the rate in each day of the most active and preoccupied persons. No wonder, then, that I find the continuous correspondence of "two persons" not only a growing weariness, but a terrible strain and indeed perilous handicap on time and energy for work.

A March 17 Fiona letter to Benjamin Burgess Moore, who was about to move to Paris, assured him the city had a "manifold fascination," though it lacked "the glow and colour of life in Italy and Spain and Greece." Fiona thanked him for his concern about her health and continued:

> I am much better for being in the south, but it has not been a really good winter anywhere, and I feel that I would like a year of nothing but sunshine and serene life. One tires of everything except illusions and dreams: and longs often for nothing but warm sunshine and rest.

Burgess must have written to Fiona in care of Sharp in Sicily for she concluded by bringing him up short: "Mr. Sharp is still in Sicily, but will be leaving any day: but apart from that please do not address to me again c/o him, as he does not like it, nor do I. My correspondence-address is Miss Macleod, | c/o Mrs. Wingate Rinder, | 21. Woronzow Road, | London. N. W." When Sharp suspected a correspondent might be approaching the truth, Fiona responded forcefully.

In early April, the Sharps were back in London where Sharp composed on the 25th a Fiona letter to Mosher describing plans for her writings and detailing how he planned to keep her out of the way should Mosher decide to visit Scotland and England anytime soon.

> There seems little doubt that I cannot expect to regain assured health unless I remain in the South from the early autumn till May for a year or two to come at any rate and, indeed, I am strongly advised to remain in the South (or, if not, in the Summer, on Scandinavian waters) all this year unbrokenly. Nothing is yet definitely decided: except that I shall not be staying in London or Edinburgh this season, and if in Scotland at all will only be for a flying visit to the West in September, or else much sooner instead. Later, I'll be better able to give you an idea of my whereabouts during the summer and autumn. By October, this year, at least, I hope and expect to get south again. It is extraordinary the difference in health it makes, though I fear it makes one lazy, and far more inclined to read

and dream, than to write and revise and be continually exercised by the forces of the mind and the spirit.

The travel plans are an interesting amalgam. Sharp had been advised to go south each fall for his health and stay as long as he could. The Scandinavian waters were only a means of keeping Fiona hidden, but the Sharps did go south in October with Fiona trailing behind.

The Fiona letters from mid-May to mid-June have her visiting the Lake District, going on to the Inner Hebrides (the Isles of Bute, Mull, and Iona), and then heading south again to the Lake District. Whether or not Sharp followed that itinerary, a June 6 Fiona letter to Yeats has him tracing "sculptured symbols of the Centaur and the Salmon" on "ancient Pagan stones" in the Hebrides. When he returns to London on June 14, Sharp will show Yeats "all the tracings and memda he has made." Of special interest is a tracing of a "horse-headed salmon, which Fiona supposed unique. In this section of the letter, Sharp lapsed into writing as himself.

From these Fiona letters we also know Sharp was revising and writing prefatory material for three Fiona Macleod books Thomas Mosher would publish in the fall: *Deirdrê and the Sons of Usna*, *The Divine Adventure*, and *The House of Usna: A Drama*. The first of these received special attention in a June 3 Fiona letter to Mosher: "Herewith I send you the MS of my dedicatory foreword to *Deirdrê*. Please take great care in comparison of the text in proof with this MS." As described in Chapter 21, the dedicatory foreword of *Deirdrê* was addressed to Esther Mona Rinder, Edith's daughter. The June 3 Fiona letter asked Mosher to send three unbound proof sets of the book for "birthday use." Esther would be two years old on June 26, 1903. Since the book would not be bound before that date, Sharp wanted Edith to have a copy of the book for her daughter's birthday. Esther Mona (Rinder) Harvey grew to adulthood without seeing the proofs, the book, or the dedication, and she was surprised and moved upon reading the dedication many years later.

When he returned to London, Sharp joined his wife in "temporary lodgings" at 9 St. Mary's Terrace in Paddington. Robert Farquharson Sharp, Elizabeth's brother (and William's cousin), lived nearby at 56 St. Mary's Mansions. Their mother, Agnes Farquharson Sharp, lived with Robert, and she was quite ill. Elizabeth wanted to be nearby to help as she could.

Chapter Twenty-Three: 1903

On June 22, Sharp made a day trip to Box Hill to see George Meredith. He described the visit in a letter to someone Elizabeth named only as a friend. Both men, Sharp wrote, felt this would be their last meeting; Meredith's death would mark "the passing of the last of the great Victorians." Sharp wished Meredith could know "a certain secret: but it is better not, and now is in every way as undesirable as indeed impossible." Since Sharp had taken Edith Rinder, pretending to be Fiona, to Box Hill to meet Meredith in June 1897, Sharp feared Meredith would be upset if told the truth.

> If there is in truth, as I believe, and as he believes, a life for us after this, he will know that his long-loving and admiring younger comrade has also striven towards the hard way that few can reach. What I did tell him before has absolutely passed from his mind: had, indeed, never taken root, and perhaps I had nurtured rather than denied what had taken root. If in some ways a little sad, I am glad otherwise. And I had one great reward, for at the end he spoke in a way he might not otherwise have done, and in words I shall never forget. I had risen and was about to lean forward and take his hands in farewell, to prevent his half-rising, when suddenly he exclaimed "Tell me something of her — of Fiona. I call her so always, and think of her so, to myself. Is she well? Is she at work? Is she true to her work and her ideal? No, that I know!"

Given Meredith's questions and elaborate praise, Sharp wondered if he suspected Sharp had some role in producing the Fiona writings. Meredith's final words alleviated that concern:

> It was then he said the following words, which two minutes later, in the garden, I jotted down in pencil at once lest I should forget even a single word or a single change in the sequence of the words. "She is a woman of genius. That is rare … . so rare anywhere, anytime, in women or in men. Some few women 'have genius,' but she is more than that. Yes, she is a woman of genius: the genius too, that is rarest, that drives deep thoughts before it. Tell her I think often of her, and of the deep thought in all she has written of late. Tell her I hope great things of her yet. And now … we'll go, since it must be so. Goodbye, my dear fellow, and God bless you." Outside, the great green slope of Box Hill rose against a cloudless sky, filled with a flowing south wind. The swifts and swallows were flying high. In the beech courts thrush and blackbird called continually, along the hedgerows the wild roses hung. But an infinite sadness was in it all. A prince among men had fallen into the lonely and dark way.

Sharp relished Meredith's praise and feared his death was eminent. Elizabeth noted the irony: "Goodbye it was in truth; but it was the older poet who recovered hold on life and outlived the younger by four years" (*Memoir*, 368).

In a letter dated simply "Sunday Evg," but written on July 5, Sharp thanked Richard Garnett for a copy of a new and augmented edition of his *Twilight of the Gods* which Grant Richards recently published. He was looking forward to seeing Garnett and hopefully his wife the next day — Monday, July 6 — when he and Elizabeth were hosting an "At Home" not at their St. Mary's Terrace lodgings, but at Sharp's club, the Grosvenor at the northeast corner of Dover Street and Piccadilly in central London. Amidst their social obligations, the Sharps were dealing with the illness of Elizabeth's mother who died sometime between the July 6 "At Home" and July 13, the date of a Sharp letter to Grant Richards written on black-bordered mourning stationery. In that letter, he said he meant to speak to Richards the other night during their "At Home," but the opportunity vanished in the "rapid dispersal" of their company after the "speechifying." A July 15 typed and unsigned Fiona letter to Mosher apologized for a "hurried line" as she was just returning to Edinburgh from London where she had been "on a matter of sudden urgency and illness." That Sharp had Fiona come to London from Scotland to mark his mother-in-law's final illness and death signals his affection for the woman who welcomed him to London in 1877, paved the way for his marriage to Elizabeth, and opened her Inverness Terrace house to him whenever he needed a place to stay in the city.

In a July 14 letter to Theodore Watts-Dunton, Sharp said it was difficult "to snatch a moment at this season, when there seems a mysterious social conspiracy against every hour of day and night," but he could free himself on Thursday July 16 if Watts-Dunton could manage to have tea with him in the late afternoon at his club. The July 15 Fiona letter to Mosher expressed her disappointment that he might not publish *The House of Usna, A Drama* in the fall as she had spent so much time preparing it and had taken such care over its lengthy introduction. It was the thing she cared most for. In response to this appeal, Mosher proceeded with a 1903 publication of the volume in a beautiful edition of 500 copies, 450 on handmade Van Gelder paper and 50 on Japanese vellum. It was dedicated "To Mona" (Caird) and signed by the publisher.

A June 23 Fiona letter to Mosher conveyed plans for the summer so he would know where to send correspondence and payments. Any letters directed to Edith Rinder's London address must reach her by the end of July since she and her family would be spending August and September in the Lake Tarbert area west and south of Glasgow. Sharp's mother and sisters would be near the Rinders in Kilcreggan for the month of August and return to their Edinburgh home where Mary would receive any Fiona correspondence. The Sharps would also go to Scotland in late July. After stopping near Falkirk to visit friends, they would join his family in Kilcreggan for August.

Fig. 71 The Firth of Clyde at Kilcreggan (on the right), with PS *Waverley* approaching across Loch Long. Photograph by Dave Souza (2018), Wikimedia, https://commons.wikimedia.org/w/index.php?curid=73771868, CCBY-SA-4.0.

During August Sharp continued to revise and write introductions for the three Macleod books Mosher had agreed to publish. Since the content of those books had already appeared in England, the revisions and introductions were a means of avoiding copyright problems. On August 4, he sent Bliss Perry, Editor of the *Atlantic Monthly*, an article on the remoter regions of Sicily called "The Sicilian Highlands" which appeared in the April 1904 issue of the magazine. In an August 25 letter he told Henry Alden his articles on the places nineteenth-century British writers lived and worked would be published by the Pall Mall Press as a book called *Literary Geography*. His "projected Greek book," would include "Magna Grecia as well, i.e., Hellenic Calabria and Sicily, etc." He intended to call it "Greek Backgrounds." As in the *Literary Geography* articles he would associate famous Greek writers with the places they lived and worked.

When Sharp's mother and sister left their rented Kilcreggan house at the end of August, Elizabeth and William went northeast to Perthshire to stay with Mrs. Glassford Bell, formerly Marion Sandeman, a childhood friend of Sharp's. While there, according to Elizabeth, her husband, having suffered through a wet spring and a still damper summer, "became so ill we went to Llandrindod Wells for him to be under special treatment." On September 13, the day after his forty-eighth birthday, Sharp thanked Isabella

Gilchrist, Murray Gilchrist's mother, for sending him birthday greetings. The letter projects Sharp coming to terms with the seriousness of his illness and the likelihood of his early death.

> But as one grows older, one the more recognizes that "climate" and "country" belong to the geography of the soul rather than to that secondary physical geography of which we hear so much. The winds of heaven, the dreary blast of wilderness, the airs of hope and peace, the tragic storms and cold inclemencies these are not the property of our North or South or East, but are of the climes self-made or inherited or in some strange way become our "atmosphere."

Like Mrs. Gilchrist who was sixty-three years old, Sharp will soon need to forsake physical travel for what he calls the "geography of the soul." Whether he wrote the letter in Perthshire or after he reached Llandrindod Wells, his illness influenced its content. Since Sharp could not stay long in one place, inability to travel raised thoughts of the afterlife: "The country we dream of, that we long for," he told Mrs. Gilchrist, "is not yet reached by Cook nor even chartered by Baedeker."

The journey from Perthshire to the spa town in the middle of Wales was long and difficult, but it had a desirable result. From Llandrindod Wells in late September, he described his condition to Ernest Rhys: "things have not gone well with me. All this summer I have been feeling vaguely unwell and, latterly, losing strength steadily." After arriving in Llandrindod Wells, "the rigorous treatment, the potent Saline and Sulphur waters and baths, the not less potent and marvelously pure and regenerative Llandrindod air — and my own exceptional vitality and recuperative powers — have combined to work a wonderful change for the better." It might prove to be no more than "a splendid rally," and he must not be "too sanguine." The end might be nearing, but he was not troubled: "I have lived, and am content, and it is only for what I don't want to leave undone that the sound of 'Farewell' has anything deeply perturbing."

Fig. 72 Ye Wells Hotel, Llandrindod where William Sharp received treatment for diabetes in September 1903: "the rigorous treatment, the potent Saline and Sulphur waters and baths, the not less potent and marvelously pure and regenerative Llandrindod air ... have combined to work a wonderful change for the better." Photograph by Percy Benzie Abery (193–?), Wikimedia, https://commons.wikimedia.org/wiki/File:-Ye_Wells_Hotel,_Llandrindod_(1293703).jpg, CC0.

In his annual birthday letter to E. C. Stedman following his return to London, Sharp described his illness as "a subtle malady" which had claimed him for a comrade. "His name is Diabetes, but he's no enemy, & refrains as much as he can, & even promises to disappear for a time, & be content with psychical Marconigrams [messages sent by radiotelegraphy]." A month previously, a specialist thought he had "got well into Chapter Last," but he surprised his friends and even himself by "an apparent complete recovery." It is only a "splendid rally," he continued, but "'I take it smiling,' as the lady said when she saw she 'couldn't help it,' when the amorous Brigand wooed her." Writing to Catherine Janvier on the September 30 he claimed to be "cheerful as a lark — let us say as a lark with a rheumatic wheeze in its little song-box, or gout in its little off-claw." He knew the combination of illnesses would soon claim him, but he was determined to "laugh and be glad and take life as I find it, till the end. The best prayer for me is that I may live vividly till 'Finis,' and work up to the last hour."

Shortly after writing and posting these letters, Sharp received a long letter from Stedman which raised his spirits. "It has been a true medicine," he wrote again to Stedman on October 2, "for, as I told you, I've been gravely ill. And it came just at the right moment and warmed my heart with its true affection." Sharp was also pleased by a recent visit to his doctor who had sanctioned his trip to Sicily and then to Greece for the winter. "When I'm once more in the land of Theocritus (and oh how entrancing it is)," he wrote to Stedman, "I'll be quite strong and well again… Indeed, I'm already 'a live miracle'!" Sharp then described in detail the itinerary he and Elizabeth intended to follow:

> We sail by the Orient liner "Orizaba" on the 23rd [of October]; reach Naples (via Gibraltar and Marseilles) 9 to 10 days later; and leave by the local mail-boat same evening for Messina — arrive there about 8 on Monday morning — catch the Syracuse mail about 10, change at 12 at Giarre, and ascend Mt. Etna by the little circular line to Maletto about 3,000 ft. high, and thence drive to the wonderful old Castle of Maniace to stay with our dear friend there, the Duke of Bronte — our third or fourth visit now. We'll be there about a fortnight: then a week with friends at lovely and unique Taormina: and then sail once more, either from Messina or Naples direct to the Piraeus, for Athens, where we hope to spend the winter and spring.

Sharp was glad to know there would be a loving friend waiting should another trip to America be possible.

As planned, the Sharps boarded the Orizaba on October 23, but the trip south was unpleasant. The weather was bad, the sea rough, and, according to a letter Sharp wrote to Catherine Janvier during the voyage, he suffered a heart attack soon after leaving Plymouth. After they passed Gibraltar and entered the Mediterranean, they encountered a "wild gale" in the Gulf of Lyon, "one of the wildest we had ever known," according to Elizabeth. They planned to visit briefly with the Janviers when the ship docked in Marseilles, but the storm by then had become "almost a hurricane." After taking shelter in a cove, they sailed directly to Naples. Elizabeth reproduced in the *Memoir* a short unrhymed poem, called "Invocation," her husband wrote during the storm. "It was his way of mental escape from a physical condition which induced great nervous strain or fatigue, to create imaginatively a contrary condition and environment, and so to identify himself with it, that he could become oblivious to surrounding actualities" (*Memoir*, 374–375).

A November 6 letter to Mosher in Mary's Fiona script, which she claimed to have written near Gibraltar, thanked him for sending newly printed copies of *The House of Usna* to Edinburgh where Mary forwarded at least one copy to Fiona. In fact, Sharp received this book when he reached Hood's Castle Maniace in the first week of November, where he drafted the Fiona letter and sent it for Mary to copy and mail from Edinburgh. He was establishing the fiction that Fiona was a week or so behind him in her travels. After spending a few days in Algeria, she would sail to Athens for a month or so with the Sharps. By shadowing his own travels with the imagined travels of Fiona, Sharp was able to describe the same people and places in both sides of the double correspondence. He could also keep Fiona on the move, carefully track her travels, and avoid the possibility of anyone asking to meet her. In the same vein, Fiona's various ailments shadowed his own with one important exception. He did not suffer the neurology in his writing hand that made it difficult for Fiona to write and thus explained the typed letters that were sometimes necessary.

In a November 11 letter to Mrs. Philpot from Castle Maniace, Sharp described how the location did not appeal to him at that time of year. It was "too high between 2,000 and 3,000 feet." And it was "too much under the domination of Etna, who swings vast electric current, and tosses thunder charged cloud-masses to and fro like a Titan acolyte swinging mighty censers at the feet of the Sun." Nonetheless, he looked forward to an excursion planned for the next day which he described in vivid detail:

> Tomorrow if fine and radiant we start for that absolutely unsurpassable expedition to the great orange gardens a thousand feet lower at the S. W. end of the Duchy. We first drive some eight miles or so through wild mountain land till we come to the gorges of the Simeto and there we mount our horses and mules and with ample escort before and behind ride in single file for about an hour and a half. Suddenly we come upon one of the greatest orange groves in Europe — 26,000 trees in full fruit, an estimated crop of 3,000,000! stretching between the rushing Simeto and great cliffs. Then once more to the saddle and back a different way to

barbaric Bronte and thence a ten-mile drive back along the ancient Greek highway from Naxos to sacred Enna.

Fig. 73 Valle del Simeto, Catania. Photograph by Davide Restivo (2007), Wikimedia, https://commons.wikimedia.org/wiki/File:Valle_del_Simeto_3.jpg#/media/File:Valle_del_Simeto_3.jpg, CC BY-SA 2.0.

Sharp also looked forward to the following Tuesday when they would go down to Taormina and its

> divine beauty and not less divinely balmy and regenerative climate sitting as she does like the beautiful goddess Falcone worshipped there of old, perched on her orange and olive-clad plateau, hundreds of feet above the peacock-hued Ionian Sea, with one hand as it were reaching back to Italy (Calabria ever like opal or amethyst to the North-east), with the other embracing all the lands of Etna to Syracuse and the Hyblaean Mount, the lands of Empedocles and Theocritus, of Aeschylus and Pindar, of Stesichorus and Simonides, and so many other great names — and with her face ever turned across the Ionian Sea to that ancient Motherland of Hellas, where once your soul and mine surely sojourned.

This may be the most elaborate and geographically correct description Taormina has received.

After stopping there for ten days or so, the Sharps left for Athens. When they arrived at the end of November, the weather turned cold, and Sharp suffered a relapse. In a late December letter, he told Mrs. Philpot, in whom he had found a kindred spirit and confidant, "I've come out of my severe feverish attack with erect (if draggled) colors and hope to march 'cock-a-hoopishly' into 1904 and even further if the smiling enigmatical gods permit!" He described his pleasure in reading the works of the ancient Greek dramatists in the theatre where they were first performed. There he could imagine hearing "upon the wind the rise and fall of the ancient lives, serene thought-tranced in deathless music." He was trying to remain focused on material for the book he was planning which had expanded in scope. It would be a close "study of the literature and philosophy and ethical concepts and ideals of ancient Hellas and of mythology in relation thereto." It would address other aspects of the life and culture of ancient Greece, 'from sculpture to vase paintings, from Doric and Ionic architecture to the beauty and complex interest of the almost inexhaustible field of ancient Greek coins." Finally, he wanted to describe in his book, or in succeeding books, Graecia Magna, the remnants of the extensive Greek settlements in southern Italy and Sicily.

On December 29, he sent New Year's greetings to Richard Garnett and told him he and Elizabeth were comfortably settled in a "pleasant large house' within walking distance of the Temple of Olympian Zeus and "the banks of the river Ilissos (alas, usually as void of original matter as an Essay by Sir John Lubbock or a poem by Sir Lewis Morris)," two British writers whose work he thought derivative. They had met members of the British community and several Greek friends, "(one of whom, named Embiricos, claims unbroken descent from a friend & a pupil of Plato!)." He ended his letter to Garnett by referencing two lines from Pindar's "Nemean Ode" which can be translated as: "Respite is sweet in every deed. Even honey may cloy, and the delightful flowers of Aphrodite." Echoing his time with Edith Rinder in Rome a decade earlier, Sharp had met a young woman in Athens whose love warmed the landscape and lifted temporarily the weight of his physical condition.

Chapter Twenty-Four

1904

During his brief visit to Greece in January 1903, Sharp fell in love with the landscape, the classical monuments, and a young American archaeologist. When he returned to Greece in late November 1903, this time with Elizabeth, he stayed four months. Besides renewing his friendship with the young woman, he intended to make additional notes for his projected "Greek Backgrounds" and for a travel book for English speaking visitors. Shortly after arriving, his plans were cut short by illness. According to Elizabeth, "the winter was very cold and at first my husband was very ill — the double strain of his life seemed to consume him like a flame" (*Memoir*, 374). In a late December letter, he assured Mrs. Philpot he had come out of his "severe feverish attack with erect (if draggled) colours." He hoped "to march 'cock-a-hoopishly' into 1904 and even further if the smiling enigmatical gods permit." Today, he continued,

> I heard a sound as of Pan piping, among the glens on Hymettos, whereon my eyes rest so often and often so long dream. Tomorrow I'll take Gilbert Murray's fine new version of Hippolytus or Bacchae as my pocket companion to the Theatre of Dionysus on the hither side of the Acropolis; possibly my favourite Oedipus at Kolonos and read sitting on Kolonos itself and imagine I hear on the wind the rise and fall of the lonely ancient lives, serene thought-tranced in deathless music. And in the going of the old and the coming of the new year, a friend's thoughts shall fare to you from far away Athens

The optimism of this letter was short-lived. He became ill again and remained so through most of January.

Late in the month, he began to feel better and described for Ernest Rhys his plan to travel southeast to "Mycenae and Argos & Tiryns" and then "to Nauplia and if possible, to Sparta." Rhys included portions of this letter in his *Letters from Limbo* (80) and described Sharp as "wandering abroad after his deadly enemy diabetes had attacked him." This observation led to an insightful comment about Sharp's attitude toward the disease which would soon claim his life:

> Not a bad way-bill for a sick wanderer, but whatever else he might be he always took his ailments and his threatened fate with courage and at times with a histrionic relish of his own predicament. […] In truth it might be said he took both his mortal ailment and his early death with a light heart, and he would do nothing to delay the step of fate. He ate a pound of Turkish delight in Athens one day when the doctor had warned him he must eat nothing sweet, and at Newport, Isle of Wight, he took a plate of cakes one day out of a confectioner's window and ate them all with amazing gusto.

Elizabeth recalled that despite her husband's illness they enjoyed "pleasant companionship" with Robert Carl Bosanquet, Head of the English School of Archaeology, Henry Fowler, Head of the American School, and Dr. Wilhelm, Head of the Austrian School. They also befriended a Greek poet, at whose house they met "several of the rising Greek men of letters, and other residents and wanderers" (*Memoir*, 375–378). "With Spring sunshine and warmth," Elizabeth wrote "my husband regained a degree of strength, and it was his chief pleasure to take long rambles on the neighboring hills alone, or with the young American archaeologist, Mrs. Roselle L. Shields, a tireless walker." Sharp described one of those walks in a late February letter to Rhys:

> Yesterday I had a lovely break from work, high up on the beautiful bracing dwarf-pine clad slopes of Pentelicos, above Kephisia, the ancient deme of Menander — and then across the country behind Hymettos, the country of Demosthenes and so back by the High Convent of St. John the Hunter, on the north spur of the Hymettian range, and the site of ancient Gargettos, the place of Epicurus' birth and boyhood. At sundown I was at Heracleion, some three or four miles from Athens — and the city was like pale gold out of which peaked Heracleion rose like a purple sapphire. The sky beyond, above Salamis, was all grass-green and mauve. A thundercloud lay on extreme Hymettos, rising from Marathon: and three rainbows lay along the violet dusk of the great hill-range.

Fig. 74 Mount Pentelicus is a mountain in Attica, Greece, situated northeast of Athens and southwest of Marathon. The mountain is covered in large part with forest (about 60 or 70%), and can be seen from southern Athens (Attica). Marble from Mount Pentelicus is of exceptionally high quality and was used to construct much of the Athenian Acropolis. *Photograph* by Dimorsitanos (2008), Wikimedia, https://commons.wikimedia.org/w/index.php?curid=3921687, CC BY-SA 4.0.

Sharp assured Rhys he felt much better: "I am apparently well and strong again, hard at work, hard at pleasure, hard at life, as before, and generally once more full of hope and energy."

A Sharp letter to E. C. Stedman many months later (August 29) casts further light on his illness in Greece and his recovery:

> I was all but done for in the autumn by a severe seizure of a form of diabetes, and after the rigorous treatment at Llandrindod Wells & elsewhere I went to Greece for the winter & spring. I got worse & worse all the same till about February. Then spring came over Hymettos, and new life came to me, & in more ways than one, & Attica became a garden of Eden, & I grew swiftly and continuously better. A heavenly trip in the Peloponnesus put an additional touch to it and a month or so later I sailed from Athens a new man.

"Hard at pleasure," "hard at life, as before," "a new life came to me, & in more ways than one, & Attica became a garden of Eden." In writing to Rhys and Stedman, Sharp often adopted the persona of a romantic Lothario. In this instance, there was some truth behind those phrases for Sharp was captivated by Roselle Lathrop Shields, the young American archaeologist.

A previously unknown letter dated February 9, 1906 (following Sharp's death in December 1905) from Catherine Janvier to Mrs. Roselle Shields, casts further light upon their relationship. Having sent Roselle an inscribed copy of her book about cats, *London Mews*, Catherine wrote on February 8 to say, "the cats are crossing the ocean and I hope will reach you safely." The letter, along with a newspaper clipping of a portrait of Sharp, was in Roselle Shields' copy of the cat book when it sold a few years ago. She had written to Catherine about her regret in not being with Sharp at Alexander Hood's Castle Maniace in Sicily when he died. Catherine responded: "My dearie, I am beginning to think that it is you and I who best know and understand our dear boy. Do not be influenced by others or their opinions. How I wish you could have been with him." She then expressed her regret at not receiving any letters from Sharp after his final arrival at Maniace:

> How I envy you your four last letters — had I but one! Well, I feel I know how he longed for his wee "Roseen." How weary he was of many things. It breaks my heart to think of him there — alone — I know that the best of care was taken of him, that every comfort was his, but I know that he was "alone," he knew too, I am sure, that it had to be.

Of the many letters Catherine received from Sharp since their first introduction in 1889, only a small number remained; "many letters were destroyed, otherwise he would not have written with the freedom that he did." She does not know what Sharp did with her letters. "Should E. [Elizabeth] read them, if he kept them, she will be greatly puzzled."

Catherine continued:

> What you say about P. and Mary and E. not knowing coincides with what I thought. In the letter that never was written he promised full details of P. and directions as to some matters — I never can know now. How I wish I were near, there is so much to ask, so much for us — you and I — to talk of.

The "E." who did not know — presumably how close Roselle's relationship with Sharp had been — was Elizabeth since Catherine referred to her as "E." earlier in the letter. The "Mary" was either Sharp's sister who provided the Fiona handwriting or Mary Wilson who accompanied the Sharps to Italy, perhaps to help Elizabeth care for her husband whose health was failing quickly. The "P" may have been

Mrs. J. H. Philpot with whom Sharp had been sharing his thoughts in correspondence and who loaned some of her letters, including one from Greece dated December 1903, to Elizabeth for the *Memoir*. Catherine agreed with Roselle that neither P., nor Mary, nor E., were aware of the intimacy of Sharp's relationship with Roselle. She also shared Roselle's regret that the woman he loved [Roselle] and the woman who often acted as his mother confessor [Catherine] could not be with him during his last hours.

Catherine's purpose was to console Roselle and assure her that despite Sharp's close relationships with other women, she, Roselle, was his true love. After describing what Sharp had left for her during his visit to New York in late November 1904, including the handwritten manuscript of the long Fiona dedication to her ("Prologue to Kathia") in *The Washer of the Ford* (1896), Catherine concluded, "as soon as I can, I will hunt up all he said of you. Unfortunately, much is destroyed." Then she affixed this postscript:

> Sunday Oct. 22. Venice — 1905 (In reference to our, yours and my, first meeting) "Remember that her all surrounding love saved me, I am sure, in far away Greece, and what it has meant ever since to me." I cannot get at the earlier ones yet.

To interpret, Catherine received a letter from Sharp written on October 20, 1905, less than two months before he died, when he and Elizabeth were in Venice on their way to Sicily. In it, according to Catherine, he said Roselle's love saved his life in Greece in the spring of 1904. Assuming the accuracy of Catherine's postscript, Sharp's relationship with Roselle echoes that with Edith Rinder which began a decade earlier. His "long rambles" among classical ruins with Roselle in Greece were like those with Edith in the Roman Campagna in 1891. His relationship with Edith lasted many years and led to the birth of Fiona Macleod. By the time Edith gave birth to a baby girl in 1901, it had begun to cool and devolve into one of close friendship. How his relationship with Roselle would have developed had Sharp lived longer, we cannot know, but it brought a measure of joy and happiness — a welcome renewal of youth — to his final years.

Two photographs of Sharp illustrate the toll taken by his illnesses. In the 1894 photograph, he was a forty years old, handsome, virile man with dark hair. In fewer than ten years, at the age of fifty, he had become an old man with grey hair and a sad and worried demeanor.

Fig. 75 Photograph of William Sharp by Frederick Hollyer (1894). Reproduced from *Poems by William Sharp*. Selected and arranged by Mrs. William Sharp (London, William Heinemann, 1912). Wikimedia, https://commons.wikimedia.org/wiki/File:William_Sharp_1894.jpg#/media/File:William_Sharp_1894.jpg, Public Domain.

Given the contrast between these two portraits, we must assume Sharp's relationship with Roselle Shields in Athens lacked the ardor of his relationship with Edith Rinder in Rome. Since he had become an old man suffering a fatal illness, it likely resembled that between a father and daughter. From Catherine Janvier's recently discovered letter, nevertheless, we can conclude Roselle Shields brought a ray of sunshine into Sharp's life that dispelled for a time his thoughts of declining health and imminent death.

In 1906, shortly after Sharp died, Catherine Janvier began an essay describing the genesis of Fiona Macleod and her discovery upon reading the first Fiona book (*Pharais*) that Sharp was its author. Her essay began as a paper read to the Aberdeen branch of the Franco-Scottish society in

Fig. 76 Photograph of William Sharp, taken by Alexander Nelson Hood, the Duke of Bronte, at his Castle Maniace in November 1903. Reproduced by Elizabeth Sharp in her *Memoir* (358).

June 1906 and became a lengthy article in the *North American Review* in April 1907. After reproducing parts of her surviving letters from Sharp in the article, Catherine made some of them available to Elizabeth for use in the *Memoir*. Roselle Shields also shared some of her letters with Elizabeth as she is the unidentified friend to whom he addressed letters near the end of his life. Elizabeth maintained a friendship with Roselle and facilitated the publication by Thomas Mosher in 1908 of *A Little Book of Nature Thoughts*, poems by Fiona Macleod selected by Mrs. William Sharp and Roselle Lathrop Shields with a foreword signed R. L. S.

Returning to Sharp's experience in Greece in the first three months of 1904, he wrote in early February a Fiona letter to the Celtic scholar and London publisher, Alfred Nutt, which he sent to Edinburgh where Mary copied and dated it February 18. Nutt had written to ask Fiona if she would like to write a comprehensive retelling of Gaelic stories which he thought Lady Gregory had done only partially and not very well in *Poets and Dreamers: Studies and Translations from the Irish*, published in 1903. Writing as Fiona, Sharp reflected the distance that had developed between the Scottish and the Irish Celtic movements. Fiona had recently reread Lady Gregory's book and found it

> not nearly so "original" as I thought it — I mean, in the sense that far more of the book is "lifted," as you say, than I had first noticed. And more than ever I realized how often the old is weakened in the retelling. There are certain episodes and even chapters which I reread with a chill indifference, when not with impatience. More and more I realise that these beautiful old Gaelic tales must be given either in the crude simplicity of direct translation or else in a modern retelling that shall be as far as possible identical in erudition and outlook and as exactly correspondent as is practical in another and more modern language and in other and more complicated exigencies of art.

Were she to attempt the retelling Nutt proposed, she would proceed with the "utmost simplicity and directness, and not at all unless in imaginative recovery of mood."

She shared Nutt's wish to have the project done, but her "dreams and hopes" were hampered by her private circumstances, and she doubted her ability to accomplish with "finality of achievement what otherwise is best left undone." Nutt must have asked Yeats to undertake the project before approaching Fiona.

> I too had hoped Mr. Yeats might do this thing. It is not to be thought of from him, now: not from lack of genius, or even scope of vision, but from his growing preoccupation with so many matters and conflicting interests and perhaps too from his lack of withdrawal from continuous personal influences, which rarely do much for the imaginative writer but oftener disintegrate what isolation has achieved.

Sharp believed Yeats was wasting his time and talent. His involvement in the cause of Irish nationalism and his relationship with Maud Gonne, an active Nationalist, interfered, so Sharp believed, with his imaginative work. Fiona could not think of others fitted for the work, but she offered the possibility that someone who has been influenced by her own imaginative work will emerge. If so, she will be pleased by having done a "truly good thing." Some day she might be able to take up Nutt's "great task," but she could do so only "with an inward certainty" that she, and she alone could do it.

Fiona proceeded to complement Nutt for his work in resurrecting the Gaelic past: Were she to attempt the project, it would only be because Nutt and others have generously revealed to her the "old and beautiful ideal." Responding to another question from Nutt, she was not thinking of issuing "Celtic Runes" which he may have been interested in publishing, but she was busy finishing a volume of essays [which became *The Winged Destiny*] and preparing a volume of verse that appeared only after Sharp died. This letter describes how Sharp would have handled the retelling of old Celtic tales; its length and tone of regret suggest Sharp would have undertaken the project were he younger and more energetic. After all, a major publisher, himself a Celtic specialist, asked him to undertake a project that would cement Fiona's reputation as a Celtic specialist. Though not expressed in the letter, he was simply too weak, too exhausted, too ill to undertake a project of that dimension however desirable the financial package might have been.

When the Sharps left Greece on March 24, 1904, their destination was the French Riviera. They travelled by ship at least part of the way, and a Fiona letter to Mosher dated March 30 and written "At Sea" suggests they may have stopped briefly in Naples. When she "put in" there, Fiona wrote, she found in her forwarded mail Mosher's April *Bibelot* which contained "a too generously worded appreciation" of her work. It also contained a Fiona essay entitled "Sea Magic and Running Water" which caused Sharp to draft the March 30 Fiona letter and send it not to Edinburgh but, in order to save time, to London for Edith Rinder to type and mail to Mosher. Fiona had not authorized him to publish that essay since it was to appear in *The Winged Destiny*, a volume Chapman & Hall planned to publish later in 1904 both in England and the United States. Were the publisher to see the *Bibelot*, he would probably delay English publication and reconsider an American edition. In his introduction to "Sea Magic and Running Water" in the *Bibelot*, Mosher wrote: "Later we hope to give some further studies, should what is here reprinted find favour, — more especially three very beautiful contributions to recent English reviews." He listed them: "The Magic Kingdoms" (published in the *Monthly Review* of 10 January 1903, 100–111); "The Sunset of Old Tales" (published in the *Fortnightly Review* of April 1, 1903, 1087–1110); and "The Woman at the Crossways" (published in the *Fortnightly Review* of November 2, 1903, 869–873). Since these essays would also be included in *The Winged Destiny*, Fiona told Mosher not to print them in his *Bibelot*. "If people in America," Fiona wrote, "can buy the best part of my new book for 10 cents, [the price of a single issue of the *Bibelot*] they will not be likely to pay for imported copies [of the book] at a dollar and a half or whatever the selling price may be." She went on to mention essays not destined for *The Winged Destiny* which Mosher could print in the *Bibelot*.

On their way to the French Riviera, the Sharps may have stopped in Bordighera on the Italian Riviera to see Dr. Goodchild as they had done in the spring of 1903. As Elizabeth recalled in the *Memoir*, they "loitered" for a time in Hyeres on the French Riviera "in the month of cherry blossoms." After stopping for a time with the Janviers and other friends in Provence, they continued northwest toward Bordeaux. Writing to Catherine Janvier from La Puy on April 18, Sharp described the "magnificent old feudal rock-Chateau fortress of Polignac, erected on the site of the famous Temple of Apollo (raised here by the Romans on the still earlier site of a Druidic Temple to the Celtic Sun God)." His time in Sicily and Greece had quickened his interest in the remains of Druidic and Roman civilizations in Western Europe. The site caused him to realize "how deep a hold even in the France of today is maintained by the ancient Pagan faith." By early May, the Sharps were back in London where they rented rooms for the summer in Bayswater's Leinster Square.

In June, Alexander Jessup asked Sharp if he would like to write a volume in a *French Men of Letters* series he was editing for the J. P. Lippincott Company in Philadelphia. Sharp responded enthusiastically on June 14: he was a specialist in "Sainte-Beuve in criticism, Hello in philosophy & criticism, Leconte de L'Isle, Baudelaire, and Villiers de L'Isle Adam — These with Chateaubriand, of whom I have long been intimate, are the names with which I am most at home." For the pleasure he would have in writing and because of concurrent work, he would prefer to write a volume on Mistral, Leconte de L'Isle, or Villiers de L'Isle Adam. Before committing, he would need to know and approve the terms. If satisfactory, he would begin drafting the book in the coming winter and finish it by mid-summer. It was decided he would do the Leconte de L'Isle volume, and he began collecting material for it during the summer. His undertaking this work indicated both his continuing need for money and his recurring optimism about his health. It was a much easier project than the comprehensive retelling of Gaelic stories Alfred Nutt proposed for Fiona in February.

Sharp remained well throughout July and into August, but his thoughts were on the nature and quality of his accomplishments as a writer. In early July, he wrote under his own name to an unidentified friend who was also a writer and who knew he was Fiona. He thanked the friend for feeling "so deeply the beauty that has been so humbly and eagerly and often despairingly sought." He then reflected on the "long road, the road of art":

> those who serve with passion and longing and unceasing labour of inward thought and outward craft are the only votaries who truly know what long and devious roads must be taken, how many pitfalls have to be avoided or escaped from, how many desires have to be foregone, how many hopes have to be crucified in slow death or more mercifully be lost by the way, before one can stand at last on "the yellow banks where the west wind blows," and see, beyond, the imperishable flowers, and hear the immortal voices (*Memoir*, 382–383).

He concluded with a reference to Fiona's *The Winged Destiny* which was about to appear:

> Destiny puts dust upon dreams, and silence upon sweet airs, and stills songs, and makes the hand idle, and the spirit as foam upon the sea. For the gods are jealous, O jealous and remorseless beyond all words to tell. And there is so little time at the best ... and the little gain, the little frail crown, is so apt to be gained too late for the tired votary to care, or to do more than lie down saying "I have striven, and I am glad, and now it is over, and I am glad!"

Reflecting on his life, Sharp recognized it might soon be over.

On the second of August he wrote again to the same friend (*Memoir*, 385–386). Yesterday had been "one of the loveliest days of the year, with the most luminous atmosphere I have seen in England — the afternoon and evening divinely serene and beautiful." He spent the day in the "glowing warmth and wonderful radiance" of Glastonbury and its neighborhood. His companion was John Goodchild who put him "unknowing to a singular test." Goodchild hoped

> with especial and deep hope that in some significant way I would write or utter the word "Joy" on this 1st day of August (the first three weeks of vital import to many, and apparently for myself too) — and also to see if a certain spiritual influence would reach me. Well, later in the day (for he could not prompt or suggest and had to await occurrence) we went into the lovely grounds of the ancient, ruined Abbey, one of the loveliest things in England, I think. I became restless and left him and went and lay down behind an angle of the East end, under the tree. I smoked, and then rested idly, and then began thinking of some correspondence I

had forgotten. Suddenly I turned on my right side, stared at the broken stone of the angle, and felt vaguely moved in some way. Abruptly and unpremeditatedly, I wrote down three enigmatic and disconnected lines. I was looking curiously at the third when I saw Dr. G. approach. "Can you make anything out of that," I said — "I've just written it, I don't know why." This is the triad.

> From the Silence of Time, Time's Silence borrow.
> In the heart of To-day is the word of To-morrow.
> The Builders of Joy are the Children of Sorrow.

With Goodchild, Sharp could indulge his belief, as he had earlier with Yeats, that the spirit world surrounds and sometimes intervenes in the natural world.

Sharp's fascination with the realm of spirits is a controlling motif in the stories and essays in *The Winged Destiny* which began with a "Dedicatory Introduction" to Goodchild (vii–xii). The spirit of the book and the nature of Sharp's relationship with Goodchild are exemplified by the last paragraph though Goodchild was unaware it was Sharp speaking through Fiona:

> But you — you are of the little clan, for whom this book is: you who have gone upon dark ways, and have known the starless road, and perchance on that obscure way learned what we have yet to learn. For you, and such as you, it is still a pleasure to gather bindweed of thoughts and dreams, these thoughts, to the airs and pauses and harmonies of considered speech. So, by your acceptance of this book, let me be not only of your fellowship but of that little scattered clan to whom the wild bees of the spirit come, as secret wings in the dark, with the sound and breath of forgotten things.

Elizabeth included in the *Memoir* (385) part of a July letter from Goodchild which she called his "first acknowledgement of the dedication." The official publication date of *The Winged Destiny* was October 7, 1904. If Elizabeth's dating is correct, Goodchild saw a draft or a proof of the dedication three months earlier.

Some of the stories and essays in *The Winged Destiny* were written in the summer of 1902 in the west of Scotland (*Memoir*, 344). In an August 23, 1902, letter, he told Alexander Hood the book — then to be called "The Magic Kingdom" — had been postponed until the following year. In an October 1902 letter to Catherine Janvier, he said he intended to put together a volume of Gaelic essays and Spiritual studies called *For the*

Beauty of an Idea. In Fiona's March 30, 1904, letter to Mosher, the book had become *The Winged Destiny* and "For the Beauty of an Idea" had become a section containing the essays "Celtic" and "The Gaelic Heart." The beautiful idea set forth in these two essays and the "Preface" to the section is that of pan-Celticism, that writers in Scotland, Wales, and especially Ireland should set aside their nationalistic passions and support each other as they write in English about myths and legends of the Gael, thereby contributing to the large canon of British literature. Most of the book's essays had appeared in British periodicals, but Sharp made some revisions and additions and settled on the internal arrangement of the book while he was in Greece. He thought Chapman & Hall would publish it in April or early May 1904, but it was delayed until October

One story in *The Winged Destiny*, "The Lynn of Dreams" (134–140), had a special meaning for Sharp. It tells the story of a writer — "let us call him John o'Dreams" — who loved words and was able to do marvellous things with them. "But he had a fatal curiosity. Year by year this had grown upon him. He wanted to know "the well-springs of all literature." He sought it everywhere in the great masters of literature and failed to find it. One day as he lay dreaming by a pool in the woods, "Dalua, the Master of Illusions, the Fool of Faery" appeared and offered to take him to the Lynn of Dreams where he would reveal "the souls of words in their immortal shape and colour, and how the flow of a secret tide continually moves them into fugitive semblances of mortal colour and mortal shape." Reaching the Lynn of Dreams, John o'Dreams saw "his heart's desire bending like a hind of the hill and quenching her thirst." He saw the "mortal shape and colour of words" and, looking deeper, he saw "the souls of words, in their immortal shape and colour." Having found paradise, "his soul cried out for joy." But soon Dalua reappeared and told him to drink from "the Cup of which Tristran drank when he loved Yseult beyond the ache of mortal love, the Cup of Wisdom that gives madness and death before it gives knowledge and life." After drinking from the cup, the writer lost all his creative ability, "the master-touch, the secret art, the craft. He became an 'obscure stammerer.' At the last he was dumb. And then his heart broke, and he died." Sharp identified with John o'Dreams who came to realize perfection in art, as in life, is inseparable from death. Writing through the Fiona persona enabled him to tell his personal story while avoiding the tincture of autobiography.

The first half of the book's final essay, "The Winged Destiny" (341–364), reproduced the "Foreword" to Fiona's "The House of Usna" which Thomas Mosher published as a book in 1902. It asserts the need to move beyond Ibsen's realism to plays like "The House of Usna" which portray the mystery of life and the spiritual forces at work in the world. Sharp wrote the play in response to Yeats' 1896 request that Fiona join him in producing dramas about mythological Celtic figures and the spiritual forces that moved them.

The second half of "The Winged Destiny" essay was written in Greece. Sharp borrowed the name Agathŏn a well-known Greek poet and dramatist, for a sculptor who created at Delphi for a "Thracian prince" a statue of Destiny. She was a woman with the "brows and mien of Athena herself," whose "down-looking eyes were all but closed." . A young sculptor, who may have been a student of Agathŏn, created at Delphi a year later another statue of Destiny, which was "held to be more beautiful, to be strange and beautiful to disquietude, to trouble the soul." This statue was a youth

> with upward lifted face, and eyes looking out through time and change and circumstance: young, yet with weight of deep thought on the brows: serene. yet somehow appalling, as though a most ancient presence out of eternity looked from the newly carved marble. He was winged too, with great wings, as though he had come from afar, and was but a moment earth-lit.

People wondered if the youth was the "ancient and dreaded god, imaged in changeless youth, Eros. Or was he "Anteros, the god of requited love, brother of Eros, the god of unrequited love. "The sculptor had suddenly laid aside his life when he laid aside his chisel," but his handyman said the statue was The Winged Destiny. Years later, a wandering priest decreed "the Stern Mistress of the veiled eyes was Fate and Retribution; the Divine Youth was Love and Redemption. The one was born of Man and the Spirit of Time; the other was born of God and the Spirit of Eternity."

Since neither statue exists at Delphi, we may wonder where Sharp found The Winged Destiny that gave his book its title. One need look only as far as London's Piccadilly Square and the figure Albert Gilbert sculpted for the top of the Lord Shaftesbury Memorial Fountain. Commonly called Eros, the figure was designed to be Anteros, his opposite, which Gilbert described "as portraying reflective and mature love, as opposed to Eros or Cupid, the frivolous tyrant." It was erected in 1893 to commemorate the philanthropic works of Anthony Ashley Cooper, seventh Earl of Shaftesbury (1801–1885), who expressed his "forward-looking love" by establishing schools for childhood education and eliminating the scourge of child-labor.

Fig. 77 Statue of Anteros, Shaftesbury Memorial, Piccadilly Circus, London. Sculpted by Alfred Gilbert and erected in 1893. Photograph by Diego Delso (2014), Wikimedia, https://commons.wikimedia.org/wiki/File:Fuente_Eros,_Piccadilly_Circus,_Londres,_Inglaterra,_2014-08-11,_DD_159.JPG, CC BY-SA 4.0.

After ruminating on the mystery of Fate, Sharp/Fiona declared there are two mighty forces at work in what we call Destiny. First, there is the "sombre and inscrutable Genius of this world, which weaves with time and races and empires, with life and death and change, and in the weft of whose web our swift-passing age, our race, our history, are no more than vivid gleams for a moment turned to the light."

Second, there is a

> Winged Destiny, a Creature of the Eternal, inhabiting infinitude, so vast and incommensurable that no eye can perceive, no imagination limn, no thought overtake, and yet that can descend upon your soul or mine as dew upon blades of grass, as wind among the multitudinous leaves, as the voice of sea and forest that can rise to the silence of mountain-brows or sink in whispers through the silence of a child's sleep — a Destiny that has no concern with crowns and empires and the proud dreams of men, but only with the soul, that flitting shadow, more intangible than dew, yet whose breath shall see the wasting of hills and the drought of oceans.

Beyond the lower force of Fate and the higher force of Destiny there is a Winged Destiny that leans

> from Eternity into Time, and whispers to the soul through symbol and intuition the inconceivable mystery of the divine silence. […] the Shepherd with whom, in the dark hour, we must go at last, to whose call we must answer when the familiar passions and desires and longings are as dust on the wind, and only that remains which so little we consider, only that little shaken flame of the spirit, which is yet of the things that do not pass, which is of the things immortal.

These passages reveal what was on Sharp's mind as he finished the essay in the spring of 1904. He knew he did not have long to live, and he must have shared his thoughts about the Winged Destiny, about the end of life, with Roselle Shields who, he said, saved his life during their long walks in the Grecian landscape.

In the "Foreword" of *A Little Book of Nature Thoughts* (i–xi), Roselle Shields asserted the ancient Greeks "felt and showed Beauty is the essence of life." Sharp convinced her the Celtic vision was a "reawakening of the old Hellenic harmony between the eternal love of beauty and the passionate longing for truth." With Elizabeth's help, Roselle selected and reproduced three quotations — one from Richard Jeffries and two from Emerson — which equate the highest life with the search for Beauty. "The Lynn of Dream" expressed the belief that the attainment of perfect beauty is synonymous with death. The conclusion of Fiona's "The Winged Destiny" expressed the belief that a shepherd descends at the moment of death and leads the spirit into the realm of immortals. Roselle Shields stated in the "Foreword" her belief in an "indefinable something, veiled, exquisite, and sombre, which hovers above the commonplace and illumines the sentiments and passions." In this context, her disappointment in not being with Sharp when he died is understandable. She missed the chance to hold his hand and comfort him as the shepherd descended and led his soul across the boundary that separates life and death. Such was the power Sharp exercised through the Fiona writings and the force of his presence over many women and men who returned the love he, like Anteros, expended.

Following "an ideal summer of warmth and radiance," Sharp fell ill again. On August 29, he wrote to E. C. Stedman

> And now I am again at Llandrindod Wells in Wales [where he had gone to recuperate the previous fall], & under the specialist's rigorous regime as to waters, diet, exercise, & so forth — but (despite a recent & sudden & somewhat severe access of the ailment, now got well in hand however) more precautionarily than of necessity. Damp & raw cold are my worst enemies, & so, as for years past, there is no thought of our spending the winter in England. But being in so much greater general health than I was last year (in Sept. last the specialist gave me "a few months!") it is not necessary to leave at October-end for Sicily, Greece, or Egypt. In fact, we had projected going to Stockholm, & then via Berlin & Leipzig to Dresden & Munich: & then later to Italy. It is still our intention to spend January, February, & March in Rome — which for me is the City of Cities. But we are going to it via New York!

He and Elizabeth intended to leave England near the end of October, spend six weeks or so in New York, and then sail directly to the Mediterranean. He asked if it would be convenient for them to stay with the Stedmans for a few days upon arrival "till we are able to look about & see what we can settle as to quarters within the limited reach of our very restricted finances." He mentioned his "Literary Geography" articles, which had been running serially in the *Pall Mall Magazine*, would be out in book-form in October. Elizabeth's little book on *Rembrandt* (London, Methuen & Company, 1904) was having an exceptionally good reception. He was busy collecting and revising his literary essays which had appeared in various periodicals over the years. He and Elizabeth would return to London in a week or two "for a month's hard work before [getting ready] for New York."

In a September 20 letter to Alexander Jessup, he withdrew his plan to write a book about Leconte de L'Isle for the *French Men of Letters* series. His deteriorating health had forced him to reduce his commitments:

> Several of my immediate plans and later projects have to be relinquished, materially modified, or indefinitely postponed. My health, which despite a strong physique has long been far from what it ought to be, is now seriously complicated by what the doctors have discovered, namely an acute and dangerous attack of Diabetes. It has been arrested by rigorous dieting and the famous treatment at Llandrindod Wells — but it has not only weakened me and brought out certain climatic and other sensitiveness, but renders imperative the medical advice given me to lessen my work to the minimum compatible with well-being and the means to live, and to spend at least six months of the year in the South of Europe in as dry and sunny a winter-climate as I can afford to obtain. In the circumstances it is out of the question for me to consider further the writing of the Leconte de Lisle volume.

Aside from illness, he found Jessup's proposed terms unacceptable; another American, he claimed, had offered much better terms for a shorter manuscript.

Helen Bartlett Bridgman (1855–1935) an American writer and friend of Mosher, had written to Fiona, praising her work and asking why she was so reclusive. Sharp responded cordially as Fiona in mid-September. The letter has the usual excuses designed to pre-empt any requests for a meeting and one masterfully constructed sentence that cuts two ways:

> I am content to do my best, as the spirit moves me, and as my sense of beauty compels me; and if, with that, I can also make some often much-needed money, enough for the need as it arises; and, further, can win the sympathy and deep appreciation of the few intimate and the now many unknown friends whom, to my great gladness and pride, I have gained, then, indeed, I can surely contentedly let wider "fame" (of all idle things the idlest, when it is, as it commonly is, the mere lip-repute of the curious and the shallow) go by, and be indifferent to the lapse of possible but superfluous greater material gain.

Just as it was necessary for Fiona to preserve her solitude and reject wider fame so her very existence kept her creator from the fame he deserved.

By September 22, Sharp had received a letter from Mrs. Stedman saying she and her husband were not well enough to have overnight house guests, but her granddaughter would try to find suitable lodgings for the Sharps in the city. In his reply on the twenty-second, Sharp expressed sorrow in hearing about their illnesses and assured her he understood why they could not have guests. In his August 29 letter to Stedman, Sharp said they intended to spend six weeks in New York, but now, "for health's sake & other reasons," they would spend only a month in America and part of that in Boston. They would be glad to have Laura Stedman, Mrs. Stedman's granddaughter, help them find modestly priced adjacent rooms, "if possible roomy & pleasant enough to use also occasionally for writing in," centrally located and "preferably well up Central Park Way." On November third they would board the *S.S. Menominee* which was due in New York on the thirteenth. By the end of September, their New York plans had crystallized. The Janviers were going to Mexico in mid-November, Sharp explained, and had offered their rooms: "They will be back by about the 1st or 2nd of December — & as we don't sail from New York for the Mediterranean till either December 10th or 12th (12th I think is the date — & the last date the doctors want me to be in a cold & damp climate, where I shouldn't be at all, tho' I am wonderfully better) we'll see something of them." By late October, the couple had decided to spend the last week of their American visit in Boston and sail from there to Naples on December 10.

The trip's "immediate object," Elizabeth wrote, "was that I should know in person some of the many friends my husband valued there, and I was specially interested to make the acquaintance of Mr. and Mrs. Stedman, who gave me a warm welcome, of Mr. and Mrs. Alden, Mr. and Mrs. R. Watson Gilder, Mr. John Lafarge, Mrs. Julia Ward Howe, and Miss Caroline Hazard whom we visited at Wellesley College" (*Memoir*, 393). Upon arriving in New York, they went directly to the Janvier's apartment on West 49th Street and were entertained during the following weeks by, amongst others, the Aldens in Hoboken and the Gilders in New York. They spent Thanksgiving Day with the Stedmans in Bronxville, and Sharp used a piece of their "Lawrence Park" stationery for a letter to Bliss Perry at the *Atlantic Monthly* in Boston. Enclosing a note of introduction from Stedman, Sharp asked Perry if he could see him on one of the four days he would be in Boston before sailing for Italy.

Soon after the Janviers returned to reclaim their apartment, the Sharps, on December 1, went to Newport, Rhode Island to spend a long weekend with Mr. and Mrs. Arthur Livingston Mason. Arthur Mason derived a fortune from The Rhode Island Locomotive Company which produced more than 3,400 steam locomotives between 1866 and 1899. The Masons lived in Halidon Hall, a twenty room Gothic structure with a commanding view of the harbor. The invitation came from Arthur's wife, Edith Bucklin Hartshorn Mason, a formidable woman who founded the Rhode Island chapter of the National Society of Colonial Dames and served on the board of the Rhode Island Sanitary and Relief Association which provided aid and comfort to men fighting in the Spanish American War. Catherine Janvier arranged the invitation, either directly or through her friend Caroline Hazard who was President of Wellesley College and a native of Newport. In any case, the Sharps enjoyed a long weekend amid the cream of Newport society. On Monday, December 5 they boarded a train to Boston to have dinner and spend the night with Caroline Hazard in the house she built with her own funds for herself and future Presidents of Wellesley College. That evening they joined the celebration of the opening of a new residence hall on the campus. On the sixth, they moved to the Thorndike Hotel where they spent four days before boarding their ship.

President Hazard's hospitality was boundless. She arranged for Elizabeth Sharp to tour Wellesley on Monday and Radcliffe College on Wednesday; for both Sharps to call on Julia Ward Howe on Thursday; and, best of all, to visit "Fen Hall to see Mrs. Gardiner's Collection" on Friday. Isabella Stewart Gardner (1840–1924) was a wealthy art collector, philanthropist, and patron of the arts who was said to be the model for Isabel Archer in Henry James' *Portrait of a Lady*. After marrying John Lowell "Jack" Gardner in 1860, they settled in Boston. When Isabella's wealthy father died in 1891, she received a large inheritance, and they began building a world class collection of paintings, statues, tapestries, photographs, silver, ceramics, and manuscripts. Following her husband's death in 1898, Isabella carried through his plans to build a home for their collection. Modelled on the Renaissance palaces of Venice, especially the Palazzo Barbaro, and located in the fens area of Boston, the building, called Fenway Court, surrounds a glass-covered garden courtyard, the first of its kind in America. Isabella designed for herself an apartment on the building's top floor which now serves as the offices of the Isabella Stewart Gardner Museum. For the museum's opening night — January 1, 1903 — she invited four hundred guests who were entertained by members of the Boston Symphony. Only two years after its opening, the Sharps, both former London art critics, received a private tour of Fenway Court, the beautiful building and its world class collection.

Fig. 78 Interior Courtyard of Boston's Isabella Stewart Gardner Museum which was built in 1903 to house the Gardner collection. The building replicates a fifteenth-century Venetian palace. The Sharps toured the building only a year after its completion and well before the collection achieved its zenith. Photograph by Sean Dungan (2017). Wikimedia, https://commons.wikimedia.org/wiki/File:Courtyard,_Isabella_Stewart_Gardner_Museum,_Boston.jpg#/media/File:Courtyard,_Isabella_Stewart_Gardner_Museum,_Boston.jpg, CC BY 4.0.

Sharp's correspondence before and during the American trip reflects his continuing concern about money, and he managed to meet with editors of some of the country's most prominent magazines with proposals for articles he would not live to write. When he called on Bliss Perry at the *Atlantic* on December 6, he was introduced to Roger Livingston Scaife (1875–1951), one of the Editors and a Director of Messrs. Houghton Mifflin & Co. Following this meeting, he stayed up late to write a detailed letter to Scaife proposing the publication of his "Greek Backgrounds" in two volumes, the first describing Greek remains in Sicily and Cambria and the second those in Greece itself. The editors accepted the proposal for the first of two volumes with the second contingent on the success of the first. Sharp acknowledged the acceptance in a letter from the Thorndike Hotel late Friday night before boarding his ship on Saturday.

On November 28, Sharp wrote to Thomas Mosher from New York to ask if he could come to Boston from Portland, Maine on one of the four days Sharp would be there. Fiona had asked him to meet Mosher, and a letter to Mosher from Fiona on December 28, indicates the meeting took place, on Friday, December 9. Given the close bond Mosher and Fiona had formed through their correspondence and with Mosher unaware he was meeting the author of all the Fiona letters he had received and the Fiona books he had published, and with Sharp conveying proposals for even more Fiona books, one can only wish to have overheard their conversation. Through it, Sharp managed to maintain the secret since Mosher remained in the dark until Sharp died. In addition to conveying directly to Mosher several proposals from Fiona, Sharp during his month in America, proposed articles to the editors of three important periodicals and obtained a commitment from Houghton, Mifflin for one and possibly two books. The Sharp's visit to America was a social and commercial success, but the good feelings that marked their departure soon began to fade.

They boarded the *Romantic* on December 10 during a snowstorm, an ominous start for what became a rough passage. They arrived in Naples in time to travel by train to Bordighera on the Italian Riviera to spend Christmas with John Goodchild. From there Sharp wrote to his friend Murray Gilchrist: "we are back from America (thank God) and are in Italy (thank Him more)… For myself I am crawling out of the suck of a wave whose sweep will I hope be a big one of some months and carry me far." The cold waves of the crossing had so penetrated his consciousness they became a metaphor for his physical and mental condition. The Sharps remained in Bordighera until mid-January when they went south to Rome and rented rooms at the top of a hotel on the Via Sallustiana where they planned to stay for two or three months.

Chapter Twenty-Five
1905

In a January 4 letter from Bordighera, Sharp told Thomas Hardy he had been to San Remo to visit William Dean Howells who ranked Hardy's work as "foremost of all contemporary work in fiction." Howells was pleased to hear Hardy valued the "faithful realism" of his work. Sharp told Hardy he and Elizabeth had just returned from New York and Boston and were glad to be back in Italy though they had "a delightful time in the States." In mid-January, they left the Italian Riviera for Rome where they hoped to stay through March in rented rooms in a hotel on the Via Sallustiana. Sharp described their location in a letter to Howells:

> We are settled here (instead of in rooms, or an apartment with a servant — which we found not to be had in accordance with our desires & needs & means) in a pleasant little suite of 3 or 4 rooms at the top of a sunny & charming new small hotel in the sunniest & healthiest part of Rome. Our rooms all face S.E. & S.W. — and so we have unbroken sunshine from sunrise till sunset: & from our windows & balconies of our Salotto we have superb views over Rome and to the hills & to the Campagna.

Despite the rooms and the views, the Sharps found Rome less desirable than anticipated. It was much colder than usual, and shortly after they arrived the flu overtook Elizabeth and spread to her husband with dire consequences for his diabetes.

Writing to Howells again in mid-January, Sharp said they knew too many people in Rome, "Italian, English, Russian, American, & French — Society & Bohemia in a perpetual league against work." He doubted they would remain in Rome beyond the end of February: "I'm afraid Italy is not a good place for work: I think we of the Anglo-Celtic stock need the northern bite of Great Britain or North America to do our best in the best way." According to Elizabeth, they "saw a few friends — in particular Mr. Hichens who was also wintering there; but my husband did not feel strong enough for any social effort." By the time Sharp wrote again to Howells in late January, they had decided to leave at the end of February. He was sorry to cut their stay short, but he could not afford to be any place he couldn't work, and "in every way Rome is about the last place for that."

In a February 5 birthday letter to Lauretta Stedman, E. C. Stedman's granddaughter, Sharp described their charming rooms and continued,

> For reasons of health (for my perilous diabetic ailment has been seriously touched up again, in consequence I suppose) & also for work-conditions, & other reasons, we have decided to leave Italy at the end of February for "The English Riviera," in other words for Ventnor in the South of the Isle of Wight — where, indeed, we think of some day making a home.... I am tired of so many years of continuous wandering, & I'm sure Mrs. Sharp is eager for a home, tho' she loves being in Italy also. For work's sake, too, (& I don't mean the financial side of the question) it is in all ways better for me to be more in touch with my own country.

For six years, the Sharps had been without a permanent residence; their furniture and belongings had been in storage since 1899. That he was thinking about ceasing his constant travel and finding a permanent home in Ventnor signaled his waning energy, but also his expectation of a longer life. Given its climate and his illness, the Isle of Wight was an unlikely place to settle permanently, but he may have chosen it as the southern-most reach of his "own country." He concluded by asking Lauretta to convey greetings to her grandparents and apologized for such a short letter, but he was not well and "under exhausting pressure of accumulated work & correspondence."

In a February 21 letter to Thomas Mosher, whom he met in Boston in December, Sharp thanked him for the leather-bound little books. Both he and their author [Fiona] preferred them to the parchment-bound copies, "both to handle and to look at." They are a reminder of their pleasant December meeting in Boston. He continued:

> I am very glad we had time for that confidential chat, too, and I think you will now better understand certain reserves & puzzling things, & the more readily see, or at any rate *feel*, how they are not all by any means

arbitrary or foolish, but more or less inevitable. I have of course seen a good deal of my friend since I came to Italy, and before she left Rome the other day I explained to her about our talk, & how that whatever she wrote to you at any time in privacy would be kept absolutely private by you. I dare say now, too, you understand a good deal more than what was said, by inference. When we meet again, or someday, things may be made still clearer to you.

This passage suggests Sharp told Mosher he and Fiona were lovers to explain their frequent, furtive meetings and her allusiveness. What might someday be made "still clearer" to Mosher was the true relationship between Sharp and Fiona, the woman he claimed to love.

Before leaving Rome, Sharp completed a two-part travel guide for Americans visiting Sicily and sent it to Richard Watson Gilder, editor of the *Century Illustrated Magazine.* Gilder accepted Sharp's proposal for this article when they met in New York in December. It was published posthumously in three parts in the March, April, and May 1906 issues of the *Century.* In a letter transmitting the article, Sharp asked for quick payment since he would need the money when he reached Ventnor. The Sicilian articles were preceded in the February 1906 issue of the *Century* by "Portraits of Keats: With Special Reference to those by Severn," the article Sharp wrote in the summer of 1904. Immediate payment was not forthcoming, but these four articles helped allay Elizabeth's financial circumstances following her husband's death.

The Sharps left Rome in late February and arrived in Ventnor via Paris in mid-March where Sharp worked on several articles that appeared in *Country Life* under his own name and several Fiona books published by Mosher in the United States. Not lingering long in Ventnor, the Sharps departed at the end of March and rented rooms at 5 Gordon Place between Kensington Church Street and Holland Park. After a few days in the city, Sharp went to Edinburgh to visit his mother and convinced his sister Mary to go with him to the Inner Hebrides. They made their way west to the small island of Lismore in Loch Linnhe north of Oban to stay with the MacCaskills, the elderly Gaelic-speaking couple Sharp had known for years. On April 19, the day after their arrival, he described to Elizabeth, who had accompanied him to Lismore in the summer of 1902, his pleasure in being there again and in the stories of strange apparitions which his host recounted by the fire at night. The weather was a drawback:

> The cold is very great, & as it is damp <u>cold</u> you'd feel it hard. Even with a warm blanket below me, & <u>six</u> above I was cold — & when I got up and had a partial bath (for I scooted out of it to dress) my breath <u>swarmed</u> about the room like a clutch of phantom peewits. No wonder I had a dream I was a seal with my feet clammed on to an iceberg. You couldn't stand it. Even Mary said it was like mid-winter. A duck went past a little ago seemingly with one feather & that blown athwart its beak, so strong was the north wind blowing from the snowy mass of Ben Nevis.

Having arrived on Lismore on Tuesday, April 18, he told Elizabeth it was almost certain they would leave the next Tuesday as he could not stand the penetrating cold much longer. He was glad to have come as it was unlikely he would ever be in Scotland again so early in the year.

On April 23, he told Elizabeth he had decided not to go out to Iona as his presence there would be noted by islanders on the lookout for Fiona Macleod. Anything he heard there and later used in the Fiona writings could be traced to him. Neither would he visit other islands since he had much of what he wanted, "above all, the atmosphere: enough to strike the keynote throughout the coming year and more, for I absorb through the very pores of both mind and body like a veritable sponge." He added: "I love that quiet isolated house on the rocks facing the Firth of Lorne." The weather played a major part in his decision to forego other islands and return Mary to the warmth of her Edinburgh home.

Fig. 79 The Lismore ferry in winter. This ferry was not available to Sharp and his sister in 1905. Photograph by Magnus Hagdorn (2012), Wikimedia, https://commons.wikimedia.org/wiki/File:Lismore_Ferry_(8120112835).jpg, CC BY-SA 2.0.

Despite the cold that required a large fire burning all day, Sharp was able to put the finishing touches on a revision of his "Iona" essay and send it to Mosher with a long letter copied by Mary into the Fiona handwriting. Fiona preferred *Iona* as a title for the volume in which it would appear, but Mosher settled on *The Isle of Dreams,* Fiona's second choice, and published it in his *Old World* Series before the close of the year. When they met in Boston, Sharp, acting on behalf of Fiona, obtained Mosher's agreement to publish a book of previously unpublished Fiona Macleod poems. In the Lismore letter, Fiona told Mosher the volume would not be ready until late May as she had to go to Wales "to be near one dear to me," one who was seriously ill. Sharp did not want Mosher to believe Fiona was ill, as that would threaten the flow of money. The one dear to her was, of course, Sharp, and it was he who had taken the cure for diabetes in Wales (at Llandrindod) in September 1903 and 1904. His proposal of *Runes of Women* as the title of the volume of new poems suggests it would contain at least some of the runes, perhaps altered, that were in the first edition of *From the Hills of Dream* which Patrick Geddes and Colleagues published in 1896 and which Mosher, through arrangements with the Geddes firm, published in America in 1901 with new editions in 1904, 1907, 1910, and 1917. Those volumes did more than any others to expand readership of Fiona in the United States. The volume of new poems discussed in his letter to Mosher materialized only after Sharp's death when Mosher, in 1907, published *The Hour of Beauty: Songs and Poems*, which contained poems written between 1901 and 1905.

While on Lismore, Sharp learned Fiona had been made an honorary member of the French League of Writers "devoted to the rarer and subtler use of Prose and Verse." In an April 20 letter, he told Elizabeth he just received "a charming letter from Paul Fort acting for his colleagues." Fort was a well-known poet who founded and edited a literary review appropriately called *Vers et Prose*. He was writing to Fiona on behalf of his colleagues, members of the League and well-known French writers, among them: Jean Moréas (1856–1910) who founded the periodical *La Symboliste* in 1886 and played a leading role in the French Symbolist Movement; Emile Verhaeren (1855–1916), a Belgian poet who wrote in French; and René François Armand (1839–1907), a Parnassian poet who won the Nobel Prize for literature in 1901. Receiving this honor as Fiona must have caused Sharp to reflect on what might have been had he been able to claim the writing as his own. In addressing Elizabeth, there was no remorse: "We're glad, aren't we, you and I? She's our daughter, isn't she?" In the late 1890s, Sharp sometimes cast Fiona as his daughter with Edith Rinder. This stopped when Edith became pregnant and gave birth to a real daughter in 1901. Referring to Fiona as Elizabeth's daughter signaled Sharp's renewed love for her in the year of his death. It was Elizabeth after all who had nursed him through illnesses, and it was she who would hold him in her arms as he died.

After their week on Lismore, Sharp and Mary crossed to the mainland on April 24, spent the night in Oban, and took the train back to Glasgow. During the train ride, Sharp wrote a note to Elizabeth that humorously echoed MacCaskill's speech: "Tarling | It will pe ferry difficult to write in this unusually shaky train, which to use a slight hyperbole will almost pe hitting the horizon on each side in its ferry pad swayings." He marveled at the isolation of the MacCaskills. Mrs. M had not made the brief trip across the water to Appin for six years.

> From year end to years end, life is the same, save for the slow change of seasons, & the slower invisible movements of the tides of life. Such isolation is restful for a time, but wd. be crushing after a spell, & mean stagnation for any not accustomed to daily manual toil or without local engrossing work. They on the other hand look with mingled awe & amusement at the to them inexplicable longing to get away from such conditions, & for the already strong desire to leave this gloomy & dull climate for abroad, where life is (for us) so far far easier as well as happier now. But even when I told MacC. that it was a matter of prolonged life & energy & "youth" for me, & that I invariably recede on an ebbing tide over here, & go high on a strong flowing tide over yonder, he'd only shake his head & say Ishe miann na lach an loch air nach bi I (i.e., in effect, the duck's desire is to be on some other loch then that on which she happens to find herself!)

Sharp was glad to have stayed with the MacCaskills on Lismore again and sorry to leave as it might be the last time in the Gaelic West at any time of year. His friend and host was equally sad as he sensed it would be their last meeting. After dropping them off at Port Appin, MacCaskill "shook hands (with both his)" and said in Gaelic "My blessing on you — and goodbye now!" and then "he turned away & went down the pier-side & hoisted the brown sail & went away across the water, waving a last farewell."

Having said this might be his last time in the Gaelic West, Sharp added parenthetically:

> I don't say this "down-ly" — but because I think it likely: and, in a way I'll explain later, am even glad. There is much I want to do, and now, as much by W. S. as F. M., & that I realize must be done abroad where alone (save for spring-time in London) can I keep well — & and mentally even more than physically. (How I hope Fontainebleau may someday suit us.)

This comment is interesting not only for his recognition of the limitations imposed by his physical and mental health. It is the only surviving instance of his admitting a waning interest in Fiona Macleod and all she represented. He had found an audience for the travel writings of William Sharp which were as remunerative as the stories and poems of Fiona Macleod, if not more so. He hoped his income from those writings would be sufficient to enable them some day to enjoy the beauty and manage the expense of living in Fontainebleau.

He told Elizabeth he had learned a great deal of Gaelic lore on Lismore, but nothing about his current interest in Gaelic astronomy. Surprisingly, the man opposite him on the train was Ralph Copeland, the Astronomer of the Edinburgh Observatory. He was surprised by what Sharp knew: "When I told him about certain groups & constellations & said I had lists of many Gaelic star-names, gathered at long intervals, & thro' a hundred sources, he hinted he would like to know who I was, for, as he said, he hardly ever met anyone away from astronomical sets interested in these things." The two men lunched together and enjoyed each other's company. Unfortunately, both would die before the year's end: Copeland in October and Sharp in December.

When Sharp returned to London at the end of April, his health was in decline. Elizabeth attributed it to the cold weather on Lismore and said his doctor advised him to go to Bad Neuenahr in Germany for treatment of his diabetes (*Memoir*, 399). It was June before he could get away as he felt compelled to spend May in London writing an article on Joseph Severn's portraits of John Keats. He had proposed the article to the editors of the *Century* when they met in New York the previous December, and he needed the money. He sent the article to New York on May 27 along with copies of Joseph Severn's portrait of Keats and a rendition of that portrait by William Hilton which, according to Sharp, was favored by many over that of Severn. Though Sharp may have been paid upon submission of the manuscript, the article, "The Portraits of Keats: with special reference to those by Severn," did not appear until February 1906 (Volume LXXI, 535 and following).

Fig. 80 John Keats (1793–1879), by Joseph Severn (1819). Oil on ivory miniature, 105 x 79 mm, National Portrait Gallery. Wikimedia, https://commons.wikimedia.org/wiki/File:JohnKeats1819_hires.jpg, Public Domain.

Fig. 81 John Keats, by William Hilton (c. 1822). Oil on canvas, 76.2 x 63.5 cm, National Portrait Gallery. Wikimedia, https://commons.wikimedia.org/wiki/File:John_Keats_by_William_Hilton.jpg, Public Domain.

Chapter Twenty-Five: 1905

Sharp left London on June 10 or 11 and planned to spend four weeks at the Villa Elsner in Bad Neuenahr. The warmth and beauty of the Villa, its gardens, and the strict diet produced a dramatic improvement in his emotional and physical health. While there and on his way home, Sharp wrote a series of letters to Elizabeth which she exempted from the mass of Sharp's papers she burned before she died in 1932. In preserving these letters (now in the National Library of Scotland) and printing portions in her *Memoir*, Elizabeth wanted to demonstrate his continuing love for her and emphasize the happy times of her husband's last year.

In his first letter, Sharp told Elizabeth the Villa Eisner was "deliciously quiet and reposeful." He had not undergone any treatments, but he was already feeling better due to

> rest of mind & body, the <u>sense</u> of reposefulness, the escape from the perturbing & exhausting forces & influences of town life especially at this season, the absence at night and by day when I am in my room or in the garden of all noise, no sounds save the susurrus of leaves and the sweet monotony of the rushing Ahr, & the cries & broken songs of birds.

He had not realized how much "nervous harm" he'd "had for long, & especially at the Gordon Pl. rooms, where the whole nervous system was frayed by the continual noise and old-exhaustedness of everything, from the air to the rooms themselves & the gas-poisoned atmosphere." A doctor at the Villa could not understand why, given his condition, he was not more anxious. He explained his physical troubles meant little to him. They were "the bodily effect of other things, & might be healed far more by spiritual wellbeing than by anything else: also that nature & fresh air & serenity & light & sun warmth & nervous rest were worth far more than all else." He wanted to be helped "but all the waters in the world & all the treatment in the world can only affect the external life."

The treatment he was about to receive would, nonetheless, enable him to keep well when "away from England for the autumn to spring months." Even in Germany the "difference climatically" was very great; he felt the immediate gain, and the "balmy warmth" suited him. He was convinced he and Elizabeth could regulate their lives better than any doctor. They would continue to plan their future as though they had many years to live. In a brief note, he told Alexander Nelson Hood he had a "narrow squeak, […] a hard tussle at the brink of 'Cape Fatal' and a stumble across 'Swamp Perilous.'" That was all behind him now.

He assured Hood he would soon "be as well in body" as he is "happy and serene in mind." He knew it was only "a reprieve, not a lifetime-discharge," but he hoped it would be an extended furlough. He knew his diabetes and weak heart could end his life at any moment; early death was inevitable. But he took what cures he could, and he was "well content," determined to enjoy the world and his life until the end.

The positive effects of the month at Villa Elsner cure were dimmed in the final week by the excruciating pain of a passing kidney stone. He did not want Elizabeth to know about the incident, but someone at the Villa sent her a telegram. The stone passed on Saturday, July 8 shortly before he boarded a train in Neuenahr bound for Doorn in Holland where he stopped to visit the Grandmonts, a couple he and Elizabeth met in Taormina. Shortly before noon on July 9, the day after his arrival, he told Elizabeth he had "a beautiful and restful afternoon and evening in this most charming and simpatica home of dear and good friends — and a long sleep from about 9:30 p.m. till about 8 this morning, I feel perfectly well again." He regretted she had known about the kidney stone before it was a thing of the past. It troubled him to think of the distress of her "dear tender heart." He hoped his telegrams first from Neuenahr and then Doorn had reassured her. After a good breakfast, he was feeling fine.

> Today there is not a trace of any kind of trouble. As I told you [in the telegrams] the stone penetrated no intestinal or other complications — & I am now of course ever so much better for having got rid of it & all the allied uric acid poison. Last night there was naturally the diabetic symptom of continuous thirst — but that was natural after the longish journey in great heat & in the vibration of a train. Today, despite that I woke to 75 degrees in my room (with both front and side French-windows wide open all night, and a large shadowy spacious room outlooking on sunlit green forest-glades a stone's throw away) I have had no thirst, no symptoms of any kind. The heat is very great, but to me most welcome and regenerative and strengthening.

Having briefly described his survival of the kidney stone and a minor diabetic episode, Sharp pivoted to the beauty of his surroundings and the hospitality of his hosts. He planned to stay the week and leave on Saturday, July 15.

The Grandmonts were an established Dutch family who, like many wealthy Europeans, wintered in Taormina, and Witte Huis, their home in

Doorn, was a large white structure in a park-like setting. Sharp's hostess was a well-known painter with an exceedingly long name: Abrahamina Arnolda Louise "Bramine" Hubrecht (Donders) (Grandmont) (1855–1913). In 1888, Bramine Hubrecht, as she was known, married Professor Franciscus Donders (1818–1889) an ophthalmologist, a professor of physiology at the University of Utrecht, and a highly-regarded authority on eye diseases. He died shortly after their marriage, but not before she painted his portrait. Four years later, in 1902, Bramine married Dr. Alphons Marie Antoine Joseph Grandmont (1837–1909) (who was sixty-five; she was forty-seven). She painted him reading to two young women sometime before he died in 1909. Bramine's paintings of her two husbands reveal her considerable skill as an artist.

Fig 82 Professor Franciscus Donders (1818–1889), by Bramine Hubrecht (1888). Oil on canvas, 142 x 95 cm, Rijkmuseum. Wikimedia, https://commons.wikimedia.org/wiki/File:Professor_Franciscus_Donders_(1818-89)._Fysioloog_en_oogheelkundige_Rijksmuseum_SK-A-2508.jpeg, Public Domain.

Fig. 83 Alphons Marie Antoine Joseph Grandmont (1837–1909), by Bramine Hubrecht (1900–1909). The painting depicts the artist's second husband tutoring two Italian girls. Oil on canvas, 100 x 100 cm, Rijksmuseum. Wikimedia, https://commons.wikimedia.org/wiki/File:Alphons_Marie_Antoine_Joseph_Grandmont_(1837-1909)._Tweede_echtgenoot_van_de_schilderes,_lesgevend_aan_twee_Italiaanse_meisjes_Rijksmuseum_SK-A-2794.jpeg, Public Domain.

In his letter to Elizabeth on the morning of Monday, July 10, Sharp praised his hosts: "How good and dear the Grandmonts are. She is so thoughtful and tender, too; and so good when I was tired after my journey and yesterday in bringing cushions when I was lying in a chair outside — and seeing to everything about food, often at no little trouble here." In addition to executing over a hundred well-regarded paintings, Bramine had a full social life and an especially high regard for elderly, infirm men. His July 10 letter to Elizabeth is addressed to "Linky Blue Dear, | How you'd love to be here!" Now he planned to leave Wednesday July 12, since the Grandmonts had to go to Utrecht. After four days of leisure in a beautiful setting, Sharp took a train north to Rotterdam on the twelfth and an overnight ferry to England from Hoek von Holland on Saturday, July 15.

Chapter Twenty-Five: 1905

In London Sharp found a letter from Richard Underwood Johnson requesting revisions in the Severn article and asking if Sharp could obtain photographs of another Severn portrait of Keats mentioned in the article. Coincidentally, Sharp also had a letter from Nigel Severn — son of Walter Severn and grandson of Joseph Severn — asking him to examine and authenticate what he thought was the death mask of Joseph Severn. On Sunday July 16, Sharp asked if he could call the following Tuesday and added: "You have I suppose no other Keats-Severn portraits of any kind?" It turned out he had two — one a miniature that resembled Joseph Severn's portrait of Keats in the National Portrait Gallery and the other a painting, now well-known, titled "Keats and the Nightingale (the Spaniards, Hampstead Heath)." Sharp observed these two paintings and the death mask sometime during the week of July 16, revised his Severn article for the *Century Magazine*, and arranged for Frederick Hollyer to photograph the two paintings for inclusion in the article. On Tuesday, July 25, Sharp mailed the revised manuscript to Johnson and left to visit friends in Yorkshire. The two Hollyer photographs caught up with him there, and he sent them on to Johnson for inclusion in his article. Sharp accomplished a good deal during his ten days in London, but they took a toll. In a July 27 letter to Johnson, he said he was glad to be out of the city again, and "With rest and fresh air and early hours" he would soon be well again. His recuperation in Germany and Holland was short-lived.

By July 30, Sharp was in Edinburgh writing apocalyptically to Dr. John Goodchild, his friend in all things mystical: "Between now and September-end (perhaps longer) many of the Dark Powers are going to make a great effort. We must all be on guard — for there will be individual as well as racial and general attack. But a Great Unloosening is at hand." Having stayed on in London, Elizabeth arrived in Edinburgh by train on the thirtieth. Sharp boarded her train, and they proceeded north to Nairn, a market town east of Inverness where they had taken a cottage on the shore of the North Sea. Before leaving Edinburgh, Sharp received a letter from Thomas Janvier informing him of the death of Laura Stedman, E. C. Stedman's wife. On November 24, 1904, the Stedmans entertained the Sharps in their substantial Lawrence Park home in Bronxville, New York for Thanksgiving Day dinner. Sharp wrote a deeply moving letter of sympathy to Stedman from the North British Station Hotel while waiting for Elizabeth's train.

> I cannot let the first available mail go without sending you my deep and loving sympathy — to you and Lauretta and your daughter-in-law, but to you most who have lost a tender and loving and life-long companion. Nor is it only deep regret for you, dear friend, but on my own account, for I have ever had the truest affection for dear Mrs. Stedman. I know too how sorry my wife will be when she hears (I join her Mail Train for the North tonight) — for she drew closely to your dear wife during our recent visit.

Sharp had a genuine affection for Stedman who introduced him to American editors and writers and paved the way for his American publications. The perilous state of his own health weighed heavily on his mind: "I am here in Edinburgh enroute for the North (after a narrow squeak for my life, with two distinct illnesses, & treatment for a month in Germany)."

In Nairn, Sharp found time to read a collection of John Masefield's stories, *A Mainsail Haul*, and to thank Masefield for sending him a copy of the book which was "rich in atmosphere" and written with "delicate art." Still, he had some suggestions for improvement: "Is it not a mistake to introduce in 'Sea Superstition' words such as 'august' and 'wrought' in a sailor's mouth?" On August 19, Masefield replied to Sharp from Greenwich that he would make use of his suggestions if the book went to a second edition (*Memoir*, 404–405). It was, he said, a product of his youth, and he had now passed into manhood. "Between those two times (forgive me for echoing Keats) one has little save a tag or two of cynicism, a little crude experience, much weariness, much regret, and a vision blurred by all four faults. One is weakened too by one's hatreds." In 1905, Masefield (1878–1967) was twenty-seven — half Sharp's age — and willing to accept advise from the older writer. Named Britain's Poet Laureate in 1930, Masefield held that position until he died thirty-seven years later. Elizabeth quoted Masefield writing of Fiona to a friend: "I think the genius of a dead people has found re-incarnation in her" (*Memoir*, 404). His life and work spanned the great divide between the late romanticism of the 1890s and the post-war modernism of the 1920s and beyond.

After two weeks in Nairn, the Sharps returned to his mother and sisters in Edinburgh. From there, according to Elizabeth they visited, among other friends, Mary Wilson, D. Y. Cameron, and David Erskine. Mary Georgina Wade Wilson (1856–1936) was an accomplished artist who specialized in garden scenes. Her paintings, some depicting Venice and other locations in Italy, are still valued by collectors and museums. She was the daughter of John Wilson (1815–1881) who had at the age of twenty-one inherited his father's coal mining business and turned it into one of the most profitable companies in Scotland. In 1860, he built South Bantaskine House on the field of the Battle of Falkirk to house his family of eight girls and one boy. Mary was about Elizabeth Sharp's age. Unmarried, she lived on the family estate with several sisters, also unattached. She and Elizabeth may have met when they were young girls. More likely, Elizabeth's position as the London art critic for the *Glasgow Herald* brought them together. They must have been close friends since Mary, in October, went to Italy with the Sharps and she was with Elizabeth at the Castle Maniace when Sharp died. D. Y. Cameron was, at the time, one of Scotland's most accomplished painters and engravers and a close friend of the Sharps. They had come together in the mid-nineties at the height of the Celtic revival in Edinburgh. The origin of David Erskine's friendship with the Sharps is unknown, but his family and their estate in Linlathen near Dundee were deeply entrenched in Scottish history.

At the end of August, the Sharps returned to London and began preparing for Italy. On his birthday, September 12, Sharp posted two letters, one from Will to Fiona and another from Fiona to Will. He sent these letters every year, but only one other seems to have survived — a letter to W. S. from F. M. dated September 12, 1897. The letters, according to Elizabeth, helped him retain the separate identity of Fiona and take stock of the year's literary output. The 1897 Fiona letter to William Sharp was hard on "dear Billy":

> I am very disappointed with you this past year. You have not been well, it is true: but you have also been idle to a painful degree, and your lack of method makes me seriously anxious. [...] But do for heaven's sake put your shoulder to the wheel, and get soon in good working trim at something worth doing. You ever put pleasure first, and think so much of youth that you don't like billiards merely because the balls are bald. This is sad, Billy.

The 1905 Fiona letter is hard but also resigned to the inevitable:

> I note not only an extraordinary indolence in effort as well as unmistakable laziness in achievement. Now, either you are growing old (in which case

> admit dotage, and be done with it) or else you are permitting yourself to remain weakly in futile havens of ignoble repose or fretful pseudo rest. You have much to do, or that you ought to do, yourself: and as to our collaboration I see no way for its continuance unless you will abrogate much of what is superfluous, curtail much that can quite well be curtailed, and generally serve me loyally as I in my turn allow for and serve <u>you</u>.

Unless he can summon the strength to persevere in the face of declining health and attendant indolence, his own writing will suffer and that of Fiona will disappear.

Sharp's 1905 letter to Fiona projects a stronger sense of declining powers and a tone of regret that verges on the elegiac:

> All that is best in this past year is due to <u>you</u>. [...] I have not helped you nearly as much as I could: in this coming year I pray, and hope, it may be otherwise. And this none the less tho' I have much else I want to do apart from <u>our</u> work. But we'll be one and the same <u>au fond</u> even then, shall we not, Fiona dear? [...] You say I can give you what you have not: well, I am glad indeed. Together we shall be good <u>Sowers</u> [...] I wish you Joy and Sorrow, Peace, and Unrest, and Leisure, Sun, and Wind, and Rain, all of Earth and Sea and Sky in this coming year. And inwardly swell with me, so that less and less I may fall short of your need as well as your ideal. And may our "Mystic's Prayer" be true for us both, who are one.

Sharp wanted to do more of his own work apart from the Fiona writings which he calls "our" work. He then suggests Fiona also takes part in the Sharp writings. Will they become "one in the same"? Probably not, so Sharp will try to give Fiona more of what she lacks. He hopes she will swell with him so he will not fall short of her need, her ideal. If that sounds confusing, it is. Near the end of his life, Sharp, encouraged by his wife, was trying to resolve the contradictions he had created when he decided to give life and form to a pseudonym. He was struggling to merge the two identities that produced two separate bodies of work into a single identity who could produce a single, unified body of writings, some to be signed William Sharp and others Fiona Macleod. Failure in that struggle was inevitable. Preserving Fiona and continuing to publish under that name was essential, financially and to avoid derision, but Sharp was losing interest in the Celtic cause, especially its growing association with nationalism — Irish, Scottish, and Welsh. With only a few months of life remaining, Sharp faced a conundrum with no obvious path of escape.

In the eight brief lines of "The Mystics Prayer," which, he asserted, was written by both William and Fiona, they pray "both, who are one" may awake with the ability to see things clearly:

> Lay me to sleep in sheltering flame
> O Master of the Hidden Fire!
> Wash pure my heart, and cleanse for me
> My soul's desire.
> In flame of sunrise bathe my mind,
> O Master of the Hidden Fire,
> That, when I wake, clear-eyed may be
> My soul's desire.

The object of William Sharp's desire was a marriage of souls, an integration of the male and female aspects of his being. The poem is a final testimony to the failure of integration in this world; the speakers hope to reach the object of their souls' desire in the afterlife. Fittingly, Elizabeth placed the poem at the end of the Uniform Edition of the Fiona Macleod poems in 1910.

In a letter dated September 15, Sharp, writing as Fiona, responded to an unknown correspondent who asked to meet her and who sensed there was a great deal of Fiona's own life in her writings. Sharp's Fiona response to the first issue was, of course, negative, and brief. A meeting is not possible but they may meet in the Isles of Peace:

> the quiet isles beyond the foam where no memories could follow [...] and where old thoughts, if they came, were like phantoms on the wind, in a moment come, in a moment gone. I failed to find these Isles, and so have you: but there are three which lie nearer, and may be reached, Dream, Forgetfulness, and Hope.

Since the Isles of Peace are unreachable in this life, Sharp was again contemplating his death. His response to the second issue is significant because it was his most direct admission that his Fiona's writings were intensely autobiographical:

> There is a personal sincerity, the direct autobiographical utterance, in even, as you say, the most remote and phantastic of my legends as in the plainest of my words. But because they cover so much illusion as well as passion, so much love gone on the wind as well as love that not even the winds of life and death can break or uproot, so much more of deep sorrow (apart from the racial sorrow which breathes through all) than of Joy save in the deeper spiritual sense, they were thus raimented

in allegory and legend and all the illusion of the past, the remote, the obscure, or the still simpler if more audacious directness of the actual, the present, and the explicit.

Knowledge of Sharp's relationship with Edith Rinder uncovers the autobiographical dimension of the Fiona Macleod stories and poems. Given the excesses of much of those writings, the next sentence is also revealing: "There is, perhaps, a greater safety, a greater illusion, in absolute simplicity than in the most subtly wrought art." The sentence demonstrates the lingering effect of the admonition in Yeats' letter to Fiona of November 23, 1901: "when you use elaborate words you invent with less conviction, with less precision, with less delicacy than when you forget everything but the myth. [...] You, as I think, should seek the delights of style in utter simplicity, in a self-effacing rhythm and language, in an expression that is like a tumbler of water rather than a cup of wine" (*Collected Letters III*, 124). After receiving this advice, Sharp strove for greater concision and fewer flourishes in what he wrote as Fiona.

In the last of his many birthday letters to E. C. Stedman, Sharp frankly described the failing state of his health: "I all but 'went under' this summer from a severe access of my Diabetes malady — but a month's special treatment at Neuenahr in Germany tided me over — & in July & August I was not only convalescent but (in August) became wonderfully well." In mid-September, however, he experienced the "ebb-tide again," and now he had to leave Britain's "damp climate at once." He and Elizabeth planned to leave "in a few days" and go first to Venice, then to Sicily until late December and then "for 3 months to Algeria (mostly Biskra in the Sahara) for a thorough 'warming' & 'drying', for my chest is menaced." This ambitious itinerary was abruptly interrupted in mid-December.

Before leaving for Italy, Sharp wrote a Fiona letter to the Duchess of Sutherland (1867–1955) which described in the guise of advice what he has attempted to achieve in the Fiona writings: "Style (that is, the outer emotion that compels and the hidden life of the imagination that impels and the brooding thought that shapes and colours) should, spiritually, reflect a soul's lineaments as faithfully as the lens of the photographer reflects the physiognomy of a man or woman." This letter was a response to a volume of stories, *The Wind of the World: Seven Love*

Stories, the Duchess published as Millicent Sutherland in 1902. Despite her elevated social position and attendant obligations, the Duchess was an aspiring writer, a fellow Scot, and a devotee of Fiona Macleod. Though she did not know Fiona was Sharp, he had come to know her by claiming he was a relative of Fiona. In the summer of 1902, he included her among possible advocates when he sought (unsuccessfully) a Civil List Pension.

Fig 84. Portrait of Millicent Leveson-Gower, Duchess of Sutherland, by John Singer Sargent (1904). Oil on canvas, 254 x 146 cm, Thyssen-Bornemisza Museum. Wikimedia, https://commons.wikimedia.org/wiki/File:John_Singer_Sargent_-_Portrait_of_Millicent_Leveson-Gower,_Duchess_of_Sutherland.jpg, Public Domain.

Writing here as one female author to another, Sharp encouraged the Duchess to aspire higher than she had in the 1902 volume. He sensed in her work

> An instinct for beauty, a deep longing for beautiful expression and because I believe you have it in you to achieve highly in worth and beauty that I write to you thus. [...] There is that Lady of Silence, the Madonna of Enigma, who lives in the heart of many women. Could you not shape something under *Her* eyes — shape it and colour it with your own inward life, and give it all the nobler help of austere discipline and control which is called art?

Insights, unique to the hearts of women — shaped, disciplined, controlled — may produce beautiful expressions that reach the status of art. It is tempting to believe Elizabeth included part of this letter in the *Memoir* to show her husband's connections with the paragons of British aristocracy, but that was not Elizabeth's nature. Her aim was to show the ideal to which her husband aspired in the poetry and fiction of Fiona Macleod. The revelation that Fiona was, in fact, Sharp and the attendant prejudices obscured, and still obscures, the fine quality, the "worth and beauty," of much of the writing, especially the lyric poetry, Sharp published under the female pseudonym.

In early October, the Sharps, accompanied by Mary Wilson, their painter friend from South Bantaskine, travelled by train to Zurich, then to Innsbruck, and finally to Venice. In transit, Sharp drafted a letter to Helen Hopekirk, the American pianist/composer, and sent it to Edinburgh for Mary to copy. Hopekirk had written to ask if she could rearrange the verses of Macleod's "The Lonely Hunter" in setting the poem to music. Fiona gave her permission to make whatever changes she wished: "I do not think the needs or nuances of one art should ever be imposed upon the free movement of another in alliance." We do not know if the American novelist Carson McCullers adopted the title of her first and most widely read novel, *The Heart is a Lonely Hunter* (1940), directly from the Fiona poem or from Helen Hopekirk's song. The poem, which appeared in the first (1896) and subsequent editions of *From the Hills of Dream*, is one of Sharp's loveliest. Its final quatrain reveals its haunting cadence:

> O never a green leaf whispers, where the green-gold branches swing:

> O never a song I hear now, where one was wont to sing
> Here in the heart of Summer, sweet is life to me still.
> But my heart is a lonely hunter that hunts on a lonely hill.

Fiona told Hopekirk she would soon be going to "Italy, and to friends, and to beautiful places in the sun, there and in Sicily and perhaps in Algeria." This was the itinerary the Sharps followed, though they did not make it to Algeria. Usually careful to place Fiona in places other than those he planned to visit, Sharp must have decided Hopekirk in America was too far away to matter.

After granting Helen Hopekirk permission, Fiona shared her sense of a foreshortened life:

> I think outward change matters less and less as the imagination deepens and as the spirit more and more "turns westward." I love the South; and in much, and for much, am happy there: but as the fatally swift months slip into the dark I realize more and more that it is better to live a briefer while at a high reach of the spirit and the uplifted if overwrought physical part of one than to save the body and soothe the mind by the illusions of physical indolence and mental leisure afforded by long sojourns in the sun lands of the South.

After describing her love of contemporary French poetry and music, loves reflecting those of both Sharps, Fiona concluded by saying she would send Hopekirk a copy of her new Tauchnitz volume, *The Sunset of Old Tales*, which was about to be published in Germany. She wanted her to have "something direct from a writer whom (to her true pleasure) you so truly care for, and who, as you say, has opened gates to you with others."

From Venice, the Sharps went to Florence where they stayed with the Eugene Lee-Hamiltons. During this last visit to the Villa Palmerino, a few miles north of Florence, the Sharps found their host ill and frail. He would suffer a debilitating stroke and die in 1907. From Florence, the Sharps went to Rome where Sharp wrote a note to Anna Geddes, promising to write more when they reached Sicily and expressing his hope to see Patrick Geddes on the Riviera after Christmas as they had decided to go there instead of Algeria, partly for "health reasons" and partly for "purse reasons." From Rome they went to Taormina where they spent the rest of November among friends, and then, on November 27, they went up to the Castello Maniace where they planned to spend

December with Alexander Nelson Hood. Sharp described their journey in a December 4 letter to Roselle Lathrop Shields:

> We left Taormina in a glory of mid-summerlike warmth and beauty — and we drove down the three miles of winding road from Taormina to the sea at Giardini; thence past the bay and promontory of Naxos, and at the site of the ancient famous fane of Apollo Archagêtês turned inland. Then through the myriad lemon-groves of Al Cantara, till we crossed the gorges of the Fiumefreddo, and then began the long ascent, in blazing heat, by the beautiful hill road to the picturesque mountain-town of Piedemonte. There we caught the little circum-Ætnean mountain loop-line, and ascended the wild and beautiful slopes of Etna. Last time we went we travelled mostly above the clouds, but this time there was not a vestige of vapour in the radiant air, save for the outriders' trail of white occasionally flare-coloured, smoke from the vast 4-mile-wide mouth of snow-white and gigantically-looming cone of Etna. At the lofty mediaeval and semi-barbaric town of Randazzo we were delayed by an excited crowd at the station, on account of the arrest and bringing in by the carabinieri of three chained and heavily manacled brigands, one of them a murderer, who evidently had the sympathy of the populace. A woman, the wife of one of the captured men, outdid any lamenting Irish woman I ever saw: her frenzy was terrible — and of course the poor soul was life-desolate and probably punished and would likely never see her man again. Finally she became distracted with despair and fury, and between her appeals and furious curses and almost maniacal lamentations, the small station was anything but an agreeable stopping place. The captive brigands were absolutely impassive: not a glance: only, as the small train puffed onward, one of them lifted a manacled arm behind one of the carabinieri and made a singular sign to someone.
>
> Thereafter we passed into the wild and terrible lava-lands of the last frightful eruption, between Randazzo and the frontier of the Duchy of Bronte: a region as wild and fantastic as anything imagined by Doré, and almost terrifying in its somber deathfulness. The great and broad and sweeping mountains, and a mightily strath — and we came under the peaked rocks of Maletto, a little town standing 3000 feet high. Then the carriage, and the armed escort, and we had that wonderful drive thro' wild and beautiful lands of which I have heretofore written you. Then about four we drove up to the gates of the Castle, and passed into the great court just within the gates, and had the cordial and affectionate welcome of our dear host.
>
> A few minutes later we were no longer at an ancient castle in the wilds of Sicily, but in a luxurious English country house at afternoon tea.

On December 8 Sharp wrote a second letter to Roselle which signaled his rapidly fading health. When he tried to sit down to his writing a "mental nausea seized" him and even "a written chat to a friend seemed […] too exhausting." His need to continue writing was terribly pressing, but he confessed, "I simply can't."

He did manage, in addition to his letter to Shields, a long letter to Robert Hichens on the eighth. It was a response to a letter from Hichens expressing his regret that Sharp's physical condition would prevent him from going to North Africa in January. Elizabeth explained in the *Memoir*: "It had been planned that after the New Year Mr. Hood, Mr. Hichens, my husband and I should go together to Biskra. But as the autumn waned, we realized the unwisdom of making any such plans" (*Memoir*, 413). Sharp described the changed plans in a December 7 letter to W. B. Yeats: they expected to remain at Maniace until after Christmas and then go to the French Riviera for three months. In this final letter, his last to Yeats, he was responding to a November 4 letter from Yeats. Hurt by Yeats's "continuous and apparently systematic ignoring of any communication," Sharp had made up his mind "to keep silence henceforth." After writing often to Sharp and Fiona for many years about his Celtic Mystical Order, Yeats had become distracted by his involvement in the creation of a theater in Dublin. He seems not to have communicated with Sharp since April 1904, when he said he had found many admirers of Fiona Macleod during his trip to America. Now he wrote to ask what messages Sharp had been receiving from the spirit world and to probe further his relationship with Fiona. Having finally heard from Yeats, Sharp expressed his "strong feeling as to the Noblesse-oblige of friendship" and informed Yeats he did not consider him "a mere acquaintance." Since Yeats had now written and Sharp has expressed his feelings in this letter, he will endeavor to put them "aside among the discharged things."

Sharp proceeded to tell Yeats he could not write about any visitations or about Fiona but would discuss those matters when next they met, perhaps in Paris, in the Spring.

> I may add, however, that neither I nor any person <u>personally</u> known to me "sent" any one to you on a veiled mission. At the same time — that a certain person sought you and that you did not recognize the person, the occasion, or the significance. [That sentence is crossed out but still legible

in the letter.] As you know, we are in a crucial period of change in many ways, and there are circles within circles, veiled influences and good and evil (and non-good and non-evil) formative and disformative forces everywhere at work. Obscure summons, obscure warnings, meetings & partings, veiled messages, come to us all. All which sounds very absurd, or mysterious, or conveniently vague. However, you'll understand. Also my present silence.

It is quite amazing that, less than a week before he died, Sharp was able to revert so easily to his spiritualist exchanges with Yeats. He concluded by asking about the meaning of a dream he may or may not have had:

I dreamt of you some time ago as going thro' a dark wood and plucking here and there in the darkness seven apples (as you thought) — but they were stars. And you came to the edge or cliff and threw three away, & listened, and then hearing nothing threw three more idly away. But you kept, or forgot, one — & it trickled thro' your body and came out at your feet, and you kicked it before you as you walked, & it gave light, but I do not think you saw the light, or the star. What is your star, here, — do you know? Or can you interpret the dream?

In describing this dream, Sharp must have had in mind the ending of Yeats's "The Song of Wandering Aengus": "And pluck till time and times are done | The silver apples of the moon, the golden apples of the sun." This poem appeared first in *The Sketch* on August 4, 1897 where it was called "A Mad Song," and then in 1899 in Yeats' *The Wind among the Reeds*.

One paragraph of Sharp's letter is particularly moving as it refers to both his physical and his mental illness:

For many months this year I was ill — dying — but there were other than physical reasons for this, & I survived thing after thing and shock after shock like a swimmer rising to successive waves — & then suddenly to every one's amazement swam into havens of relative well-being once more. But the game is not over, of course: and equally of course is a losing game. Nevertheless I'm well content with things as they are, all things considered.

In his diary on December 8, Sharp said he and Elizabeth had that afternoon "a lovely drive," and she described that "fatal" drive in the *Memoir* (418).

We drove far along a mountain pass and at the furthest point stopped to let him look at the superb sunset over against the hillset town of Cesaro. He seemed wrapt in thought and looked long and steadfastly at the wonderful glowing light; it was with difficulty that I persuaded him to let us return. On the way back, a sudden turn of the road brought us in face to the snow-covered cone of Aetna. The wind had changed and blew with cutting cold straight off the snow. It struck him, chilling him through and through. Half-way back he got out of the carriage to walk and get warm. But the harm was done.

When they returned to Maniace, he told Elizabeth he planned to talk a great deal that evening to "amuse" Alex Hood who seemed depressed. And Hood, as he said goodnight to Elizabeth, said "I have never heard Will more brilliant than he has been tonight." The next morning Sharp had a severe pain — perhaps a diabetic attack, perhaps a heart attack, perhaps both — which Elizabeth believed to be caused by the chill during their drive. A doctor was summoned, but he could only relieve the pain; Sharp died three days later — in the afternoon of December 12. Elizabeth described his death: About 3 o'clock, with his devoted friend Alex Hood by his side, he suddenly leant forward with shining eyes and exclaimed in a tone of joyous recognition, "Oh, the beautiful 'Green Life' again!' and the next moment sank back in my arms with the contented sigh, 'Ah, all is well.'" He was buried in the estate's English cemetery wo days later.

Ernest Rhys wrote in his *Letters from Limbo* (80): "A pity he did not live to see his own superb funeral when he was carried by torchlight up the mountain after his death at the Duke of Bronte's Castle Maniace in Sicily. [...] He was a great romancer and died as he had lived, romancing." Rhys himself was not immune to romancing since the cemetery is not on a mountain and not far from the Castle. The procession from the residence to the cemetery made its way along a dusty road. "On the 14th," according to Elizabeth, "in an hour of lovely sunshine, the body was laid to rest in a little woodland burial ground on the hillside within sound of the Simeto,"a river running through the estate. Alex Hood read "Invocation to Peace" a poem from Fiona's *Dominion of Dreams*, over the grave. Later, he commissioned a large Celtic cross carved from the lava of Mount Etna which still marks the grave. On the cross, in accord with Sharp's instructions, is the inscription:

IN MEMORY OF WILLIAM SHARP
BORN 12TH SEPTEMBER 1855
DIED 12TH DECEMBER 1905
FIONA MACLEOD
"FAREWELL TO THE KNOWN AND EXHAUSTED
WELCOME TO THE UNKNOWN AND UNFATHOMED" W. S.
"LOVE IS MORE GREAT THAN WE CONCEIVE
AND DEATH IS THE KEEPER OF UNKNOWN REDEMPTIONS"
F. M.

Fig. 85 A Celtic Cross marking William Sharp's Grave. Castello Nelson's Protestant Cemetery, Sicily. Photograph by Warwick Gould (2016), reproduced with his permission.

Appendix 1

William Butler Yeats and Elizabeth Amelia Sharp

News of Sharp's death was wired to Edith Rinder in London, and she passed it to the newspapers with the information that Sharp was the author of the writings of Fiona Macleod. Six years before he died, Sharp wrote on small white cards a message confessing that he, and he alone, was "the author — in the literal and literary sense — of all written under the name of Fiona Macleod." He identified individuals who were to receive the cards from Elizabeth after he died. She sent one to W. B. Yeats on December 28, and he replied on January 6 (*Collected Letters IV*, 302–303):

> I want to tell you how much I sympathize with you in your great trouble. Your husband was a man of genius who brought something wholly new into letters & thousands will feel his loss with a curious personal regret. To me he was that, & a strange mystery too & also a dear friend. To talk with him was to feel the presence of that mystery, he was very near always to the world where he now is & often seemed to me to deliver its messages. He often spoke to me of things of my personal life that were unknown to him by the common channels of sense. I knew he was ill — but never knew how ill. I had a letter from him only two days before I saw his death in the paper. I had been looking forward to seeing him again very shortly. I feel now that one of the Gates of Wisdom has been closed for much as I admire his writing he was, as a man should be, more than his writing. What must you feel at so great a loss. You must however know that one, who was so often as it seemed out of the body while he lived, cannot have undergone any unrecognizable change or gone very far away. Blake said of death that it was but going into another room. He was certainly the most imaginative man — I use the word in its old & literal sense of image making — I have ever known, not like a man of this age at all.

This letter was written to comfort Elizabeth in her grief. Read in the context of Sharp's last letter to Yeats which admonished him for his long silence, it may also have been motivated by guilt. Yet admiration for the life and work of a fellow writer comes through clearly and sincerely.

Elizabeth began planning a book about her husband's life and work shortly after he died. She asked some of his correspondents if she could see and use some of his letters in what became her *Memoir*. Yeats was one of those, but Elizabeth had a special request of him. Among Sharp's papers she had come upon what looked like a Masonic rite, and she wondered if Yeats could cast some light on it. She was also curious to know if her husband had written or spoken to Yeats about any visions. Initially she was skeptical about her husband's effort to see visions and interact with spirits, but gradually she had come to share his beliefs. After he died, she began searching for a means of contacting him.

Writing from Lady Gregory's Coole Park on July 21, 1906, Yeats told Elizabeth he had intended to call on her when he was in London in the Spring, but other matters intervened (typed letter signed, Private collection). He will see her in the fall when he will have found and sorted out his letters from Sharp and Fiona: "I think there are one or two visions recorded amongst them," he wrote, "but I am not sure."

> I think too that I have some notes of a vision of your husband's, but it took place five or six years ago, and I am not certain that I should be able to understand the notes. I made a search through my papers when I was in London, but I have not yet found a bundle of rather interesting letters which your husband wrote me at the outset of the Fiona Macleod books. "The Masonic Rite" you speak of was made in the first instance by me and then after a vision which your husband had working with me, was worked by him. He never sent it to me, and I would be very much obliged if you would let me see it. There are a good many things I can tell you about this rite and others of the same sort, and there are still more matters which I am most anxious to ask you about.

His "absorption in the theatre" had caused interests he shared with Sharp to fade into the background, and he had drifted farther apart from Sharp than he liked. When his theatre work becomes "instinctive," he will return "to what are still to me the supreme interests." Irish Nationalism and the creation of an Irish National Theatre had intervened, but he had not abandoned his effort to establish a Celtic Mystical Order in the West of Ireland and obtain its rites through dream and vision.

Yeats called on Elizabeth in London not in the fall but in the first week of January 1907, and he described their meeting in a letter to Maud Gonne dated January 14 (*Collected Letters IV*, 591–594). He now knew a great deal more about the Fiona Macleod mystery. It was as he thought:

> Fiona Macleod was so far as external perception could say a secondary personality induced in Sharp by the presence of a very beautiful unknown woman whom he fell in love with. She, alas! has disappeared from everyone's sight, no one having set eyes on her except George Meredith who says she was the most beautiful woman he ever saw. Whether there was more than this I do not know but poor Mrs. Sharp, though generous and self-sacrificing as I can see does not want to enlarge that unknown woman's share. A great deal, however, which Sharp used to give in letters as an account of Fiona's doings were she insists a kind of semi-allegorical description of the adventures of his own secondary personality and its relation with the primary self.

Yeats then recalled an instance in which Sharp wrote to say he would leave Yeats' letter for Fiona to read when she woke up. According to Elizabeth this meant the secondary personality would read it and respond when it awoke. That response from Fiona, Yeats said, though written for her by Sharp, was "much more impassioned" than the rest of the letter. Yeats doubted there would be much of this in the biography Elizabeth intended to write because when he suggested she tell the whole story, she said "How can I! Other people are so much involved."

The Sharp letter Yeats remembered was written on May 5, 1898 in St. Margaret's Bay near Dover where Fiona's sudden illness was invented to prevent Sharp from taking her across the channel to meet Yeats and others in Paris (*Letters to Yeats II*, 394–396). After his conversation with Elizabeth, Yeats thought the woman who would read his letter when she woke up was not Sharp's secondary personality but the "beautiful unknown woman" he loved, the woman who "awakened" the secondary personality. Elizabeth "never talked quite openly about things," he continued, "except it being a secondary personality, but told things in a series of hints and yet, at the same time, quite clearly. I noticed that each time she said this personality was awakened in him by a beautiful person she would add as if to lessen the effect, 'and by beautiful scenery.'" We can now see Elizabeth was trying to be as truthful as she could without revealing that Edith Wingate Rinder was the beautiful woman who induced Fiona Macleod, the beautiful woman

Sharp introduced to George Meredith as Fiona Macleod, the beautiful woman who refused to accompany Sharp to Paris, the beautiful woman who, according to Yeats, has disappeared from everyone's sight.

It is now apparent the beautiful woman had not disappeared. In fact, Yeats must have been among the friends of the Sharps who met her at the parties and "at homes" given by the Sharps and Mona Caird. Among their friends in Rome in the winter of 1890–1891, including Mona Caird, Elizabeth mentioned "Mrs. Wingate Rinder" who joined them for three weeks. "With her," she wrote, "my husband greatly enjoyed long walks over the Campana and expeditions to the little neighboring hill towns" (*Memoir*, 173). She did not say many of the poems he wrote and privately published in Italy in 1891 as *Sospiri di Roma* were written about Mrs. Rinder, their long walks through hills near Rome and his love for her. Elizabeth saw those poems, nonetheless, as the "turning point" in his career as a writer.

> [They] are filled not only with the passionate delight in life, with the sheer joy of existence, but also with the ecstatic worship of beauty that possessed him during those spring months we spent in Rome, when he had cut himself adrift for the time from the usual routine of our life, and touched a high point of health and exuberant spirits (*Memoir*, 222).

He found there, Elizabeth continued, "the desired incentive towards a true expression of himself in the stimulus and sympathetic understanding of the friend to whom he dedicated the first of the books published under the pseudonym." That book was *Pharais*, and it was dedicated to E. W. R.

In the dedication, Sharp, writing as Fiona, said he and the dedicatee met a long while ago in a "resting place" of friendship and "found that we loved the same things, and in the same way." The place they met was paradisal, thus *Pharais*, and there "we both have seen beautiful visions and dreamed dreams. Take, then, out of my heart this book of vision and dream." Edith appeared often in the Fiona writings but always by her initials or as an anagram, a made-up name, or a fictional character. In the *Memoir*, Elizabeth said her husband's friendship with the woman to whom he dedicated *Pharais* began in Rome and "lasted throughout the remainder of his life." Although there are hints throughout her *Memoir* and the Fiona writings, Elizabeth refrained from describing the true nature of that friendship.

Before Sharp went to America in 1896, he left Elizabeth a "letter of instructions concerning his wishes in the event of his death." In it he said he owed his development as Fiona Macleod to Edith Rinder. "Without her," he said, "there would have been no Fiona Macleod." Recalling that letter, Elizabeth said of this woman without identifying her:

> Because of her beauty, her strong sense of life and of the joy of life; because of her keen intuitions and mental alertness, her personality stood for him as a symbol of the heroic women of Greece and Celtic days, a symbol that, as he expressed it, unlocked new doors in his mind and put him "in touch with ancestral memories" of his race (*Memoir*, 222).

It is revealing of Elizabeth's character that she included in her *Memoir* this description of the woman her husband deeply loved for many years. It is a well-deserved tribute to a remarkable woman, and now that Edith has remerged in the life of William Sharp, she may be recognized as an accomplished writer, translator, and editor. Elizabeth's description of Edith is also a lasting tribute to the remarkable qualities of the woman Sharp married. Elizabeth preserved long after her death the secret of Edith's identity by burning most of her husband's papers before she died. Through all the years between her husband's death in 1905 and hers in 1932, Elizabeth maintained a close friendship with Edith and Frank Rinder.

Elizabeth respected Edith's determination to erase from the historical record her role in the birth of Fiona Macleod, in the Fiona writings, and in the life of William Sharp. The relationship between William and Edith had begun to cool before Edith gave birth to a baby girl in July 1901, but the friendship between the Sharps and Rinders remained solid. Edith became Sharp's point of contact in London for the Fiona correspondence and functioned for several years as his secretary. After the turn of the century, Sharp came to regret his embrace of New Paganism in the early 1990s and his opposition to the restraints society placed upon marriage. Following the trial of Oscar Wilde in 1895 and events surrounding it, there was a seismic shift in attitudes towards what came to be called the "decadence." The desire to erase the nature of the relationship between Edith Rinder and William Sharp was motivated also by the desire to shield Edith's daughter from any recriminations that might befall her from what she came to call the "advanced views" of her parents and their close friends. Sharp was seldom mentioned in her presence, and as a child she was warned not to touch any of the Sharp or Fiona books in her parents' library. When her mother died in 1962, all those books, many containing authors' inscriptions, had been removed and destroyed.

Given the course of events before and after Sharp's death, it is no wonder Elizabeth responded "How can I! Other people are so much involved" when Yeats suggested in his January 1906 meeting that she tell "the whole story" in her *Memoir*. Yeats concluded his description of that meeting by asking Maud Gonne to keep his letter: "For I am fresh from seeing Mrs. Sharp [...] and this will be a record. Put it in some safe place and I may ask you for it again some day for it is a fragment of history."

Fig. 86 Photograph of William and Elizabeth Sharp in 1904, unknown photographer. Gift of Noel Farquharson Sharp to William F. Halloran in 1968.

Yeats's meeting with Elizabeth did not unravel the mystery of Fiona Macleod. He remained perplexed. Was she a second personality or a female spirit speaking through Sharp? Yet he came away from his conversation with Elizabeth believing a real woman was intimately involved in the personality Sharp projected as Fiona Macleod and in the writings Sharp published under the female pseudonym. Yeats's description of his meeting with Elizabeth paints an intimate picture of her feelings about her husband's relationship with Edith. In reading

Yeats's account of the meeting, which he saw as a fragment of history, it is impossible not to share the sympathy for Elizabeth that breathes through his words. In her own writings and what others have said about her, Elizabeth emerges as an intelligent and accomplished woman who retained her patience and enthusiasm for life and her love for the cousin she met as a girl during summer vacations in Scotland, the cousin who proposed to her in an Edinburgh cemetery, the cousin she eventually married despite the concerns of their families, the cousin she followed all over Britain, continental Europe, and Northern Africa, and the cousin mediums brought to life for her many years after she buried him on the slopes of Etna in the Sicilian wilds.

Appendix 2

Catherine Ann Janvier and Roselle Shields

The letter transcribed below casts light on the final two years of William Sharp's life. It was written by Catherine Ann (Drinker) Janvier — an American painter, writer, and close friend of Sharp — to Roselle Lathrop Shields, a young American working in Greece as an assistant to an archaeologist when Sharp met her during a two-week visit to Greece in the winter of 1903 and came to know her well during the four months the Sharps spent in Greece the following year (December 1903–March 1904).

Born in 1841, Catherine Ann Drinker of Philadelphia married Thomas Janvier in 1878. Originally from New Orleans, he was a short story writer and journalist. They lived a peripatetic life alternating between New York's Greenwich Village, Mexico, England, and the south of France. Sharp was introduced to the Janviers during his first visit to New York in 1889, and a close friendship developed in the 1890s as they and the Sharps visited back and forth in England and France. Fourteen years older than William Sharp, Catherine became particularly fond of him, and he shared with her some of his deepest thoughts and feelings. The Janviers were childless, and the relationship she developed with Sharp resembled that between a mother and son.

Sharp sent her a copy of the first Fiona Macleod book, *Pharais, A Romance of the Isles* when it was published in 1894 and claimed it was the work of a friend. She recalled Sharp mentioning in 1893 he was working on a novel called *Pharais*, and she confronted him with the fact that he was Fiona. He prevailed upon her to keep his secret, and the confidence they shared cemented their relationship. Following his death, which affected her greatly, she delivered a paper about Sharp's life and work to the Aberdeen Branch of the Franco-Scottish Society on June 8, 1906. She refined and expanded that paper into an article titled "Fiona Macleod and Her Creator William Sharp," which appeared in the *North American Review* of April 5, 1907 (Volume 184, 718–732). For the article, she depended on letters she had received from Sharp, their conversations, and her careful and sympathetic reading of the work Sharp published under the female pseudonym.

Two months after Sharp died, Catherine wrote a letter to Roselle Lathrop Shields which shines a light on the last two years of his life. Roselle Lathrop was born in Bridgeport, Connecticut in 1877. As a young woman she made her way to England where, in 1900, she married James Van Allen Shields. Born in Washington, D.C. in 1871, he worked in London for the Columbia Record Company. Twenty-two years younger than Sharp, Roselle was much taken by him, and they maintained contact through the year. They met again in December 1903 when the Sharps arrived in Greece. In her *Memoir* (378), Elizabeth said her husband became ill upon their arrival, but his health improved after the turn of the year: "With Spring sunshine and warmth my husband regained a degree of strength, and it was his chief pleasure to take long rambles on the neighboring hills alone, or with the young American archaeologist, Mrs. Roselle L. Shields, a tireless walker." Elizabeth printed in the *Memoir* (413–416) parts of two letters Sharp wrote to an unnamed friend during the last two weeks of his life. It has been speculated these letters were written to Edith Rinder, but they were two of the four letters mentioned in the letter below Sharp wrote to Roselle Shields in the waning days of his life. Having met in Greece, Roselle and Elizabeth Sharp, both Londoners, became friends, and Roselle shared at least these two letters with Elizabeth to use in the *Memoir*. They also cooperated in preparing *A Little Book of Nature Thoughts*, from the writings of Fiona Macleod, selected by Mrs. William Sharp and Roselle Shields, with a foreword by R. L. S. (Roselle Lathrop Shields), which Thomas Mosher published in 1908 and for which he paid Elizabeth £50.

Catherine Janvier wrote a nicely illustrated book called *London Mews* containing rhymes about cats which was published on January 1, 1904 by Harper & Brother in New York. She sent a copy of that book to Roselle Shields as a Christmas gift in 1905. Her letter to Shields was in that copy when it recently appeared for sale. The cat book was on its way across the ocean to Shields which explains the letter's reference to cats in its second paragraph. Here is a transcription of the letter Roselle saved in the cat book.

Catherine Ann Janvier to Roselle Lathrop Shields, February 8, 1906

8 February 1906

My dearie

I have been putting off writing to you hoping to be able to get a long hour to give you. It was a mistake, and in future I shall send you short letters when I cannot have time for long ones.

The cats are crossing the ocean and I hope will reach you safely. "The Mews" really is not a book exclusively for children, though generally it seems so to be considered.

Thank you for your letter. My dearie, I am beginning to think that it is you and I who best know and understand our dear boy. Do not be influenced by others or their opinions. How I wish you could have been with him. It always will be a bitter pain to me that he put off writing to me, so that I have nothing of any account after he went to Maniace. On the other hand, I have a treasury of letters dating back to 1889 — what I have is but a small part, too, because many letters were destroyed. Otherwise he would not have written with the freedom he did. I do not know what he did with my letters. Should E. have them, if he kept them, she will be greatly puzzled.

What you say about P. and Mary and E. not knowing coincides with what I thought. In the letter that never was written he promised full details of P. and directions as to some matters. I never can know now. How I wish I were near, there is so much to ask, so much for us — you and I — to talk of.

How I envy you your four last letters — had I had but one! Well, I feel I know how he longed for his wee "Roseen." How weary he was of many things. It breaks my heart to think of him there — alone — I know that the best of care was taken of him, that every comfort was his, but I know that he was "alone," he knew too, I am sure, that it had to be.

Do not forget to tell me the full story of the seal — I mean what he told you to do about it, and how, as far as you know, he came to think of it. He wrote me the meaning of the device. That — at least — I have, but if I could have had my letter!

Tell me what you can about that last week's letters when you can.

I told Elizabeth ~~yesterday I think~~ in my last letter to her that I was writing a little article in appreciation of him, but went into no details, so you need know nothing as yet.

I have had to stop short in the middle to do some translating for T. A. J., but hope to start fresh and keep on by the end of this week.

How I wish you were here to go over the old letters with me. You are the only person in the world to whom I would show them. I know he would be willing. The whole evolution of Fiona Macleod practically is in those that I have kept, although much is lost by the destruction of letters too personal to keep.

You must understand that this collection — that is three or four letters absolutely proving him to be Fiona — was put away to keep with his approbation. The last time we were together here, he entirely approved of what I had arranged as to their disposition in case of my sudden death.

He gave me the ms. of the dedication to me of "The Washer of the Ford' — the long Prologue to Kathia. Also some ms. (all this in his own handwriting) of various other articles of Fiona's and some poems. He hoped against hope — the dear one — that the secret might be kept for years — but if not, and he had small hope of it then, that it was well for me to keep and use, if needful, or if I pleased these incontrovertible proofs. You will see by my little article how interesting his confession in 1894 is, as to being F. M.

I have not mentioned these letters to <u>anyone</u>, as yet, and wish to finish and send off my article before they are known. What a life! could I write it out! What a wonderful life!

As soon as I can, I will hunt up all he said of you. Unfortunately much is destroyed.

Your Kathie

Sunday Oct. 22 Venice–1905 (In reference to our, your and mine, first meeting) "Remember that her all surrounding love saved me, I am sure, in far away Greece, and what it has meant ever since to me."

I cannot get at the earlier ones yet —

Autograph signed letter, Private collection

Bibliography

This bibliography lists articles and books mentioned in the text except those of William Sharp. The best bibliography of Sharp's writings remains that by Elizabeth A. Sharp at the end of the two-volume edition of her *Memoir* (New York: Duffield & Co., 1812). The revision and expansion of that bibliography will be a major undertaking that is beyond the scope of this biography.

Alaya, Flavia, *William Sharp — "Fiona Macleod, 1955–1905* (Cambridge, Massachusetts: Harvard University Press, 1970).

Allen, Grant, *The Woman Who Did* (London: Grant Allen, 1895).

— *The Type-Writer Girl* [pseudonymously by Olive Pratt Rayner] (London: Grant Allen, 1897).

Allen, Vivien, *Hall Caine: Portrait of a Victorian Romancer* (Sheffield: Sheffield Academic Press, 1997).

Balmires, Steve, *The Little Book of the Great Enchantment* (Arcata, CA: R. J. Stewart Books, 2008).

Cameron, Mrs. Lovett [Emily Lovett], *The Triumph of a Snipe Pie* [better known as *The Man Who Didn't*] (London: 1895).

Crosse, Victoria [pseudonym of Vivian Cory], *The Woman Who Didn't* (London: John Lane, 1895).

Denisoff, Dennis, "*The Pagan Review* in Context", *Yellow Nineties 2.0*, Edited by Dennis Denisoff and Lorraine Janzen Kooistra (2010), https://1890s.ca/tpr-general-introduction/

Dowden, Edward, *Shakespeare*: *A Critical Study of His Mind and Art* (London: H. S. King & Co., 1875).

Foster, R. F., *W. B. Yeats, A Life, I: The Apprentice Mage, 1865–1914* (Oxford: Oxford University Press, 1997).

— *W. B. Yeats — A Life, II: The Arch-Poet 1915–1939* (Oxford: Oxford University Press, 2003).

Lee-Hamilton, Eugene, *Apollo and Marsyas, and Other Poems* (London: Elliot Stock, 1885).

Gilchrist, Robert Murray, *The Basilisk and Other Tales of Dread*, Edited by John Pelan and Christopher Roden (Ashcroft, BC: Ash Tree Press, 2003).

— *Frangipanni: The Story of Her Infatuation* (Derby: Frank Murray Press, 1893).

Green, Ernest, "Book of the Week," *The New Age*, 4.13 (January 21, 1909), 166–167.

Gregory, Lady [Augusta], *Poets and Dreamers: Studies and Translations from the Irish* (Dublin: Hodges and Figgis, & Co. and London: John Murray, 1903).

— *Lady Gregory's Diaries, 1892–1902*, Edited and Introduced by James Pethica (Oxford: Oxford University Press, 1996).

Halloran, William, "Yeats and Fiona Macleod, Part I," in *Yeats Annual No. 13*, Edited by Warwick Gould (London: Palgrave Macmillan, 1998), 62–109.

— "W. B. Yeats, William Sharp, and Fiona Macleod: A Celtic Drama, 1897," in *Yeats Annual No. 14*, Edited by Warwick Gould (London: Palgrave Macmillan, 2001), 159–208.

— *The Life and Letters of William Sharp and "Fiona Macleod," Volume 1: 1855–1894*, Transcribed, Edited, and Introduced by William Halloran (Cambridge, UK: Open Book Publishers, 2018), https://doi.org/10.11647/OBP.0142

— *The Life and Letters of William Sharp and "Fiona Macleod," Volume 2: 1895–1899, Volume 3: 1900–1905*, Transcribed, Edited, and Introduced by William Halloran (Cambridge, UK: Open Book Publishers, 2020), https://doi.org/10.11647/OBP.0196

— *The Life and Letters of William Sharp and "Fiona Macleod," Volume 3: 1900–1905*, Transcribed, Edited, and Introduced by William Halloran (Cambridge, UK: Open Book Publishers, 2020), https://doi.org/10.11647/OBP.0221

Hood, Alexander Nelson, *Adria, A Tale of Venice* (London: John Murray; New York: E. P. Dutton & Co., 1904).

Jackson, Holbrook, *The Eighteen Nineties, A Review of Art and Ideas at the Close of the Nineteenth Century* (New York: Mitchell Kennerley, 1914).

Janvier, Catherine, "Fiona Macleod and Her Creator William Sharp," *North American Review* (April 5, 1907), 718–732.

Janvier, Thomas, *The Uncle of an Angel, and Other Stories* (New York: Harper Brothers 1891).

Le Gallienne, Richard, *Volumes in Folio* (London: C. Elkin Mathews, The Bodley Head, 1889).

— *Travels in England* (London: John Lane, The Bodley Head, 1900).

— *The Romantic '90s* (London and New York: G.P. Putnam's Sons, 1925).

Meyers, Terry L., *The Sexual Tensions of William Sharp, A Study of the Birth of Fiona Macleod. Incorporating Two Lost Works, Ariadne in Naxos and Beatrice* (New York: Peter Lang, 1996).

Paget, Violet [pseudonymously by Vernon Lee], *Miss Brown* (Edinburgh and London: William Blackwood and Sons, 1884).

Philpot, Mrs. J. H., *The Sacred Tree in Religion and Myth* (London and New York: Macmillan, 1897).

Rhys, Ernest, *The Fiddler of Carne, A North Sea Winter's Tale* (Edinburgh: Patrick Geddes and Colleagues, 1896).

— "William Sharp and 'Fiona Macleod,'" *Century Magazine*, 74 (May, 1907), 111–117.

— *Everyman Remembers* (London and Toronto: J. M. Dent and Sons, 1931).

— *Letters from Limbo* (London: J. M. Dent and Sons, 1936).

Richards, Grant, *Author Hunting by an Old Literary Sportsman* (New York: Coward-McCann, 1934).

Rinder, Edith Wingate, *The Massacre of the Innocents and Other Tales by Belgian Writers*, Translated and Introduced by Edith Wingate Rinder (Chicago: Stone and Kimball, 1895).

— *The Shadow of Arvor: Legendary Romances and Folk-Tales of Brittany*, Translated and Retold by Edith Wingate Rinder (Edinburgh: Patrick Geddes and Colleagues, 1896).

— Charles Le Goffic, *The Dark Way of Love* [Le Crucifié de Keraliès], Translated by Edith Wingate Rinder (London: Archibald Constable & Co., 1898).

Sharp, Elizabeth, *Lyra Celtica, An Anthology of Representative Celtic Poetry*, Edited by Elizabeth A. Sharp with an Introduction and Notes by William Sharp (Edinburgh: Patrick Geddes and Colleagues, 1896).

— *William Sharp (Fiona Macleod), A Memoir* (London: William Heinemann; New York: Duffield & Co., 1910).

Stanton, Elizabeth Cady, *Eighty Years and More: Reminiscences 1815–1897* (New York: European Publishing Company, 1898).

Traubel, Horace, *With Walt Whitman in Camden, Volume I: March 28–July 14, 1888* (Small, Maynard & Cany, Boston, 1906).

Walpole, Hugh, *The Apple Trees: Four Reminiscences* (Waltham Saint Lawrence, Berkshire: Golden Cockerel Press, 1932).

Watts-Dunton, Theodore, *Aylwin* (London: Hurst and Blackett, 1898).

Yeats, William Butler, *The Wind among the Reeds* (London: Elkin Mathews, 1899).

— *Autobiographies* (London: Macmillan, 1955).

— *Memoirs*, Transcribed and Edited by Denis Donoghue (London: Macmillan, 1972).

— *Letters to W. B. Yeats, Volume I*, Edited by Richard Finneran, George Mills Harper, and William M. Murphy (New York: Columbia University Press, 1977).

— *The Collected Letters of W. B. Yeats, Volume II, 1896–1900*, Edited by Warwick Gould, John Kelly, and Deidre Toomey (Oxford: Oxford University Press, 1997).

— *The Collected Letters of W. B. Yeats, Volume IV, 1905–1907*, Edited by John Kelly and Ronald Schuchard (Oxford: Oxford University Press, 2005).

List of Illustrations

Fig. 1   Dante Gabriel Rossetti in 1850 at age twenty-two. A portrait by William Holman Hunt (c. 1883), Wikimedia, https://commons.wikimedia.org/wiki/File:William_Holman_Hunt_-_Portrait_of_Dante_Gabriel_Rossetti_at_22_years_of_Age_-_Google_Art_Project.jpg, Public Domain.   5

Fig. 2   An albumen print of Dante Gabriel Rossetti. Taken by Charles Lutwidge Dodgson (Lewis Carroll) (1863), Wikimedia, https://commons.wikimedia.org/wiki/File:Dante_Gabriel_Rossetti_001.jpg, Public Domain.   6

Fig. 3   Hall Caine, The Manxman, as caricatured in *Vanity Fair*. John Bernard Partridge (1896), Wikimedia, https://en.wikipedia.org/wiki/File:Hall_Caine_Vanity_Fair_2_July_1896.jpg, Public Domain.   11

Fig. 4   Photograph of William Sharp taken by an unknown photographer in Rome in 1883. Reproduced from *William Sharp: A Memoir*, compiled by Elizabeth Sharp (London: William Heinemann, 1910).   13

Fig. 5   Photograph of Edward Dowden Robinson (c. 1895), Wikimedia, https://commons.wikimedia.org/wiki/File:Portrait_of_Edward_Dowden.jpg, Public Domain.   22

Fig. 6   Alice Mona (Alison) Caird (1854–1922) Engraving based on a photograph by H. S. Mendelssohn Wikipedia, https://en.wikipedia.org/wiki/Mona_Caird   35

Fig. 7   George Meredith in *Robert Louis Stevenson: A Bookman Extra Number 1913* (London: Hodder & Stoughton), p. 138, Wikimedia, https://commons.wikimedia.org/wiki/File:George_Meredith%27s_Portrait.jpg, Public Domain.   36

Fig. 8   Richard Le Gallienne (1866–1947). Photograph by Arthur Ellis (1894). Wikimedia, https://commons.wikimedia.org/wiki/File:Richard_Le_Gallienne,_by_Alfred_Ellis.jpg, Public Domain.   38

Fig. 9	An 1897 photograph of Edmund Clarence Stedman (1833–1908), an American poet, critic, essayist, banker, and scientist. Wikimedia, https://commons.wikimedia.org/wiki/File:Edmund_Clarence_Stedman_cph.3a44372.jpg, Public Domain.	44
Fig. 10	A self portrait of Theodore Roussel (1847–1926) a French painter, who moved to London in 1878 and two years later married the widow Frances Amelia Smithson Bull (1844–1909). A close friend of James McNeill, he was William Sharp's "most intimate friend" in 1890. Wikipedia, https://commons.wikimedia.org/wiki/File:Theodore_Roussel_(autorretrato)_(1).jpg	57
Fig. 11	John Robert Cozens, *Lake Nemi* (1777). © Tate, https://www.tate.org.uk/art/artworks/cozens-lake-nemi-t00982, CC-BY-NC-ND 3.0.	65
Fig. 12	Joseph Mallord William Turner, *Lake Nemi* (c. 1827–1828). Turner visited Lake Nemi in 1819 and painted this sketch from memory in Rome in 1828. © Tate, https://www.tate.org.uk/art/artworks/turner-lake-nemi-n03027, CC-BY-NC-ND 3.0.	66
Fig. 13	Lake Nemi, Engraved by Middiman and Pye in 1819 after a sketch by Joseph Mallord William Turner. Transferred from the British Museum to Tate Britain in 1988, https://www.tate.org.uk/art/artworks/turner-lake-of-nemi-engraved-by-middiman-and-pye-t06023, CC-BY-NC-ND (3.0 Unported)	66
Fig. 14	Sir Charles Holroyd's etching of William Sharp, which Sharp reproduced for insertion opposite the title page of *Sospiri di Roma*, the book of poems he wrote in Rome in January/February 1891 and published privately in Tivoli in March 1891, https://www.google.co.uk/books/edition/Sospiri_di_Roma/jT9DAQAAMAAJ?hl=en&gbpv=1	69
Fig. 15	A pastel painting of William Sharp by the Norwegian painter Charles M. Ross. Sharp sat for this portrait in Rome in early March 1891. This is a photograph of the copy Elizabeth Sharp reproduced in her *Memoir*, taken by William Halloran (2021).	70
Fig. 16	Blanche Willis Howard, in F. E. Willard, *A Woman of the Century: Fourteen Hundred-Seventy Biographical Sketches Accompanied by Portraits of Leading American Women in All Walks of Life* (Buffalo, N. Y.: Moulton, 1893), 735. Wikipedia, https://commons.wikimedia.org/wiki/File:BLANCHE_WILLIS_HOWARD_VON_TEUFFEL._A_woman_of_the_century_(page_745_crop).jpg, Public Domain.	74

List of Illustrations 431

Fig. 17	Photograph of Walt Whitman and his nurse Fritzenger (1890). Wikimedia, https://commons.wikimedia.org/wiki/File:Whitman,_Walt_(1819-1892)_and_his_male_nurse_Fritzenger.JPG, Public Domain.	80
Fig. 18	Photograph of Horace Traubel (c. 1912). Wikimedia, https://commons.wikimedia.org/wiki/File:Portrait_of_Horace_Traubel.jpg, Public Domain.	81
Fig. 19	Early twentieth-century photograph of the house across the road from the Sharp's Phenice Croft in Bucks Green, Rudgwick Sussex. © Rudgwick Preservation Society. Courtesy of Roger Nash, Chair, Rudgwick Preservation Society, https://www.rudgwick-rps.org.uk	89
Fig. 20	Mid-twentieth-century photograph of Bucks Green, Rudgwick, Sussex. Phenice Croft, now the Toll House, is across the road from the building, now white, which housed the shop. © The Francis Frith Collection, https://www.francisfrith.com/bucks-green/bucks-green-the-village-c1965_b587001	95
Fig. 21	Park House, Horsham, Sussex. Photograph by Whn64 (2013), Wikimedia, https://commons.wikimedia.org/wiki/File:Horsham_-_horsham_park.jpg, CC BY-SA 3.0.	95
Fig. 22	Photograph of Edith Wingate Rinder known as "My Lady Greensleeves" reflecting the green velvet dress she wore for the sitting (c. 1894). The pose mirrors many of the paintings of the Pre-Raphaelite Brotherhood, especially those of Dante Gabriel Rossetti. Photographer unknown. Courtesy of Fig the Rinder family.	100
Fig. 23	Daniel Gabriel Rossetti, *My Lady Greensleeves* (1872). Oil on panel, 33 x 27.3 cm. Harvard Art Museums, Fogg Museum. Wikimedia, https://commons.wikimedia.org/wiki/File:Dante_Gabriel_Rossetti_-_My_Lady_Greensleeves_-_1943.203_-_Fogg_Museum.jpg, Public Domain.	100
Fig. 24	The Great Bridge in Constantine Algeria 1899.jpg Silverbanks Pictures Image Archive, Photographer unknown. Wikimedia Commons, https://www.flickr.com/photos/159714170@N02/48311372867/	113
Fig. 25	Ruins of the Baths of Antonius Pius, Carthage, Algeria. Photograph by BishkekRocks (2004), Wikimedia, https://commons.wikimedia.org/wiki/File:Karthago_Antoninus-Pius-Thermen.JPG, Public Domain.	114

Fig. 26   Portrait of Mary Beatrice Sharp, William Sharp's youngest sister taken in the Davis Studios in Edinburgh in 1906. Mary provided the handwriting for Fiona Macleod's extensive correspondence. Courtesy of the Department of Rare Books and Special Collections, Dulles Reading Room, Firestone Library, Princeton University.   135

Fig. 27   Verso of Fig. 23 in Mary Sharp's handwriting (the handwriting of Fiona Macleod). The photograph is inscribed "To the Reverend R. Wilkins Rees. Yours Sincerely, Mary B. Sharp. Fiona Macleod's sister, who did all the writing of the Fiona Macleod work and carried on the correspondence connected with it." Reverend R. Wilkins Rees was the author of ghost stories, among them "Ghost-Layers and Ghost-Laying," in *The Church Treasury of History, Custom, Folk-lore, Etc.*, ed. William Andrews (London: William Andrews & Company, 1898), 241–274.) Courtesy of the Department of Rare Books and Special Collections, Dulles Reading Room, Firestone Library, Princeton University.   136

Fig. 28   Photograph of Grant Allen (1848–1899) by Elliott & Fry (c. 1899), Wikimedia, https://commons.wikimedia.org/wiki/File:Portrait_of_Grant_Allen.jpg, Public Domain.   138

Fig. 29   Photograph of William Sharp by Frederick Hollyer (1894). Reproduced from *Poems by William Sharp*. Selected and arranged by Mrs. William Sharp (London, William Heinemann, 1912). Wikimedia, https://commons.wikimedia.org/wiki/File:William_Sharp_1894.jpg#/media/File:William_Sharp_1894.jpg, Public Domain.   142

Fig. 30   Portrait of Henry Mills Alden (1836–1919), who edited *Harper's Magazine* for fifty years, in 1910. Unknown photographer. Wikimedia, https://commons.wikimedia.org/wiki/File:Henry_Mills_Alden_portrait_in_In_After_Days_(1910).jpg, Public Domain   143

Fig. 31   Sir Patrick Geddes (1854–1932). Photograph by Lafayette, 30 December 1931. © National Portrait Gallery, London. Some rights reserved.   149

Fig. 32   Winter on the Isle of Arran. By Archie46 — Own work, CC BY-SA 3.0, Wikimedia Common, https://commons.wikimedia.org/w/index.php?curid=30013029   154

Fig. 33   "Apollo's School Days," John Duncan, in *The Evergreen: A Northern Seasonal, The Book of Spring* (Edinburgh: Patrick Geddes and Colleagues, 1895). Photograph by William F. Halloran of his copy in 2020   158

List of Illustrations 433

Fig. 34 The Outlook Tower, Castlehill, Edinburgh., locus of the Scottish Celtic Revival. Photograph by Kim Traynor (2013), Wikimedia, https://commons.wikimedia.org/wiki/File:Outlook_Tower,_Castlehill,_Edinburgh.JPG#/media/File:Outlook_Tower,_Castlehill,_Edinburgh.JPG, CC BY-SA 3.0. 160

Fig. 35 An example of a Patrick Geddes and Colleague book: *The Shadow of Arvor: Legendary Romances and Folk-Tales of Brittany*, Translated and Retold by Edith Wingate Rinder (Edinburgh: Patrick Geddes & Colleagues, 1897). Printed by W. H. White and Co. Ltd., Edinburgh Riverside Press. Photograph by William F. Halloran (2019). 163

Fig. 36 Title page of the first edition of *Lyra Celtica, An Anthology of Representative Celtic Poetry*, edited by Elizabeth A. Sharp, with an Introduction and Notes by William Sharp (Edinburgh: Patrick Geddes and Colleagues, 1896), https://archive.org/details/lyracelticaantho00shar/mode/2up 165

Fig. 37 "The Croft," Grant Allen's House in Hindhead, Haslemere, Surrey (1906). © The Francis Frith Collection, https://www.francisfrith.com/hindhead/hindhead-grant-allen-s-house-1906_55569 170

Fig. 38 Ramsay Gardens from Princes' Street, Edinburgh. The Outlook Tower is on the High Street behind this impressive group of buildings. Photo by David Monniaux (2005), Wikimedia, https://commons.wikimedia.org/w/index.php?curid=228032#/media/File:Edinburgh_old_town_dsc06355.jpg, CC BY-SA 3.0. 174

Fig. 39 Fiona Macleod, *The Sin-Eater and Other Tales* (Edinburgh: Patrick Geddes & Colleagues, 1895). Photograph by William F. Halloran (2019). 177

Fig. 40 William Butler Yeats (1865–1939). Photograph by Alice Boughton (1903), Wikimedia, https://commons.wikimedia.org/wiki/File:Yeats_Boughton.jpg#/media/File:Yeats_Boughton.jpg, Public Domain. 209

Fig. 41 The first American edition of Fiona MacLeod's *Green Fire. A Romance* (New York: Harper & Brothers, 1896). Photograph by William F. Halloran (2019). 213

Fig. 42 Poster advertising the premiere of *Esclarmonde*, libretto by Alfred Blau and Louis de Gramodt, music by Jules Massenet's, Paris, May 1889. August François-Marie Gorguet, *Esclarmonde* (1889), chromolithograph. Wikimedia, https://commons.wikimedia.org/wiki/File:Esclarmonde.jpg#/media/File:Esclarmonde.jpg, Public Domain. 216

Fig. 43 Cover and title page of the first edition of Fiona Macleod's *From the Hills of Dream* (Edinburgh: Patrick Geddes & Colleagues, 1896). Photograph by William F. Halloran (2019). 218

Fig. 44 Fiona Macleod stories reissued in paperbacks by Patrick Geddes and Colleagues in 1896. Photograph by William F. Halloran (2019). 228

Fig. 45 Coulson Kernahan (1853–1943). Photography by Elliot and Fry (1903). Public Domain. Wikipedia, https://commons.wikimedia.org/wiki/File:Coulson_Kernahan_by_Elliott_%26_Fry.jpg 230

Fig. 46 An etching of William Sharp, dated about 1897, by William Strang (1859–1921). Printed by David Strang (1887–1967), the artist's son. Photograph by William F. Halloran of his copy (2019). 233

Fig. 47 Cartledge Hall, Holmesfield, Derbyshire. Home of R. Murray Gilchrist and family. Photograph by Dave Hobson (2014). Courtesy of Vale of Belvoir Ramblers, https://vbramblers.blogspot.com/2014_04_01_archive.html 235

Fig. 48 This photograph of William Sharp was taken in Dublin in late September 1897, and sent to Henry Mills Alden, editor of *Harper's Magazine* and Sharp's friend, at Christmas, 1897. Courtesy of the University of Delaware Library (The Henry Mills Alden Papers), Public Domain. 240

Fig. 49 Maud Gonne McBride (1866–1953). Wikimedia https://commons.wikimedia.org/wiki/File:Maude_Gonne_McBride_nd.jpg#/media/File:Maude_Gonne_McBride_nd.jpg, Public Domain. 251

Fig. 50 Moina Mathers (1865–1928), the wife of Macgregor Mathers and sister of Henri Bergson, was an artist, occultist, and founder of the Alpha et Omega Lodge of the Golden Dawn. Left: Moina Mathers from her performance in the Rites of Isis in the Paris Lodge of the Golden Dawn (1899), Wikimedia, https://commons.wikimedia.org/wiki/File:Picture_of_Moina_Mathers_from_her_performance_in_the_Rites_of_Isis_in_Paris.jpg, Public Domain. Right: Moina Mathers (c. 1887). Public Domain. Wikimedia, https://commons.wikimedia.org/wiki/File:Moina_Mathers.jpg 255

Fig. 51 The elaborate cover design of *The Dark Way of Love*, Edith Wingate Rinder's translation of C. Le Goffic's *Le Crucifié de Keraliès*, published by Archibald Constable in 1898. Photograph by William F. Halloran of his copy. 268

List of Illustrations 435

Fig. 52   Dame Edith Sophy Lyttelton (née Balfour) after a picture by Romney; by Lafayette, photogravure by Walker & Boutall, 1897; published 1899. © National Portrait Gallery, London. Some rights reserved.   277

Fig. 53   Recent photograph of Wharncliffe, Chorleywood, London, http://www.hertfordshire-genealogy.co.uk/images/!/c/chorleywood/chorleywood-wharncliffe-google.jpg   292

Fig. 54   Benedictine Abbey on Iona, Inner Hebrides, constructed in 1203 AD on the site of the Celtic Church which St. Columbo built after he settled on Iona in 563 AD and began to establish Christianity in Scotland. Photograph by Paul T. (Gunther Tschuch) (2019), Wikimedia, https://commons.wikimedia.org/wiki/File:Iona_07.jpg, CC BY-SA 4.0.   303

Fig. 55   Map of the Isle of Mull in Scotland's Inner Hebrides. Iona is the tiny island located off Mull's eastern-most tip. Wikimedia, https://commons.wikimedia.org/wiki/File:Ordnance_Survey_1-250000_-_NM.jpg, OGL v.3. Contains OS data © Crown copyright and database right (2021).   *304*

Fig. 56   Taormina on the east Coast of Sicily with Mt. Etna in the distance. Photograph by Miguel Torres (2011), Wikimedia, https://commons.wikimedia.org/w/index.php?curid=17133090#/media/File:Taormina_and_Mt_Etna.jpg, CC BY-SA 3.0.   316

Fig. 57   Bust and portrait of the 5th Duke of Bronté, Alexander Nelson Hood (1854–1937), on display in the Castello Nelson (formally the Castello Maniace). Photographs by Warwick Gould (2014), reproduced with permission.   318

Fig. 58   The Greek Theater in Syracuse, Sicily. Built about 470 B. C., it is the largest surviving theater of the ancient world. Photograph by Michele Ponzio (2006), Wikimedia, https://commons.wikimedia.org/wiki/File:Teatro_greco_di_Siracusa_-_aerea.jpg, CC BY-SA 2.0.   318

Fig. 59   A recent photograph of the beautifully restored Villa Il Palmerino in Settignano, north-east of Florence, where Eugene Lee-Hamilton and Vernon Lee lived for many years. Photograph by Sailko (2016), Wikimedia, https://commons.wikimedia.org/wiki/File:Il_palmerino,_esterno_04.jpg, CC BY 3.0.   320

Fig. 60   Baron Christian Karl Bernard Tauchnitz (1841–1921). Portrait by Vilma Lwoff-Parlaghy (1901). Wikimedia, https://commons.wikimedia.org/wiki/File:Tauchnitz_Christian_Karl_001.jpg#/media/File:Tauchnitz_Christian_Karl_001.jpg, Public Domain   323

Fig. 61	Theodore Watts-Dunton (1832–1914). Portrait by H. B. Norris (1902). Public Domain. Wikimedia, https://commons.wikimedia.org/wiki/File:Theodore.watts-dunton.jpeg	331
Fig. 62	Maude Valérie White. Photograph by Herbert Rose Barraud, published by Eglington & Co. Carbon print, published 1889. © National Portrait Gallery, London. Some rights reserved.	334
Fig. 63	Photograph of the Hotel Castello-a-Mare taken in 1937. William and Elizabeth Sharp stayed here in April 1902, and he described the view from the terrace outside his window in an April 3 letter to Mrs. J. H. Philpot. Photograph of postcard taken by William F. Halloran (2021). Original photographer unknown.	337
Fig. 64	Taormina as seen from the Saracen castle overlooking the town. The Hotel Castello-a-Mare is at the far left. The Greek theater is in the background. Photograph by Solomonn Levi, Wikimedia, https://en.wikipedia.org/wiki/File:Taormina_as_seen_from_the_castle_overlooking_the_town..jpg, CC BY-SA 4.0.	337
Fig. 65	North Lismore from Port Appin on the mainland with the hills of Kingairloch beyond. Photograph by Alan Partridge (2004), Wikimedia, https://commons.wikimedia.org/wiki/File:Lismore_Island.jpg, CC BY-SA 2.0.	342
Fig. 66	The Ferrovia Circumetnea is a narrow-gauge railway which encircles Mount Etna. From its terminal in Catania the line loops around Mount Etna and eventually reaches the other terminal at the seaside town of Riposto. Its rolling stock has been updated several times, but the route is the same as when the Sharps boarded the train to travel back and forth between Taormina and the Castello Maniace in the early twentieth century. Photograph by Arbalete (2011), Wikimedia, https://commons.wikimedia.org/wiki/File:Mappa_ferr_Circumetnea.png, CC BY-SA 3.0.	346
Fig. 67	The Randazzo station of the Ferrovia Circumetnea where the Sharps entered and left the train on their trips to the Castello Maniace. Photograph by LuckyLisp (2005), Wikimedia, https://commons.wikimedia.org/wiki/File:Circumetnea_stazione_di_randazzo.jpg, CC BY-SA 3.0.	346
Fig. 68	Sir Alexander Nelson Hood, Fifth Duke of Bronté (1854–1937). "The Princess's Private Secretary," Caricature by Spy (Leslie Ward), published in *Vanity Fair* in 1905. Wikimedia, https://en.wikipedia.org/wiki/Alexander_Hood,_5th_Duke_of_Bronté#/media/File:Alexander_Nelson_Hood,_Vanity_Fair,_1905-10-26.jpg, Public Domain.	348

List of Illustrations 437

Fig. 69   Robert Smythe Hichens (1864–1950). Photograph by unknown photographer (1912), in Frederic Taber Cooper, *Some English Story Tellers* (New York: Henry Holt & Co, 1912). Wikimedia, https://commons.wikimedia.org/wiki/File:Robert_Hichens_001.jpg#/media/File:Robert_Hichens_001.jpg, Public Domain.   350

Fig. 70   View over the excavation site towards Eleusis, the site of the Eleusinian Mysteries, or the Mysteries of Demeter and Kore, which became popular in the Greek-speaking world as early as 600 BC and attracted initiates during the Roman Empire before declining in the fourth century AD. Photograph by Carole Raddato (2005), Wikimedia, https://commons.wikimedia.org/wiki/File:General_view_of_sanctuary_of_Demeter_and_Kore_and_the_Telesterion_(Initiation_Hall),_center_for_the_Eleusinian_Mysteries,_Eleusis_(8191841684).jpg, CC BY-SA 2.0.   352

Fig. 71   The Firth of Clyde at Kilcreggan (on the right), with PS *Waverley* approaching across Loch Long. Photograph by Dave Souza (2018), Wikimedia, https://commons.wikimedia.org/w/index.php?curid=73771868, CCBY-SA-4.0.   357

Fig. 72   Ye Wells Hotel, Llandrindod where William Sharp received treatment for diabetes in September 1903: "the rigorous treatment, the potent Saline and Sulphur waters and baths, the not less potent and marvelously pure and regenerative Llandrindod air … have combined to work a wonderful change for the better." Photograph by Percy Benzie Abery (193-?), Wikimedia, https://commons.wikimedia.org/wiki/File:-Ye_Wells_Hotel,_Llandrindod_(1293703).jpg, CC0.   359

Fig. 73   Valle del Simeto, Catania. Photograph by Davide Restivo (2007), Wikimedia, https://commons.wikimedia.org/wiki/File:Valle_del_Simeto_3.jpg#/media/File:Valle_del_Simeto_3.jpg, CC BY-SA 2.0.   362

Fig. 74   Mount Pentelicus is a mountain in Attica, Greece, situated northeast of Athens and southwest of Marathon. The mountain is covered in large part with forest (about 60 or 70%), and can be seen from southern Athens (Attica). Marble from Mount Pentelicus is of exceptionally high quality and was used to construct much of the Athenian Acropolis. *Photograph* by Dimorsitanos (2008), Wikimedia, https://commons.wikimedia.org/w/index.php?curid=3921687, CC BY-SA 4.0.   367

Fig. 75 Photograph of William Sharp by Frederick Hollyer (1894). 370
Reproduced from *Poems by William Sharp*. Selected and arranged by Mrs. William Sharp (London, William Heinemann, 1912). Wikimedia, https://commons.wikimedia.org/wiki/File:William_Sharp_1894.jpg#/media/File:William_Sharp_1894.jpg, Public Domain.

Fig. 76 Photograph of William Sharp, taken by Alexander Nelson 371
Hood, the Duke of Bronte, at his Castle Maniace in November 1903. Reproduced by Elizabeth Sharp in her *Memoir* (358).

Fig. 77 Statue of Anteros, Shaftesbury Memorial, Piccadilly Circus, 379
London. Sculpted by Alfred Gilbert and erected in 1893. Photograph by Diego Delso (2014), Wikimedia, https://commons.wikimedia.org/wiki/File:Fuente_Eros,_Piccadilly_Circus,_Londres,_Inglaterra,_2014-08-11,_DD_159.JPG, CC BY-SA 4.0.

Fig. 78 Interior Courtyard of Boston's Isabella Stewart Gardner Museum 385
which was built in 1903 to house the Gardner collection. The building replicates a fifteenth-century Venetian palace. The Sharps toured the building only a year after its completion and well before the collection achieved its zenith. Photograph by Sean Dungan (2017). Wikimedia, https://commons.wikimedia.org/wiki/File:Courtyard,_Isabella_Stewart_Gardner_Museum,_Boston.jpg#/media/File:Courtyard,_Isabella_Stewart_Gardner_Museum,_Boston.jpg, CC BY 4.0.

Fig. 79 The Lismore ferry in winter. This ferry was not available to 390
Sharp and his sister in 1905. Photograph by Magnus Hagdorn (2012), Wikimedia, https://commons.wikimedia.org/wiki/File:Lismore_Ferry_(8120112835).jpg, CC BY-SA 2.0.

Fig. 80 John Keats (1793–1879), by Joseph Severn (1819). Oil on 394
ivory miniature, 105 x 79 mm, National Portrait Gallery. Wikimedia, Domain, https://commons.wikimedia.org/wiki/File:JohnKeats1819_hires.jpg, Public Domain.

Fig. 81 John Keats, by William Hilton (c. 1822). Oil on canvas, 76.2 x 63.5 394
cm, National Portrait Gallery. Wikimedia, https://commons.wikimedia.org/wiki/File:John_Keats_by_William_Hilton.jpg, Public Domain.

Fig 82 Professor Franciscus Donders (1818–1889), by Bramine 397
Hubrecht (1888). Oil on canvas, 142 x 95 cm, Rijkmuseum. Wikimedia, https://commons.wikimedia.org/wiki/File:Professor_Franciscus_Donders_(1818-89)._Fysioloog_en_oogheelkundige_Rijksmuseum_SK-A-2508.jpeg, Public Domain.

Fig. 83   Alphons Marie Antoine Joseph Grandmont (1837–1909), by Bramine Hubrecht (1900–1909). The painting depicts the artist's second husband tutoring two Italian girls. Oil on canvas, 100 x 100 cm, Rijkmuseum. Wikimedia, https://commons.wikimedia.org/wiki/File:Alphons_Marie_Antoine_Joseph_Grandmont_(1837-1909)._Tweede_echtgenoot_van_de_schilderes,_lesgevend_aan_twee_Italiaanse_meisjes_Rijksmuseum_SK-A-2794.jpeg, Public Domain.   398

Fig 84.   Portrait of Millicent Leveson-Gower, Duchess of Sutherland, by John Singer Sargent (1904). Oil on canvas, 254 x 146 cm, Thyssen-Bornemisza Museum. Wikimedia, https://commons.wikimedia.org/wiki/File:John_Singer_Sargent_-_Portrait_of_Millicent_Leveson-Gower,_Duchess_of_Sutherland.jpg, Public Domain.   405

Fig. 85   A Celtic Cross marking William Sharp's Grave. Castello Nelson's Protestant Cemetery, Sicily. Photograph by Warwick Gould (2016), reproduced with his permission.   412

Fig. 86   Photograph of William and Elizabeth Sharp in 1904, unknown photographer. Gift of Noel Farquharson Sharp to William F. Halloran in 1968.   418

Index

Aberdeen 39, 58, 370, 421
A Fellowe and His Wife 73, 82–83, 108, 122
Africa 105, 111–114, 116, 142, 349, 351, 419
Alaya, Flavia xiv
Alden, Annie 172–173
Alden, Henry Mills 51, 81–82, 117, 142–143, 212, 240, 324, 338, 343, 357, 383
Algeria 113–114, 313, 351, 361
Algiers 111, 301, 313
Alison, Mona 4
Allen, Grant 35, 51, 137–139, 148, 169–171, 173, 189–190, 247, 267, 292, 295, 298
Allen, Nellie 189–190, 192–193, 267, 295
American xiv, xvi, 34–35, 43–45, 49, 51–52, 54, 56, 59, 69, 74, 82, 108, 112, 121, 134, 141, 152, 161, 169, 176, 196, 198, 201, 211–213, 221, 223, 227, 231, 234, 262–263, 271, 285, 319, 321, 325, 330, 343, 347, 365–367, 371, 373, 382–385, 421–422
America, visits to xvii, 12, 20, 43, 45, 48–49, 73, 76–77, 79, 81, 108–109, 118, 121, 134, 157, 169, 172, 198, 211–212, 217, 220, 236, 285, 296, 331, 340, 360, 373, 383–384, 386, 417
Anglo-Celtic 157, 265
Anteros 378–379, 381
Antrim 285–286
Arab 112–113, 115–116
Archibald Constable and Co. 178, 212, 237–238, 261

Argyll 21, 27, 58, 166, 175, 235, 324, 330
Arnold, Matthew 186, 189, 193, 202, 308
Arran, Isle of 1, 13, 119, 153–156, 238–239, 284, 342
Arrochar 119
Athens 351, 360–363, 365–367, 370
Austin, Alfred 47, 104–105, 338
Australia xi, 4, 7, 24, 338
Australian 25, 43–44, 104
Austria 49, 347
autobiography xvii, 23, 226, 288, 294–295, 301–302, 378

Balfour, Arthur 105, 338–339, 341
Balmires, Steve xiv
Balzac, Honoré de 68
Bayswater Road 4, 61
Beardsley, Aubrey 159
Belgian literature 54, 142, 175, 177, 189, 246
Belgium 98, 133, 246
Black Sea 116
Blake, William 23, 121, 133, 413
Blavatsky, Madame 15, 341
Bohemianism 87, 95
Boston 43, 49, 51, 76–77, 81, 84, 109, 141, 220, 259, 383–386
Bouguereau, Adolphe 15
Bourget, Paul 15
Bowen, Henry Chandler 51
Breton, Jules 15, 50, 164, 175, 297, 306
Britain 57, 66, 73, 149, 157, 186, 202, 212, 220, 271, 300, 340–341, 347, 419

British xvi, 20, 43–44, 49, 56, 66, 68, 70, 77, 80, 82, 84, 96, 112, 176, 189, 201, 244, 247, 259, 306, 309, 316–317, 319, 324, 333, 340, 349, 357, 363, 377
Brittany 162–163, 173, 175, 191, 213–215, 219, 297–298, 336
Brooks, Katherine xi, 1
Brooks, W. H. 94, 103
Brown, Ford Madox 19, 29, 31, 53
Browning, Robert xi, 17, 24, 47, 52–54, 56, 68, 178
Bucks Green 84, 88–90, 93–94, 101, 105, 116, 118, 128–130, 132
Burns, Robert 23

Cady Stanton, Elizabeth 34
Caine, Hall 6, 9–11, 13–16, 27, 32–34, 39, 46–47, 52, 55, 96, 131, 185, 250, 347
Caird, Mona xii, xiii, 4, 28, 31–32, 34–35, 49, 56, 61–62, 116, 151, 161–162, 179, 189, 208, 238, 249, 322, 356, 416
Camden 79–80
Camelot Classics Series 22–23
Campagna, Roman 63, 71, 84, 86, 98, 369
Canada 29, 43, 49–50, 52–53, 164, 319–320
Canadian 49, 52–53, 141
Canterbury Poets Series 15, 21–25, 35, 38, 43, 54, 56, 193, 202
Carman, Bliss 50, 53–54, 69, 73–74, 77, 82, 104, 141, 164
Carmichael, Andrew 219, 311–312
Carpenter, Edward 103–104
Castle Maniace xiii, 317–318, 330, 333, 345–346, 348, 361, 368, 371
Catholic 189, 232, 327
Celtic xiii, xiv, 1, 21, 23, 28, 37, 41, 58, 62, 113, 119–124, 134–135, 137, 141, 144, 147–148, 150, 152, 156–158, 160, 162–165, 173–176, 191–192, 194, 199, 201–202, 206, 210–211, 213, 218, 223–225, 227, 231, 235, 237, 239, 241, 248, 250–253, 260–262, 265, 269, 271, 275, 278–280, 283–284, 290, 298, 303, 305–309, 318, 325–330, 341, 371–374, 377–378, 380, 414, 417
Celtic Dream 123

Celticism 207, 224, 265, 309, 377
Celtic Mystical Order 28, 113, 223, 225, 248, 250–251, 271, 278, 309, 325, 327–328, 330, 341, 414
Celtic Renaissance xiii, 121, 135, 144, 147–148, 150, 158, 192, 269, 284
Celtic Renascence 163, 174, 265
Celtic Revival 150, 157, 160, 162–164, 192, 202, 224, 252, 265, 271
Celtic Rites 280
Celtic Romance 120, 135
Celtic Theatre 250, 262, 279
Celtic Twilight 123
Celts 149, 202, 247, 260, 303, 305–309
Century Publishing Company 43
Chapman & Hall 295, 301, 347, 373, 377
Chatto, Andrew 39, 43
Chatto & Windus 43
Chavannes, Puvis de 15
Chicago 76, 119, 133, 153, 161, 176, 178, 192
childbirth 11–12, 93, 122, 124, 132, 179, 215, 225, 263, 306, 319–320, 322, 324, 326, 366, 369, 417
Children of Tomorrow 2, 39, 41, 43, 48–49
Chorleywood 285, 291–293, 295, 297
Christian 72, 103, 323
Christianity 143, 194, 218, 225, 247, 303, 327–328
Civil List xiii, 105, 339
Clough, Arthur Hugh 186
Clyde 1, 3, 12, 141, 205, 357
Coleridge, Samuel Taylor 23
Connecticut 51, 422
Constable, Archibald 119, 159, 178, 198, 201, 212, 237–238, 261, 266–268
Contemporary Science Series 22
Coole Park 239, 262, 279, 414
Cormon, Fernand 15
cosmopolitanism 87, 149, 164
Cotterell, George 116, 164, 178
Cotton, Joseph 35, 46
Covent Garden 7
Craik, George Lillie 6–7, 15
Crawford, Marion 330

D'Annunzio, Gabriele 54, 68
Daudet, Alphonse 15
decadence 96–98, 157, 159, 417
De Quincey, Thomas 24–26
Derby xii, 118–120, 134–135, 137
Derbyshire 103–104, 118–119, 127, 133, 178, 180, 205, 235, 237, 261, 322, 324
de Vere, Aubrey 47
diabetes xiii, 93, 359, 366–367, 382
Dickinson, Emily 43
Distant Country, The 219, 261, 273–274, 276, 287–290
Divine Adventure: Iona: By Sundown Shores: Studies in Spiritual History, The 144, 154, 226, 286, 288, 291, 294–295, 301, 303, 305, 307–308, 328, 354
Dominion of Dreams, The 213, 226, 237, 247, 261–263, 266, 271–273, 276, 279–280, 283–285, 287–288, 290
Dorset 84, 237, 311
Douglas, George 156, 186–187
Douglas, George Brisbane Scott 45–47
Dover 15, 201, 232, 243–244, 251, 356, 415
Dowden, Edward 21–22, 24, 29, 32, 47, 94, 131
dramas 25, 46, 48, 54, 71, 73, 76–77, 82, 96, 109, 114, 124, 142, 148, 151, 177, 223, 226, 232, 238–239, 250, 252, 261–262, 279, 281, 283–284, 286, 288, 298–300, 311–312, 326, 330, 336, 354, 356, 363, 378
Dreeme, Willand 96–98
drugs 28, 112, 117, 220, 240, 244, 325
Druidic 194, 374
duality 26, 117, 130, 144, 150, 155, 184, 203, 220, 223, 230, 234, 258, 288, 340–341
Dublin 21, 162, 238–240, 250, 261–262, 269, 279–280, 285, 298
Duncan, John 157, 159
Dundee 149, 161, 165, 189, 344
Dunoon 3–4, 205–206

Earth's Voices 14, 20
Eastbourne 73
Ecce Puella and Other Prose Imaginings 169, 176, 178–179, 182, 187

Edinburgh xiii, xv, 3, 14, 27, 29, 53, 57–58, 61, 72–73, 82–83, 87, 108, 118–119, 135, 137, 140–141, 146, 149–153, 157–160, 163–165, 172–177, 180, 187, 189–192, 194, 198, 201–202, 205–207, 211, 218, 223, 226, 236, 238, 263, 281, 285, 297, 300, 321, 325, 341–342, 344, 349, 353, 356–357, 361, 371, 373, 419
Egypt 313, 349, 381
Elder, Adelaide 4, 185, 287
Elder, John 185–186
Eliot, George 16
Ellis, Havelock 341
England xii, xiii, xv, xvi, 11, 23, 35, 39, 55, 61, 73, 76, 80, 101, 108–109, 116, 118, 137, 148, 178, 201, 220, 223, 228, 232, 237, 244, 247–248, 285, 300, 309, 311–312, 316, 328, 336–338, 341, 349, 351, 353, 357, 373, 375, 381, 421–422
English xiv, xv, 2, 7, 21, 23, 39, 44, 47, 50, 54, 94, 98–99, 116, 138, 157, 189, 191, 231, 265, 286, 306–309, 316–319, 321–322, 328, 333, 335, 342, 345, 350, 365–366, 373, 377
Eros 378–379
Etna xiii, 193, 315–317, 333, 335–336, 345–346, 360–362, 419
Europe xvii, 59, 112, 164, 201, 212, 352, 361, 374, 382, 419
European xiv, xvi, 112, 150, 164
Evergreen, The 152, 157–162, 172, 176, 187, 198
Everyman's Library 23

fairies xiv, 1, 55
Falkirk 2, 357
Fanshawe, W. S. 97
feminism 170, 319–320
Fergusson, Robert 147
Fife 32, 39, 173, 192, 341
fin de siècle 170
Florence 11–12, 20, 59, 70, 105, 189, 311, 319–321, 330
Flower o' the Vine 82, 84, 86–87, 108, 134
Fogazzaro, Antonio 68
For a Song's Sake and other Stories 31

Ford, Ford Madox 17, 29, 31, 53, 162–163, 177, 190, 193–194, 196–198, 201, 235, 267, 369, 424
France 15, 52, 59, 70, 72, 84, 88, 98, 118, 133–134, 137, 161, 192, 216, 220, 223, 227, 236, 246–247, 250, 271–272, 277, 286, 310, 312, 374, 421
Francillon, Robert 6–7
Frankfurt 59
French 54, 57, 59, 65, 96–98, 116, 119, 169, 177, 216, 218, 267, 297, 317, 336, 373–374, 381
From the Hills of Dream 65, 144, 163, 177, 207, 211, 217–219, 231, 235, 278, 300, 325, 328–329, 343, 347

Gaelic xiv, xvii, 1–2, 88, 120, 138, 148, 166, 181, 191, 226, 235, 260, 273, 285, 307, 324, 344, 347, 371–372, 374, 376–377
Gaels 213, 260, 301, 303, 306, 308–309, 311–313, 347, 377
Galway 238, 262
Gare Loch 1–2
Garfitt, George Alfred 103, 119, 128–129, 131, 180, 183–184, 261
Garnett, Richard 47, 94, 189, 291, 339, 356, 363
Geddes, Anna 150
Geddes, Patrick 149–153, 157–167, 171–172, 176–178, 187, 189–190, 192, 194, 198–203, 207, 217–218, 227–228, 325, 328
Genoa 311, 319, 332–333
German 7, 39, 59–60, 73, 75
Germany 52, 58–61, 73–76, 83–84, 87, 90, 93, 97, 108–109, 133
Gilchrist, Robert Murray 102–104, 118–121, 127–135, 145, 172, 176, 178, 180–185, 187, 190, 192, 194, 199, 201, 205, 211, 219, 227, 229, 235–237, 245, 247, 250, 258, 261, 292–294, 311–312, 322, 348–349, 358, 386
Gilder, Richard Watson 51–52, 55, 383
Gippsland 4

Gipsy Christ and Other Tales, The 2, 134, 144–145, 153, 161, 169, 176, 178, 187, 200
Gissing, George 171
Glasgow xi, 1–3, 12–13, 15, 19, 21, 31, 35, 47, 53–54, 56, 58, 87, 94–95, 117, 127, 132, 140, 161, 191, 193, 198, 202, 205–207, 211, 228, 281, 338, 342, 357
Glastonbury 248, 328, 341, 375
God 1, 26, 101, 129, 131, 166–167, 181, 195, 199, 235, 245, 254, 273, 303, 342, 355, 374, 378, 386
Goethe, Johann Wolfgang von 59
Golden Bough, The 65
Golden Dawn, Hermetic Order of the 225–226, 252, 255–256, 271–272, 325–326, 341
Gonne, Maud 225–226, 231–232, 244, 250–251, 253, 327, 372, 415, 418
Goodchild, John A. 247–248, 328, 332–333, 335, 340–341, 374–376, 386
Gordon, David 22–23
Gould, Warwick xvi, 318
Great Writers 22, 24, 29, 32, 39, 52–53
Great Writers Series 22, 24, 29, 32, 39, 52–53, 57
Greece 104–105, 305, 350–353, 360, 363, 365, 367, 369, 371, 373–374, 377–378, 381, 385, 417, 421–422, 424
Greek mythology 62, 65, 88, 90, 103, 124, 156, 312, 315, 318–319, 333, 336–337, 349–350, 352, 357–358, 362–363, 365–366, 378, 385
Green Fire: A Romance 198, 212–213, 215, 218–219
Green, Frederick Ernest 28, 64, 84, 88–90, 93–94, 99, 101, 105, 116, 118, 128–130, 132, 175, 177, 198, 212–213, 215, 218–219, 267–269, 342
green life 130
Green Tree Library series 175, 177
gypsies 2, 27, 74, 87, 178
Gypsy Christ 2, 134, 144–145, 153, 161, 169, 176, 178, 186–187, 200

Halkett, George 330, 343, 349–350
Hallam, Arthur Henry 186
Halswelle, Keeley 53
Hampshire 28, 31, 53, 56, 62
Hampstead 16, 34, 47, 53, 55–56, 62, 127, 132, 144, 279, 284–285
Hardy, Thomas 34, 51, 84, 96, 105, 108, 171, 311, 339
Harland, Henry 82
Harvard University xiv, 51, 77, 100, 133
Hawthorne, Julian 6–7, 56
Hebridean 135, 155, 213
Hebrides xi, xiv, 1, 55, 122, 137, 207, 213, 215, 228, 232, 245, 252, 260, 286, 303–304, 311, 354
Heidelberg xii, 59–60
Heine, Heinrich 24, 39
Herbert, George 23
Hichens, Robert 349–352
Higginson, Thomas Wentworth 43
Highlands 1–2, 21, 58, 87, 104, 191–193, 197, 205–206, 239, 260, 284, 306, 312, 341–342, 344, 351, 357
Hinkson, Katharine Tynan 143–144, 157, 189, 231–232, 234, 265
Holdsworth, Annie E. 20
Hollyer, Frederick 141–142, 370
Holroyd, Charles 69, 119
Holy Grail 248, 341
homosexuality xv, 104, 116, 184, 349
Hood, Alexander Nelson xiii, 105, 250, 316–319, 321, 330, 332–333, 335, 338–341, 345, 347–350, 352, 361, 368, 371, 376
Hopper, Nora 231, 265
Hotel Timeo 349
Houghton and Mifflin 84, 386
House of Usna, A Drama, The 261–262, 298–300, 354, 356, 361, 378
Howard, Blanche Willis 58–60, 73–75, 83, 139
Howells, William Dean 12, 51, 97
Human Inheritance, The; The New Hope; Motherhood 4, 11, 43
Hurst and Blackett 24

Hyde, Douglas 239, 310
Ibsen, Henrik 68, 378
impressionism 25, 69, 71, 97, 128, 179
Inverness Terrace 4, 15, 17, 58, 61, 330, 356
Iona 13, 141, 143–144, 154, 194, 205, 235, 284, 286, 294, 301–305, 307–308, 354
Ireland 28, 133, 143, 148, 152, 191, 208, 210, 224–225, 230–231, 238–239, 247, 271, 279, 285–286, 306–310, 325–326, 328, 377, 414
Irish 123, 143–144, 148, 152, 157, 162–164, 176, 189, 191–192, 202, 208, 231, 238–239, 241, 262, 265, 268–269, 271, 306–311, 327, 371–372, 414
Irish literary revival 239
Irish nationalism 271, 306, 308–309, 372, 414
Irish Renaissance 123
Isle of Man 10
Isle of Wight 34, 84, 117–118, 146–147, 366
Italian 12–13, 49, 54, 62, 95, 98, 178, 201, 216, 317, 332, 336, 339, 374, 386
Italian Renaissance 12, 178
Italy xii, 6, 11–13, 19, 25, 51, 55–56, 58–59, 67, 69, 95, 102, 105, 133, 179, 182, 187, 190, 192–194, 199–200, 202, 228, 247, 286, 311, 313, 316, 321, 330, 350, 353, 362–363, 368, 381, 383, 386, 416

James, Henry 19, 56, 332, 384
Janvier, Catherine Ann 52, 59–60, 70–71, 74–76, 83, 119–120, 134, 148, 156, 195–196, 221, 223, 229, 243–244, 250, 263, 315–316, 319, 335, 344–345, 347, 352, 359–360, 368–371, 374, 376, 384, 421–423
Janviers, the 52, 95, 201, 220–221, 223, 236–237, 312, 360, 374, 383, 421
Janvier, Thomas Allibone 52, 59, 71, 82–83, 87, 99, 196–197, 258, 267, 383, 421

Keats, John 37, 56, 77
Kensington 17, 34, 83–84, 116, 127, 132

Kent 6, 9, 297
Kernahan, Coulson 229–230, 276
Kilcreggan 141–142, 262, 324, 357–358
Kimball, Hannibal Ingalls 119, 133–134, 141, 144, 152–153, 161, 176–178, 186, 192, 194, 198, 200–201, 211–212, 219–220, 227–228, 246, 325

Lady Gregory 239, 241, 250, 278–279, 310, 329, 371, 414
Lamson, Wolffe and Co. 259
Lamson, Wolffe & Co. 220
Lane, John 127, 138–141, 153, 169–170
Late Victorianism xiv
Laughter of Peterkin, The 237–238
Lauritsen, John 103–104
Lee-Hamilton, Eugene 11–12, 19–20, 319–320, 343
Lee, Vernon (a.k.a. Violet Paget) 11–12, 19–20, 319–320
Le Gallienne, Richard 35, 37–39, 47–48, 116, 127, 139, 171–172, 192, 228
Leighton, Frederick 17
Leipzig 321, 381
Life and Letters of Joseph Severn 83, 108
Linlithgow 2
Linscott Publishing Company, The 297
Lismore, Isle of 120, 342–344
Little, J. Stanley xiv, 29, 53, 84, 88–90, 93–94, 99, 102, 104–105, 111, 116–119, 127, 131–132, 134, 169, 173, 185, 232, 236, 250, 297–298, 332, 347, 380, 422
Liverpool 37–38, 52, 77, 82
Llandrindod Wells 358, 367, 381–382
Loch Fyne 21, 58, 166, 207
London xi, xii, xiv, xv, xvi, 1, 3–4, 6–7, 9–10, 12–15, 17, 19, 21, 23, 25, 34, 36–40, 43, 46–49, 52–53, 55–58, 60–63, 68, 72–73, 76, 79–84, 86–88, 90, 93–94, 97–99, 103–104, 106, 111, 113, 118–119, 125, 127, 132–134, 136, 140–142, 146–147, 149–153, 157, 161–162, 164, 166, 169–170, 172, 176, 178, 180, 185, 187, 189–193, 198–201, 205, 207, 210–212, 220–221, 224–226, 229, 231–232, 236–241, 243, 245–246, 255–256, 258, 261–262, 266–267, 272, 276–277, 279, 283–285, 287, 291–293, 295, 297–298, 300–301, 310–312, 316, 319, 321–322, 325–326, 330–334, 341, 344, 347, 353–354, 356–357, 359, 368, 370–371, 373–374, 378–379, 381, 385, 413–415, 417, 422
Longley, James 50
Loti, Pierre 68
Lyttelton, Edith 276–278, 286, 295, 301

MacColl, Norman 16, 46
Macleay, John 191–193, 205–207, 215, 239, 257, 284, 287, 301, 312–313, 341, 343–344
Macleod, Fiona xii, xiii, xiv, xv, xvi, xvii, 1–2, 12–13, 15, 21, 26–28, 37, 41, 48, 52, 55, 58, 62–63, 65, 67, 73, 88, 90, 97, 101–102, 105, 116, 119–124, 128, 130, 132, 134–141, 143–150, 152–159, 161–163, 165–166, 170–181, 183, 185–187, 189–198, 200–203, 205–213, 215, 217–219, 223–224, 226–232, 234–235, 237–239, 243–244, 247–248, 250–262, 265–281, 283–291, 294–295, 298–303, 305, 307–313, 319–322, 324–332, 338–341, 343–345, 347, 349, 353–357, 361, 368–382, 386, 413–418, 421–422, 424
Madge o' the Pool: The Gipsy Christ and Other Tales 119
Maeterlinck, Maurice 83, 108, 142, 177, 246, 299
Manchester 29, 31
marriage xi, xvii, 3, 14, 16, 32, 34, 40, 49, 62, 101, 214, 217, 249, 292, 317, 322, 356, 417
Marseilles 71, 313, 360
Marston, Philip 6, 15, 31–32, 35, 37, 76, 81, 108
Martyn, Edward 238–239, 262, 279
Mary, Sharp 27
Marzials, Frank 53
Massachusetts 51
Masterpieces of Foreign Authors series 54
Mathers, Macgregor 226, 250–252, 254–255, 272

Mathers, Moina 254–255, 272
Mathews, Elkin 109, 118, 169, 176, 178, 189
Mavor, James 48–49, 54, 59
Mediterranean sea 106, 313, 360, 381, 383
Meredith, George 24, 35–36, 45, 47, 49, 58, 68, 71–72, 96, 105, 148, 164, 170–172, 232, 238, 252, 269, 299, 331, 338, 355–356, 415–416
Merrill, Stuart 96–97, 103
Meyers, Terry L. xv
Micheldever 28–29, 56, 62, 95
Milton, John 121, 184, 291
Minto, William 47, 106–107
Mistral, Frederic 15, 236, 267, 374
Moffat 4
Montreal 51
Moore, Harvey 229, 234–235, 257, 262, 276, 285, 353
Moray Press 134
Morley, Henry 47
Morocco 111, 115
Morris, William 17, 37, 363
Mosher, Thomas 65, 219, 299, 321–322, 324–325, 328–329, 331–332, 338, 343, 353–354, 356–357, 361, 371, 373–374, 377–378, 382, 386, 422
Moulton, Louise Chandler 32, 48, 74, 81, 118, 133, 232, 332
Mountain Lovers, The xii, 138–141, 144, 153, 156, 162, 170–171, 173, 187
Mull 13, 143, 304–305, 354
Murray, Frank xii, 118–122, 127, 134–135, 137, 140, 365
mythology xvii, 2, 58, 65–66, 96, 99, 195, 226, 250, 252, 271, 285, 305, 310, 324, 329, 340, 363, 377

Nash, Roger 88–90
nationalism 271, 306, 308–309, 372
nature xii, 1–3, 15, 39, 44, 55, 102–103, 117, 122, 124, 130, 137, 148–149, 184–186, 194–195, 214–215, 223, 233–234, 243, 245, 253, 260, 270–271, 278, 292, 302, 305, 312, 332, 340, 374, 376, 416–417
Naxos xv, 114, 315, 335, 362

Nemi 63–68, 71–72, 179
Newcastle 21–22
New Jersey 51, 79, 81, 172, 324
New York xiv, 43–45, 49–54, 68–69, 73, 76–77, 79, 81–83, 96, 106, 109, 137, 142–143, 194, 201, 211–213, 217, 219–220, 227, 245, 321, 324, 350, 369, 381, 383, 386, 421–422
New Zealand 185
Nichol, John 2, 94
Nicholson, Gresham 90–91
Northumberland 205
Norway 105
Nova Scotia 50
Nutt, Alfred 371–372, 374

Oban 13, 143–144, 191, 305, 342–343
occultism 2, 207, 223, 226, 274–276
O'Grady, Standish 307–310
Omar Khayyam Club 171, 293, 295
Ontario 51
Ottoman Empire 116
Ouida 12
Outer Hebrides xiv
Oxford 20

Pagan 70–72, 87, 90, 94–99, 101–104, 116, 119, 128, 134, 166, 194, 196, 214, 228, 303, 354, 374
Paganism 87, 95–97, 101–104, 167, 417
Pagan Press 103–104
Pagan Review 70, 72, 87, 90, 94–98, 101–104, 119, 128, 134
Paisley xi, 1–2
Paris 15, 31, 35, 47–48, 54, 69, 84, 87, 95, 97–99, 117, 133–134, 161, 169–170, 200, 214, 216, 223–224, 226, 231–233, 236, 246, 250–255, 257, 272, 297–298, 301, 312, 353, 415–416
  Salons 31, 35, 47–48, 54, 87, 232–233, 272, 297–298
Parliament xiii, 62, 105, 276, 309, 340–341
Pater, Walter 14, 17, 20, 45, 47, 117, 145, 147
Patmore, Coventry 53, 68
Paton, Noel 5, 7, 12–13, 287

Patrick Geddes & Colleagues 157–158, 162–163, 165, 176–177, 189, 192, 198, 202, 207, 218, 228, 325
Perry, Bliss 357, 383, 385
Persian 115
Pettycur Inn 174–175, 192, 201–203, 226, 263
Pharais, A Romance of the Isles xii, 63, 88, 119–123, 132, 134–135, 137–140, 148, 161, 169, 175–176, 186–187, 207, 370, 416, 421
Phenice Croft 88–90, 94, 102–103, 109, 116–117, 119, 122, 124–125, 127–132, 134, 145, 180, 182, 185, 220, 240, 244
Philadelphia 43, 52, 76, 79, 297, 374, 421
Philpot, Mrs J. H. 332, 336–337, 361–362, 365, 369
Piccadilly Circus 379
Pisa 70
Poe, Edgar Allan 23, 68
Portland 219, 324, 332, 386
Port Maddock 6
Pre-Raphaelite 5, 12, 64, 76, 100, 106, 108, 263
Presbyterian 2, 58
Prince Edward Island 50
Protestant xiii, 56
Provençal 216–217, 236, 267, 312
Provence 70, 72, 195–196, 201, 236, 267, 311, 313, 317, 374
pseudonym; pseudonimity xii, xvii, 1, 11, 41, 48, 63, 72–73, 82–83, 88, 94–95, 97, 121–123, 139, 148, 163, 169–170, 207, 217, 266, 319, 341, 349, 416, 418, 422

Quebec 50–51

Rea, Lillian 198–199, 227, 300, 321
Reclus, Élie 68
Regent's Library 118, 120–121, 134
religion 25, 58, 71–72, 96, 143–144, 184, 194–195
rheumatic fever xiii, 6, 14–15, 20, 26–27, 93
Rhine 59, 74

Rhys, Ernest 14–15, 23–28, 39, 66–67, 157, 162, 177, 190, 198, 243, 299, 333, 358, 365–367
Richards, Grant 127, 247, 257, 259, 263, 266–268, 272, 281, 284, 292, 300–301, 320, 344, 356
Rinder, Edith Wingate xii, xiii, 61–63, 65–68, 84, 86–87, 98–101, 104, 111, 116, 118, 123–125, 127, 131, 134, 137, 146, 156, 162–163, 173–175, 177–178, 181–187, 189–190, 193–194, 198–199, 207–208, 215–218, 226, 230, 232–234, 238, 240, 244–246, 248–250, 252–254, 256, 260–263, 267–269, 273–276, 281, 286–290, 294, 299–300, 321–322, 324, 331–332, 340, 354–355, 357, 363, 369–370, 373, 413, 415–418, 422
Rinder, Esther Mona 322, 324, 326, 354
Rinder, Frank xii, 61–62, 84, 101, 116, 127, 131, 147, 194, 197, 207, 218, 227, 273, 275, 294, 299, 302, 322, 417
Riviera, the 200–201, 221, 227, 232, 236, 267, 332, 373–374, 386
Roberts, Charles G. D. 50
Robertson, Eric 24, 26, 31, 57–58
Rolleston, T. W. 309–310
Roman 60, 63, 65, 77, 86, 95, 98, 103, 109, 351–352, 369, 374
Romantic 36–39, 41, 45, 48, 54, 72, 82, 86, 96, 109, 193, 386
Romantic Ballads and Poems of Phantasy 36–37, 39, 41, 45, 48, 54, 72, 82, 86, 96, 109
Romanticism 38–39, 41, 86, 96
Romantic School 48
Rome xii, 12–13, 55–64, 66–73, 77, 86, 88, 99, 105, 109, 116, 119, 122–123, 135, 142, 189, 333, 363, 370, 381, 386, 416
Rossetti, Christina 6, 14, 147
Rossetti, Dante Gabriel xi, 5–7, 9–12, 14–15, 17, 20, 25, 27, 37–38, 44–45, 49, 52, 56, 64, 99–100, 106, 108, 116–117, 119, 147, 185, 287
Roussel, Theodore 57, 121
Royal Academy 26
Royal Jubilee Exhibition 31

Rudgwick 88–89, 94, 118, 125, 129, 180
Ruskin, John 77, 107
Russell, George (Æ) 157, 192, 238, 255, 265, 276, 280, 306–311, 328–329

Sahara desert 111, 351
Sainte-Beuve, Charles Augustin 54, 68, 374
Saint Remy 312
Salons, Paris 31, 35, 47–48, 54, 87, 232–233, 272, 297–298
Scandinavia 133, 279
Scollard, Clinton 43
Scotland xii, xv, 1, 4, 7, 10, 12–14, 16, 20–21, 24, 39–40, 55–56, 58, 61–62, 71–72, 88, 95, 104, 118–120, 123, 133, 135, 141, 143, 146, 148–149, 152–153, 157, 159, 161, 163–164, 172–173, 175, 178, 185–186, 191–192, 195, 206–207, 211, 225–226, 231, 235–236, 238–239, 247, 262, 266–267, 280, 283–285, 298, 303–304, 311–312, 321, 332, 341, 343, 353, 356–357, 376–377, 419
Scots 148, 158, 176, 252, 308–309
Scottish xiii, 4–5, 45, 48–49, 53–54, 58, 87–88, 90, 106, 137, 144, 147–148, 150, 152, 157, 160–161, 163–164, 189, 191–192, 202, 207, 227, 231, 253, 287, 302, 306–307, 309–312, 344, 370–371, 421
Scott, Walter 15, 24, 343
Scott, William Bell 7
Scudder, Horace 77, 81–82, 147–148, 150
Severn, Joseph 56, 73, 75, 77, 83
Severn, Walter 56, 73, 76–77, 109
sexual fluidity 116
Shadow of Arvor, The 162–163, 177, 190
Shakespeare, William 21, 23, 73
Sharp, Elizabeth xi, xii, xiii, xiv, xvi, xvii, 1–7, 9–17, 19–20, 23–29, 31–32, 34, 36, 40, 44–45, 47–50, 52, 56–63, 69–71, 73, 76–77, 83–84, 87–88, 90, 93, 95, 99, 101–102, 105, 111, 116–119, 122, 124–125, 127, 130–132, 134, 138, 141, 143–144, 146–147, 150, 153, 155–157, 164–166, 169, 173–176, 178, 185–187, 189–190, 192–203, 205, 207–208, 210, 213, 217–218, 220–221, 229–230, 232–234, 236–237, 239–241, 243–250, 256, 258–259, 267, 275–276, 279, 284, 287, 293, 297, 299, 311, 315, 317, 319–320, 330, 332–333, 335, 337, 339, 341–345, 347, 351–352, 354–356, 358, 360, 363, 365–366, 368–369, 371, 374, 376, 380–381, 383–384, 413–419, 422, 424
  Lyra Celtica 162, 164–165, 177, 190, 194, 198, 201–202
Sharp, Mary xiii, 14, 16, 27, 58, 102, 116, 135–137, 174, 176, 193, 207, 211, 223, 234, 300, 319–321, 331, 349, 357, 361, 368–369, 371, 423
Sheffield 103
Shelley, Percy Bysshe xi, 15, 23–24, 29, 32, 40, 88, 93–94, 311
Sherman, Frank Dempster 43
Shields, Roselle Lathrop 29, 35, 366–371, 380, 421–423
Shorter Stories of Fiona Macleod, The 163
Sicily xiii, 88, 105, 114, 275, 313, 315–319, 324, 330, 332–333, 335, 338, 341, 344, 347, 350, 352–353, 357, 360, 363, 368–369, 374, 381, 385
Sienna 12
Silence Farm 259, 266–267, 272, 279, 283–284, 286
Silence of Amor | Prose Rhythms by Fiona Macleod, The 65, 217, 219, 343
Sin-Eater and Other Stories, The 128, 153, 162–163, 169, 176–178, 180–183, 185–187, 189, 194
Siwäarmill, H. P. 48, 83, 97, 178
Skipsey, Joseph 22–23
Skye 209–210, 213, 219
Songs and Poems, Old and New 268
Songs and Tales of St. Columba and His Age 163
Sonnenschein, William Swan 116
Sospiri di Roma xii, 63–64, 67, 69–72, 82, 84, 86, 95–97, 99, 109, 122, 179, 286, 416
Spain 133, 353
Spanish 73, 109, 384

spiritualism 325, 341
Sport of Chance, The 24
Stage Society 261, 298–299, 311–312
St. Andrews 119, 146, 173–175
St. Columba 143, 163, 194
Stedman, Arthur 81–82, 106, 111, 134
Stedman, E. C. 43–45, 49–52, 55–56, 58–59, 75–76, 79, 81–82, 84, 99, 101–102, 104–106, 108, 141, 156, 176, 211–212, 220, 226–228, 238, 245–247, 250, 252, 262–263, 359–360, 367, 381–383
Stevenson, Lionel xv, 36, 343
Stevenson, Robert Louis 36, 161–162, 311, 343
Stewart, George xiv, 51, 90, 384–385
St. Margaret's Bay 232–234, 237, 243–245, 247, 251, 253–254, 256, 258, 415
Stock, Elliot 10–11, 14, 268
Stoddard, Richard Henry 51, 79
Stoddart, J. M. 79, 120
Stone and Kimball 119, 133–134, 141, 144, 152–153, 161, 176–178, 186, 192, 194, 198, 200–201, 211–212, 220, 246, 325
Stone, FIRSTNAME 190
Stone, Herbert 133, 141, 145, 153, 161, 169, 174, 190–191, 193, 199–201, 212, 219
Story, William Wetmore 56–57, 96, 350
St. Petersburg 67
St. Remy 220–221, 223, 229, 236–237
Stuttgart 59–60, 73, 75
Surrey 35, 49, 56, 139, 169–171, 189, 192, 232, 267
Sussex 73, 84, 88–90, 93–95, 101, 104, 118, 185, 236–237
Swedish xi, 1, 95
Swinburne, Algernon 5, 25, 68, 96, 106–107, 145, 321–322, 330, 339
Switzerland 105, 349
symbolism 271, 326
Symonds, John Addington 12, 45, 145
Symons, Arthur 208, 210, 241

Syracuse 318–319, 336, 360, 362
Taormina 114, 313, 315–317, 319, 330, 333, 335–337, 344–346, 349–352, 360, 362
Tarascon 220–221, 236
Tarbert 20–21, 58, 207–208, 211, 238, 357
Tennyson, Alfred 104, 186
Teutonic 77, 79, 265
The Gipsy Christ and Other Tales 119
There is But One Love 247
Tillyra Castle 208, 210, 238–239, 241, 262, 279
Tivoli 69–71
Toronto 297
"Tragic Landscapes" 128, 130, 180, 182
Traill, H. D. 148, 330
Traubel, Horace 79, 81
travel xv, 20, 31, 39, 56, 88, 112, 116, 151, 184, 200, 259, 295, 346, 354, 358, 365, 373, 386
travel writing 112, 116, 259
Tunis 113–114
Turner, J. M. W. 65–66
Tuscany 58–59
Tynan-Hinkson, Katharine 143
Tyne Publishing Company 21

United States 43, 49, 52, 54, 57, 77, 82, 109, 124, 162, 187, 190, 201, 235, 276, 325, 373

Vedder, Elihu 68
Venice 12, 52, 194, 201–202, 345, 347, 369, 384, 424
Verlaine, Paul 87, 96
Vermont 51
Victorianism xiv, 62, 72, 95
Viking 1, 221
visions 3, 15, 71, 112, 117, 123, 130, 137, 166, 172, 195, 208–210, 224–226, 234, 239–240, 244, 250, 252, 260, 270, 289, 302, 323–326, 335, 372, 380, 414, 416
Vistas 54, 82–83, 97, 109, 116, 118–122, 127, 131, 134, 141–142, 152, 187, 229

Wales 4, 6, 23, 148, 152, 162, 191, 358, 377, 381
Walter Scott Publishing House 15, 21–24, 31–32, 36, 39–40, 49, 53–54, 57, 189, 193, 202, 296, 343
Washer of the Ford, The 162–163, 177, 190, 193–194, 196–198, 201, 235, 267, 369, 424
Watts, Theodore (a.k.a Theodore Watts-Dunton) 5, 9, 28, 36–37, 39, 45–47, 58, 105–107, 144–145, 148, 171, 291, 293–294, 296–297, 321–322, 330–331, 333, 339, 356
Webster, Augusta 47, 82–84, 87, 109, 145
Webster, Charles 82, 84, 109, 116, 118, 134
Welsh 152, 157, 162, 202, 306
Wescam 34, 46, 56, 62
Western Isles 21, 194–195
West Highlands 2, 58, 104, 284
Wharncliffe 291–292
Whelen, Frederick 298–299

Whitby 73–74
Whiteing, Richard 116, 268
White, Maude Valérie 64, 95, 116, 163, 217, 247, 333–334, 349
Whitman, Walt 79–80
Wilde, Oscar 17, 41, 52, 96, 98, 103, 184, 349, 417
Winged Destiny, The 347, 373–378, 380
Wives in Exile 190, 193, 198, 201, 219–220, 227, 259, 261, 272
Wordsworth, William 37

Yeats, W. B. xvi, 28, 113, 123, 157, 176, 192, 201–203, 208–211, 220, 223–226, 229–232, 234, 238–241, 244, 248, 250–263, 265, 268–273, 276, 278–281, 283–284, 287–290, 298–299, 306, 309–310, 324–330, 340–341, 343, 354, 372, 376, 378, 413–416, 418–419
York 73, 164, 180, 205

Zola, Emile 15

About the Team

Alessandra Tosi was the managing editor for this book.

Melissa Purkiss performed the copy-editing and proofreading.

Lucy Barned indexed the volume.

Anna Gatti designed the cover. The cover was produced in InDesign using the Fontin font.

Luca Baffa typeset the book in InDesign and produced the paperback and hardback editions. The text font is Tex Gyre Pagella; the heading font is Californian FB. Luca produced the EPUB, azw3, PDF, HTML, and XML editions — the conversion is performed with open source software freely available on our GitHub page (https://github.com/OpenBook Publishers).

This book need not end here...

Share

All our books — including the one you have just read — are free to access online so that students, researchers and members of the public who can't afford a printed edition will have access to the same ideas. This title will be accessed online by hundreds of readers each month across the globe: why not share the link so that someone you know is one of them?

This book and additional content is available at:

https://doi.org/10.11647/OBP.0276

Customise

Personalise your copy of this book or design new books using OBP and third-party material. Take chapters or whole books from our published list and make a special edition, a new anthology or an illuminating coursepack. Each customised edition will be produced as a paperback and a downloadable PDF.

Find out more at:

https://www.openbookpublishers.com/section/59/1

You may also be interested in:

The Life and Letters of William Sharp and "Fiona Macleod". Volume 1
1855–1894

William F. Halloran

https://doi.org/10.11647/OBP.0142

The Life and Letters of William Sharp and "Fiona Macleod". Volume 2
1895–1899

William F. Halloran

https://doi.org/10.11647/OBP.0196

The Life and Letters of William Sharp and "Fiona Macleod". Volume 3
1900–1905

William F. Halloran

https://doi.org/10.11647/OBP.0221

www.ingramcontent.com/pod-product-compliance
Lightning Source LLC
Chambersburg PA
CBHW062025290426
44108CB00025B/2780